Quick & Indepth

C

With Data Structures

Sudripta Nandy

[Includes changes proposed in C99 & C11]

ABOUT THE AUTHOR

Sudripta has almost 20 years of experience working on various computer technologies ranging from desktop computers to Mainframes and to data centers. He has worked on multiple projects for many Fortune 500 companies and in areas like operating system, media technologies, content protection, data processing, backup technologies, services, setup and application development. Professionally, he has spent his spare time educating and training upcoming young minds to the intricacies of programming. In the personal front, he divides his time playing with his sports fanatic son, being a couch potato and serving 'Her Majesty' - His wife :-). He can be reached at sudriptanandy@gmail.com.

ACKNOWLEDGMENTS

I may be the author of this book, but, it would have been impossible without the love and support of many people around me. People who helped me grow up, get educated, guided me, inspired me, made this book a possibility. There are so many people who touched my life, that I would need hundreds of pages to dedicate them individually. If someone is left out over here, do remember that you reside in the most precious place within me – my heart.

The first person I want to dedicate this book to, is my late grandfather, whose life principles I carry to this day. I can relate many of my characteristics to him – some may not suit this modern era but, I am proud of them. The next person who helped me shape up as a person and still doing so, is my mother. She spent so many sleepless nights when I got those asthma attacks. I slept because she stayed awake, I am alive because she stayed strong. She is my pillar of strength.

When I think about my life, its incomplete without my father – the person who never got angry on me, who died working so that I could live. The most simple yet straight forward person I know. He left a void in my heart which can never be filled.

The person who fills my life with the warmth I look for, is my son. Being a father is the best feeling a person can have. He has helped me grow so much as a person and as a father. The next person who completes me is my wife – the best friend in my entire life. The love and support, I get from her help me in life's every journey I take.

A person's life is incomplete without a sister, and I am lucky to have two. The biggest support pillars of my life, the persons I can always count on when in need. My grandmother is the person in whose lap I started off my journey called life. My niece is the person who gave me the first feelings of being the older generation – and what a beautiful feeling. Still visualize those chubby cheeks and big round eyes.

There are many others who played an important role in my life and guided me towards this journey. My father-in-law, mother-in-law, moni, mesho, mezdabhai, brothers-in-law, sister-in-law, nephews, Sumit – all helped me become the person I am today. They may not have directly helped me in writing this book but, have helped the author within me evolve.

This book is also dedicated to the many friends and colleagues I had over the years. I learned from every colleague I had during my entire professional career. The work I did within my organization also helped me grow as a professional and come to this point where I can confidently write a book.

CONTENTS

INTRODUCTION TO C

[CHAPTER-1]

'C' seems to be an odd name for a programming language. On first thought, it feels it is part of a version sequence of a programming language. You will not be totally wrong in assuming this. C is an offspring of the 'Basic Combined Programming Language' (BCPL) called 'B' in short. 'B' was developed at 'Bell Labs' in 1969 by Ken Thompson and Dennis Ritchie. B was designed for recursive, non-numeric, machine independent applications, such as system and language software. 'C' was developed by Dennis Ritchie at 'Bell Labs' between 1969 and 1973 as a successor to the 'B' language. It was originally developed to re-implement the Unix operating system. It has since become one of the most widely used programming languages of all time. C has been standardized by the American National Standards Institute (ANSI) since 1989 (as ANSI C) and subsequently by the International Organization for Standardization (ISO). C compilers are available across all major architectures and operating systems. Many languages like C++, D, Java, JavaScript, C#, Objective-C, Perl, PHP, Python have directly or indirectly borrowed extensively from 'C'. Almost all major operating systems like MS-DOS, Windows, Mac, Linux, Android, iOS have components written in C or C++ (a successor to C).

1.1 IMPORTANCE OF C

'C' is a robust language which provides a perfect balance between performance and development ease. It was designed to be compiled using a relatively straightforward compiler, to provide low-level access to memory, to provide language constructs that map efficiently to machine instructions, and to require minimal run-time support. Therefore, C was useful for many applications that had formerly been coded in assembly language, for example in system programming. The C compiler combines the capabilities of an assembly language with the features of a high level language, making it well suited for writing both system software and business packages. C being a compiler and so close to assembly language, is many times faster than most other languages. Unlike assembly language, C is highly portable. A program written for one system architecture or an operating system can be ported to another after no or very little modifications and re-compiling for the new system.

C follows the concept of structured programming requiring the user to think of the problem in terms of function modules or blocks. A proper collection of these modules would make a complete program. Another important feature of C is its ability for extensions. A C program is basically a collection of functions that are supported by the C library functions. By continuously adding new functions to the C library, the language has become more and more powerful and programming task simple.

1.2 WRITING PROGRAMS

C consists of five components - system library files, system header files, user library files, user header files and user code files.

System library files contain many important library functions which perform specific tasks. A function is a block of code which performs a specific task. A task can be a combination of the four basic tasks: Input, Output, Storage and Processing. A function may be called by another function (called the caller) requiring the later (called the callee) to perform a task on its behalf. The callee may accept parameters or arguments which may act as inputs for performing the task. The callee may also return a value which is the result of the processing. Though there can be multiple parameters to a function, there can be only one return value. Coming back to our previous discussion, system library files (like stdio, stdlib etc.) contain functions which perform such specific tasks.

System header files (like stdio.h, string.h etc.) contain the prototype or declaration of these system library functions and data types (discussed later). Prototypes or declarations provide information (like the function name, what are the parameters that the function accepts, what is its return type) regarding the function. This information not only helps the programmer to understand the requirements of the function but also helps the compiler verify the correctness of a function call.

User library files are similar to the system library files except that they are custom written by the users for extending the system library functions or to perform specific tasks not available in the system libraries. User libraries are created for porting or re-using the same functions across multiple programs without re-implementing the same across programs.

User header files contain the function declarations and data types to be shared among different user code files and user libraries.

The *user code files* define the actual program functionality utilizing the previous four components and other processing code.

1.3 OUR FIRST PROGRAM

As our first program, lets print a simple message.

```
#include <stdio.h>
int main()
{
    printf("This is my first C program.");
    return 0; /* Return 0 to indicate successful operation' */
}
```

When the above program is executed, it will generate the following output on the console:

```
This is my first C program.
```

Now, let us take a first look at the program.

The first statement (#include <stdio.h>) tells the compiler to include the system header file 'stdio.h'. This header file contains the declaration of the predefined system function 'printf' used within the program. By predefined we mean that the function body has already been written, compiled and linked with our program at the time of linking.

Take a look at the '**printf**' function call. Over here it is accepting one parameter i.e. The string to print. The prototype of the 'printf' function is declared as '*int printf (const char * format, ...)*'. The information contained within the parentheses of the printf function is called the argument or parameter of the function. The printf function returns the number of characters written to the output, which in this case is 27 (including the spaces and the dot '.').

The '**main()**' is a special function used by the C language which tells the computer where the program starts. Every program must have exactly one **main** function. If there are more than one main function, the compiler will fail to understand the beginning of the program and will raise an error.

The empty pair of parentheses following main tells the compiler that the function does not accept any arguments in this case. Though the main function can accept two arguments, but you can define a main function which accepts no arguments. The two arguments which it may accept are int and a **character pointer** which we will discuss later. Though there is no standard defined as the return type of the main function, but, it is a good practice to return an int, which refers to an integer. This return value will tell the caller program or the operating system regarding the success or failure result of the program execution. The main function like any other function may return nothing, which is marked with the 'C' keyword '*void*'. We will discuss regarding 'C' keywords a little later.

The opening curly brace '{' appearing after the main function name marks the beginning of the function main() and the closing curly brace '}' marks the end of the function. Braces group a collection of statements together and for a function mark the start and end of the function. All the statements between these two braces specify what the function wants to do and is called the *function body*. Over here the function body contains two statements where one is the *printf* function call and the other ('*return*') is a 'C' reserved keyword. The value following the return statement is the value returned by the function to its caller indicating the result of the function processing or operation.

The statement enclosed within '**/***' and '***/**' following the return statement is not processed by the compiler and is just a **comment** for the readability and understanding of the program by the developers. All lines appearing between '/*' and '*/' is ignored by the compiler. A *comment* can be inserted in any place within the program where a blank space can occur. It can appear as separate independent lines, at the start, middle or end of a line. Starting from C99 *(an extension to the language published by ISO in the year 1999)*, a single line of statement can be commented using '**//**' *(excluding the single quote pair)* at the start of the statement. Everything written after '//' on that line gets excluded from compilation. So, any symbol appearing to the right of '//' is ignored by the compiler. Some examples of such comment are given below:

```
•   int main()
    {
        printf("This is my first C program.");
        // This line is a comment, but the below line will get processed.
        return 0;
    }
```

```
• int main()
  {
      printf("This is my first C program.");
      // This line is a comment, but below 'return 0;' will be processed.
      return 0; // Starting from here all text ignored, but the below '}' is processed.
  }
• int main()
  {
      printf("This is my first C program.");
      // In this example, we are commenting multiple lines, one-line at a time.
      // This line too gets treated as a comment.
      // The below 'return 0;' will get processed.
      return 0;
  }
```

All processing statements in 'C' should end with a semi-colon (;) mark.

In place of writing '**printf**("This is my first C program.");', we could have written the statement as '**printf**("This is my\nfirst C program.");'. The '\n' refers to a new line character i.e. whenever the compiler encounters it, all characters appearing after '\n' within the printf statement will be displayed in the next line of the console. So, in this case the output will be

```
This is my
first C program.
```

We could have achieved the same result using two separate consecutive 'printf' statements like
printf("This is my");
printf("\nfirst C program.");

So, let us recollect our previous understanding regarding the program using the following image.

1.4 STRUCTURE OF C PROGRAMS

Documentation and Comment Section
[Contains information regarding your program like what it does, steps to execute the program etc.]

Preprocessor Statements
[Special instructions for the compiler for compiling the program like header file inclusions etc.]

Declaration and Definition Section
[Function prototypes, structure definitions etc.]

Global Declarations
[Global variable declarations i.e. variables declared outside the functions and applicable to the entire program]

main() Function Section

{
    Function Variable Declarations
    Executable statements
}

User-Defined Functions

1.5 EXECUTING A 'C' PROGRAM

Execution of a 'C' program involves a series of steps. They are:

- **Creating a program:** This involves writing the code of the program.
- **Compiling the program:** In this step, individual code files are compiled into individual object files.
- **Linking the program:** In this step, the individual object files are linked together to generate the executable.
- **Executing the program**.

1.6 IDENTIFIERS IN C

An identifier is a string of alphanumeric characters that begins with an alphabetic or an underscore character that is used to represent various programming elements such as variables, functions, arrays, structures, unions and so on. Identifier is a user-specified word. So, in our example 'printf' too is an identifier (called function identifier) and all variable names are also identifiers.

DATA TYPES, VARIABLES AND CONSTANTS

[CHAPTER-2]

2.1 INTRODUCTION

For a programming language, data is the information processed or stored by a computer. This data can be in the form of numbers or characters. The data is processed and information is generated in the form of some suitable output. This output can be shown to the user on the screen, printed, stored to a disk or sent over the network. The instructions or steps for processing the data is called a program. These instructions are written in some specific rules called syntax rules to make them understandable to the compiler.

2.2 CHARACTER REPRESENTATION

Characters in C are represented using **ASCII** *(American Standard Code for Information Interchange)*. ASCII specifies a correspondence between digital bit patterns and character symbols. A specific digital bit pattern corresponds to a specific character symbol. As an example the digital bit pattern *'01000001'* denotes the character 'A' and the bit pattern *'01100001'* is for the character 'a'.

ASCII reserves the first 32 codes (numbers 0–31 decimal) for control characters: codes originally intended not to represent printable information, but rather to control devices (such as printers) that make use of ASCII, or to provide meta-information about data. For example, character 13 represents a new line i.e. the cursor on the output device moves to the next line on encountering this character. Codes from 32 to 126 represent printable characters, including letters, numbers and special characters. ASCII uses only 7 bits out of a byte to represent one character, leaving 1 bit unused.

Though ASCII could represent almost all English characters, it could not do so for all characters from other languages. ASCII could represent only 95 characters which is insufficient to handle characters from other languages as they have a larger character set. So, a new character format called Unicode was defined which represented one character using more than one byte. The number of bytes used by a Unicode character depends on the compiler and the encoding mechanism used, which may be 1+ byte (UTF-8 encoding), 2 bytes (UTF-16 encoding) and 4 bytes (UTF-32 encoding). ASCII characters were incorporated in the Unicode character set as the first 128 symbols. So, the first 128 symbols are the same in ASCII and Unicode.

ASCII TABLE

Decimal	Binary	ASCII	Decimal	Binary	ASCII	Decimal	Binary	ASCII	Decimal	Binary	ASCII
0	00000000	NUL	32	00100000	Space	64	01000000	@	96	01100000	`
1	00000001	SOH	33	00100001	!	65	01000001	A	97	01100001	a
2	00000010	STX	34	00100010	"	66	01000010	B	98	01100010	b
3	00000011	ETX	35	00100011	#	67	01000011	C	99	01100011	c
4	00000100	EOT	36	00100100	$	68	01000100	D	100	01100100	d
5	00000101	ENQ	37	00100101	%	69	01000101	E	101	01100101	e
6	00000110	ACK	38	00100110	&	70	01000110	F	102	01100110	f
7	00000111	BEL	39	00100111	'	71	01000111	G	103	01100111	g
8	00001000	BS	40	00101000	(	72	01001000	H	104	01101000	h
9	00001001	HT	41	00101001	)	73	01001001	I	105	01101001	i
10	00001010	LF	42	00101010	*	74	01001010	J	106	01101010	j
11	00001011	VT	43	00101011	+	75	01001011	K	107	01101011	k
12	00001100	FF	44	00101100	,	76	01001100	L	108	01101100	l
13	00001101	CR	45	00101101	-	77	01001101	M	109	01101101	m
14	00001110	SO	46	00101110	.	78	01001110	N	110	01101110	n
15	00001111	SI	47	00101111	/	79	01001111	O	111	01101111	o
16	00010000	DLE	48	00110000	0	80	01010000	P	112	01110000	p
17	00010001	DC1	49	00110001	1	81	01010001	Q	113	01110001	q
18	00010010	DC2	50	00110010	2	82	01010010	R	114	01110010	r
19	00010011	DC3	51	00110011	3	83	01010011	S	115	01110011	s
20	00010100	DC4	52	00110100	4	84	01010100	T	116	01110100	t
21	00010101	NAK	53	00110101	5	85	01010101	U	117	01110101	u
22	00010110	SYN	54	00110110	6	86	01010110	V	118	01110110	v
23	00010111	ETB	55	00110111	7	87	01010111	W	119	01110111	w
24	00011000	CAN	56	00111000	8	88	01011000	X	120	01111000	x
25	00011001	EM	57	00111001	9	89	01011001	Y	121	01111001	y
26	00011010	SUB	58	00111010	:	90	01011010	Z	122	01111010	z
27	00011011	ESC	59	00111011	;	91	01011011	[	123	01111011	{
28	00011100	FS	60	00111100	<	92	01011100	\	124	01111100		
29	00011101	GS	61	00111101	=	93	01011101	]	125	01111101	}
30	00011110	RS	62	00111110	>	94	01011110	^	126	01111110	~
31	00011111	US	63	00111111	?	95	01011111	_	127	01111111	DEL

2.3 TOKENS IN C

In a C program, the basic element recognized by the compiler is a token or lexical unit. It is the smallest unit which is not broken further during parsing. There can be six type of tokens in C.

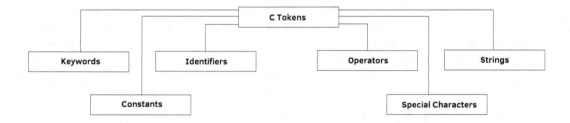

2.4 KEYWORDS

Keywords are special words with fixed meanings which cannot be changed. They are the words which are already defined in the compiler. They cannot be used as variable names i.e. no identifier can have the same spelling and case as a C keyword. Native C compiler had 32 keywords defined but many modern compilers have extended the list with some of their own. As per ANSI C (*a standard published by American National Standards Institute*), the list of C keywords are:

auto	break	case	char
const	continue	default	do
double	else	enum	extern
float	for	goto	if
int	long	register	return
short	signed	sizeof	static
struct	switch	typedef	union
unsigned	void	volatile	while

In **later** versions of C, more keywords were added to the language and they are:

_Alignas	_Alignof	_Atomic	_Bool
_Complex	_Generic	_Imaginary	_Noreturn
_Static_assert	_Thread_local	_Pragma	

2.5 CONSTANTS

Constants refer to fixed values which do not change during the execution of a program. Constants can be:

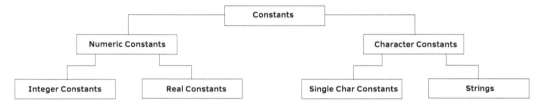

2.5.1 INTEGER CONSTANTS

An integer constant consists of a sequence of digits. An integer constant can be represented in decimal, octal or hexadecimal.

Decimal are base 10 representation and so consists of digits ranging from **0** to **9**. They can be preceded by an optional – or + sign. Example of decimal integer constants are *562, -8217, +838383, 0* and so on. Spaces, commas or any other non-digit characters are not allowed within the digits.

Octal are base 8 representation and so consists of digits ranging from **0** to **7**. They are preceded with a leading 0 to help the compiler differentiate them from decimals or hexadecimals. Example of octal integer constants are *026, 0, 015, 0264*.

Hexadecimal are base 16 representation and so consists of digits from **0** to **9** and alphabets from **A** to **F** (or **a** to **f**). They are preceded with a leading **0x** to help the compiler differentiate them from decimals or octal. Example of hexadecimal integer constants are *0x26, 0xFF, 0x5AFF*.

The largest integer constants are machine dependent . It can be $2^{32}-1$ for a 32-bit representation and

$2^{64}-1$ for a 64-bit representation. This can be increased by appending qualifiers such as U, L and UL to the constants like *3324334U* (unsigned integer constant), *2234443L* (long integer constant), *4234324324UL* (unsigned long integer constant).

2.5.2 REAL CONSTANTS

Integer constants cannot be used to represent values which can be in the decimals such as *186.56*, *176527.762872, -0.881981*. These numbers have a whole number followed by a decimal point and then the fractional part. It is possible to omit digits before or after the decimal point i.e. a value may not contain the whole number part and another value may not have the fraction part. Such numbers are called real constants. A real constant may also be expressed in exponential notation. For example, the value *678.72* may be expressed as *6.7872e2* in exponential notation where *e2* refers to multiplication by *100*. **'e'** refers to 10 and the number following 'e' refers to its power. The general mathematical representation is:

$$mantissa \times 10^n$$

Where mantissa can be any real or an integer number. **'n'** is an integer with an optional plus or minus sign. If 'n' is preceded by a minus sign, it means the resultant multiplication with the mantissa will move the decimal point to the left rather than the right.

The letter 'e' can be represented in lower or upper case.
Examples of such numbers are *727.321e2*, *0.72829e4*, *0.072828e5*, *8382.382e-1*.

Real constants are also called floating point constants and are represented in double precision. They can be made to represent single precision by suffixing them with a **'f'** or **'F'**.

2.5.3 SINGLE CHARACTER CONSTANTS

A single character constant (or character constant) contains a single character enclosed within a pair of single quotation marks such as *'A'*, *'g'*, *'2'*, *'#'*,*' '*. The constant '2' is not the same as the number 2. The character constant '2' denotes the **ASCII** value 50 (refer to the ASCII table in para 2.2). For example, the statement

printf("%c", 50);

will print the character '*2*' on the output screen and the statement

printf("%d", 'A');

will print the number *65* on the output screen. 65 is the ASCII value of the character 'A'.

Some special character constants are defined in 'C' which change their meaning and ASCII value representation. Remember, some non-printable values are also present in the ASCII table. These values carry special meanings. These constants are sometimes called *backslash character constants*. They represent only one character although they are represented using two characters (*a backslash followed by a character*). The backslash is called an escape character which changes the meaning of the character following it. The two characters (*'\' and the character following it*) are processed as a single unit and are evaluated as a single character. If we need to specify only the backslash character, it itself needs to be escaped by another backslash.

The various backslash character constants are:

Constant	Meaning	ASCII Value
'\a'	An audible alert	7
'\b'	Backspace	8
'\f'	Form feed	12
'\n'	New line (Line feed)	10
'\r'	Carriage return	13
'\t'	Horizontal tab	9
'\v'	Vertical tab	11
'\0'	NULL (marks the end of a string, file etc.)	0
'\''	Single quote	39
'\"'	Double quote	34
'\?'	Question mark	63
'\\'	Backslash	92

2.5.4 STRING CONSTANTS

A string constant is a sequence of characters enclosed in double quotes. The characters can be letters, numbers, space, backslash characters and special characters. Internally, the compiler marks the ending of the string constant using a special non-printable character called *NULL* ('\0') represented by the ASCII value *0* (zero). The character constant '*G*' is different from the string constant "*G*". A string constant does not have an equivalent integer value while a character constant has an equivalent integer value corresponding to its ASCII value.

2.6 IDENTIFIERS

An identifier is a string of alphanumeric characters that begins with an alphabetic character or an underscore character and is used to represent various programming elements such as variables, functions, arrays, structures, unions etc. An identifier can also contain an underscore and is a user-defined name given to a programming element. Though we can start an identifier with an underscore, but it is discouraged. An identifier can be of any length but two identifiers must be distinguishable in the first 31 characters. In other words the C compiler uses the first 31 characters of an identifier as the token. Case of a character within an identifier is important i.e. it is case sensitive. For example, the identifier '*NAME*' is different than the identifier '*name*'. Space is not allowed within an identifier. The identifier should not be the same as a C keyword.

2.7 VARIABLES

Variables are names used to refer to some location in memory which holds a value with which we are working. They are placeholder for a value. Before a program can utilize memory to store a variable it must claim the memory needed to store the value for a variable. This is done by declaring the variable. Before a variable is used the compiler needs to know the number of variables it needs, what they are going to be named, and how much memory they will need. When managing and working with variables, it is important to know the type of variables and the size of these types. The type determines the kind of data we are going to store in the variable, for example integer values (*0, 9828, 2827382, ...*), character values (*'G', 'M', 'a', '#', ...*), real values (*728.28, 822329.283302, 62.3738e3, ...*) etc. Unlike constants which cannot be changed during the lifetime of the program, values in variables can be changed according to the needs of the program. Variable names are governed by identifier naming convention as stated earlier. Some valid variable names are '*m_dblAverage*', '*s_fltUnitPrice*', '*ulTotal*'. Some invalid variable names are '*353dhd*', '*edfsd$22&35*', '*@*', '*4545*'.

2.7.1 VARIABLE DECLARATION

After determining variable names, we must declare the variables before using them anywhere in the program. This helps the compiler understand the memory requirements of the variable and the kind of operations to be allowed on them. Declaration helps the compiler understand the following things:

- The variable names.
- The type of data the variable will contain.
- The memory required to hold the value corresponding to the variable.
- The operations to be allowed on the variable.

Variables can also be declared using the optional '*const*' keyword which makes the value contained within the variable constant i.e. the value contained within the variable cannot be changed.

2.8 DATA TYPES

Data types are declarations for memory locations or variables that determine the characteristics of the data that may be stored and the operations that are permitted using them. ANSI C supports four classes of data types:

1. Primary (basic or fundamental) data types.
2. Derived data types.
3. Alias data types.
4. void data type.

2.8.1 PRIMARY DATA TYPES

- **int**: They hold integer values. They are whole numbers and their capacity depends on the compiler but, must use at-least 16 bits *(2 bytes)* of internal storage. Generally most modern compilers use 32 bits *(4 bytes)* of internal storage to represent an integer value allowing an int variable to hold values in the range of *-2147483648* to *+2147483647 (i.e. -2^{31} to $+2^{31}-1$)*. A signed integer uses one bit to hold the sign of the value and the rest for holding the magnitude. There are two kinds of modifiers which can be used to change the properties of the integer data – Storage modifiers and sign modifiers. Storage modifiers '***short***' and '***long***' can be used to change the range of the values stored in a variable whereas the sign modifiers '***signed***' and '***unsigned***' can be used to change the sign of the value. 'short' modifier halves the storage requirement of the value and also the range of the value. It makes the data use 16 bits *(2 bytes)* of internal storage giving it a range of *-32768* to *+32767 (i.e. -2^{15} to $+2^{15}-1$)*. 'long' modifier doubles the storage requirement and the range of the value but, is machine architecture dependent. On 32-bit machines the 'long' modifier makes the data use 32 bits *(4 bytes)* of internal storage giving it a range of *-2147483648* to *+2147483647 (i.e. -2^{31} to $+2^{31}-1$).* On 64-bit machines it makes the data use 64 bits *(8 bytes)* of internal storage giving it a range of *-9223372036854775808* to *+9223372036854775807 (i.e. -2^{63} to $+2^{63}-1$).* As the long modifier makes the range differ depending on the machine architecture, a new modifier '**long long**' was introduced in some newer compilers which makes the data use exactly 64 bits *(8 bytes)* of internal storage regardless of the machine architecture. 'signed' modifier is optional and all integer values are signed by default unless we explicitly specify 'unsigned' as the modifier. 'unsigned' modifier specifies that the value will only store 0 and positive values.

- **char:** They hold character type data like 'T', 'Q', 'h', '4', '?' etc. Characters are usually stored in 8 bits *(1 byte)* of internal storage. This is sufficient to hold all character representations in the English language, but is insufficient to hold all characters of many languages other than English. So, a new character type called 'Unicode' *(wide char denoted using 'wchar_t')* was defined which stores the value in 1 to 4 bytes *(depending on the encoding used)* of internal storage (refer **section 2.2**). We will discuss more about Unicode in our later chapters. Just like 'int', the sign modifiers '*signed*' and '*unsigned*' may also be applied to 'char'. While signed 'char' can hold values ranging from *-128* to *127*, unsigned 'char' can hold values in the range of *0* to *255*.

- **float:** They hold real numbers like *3444.3839*, *89393.33*, *83.3443e2* etc. They are stored in 32 bits *(4 bytes)* of internal storage and have 6 digits of precision. No size or sign modifier can be applied to the float data type and all float values are always signed.

- **double:** When the accuracy provided by float is not sufficient, the type 'double' can be used. They are stored in 64 bits *(8 bytes)* of internal storage and have 14 digits of precision. They hold the same type of data *(real)* as float but with double the precision, hence the name 'double'. Their precision can be further extended to use 80 bits *(10 bytes)* of internal storage by using the size modifier 'long'. The other modifiers 'short', 'signed' and 'unsigned' cannot be applied to the double data type. They are always signed.

- **Data types specific to C99 and later:** In the year 1999, some modifications were made to the C programming language to make it more robust and extend it with more features. It helped utilize the current hardware better and achieve better program optimization. It introduced new data types which were not available in earlier versions. The data types that were introduced were float_t, double_t, float _Complex, double _Complex, long double _Complex and _Bool.
  - **float_t** and **double_t**: They correspond to the types used for the intermediate results of floating-point expressions when **FLT_EVAL_METHOD** is 0, 1, or 2. *FLT_EVAL_METHOD* specifies the precision in which all floating point arithmetic operations other than assignment and cast are done. When *FLT_EVAL_METHOD* is:
    - **0 *(zero)*:** float_t and double_t are equivalent to float and double, respectively.
    - **1:** Both float_t and double_t are equivalent to double.
    - **2:** Both float_t and double_t are equivalent to long double.

- ○ **float _Complex**, **double _Complex** and **long double _Complex**: When the floating point types are followed by the '_Complex' keyword, they help store and process mathematical complex numbers. Complex numbers are numbers which are of the form 'a + bi' where 'a' and 'b' are real numbers and 'i' is an imaginary unit.
- ○ **_Bool:** _Bool is a type which is capable of holding the two values 1 and 0, where 1 signifies 'true' and 0 signifies 'false'. _Bool has been type defined as 'bool' in the header file 'stdbool.h'. So, for convenience we can also write 'bool' in place of '_Bool', if we include the header file 'stdbool.h'.

2.8.2 SIZE AND RANGE OF PRIMARY DATA TYPES

Type	Size (bytes)	Range
char/signed char	1	–128 to 127.
unsigned char	1	0 to 255.
wchar_t	2	0 to 65535 [Unicode characters].
short/short int/signed short/signed short int	2	–32768 to +32767.
unsigned short/ unsigned short int	2	0 to 65535.
int/signed/signed int	2 or 4	–32768 to +32767 when represented using 2 bytes.. -2147483648 to +2147483647 when represented using 4 bytes.
unsigned/unsigned int	2 or 4	0 to 65535 when represented using 2 bytes. 0 to 4294967295 when represented using 4 bytes.
long/long int/signed long/signed long int	4 or 8	–2147483648 to +2147483647 when represented using 4 bytes. -9223372036854775808 to +9223372036854775807 when represented using 8 bytes.
unsigned long/ unsigned long int	4 or 8	0 to 4294967295 when represented using 4 bytes. 0 to 18446744073709551615 when represented using 8 bytes.
long long/long long int/signed long long/ signed long long int / _int64	8	–9223372036854775808 to +9223372036854775807. (These types are available since C99)
unsigned long long/ unsigned long long int/ unsigned _int64	8	0 to 18446744073709551615. (These types are available since C99)
float	4	–3.4e+38 to +3.4e+38.
double	8	–1.7e+308 to +1.7e+308.
long double	10	Typically –3.4e+4932 to +1.1e+4932.

Note: *The data types with multiple size options in the 'Size (bytes)' column (ex: 2 or 4), are compiler dependent and so, the number of bytes they occupy depend on the compiler with which we are working.*

2.8.3 DERIVED DATA TYPES

These data types are either formed using a combination of primary data types or they are used to represent the primary data types in a different way. They extend the scope of C language. The most common are *pointers*, *arrays*, *union* and *structures (struct)*. We will read about them in later chapters.

2.8.4 ALIAS DATA TYPES

C allows type-definition which lets the programmer define an identifier that will represent an existing data type. In other words, we may give a new name *(alias)* to an existing data type. This alias can later be used to declare variables. There are two types of alias data types:
- Data types created using the **typedef** keyword.
- Data types created using the **enum** keyword.

'typedef' is a reserved keyword in the C programming languages. It is used to create an alias name for another data type. As such, it is often used to simplify the syntax of declaring data structures consisting of struct and union types, but can also be used to provide specific descriptive type names for the primary data types, arrays and pointers. The syntax of a typedef statement is:

typedef type identifier;

where *'type'* refers to an existing data type and *'identifier'* refers to the new typedef *(alias)* name given to the data type. The new name remains absolutely identical to the data type which it is type-defining. 'typedef' cannot create a new type but provides just an alias name for an existing type. Some examples of typedef statements and their uses are:

typedef int categories;
categories PrimaryID;
categories SubIDs[100];

Another alias data types is defined using the keyword 'enum' *(enumerated in short)*. An enumeration consists of a set of named integer constants. An enumeration type declaration gives a **name** *(optional)* and defines a set of named integer identifiers representing values which the enumerated **name** can hold. It is defined as:

Example 1:   **enum** <name>
{
    identifier1,
    identifier2,
    identifier3,
    ...
};

In the above example, the compiler internally provides an integer value of 0 to *'identifier1'*, 1 to '*identifier2*', 2 to '*identifier3*' and so on. So, if we do not provide any specific values, the enumerated identifiers will obtain values starting from 0 and increment sequentially.

'enum' can also be defined in a way so that the enumerated identifiers can attain certain specific integer values like:

Example 2:   **enum** <name>
```
                {
                    identifier1 = 10,
                    identifier2 = 11,
                    identifier3 = 12,
                    identifier4 = 20,
                    identifier5 = 21,

                    ...
                };
```

In the above example, the compiler internally provides an integer value of 10 to '*identifier1*', 11 to '*identifier2*', 12 to '*identifier3*', 20 to '*identifier4*' and so on.

We can then declare variables using the enumerated name in the following manner:

enum <*name*> v1;

enum <*name*> v2;

where the variables '*v1*' and '*v2*' can only hold values identified using the identifiers (*identifier1*, *identifier2*, ...) as mentioned in the enumeration.

Usage example:
```
                enum DayOfTheWeek
                {
                    Monday,
                    Tuesday,
                    Wednesday,
                    Thursday,
                    Friday,
                    Saturday,
                    Sunday
                };

                enum DayOfTheWeek StartDay;
                enum DayOfTheWeek EndDay;

                StartDay = Wednesday;    /* StartDay is assigned Wednesday (integer value 2). */
                EndDay = StartDay;    /* EndDay will also have the value Wednesday. */
                if (EndDay == Wednesday)
                {
                    EndDay = Sunday;    /* Now, EndDay gets assigned Sunday (integer value 6). */
                }
```

2.8.5 void DATA TYPE

The data type **void** actually refers to no value or no specific data type. A function may return void which means that it does not return anything. A function may also accept void as its parameter signifying that it does not accept any parameters or arguments. Similarly, we can have void pointers *(discussed in later chapters)*, which mean that they point to memory locations whose data type is not known.

Example:　　　void PrintVal(int I);

　　　　　　　int GetVal(void);

　　　　　　　void ShowWelcomeMessage(void);

2.9 STORAGE CLASSES

A storage class defines the scope *(visibility)* and life-time of variables within a C Program. They precede the type that they modify. They tell the compiler where to store a variable, how to store the variable, what is the initial value of the variable and life time of the variable. Consider the following example:

```
int g_Val1;
void function1(void)
{
   int iVal2;
}

int main(void)
{
   int iVal3;
   int iVal2;
   function1();
   return 0;
}
```

The variable '*g_Val1*' which has been defined outside all functions is called the **global** variable. It is accessible across all the functions within the source file. It need **not** be declared within any function to be accessible. The global variables are visible starting from the location in which they are declared to the end of the source file. Any usage of the variable before it is declared is marked as an error. Consider the below example:

```
void PrintVal(void)
{
    /* The compiler will generate an error for the below 'printf' statement, as the global
       variable 'g_iVal' is still undeclared at that location. 'g_iVal' is declared below
       this function 'PrintVal' and so is not visible within function 'PrintVal'. */
    printf("\nValue of 'g_iVal' is %d", g_iVal);
}

int g_iVal = 10;

int main(void)
{
    /* The below 'printf' statement is valid. The global variable 'g_iVal' is declared
```

```
     before the below statement, making it visible at that location. */
   printf("\nValue of 'g_iVal' is %d", g_iVal++);
   PrintVal();
   return 0;
}
```

The variable '*iVal2*' is a local variable to the function '*function1*' and is available only to this function. All other functions do not have access to this variable. Similarly, the variable '*iVal3*' is local to the the the function '*main*' and is accessible only within the function 'main'. We can see that the variable '*iVal2*' has also been declared within the '*main*' function. But, the '*iVal2*' of the function '*function1*' is different than the '*iVal2*' of the function '*main*'. Both can have different values, are stored in separate internal memory locations and are accessible only to the respective functions.

Prior to C99, all local variables must be declared at the start of the block within which it is declared. Starting from C99, a variable may be declared anywhere within a block, even at the point of its usage. We will discuss this in our later chapters.

C programs can have four storage class specifiers. They are:

Storage Class	Meaning	Default Value
auto	Local variable known only to the function in which it is declared. It is the default. **Usage Example:** *int iCount; auto double dblPrice;*	Garbage (Uninitialized)
static	The static storage class instructs the compiler to keep a local variable in existence during the life-time of the program instead of creating and destroying it each time it comes in and goes out of scope. Making local variables static enables them to maintain their values between function calls. The static modifier may also be applied to global variables upon which it causes that variable's scope to be restricted not just to a function but to the entire file in which it is declared. **Usage Example:** *static char iVal;*	0
extern	The *extern* keyword is used before a variable to inform the compiler that this variable is declared in some other source file of the same program. Global variables declared in one source file can be accessed in another using the keyword extern. For example, an integer '*iVal*' declared in the source file '*file1.c*' can be accessed in another file '*file2.c*' using the *extern* keyword. **Usage Example:** *extern long lTotal;*	0
register	Local variables which are stored in the CPU registers. For some high performance temporary operations, we may declare *register* variables. As they are stored in registers, a variable's maximum size is limited to the register size *(usually one word)*. Only few variables can be placed inside register. **Usage Example:** *register short Counter;*	Garbage (Uninitialized)

2.10 DEFINING SYMBOLIC CONSTANTS AND MACROS

We often require to use some constant values within the program. These values may need to be used repeatedly across the source files of the program. As an example, we may require to use *1.414* as the square root value of 2. We may be using it repeatedly within the program. So, to save ourselves from errors we may define it using a name, and use the defined name across all places which require that value. The general form of defining is:

#define   *symbolic-name*   *value*

where symbolic-name is the name given to the value. As an example, we may use it as:

#define   *SQUARE_ROOT*   *1.414*

The defined names are called symbolic names or symbolic constants. When the program is compiled, these symbolic names are replaced by their respective defined values by the compiler before performing the compilation. As an example, the symbolic name 'SQUARE_ROOT' is replaced by 1.414, wherever that name is encountered within the program. These statements are called **preprocessor** statements as they are processed before the compilation begins. The *preprocessor* statements begin with a '#' symbol, and do **not** end with a semicolon. The defined value may represent a numeric constant, a character constant, a string constant or even an expression. Though there is no restriction regarding the case of the symbolic name, it is considered a convention to use all UPPERCASE characters. This helps in distinguishing them from normal variable names which are written using lower case or mixed *(both lower an upper)* case characters.

The '*#define*' statement can also define an expression to be used in place of the symbolic-name wherever it is used. The expression can be something like:

#define INCREMENT(x)   *++x*

Wherever the compiler finds the symbolic name *'INCREMENT'*, it replaces the name with the expression corresponding to the name specified in the '*#define*' statement. This kind of statements are also called **macros**. A Macro is typically an abbreviated name given to a piece of code or a value. A macro is a code which has been given a name and whenever the name is used, it is replaced by the contents of the macro. The argument(s) to the macro *('x' in our example)* is replaced by the actual argument(s) specified during the macro call. There can be more than one argument to the macro. So, we may have something like:

```c
/* Header Files */
#include <stdio.h>
/* Defined Values */
#define INCREMENT(x)     ++x

void main(void)
{
    /* Variable declaration and initialization. */
    int i = 10;

    /* Now, print the incremented value. */
    printf("\nAfter increment i is: %d.\n\n", INCREMENT(i));
}
```

In the above program, the macro call *'INCREMENT'* within the *'printf'* statement will be replaced by the expression corresponding to the macro and *'i' (specified within the call)* will replace *'x'* within the macro expression. So, the macro call *'INCREMENT(i)'* will be replaced by the expression *'++i'*. The program will print the following output:

```
After increment i is: 11.
```

The following **rules** apply to the #*define* statement.
- '#' must be the first character of the line, though some modern compilers allow spaces before the '#' symbol.
- No space should be present between the '#' and the *'define'* word.
- At-least one blank space is required between '#*define'* and the symbolic name, and between the symbolic name and the constant value.
- Preprocessor statements (like #*define*) must not end with a semi-colon.
- The data type of the constant is determined by the compiler depending on its value. The '#*define'* statement does not specify any data type.
- After a symbolic name has been defined, it cannot be re-defined anywhere within the source file *(unless undefined)*. Also, **NO** value can be assigned to a symbolic name anywhere else within the program *(like SQUARE_ROOT = 1.4)*.
- '#*define'* statements can appear anywhere within the program but before they are referenced. By convention they are placed at the beginning of a source or header file.
- Separate preprocessor statements (like #*define*) must appear in separate lines. **Neither** multiple values can be defined for a symbolic name, nor multiple definitions can appear in a single line. So, the following statements are **invalid**.

```
#define  SQUARE_ROOT  1.414   1.414213
#define  SQUARE_ROOT  1.414   PI  3.141
#define  SQUARE_ROOT  1.414,  PI  3.141
```

Now, let us discuss the advantages of using the '**#define**' statements. There are primarily two advantages of using '#*define*' statements and they are:
- **Easy modifications:** If we use the square root value of *2* as *1.414* directly across multiple locations within the program, it will require an immense amount of work in case we later decide to change the value. Say, we later decide to increase the precision of the value from the existing *1.414* to *1.414213*, we will need to make changes across the entire program wherever that value gets used. If any location is missed, the program may generate erroneous output.

- **Easy understanding:** If we had used the constant value *1.414* directly within a program location, another programmer may not understand the origin of that value. Multiple programmers may work on the same program, or a program may be developed by one programmer but, maintained by another. When a new programmer starts working on the program, (s)he may not understand the origin or the reason for using that specific constant value. If a descriptive name is defined for the value and that name is used across the program, (s)he will immediately understand the reason and the origin of the value.

2.11 DECLARING A VARIABLE AS A CONSTANT

We may not want a value to be defined using the '#*define*' statement as we cannot specify its data type. We may require a value to be of a certain specific data type. So, for values like these we may use the '**const**' keyword. The '*const*' keyword is used as a qualifier during variable declaration. The variable must be declared and initialized in the same statement when using the '*const*' qualifier. This constant variable can be used as the right hand value of any assignment statement and also provided as argument to any function. No value can be assigned to the variable. If a constant variable is declared within a function, its value cannot be modified anywhere within the function, and every time the function gets invoked, the constant variable gets the same value with which it is initialized. If a constant variable is declared within a source file, its value cannot be changed anywhere within the entire source file *(including all its functions)*. Some examples of the '*const*' qualifier are:

const float fltPI = 3.141;

const int iPrice = 130;

2.12 VOLATILE VARIABLES

We can have another qualifier called '**volatile**' which gets applied during variable declaration. It tells the compiler that the value of the variable may change at any time, and even without any action being taken by the code. If not properly used, the implications of this behaviour may be quite serious. In real life we should rarely need to use the '*volatile*' qualifier. An example use of the '*volatile*' qualifier is given below.

volatile int iValue;

If a variable is declared as volatile, it can, not only be modified by external factors *(like processes, hardware operations etc.)*, but also be changed by its own program as well. To prevent the value from getting changed by the own program and yet allowing external forces to change the value, we may add the '*const*' qualifier along with the '*volatile*' qualifier as below.

volatile const int iValue = 56;

2.13 DATA OVERFLOW AND UNDERFLOW

When programming we need to be very careful regarding assigning values to variable which are larger or smaller than the variable's capacity. Data overflow occurs when we try to assign a value to a variable which is larger or smaller than the variable's capacity *(as per its data type)*. When overflow occurs, the value in the variable gets rolled over *(wrap around)*. C does not provide any warnings for data overflow. It only generates wrong results which may make the program to fail. Underflow can occur when the true result of a floating point operation is smaller in magnitude *(that is, closer to zero)* than the smallest value that can be represented in the target data type.

2.14 ALIGNING ADDRESSES

Every variable we declare is stored in the memory and assigned a memory address. When we declare variables, they are assigned any valid and unused memory address. One '*char*' variable may be assigned an address of 1757 while the next may be assigned 2240. Programs may have a requirement to align certain variable addresses to the multiples of a constant *(power of 2)*. For example, we may want some variables in our program to be aligned at 16 byte addresses. We may achieve this by using the type specifier '**_Alignas**' or the macro '**alignas**'. We will learn about these in our chapter on '*Structures And Unions*'.

2.15 SAMPLE PROGRAM

Calculation of area of circles.
Lets try to write a program where we will calculate the area of multiple circles. The radius of the circle will start from 5 and will increment sequentially till 15.

```
/*******************************************************/
/*                    Area of circles                  */
/*                  Copyright Information              */
/*******************************************************/
/* Header Files */
#include <stdio.h>

/* Defined Values */
#define  PI           3.141592
#define  MIN_RADIUS   5
#define  MAX_RADIUS   15

void main(void)
{
    /* Variable Declaration & Initialization */
    int     iRadius = MIN_RADIUS;
    double dblArea = 0;

    while (iRadius <= MAX_RADIUS)
    {
        dblArea = PI * iRadius * iRadius;
        printf("\nThe area of the circle with radius %d is %f.", iRadius, dblArea);
        iRadius = iRadius + 1;
    }
}
```

Output

```
The area of the circle with radius 5 is 78.539800.
The area of the circle with radius 6 is 113.097312.
The area of the circle with radius 7 is 153.938008.
The area of the circle with radius 8 is 201.061888.
The area of the circle with radius 9 is 254.468952.
The area of the circle with radius 10 is 314.159200.
The area of the circle with radius 11 is 380.132632.
The area of the circle with radius 12 is 452.389248.
The area of the circle with radius 13 is 530.929048.
The area of the circle with radius 14 is 615.752032.
The area of the circle with radius 15 is 706.858200.
```

OPERATORS AND OPERATIONS

[CHAPTER-3]

3.1 INTRODUCTION

An *operator* is a symbol that operates on a value or variable. It is used to perform certain mathematical or logical operations on data and variables. C language supports a rich set of built-in operators. The operators in C can be classified into the following categories.

1. Arithmetic operators
2. Increment and decrement operators
3. Assignment operator
4. Bitwise operators
5. Relational operators
6. Logical operators
7. Conditional (Ternary) operator
8. Special operators

The operations performed using the operators are also called **expressions**.

3.2 ARITHMETIC OPERATORS

C provides operators for all the basic arithmetic operations. The arithmetic operators are:

Operator	Meaning
+	Addition of two numbers or unary plus.
-	Subtraction of two numbers or unary minus.
*	Multiplication of two numbers.
/	Division of two numbers.
%	Remainder after division (Modulo division).

Arithmetic operations are always performed between two numbers. The result of an arithmetic operation between two numbers is always in the larger data type of the two numbers involved in the operation. By larger data type we mean the data type which is capable of holding a larger value or higher precision. The following rules are applied in the order given:

- If one of the number is a *long double*, the other number too is promoted to *long double* and the result will be in *long double*.
- If one of the number is a *double*, the other number too is promoted to *double* and the result will be in *double*.
- If one of the number is a *float*, the other number too is promoted to *float* and the result will be in *float*.
- If one of the number is *long int*, the other number too is promoted to *long int* and the result will be in *long int*.

- If one of the number is *int*, the other number too is promoted to *int* and the result will be in *int*.
- If one of the number is *short*, the other number too is promoted to *short* and the result will be in *short*.
- The result will be in *char*, if both the numbers are in *char*.

The arithmetic operation between two integer is called *integer arithmetic* and the expression is called *integer expression.* Integer arithmetic always yields an integer value. The integer arithmetic between two integer values 'x' and 'y' where 'x' has a value of 19 and 'y' has a value of 8, will yield the following results.

x – y = 11
x + y = 27
x * y = 152
x / y = 2 *(decimal part truncated as the result will be in integer)*
x % y = 3 *(remainder of the division)*

During division between two integer (*int*) numbers, the decimal part is truncated as the result of two integer (*int*) numbers will always be an integer (*int*). If we need the remainder, we may use the modulo *(%)* operator.

During modulo division, the sign of the result is the sign of the first operand in the operation. For example:

-19 % 8 = -3
-19 % -8 = -3
19 % -8 = 3
19 % 8 = 3

An arithmetic operation between two real numbers is called *real arithmetic operation*. A real operand may be in decimal or exponential notation. The result of such an operation is a real number. The modulo operator *(%)* cannot be used with real operands.

When in an arithmetic operation, one of the operand is a real number and the other an integer, the operation is called *mixed mode arithmetic operation*. The result of such an operation is a real number. For example:

39 / 10.0 = 3.9

3.3 INCREMENT AND DECREMENT OPERATORS

Increment and decrement operators are unary operators that add or subtract one from their operand, respectively. They are:

++ and --

The increment operator is written as **++** and the decrement operator is written as **--**. The increment operator increases the value of its operand by 1 and the decrement operator decreases the value by 1. The operands must have an arithmetic or pointer data type. They take the following forms:

++*count* or *count*++ *(Same as: count = count + 1)*

--*count* or *count*-- *(Same as: count = count -1)*

Though, ++*count* and *count*++ do the same thing, they behave a bit differently when they are put in the right hand side of an assignment statement.
Consider the following statements:
int count = 10;
int index = count++;

In the above statements, the value of 'count' will be 11 whereas the value of 'index' will be 10. So, in other words the value of 'count' is assigned to 'index' before performing the increment. The operation 'count++' is called **post-increment**, as the increment is done after the assignment.
Now consider the following statements:
int count = 10;
int index = ++count;

In the above statements, the value of 'count' will be 11 and the value of 'index' will also be 11. So, in other words the value of 'count' is incremented before assigning it to 'index'. The operation '++count' is called **pre-increment**, as the increment is done before the value is assigned.

In simple words, in case of post-increment, the operator first assigns the value to the variable on the left and then increments the operand. In case of pre-increment, the operator first increments the operand and then the result is assigned to the variable on the left. Similar behavior occurs for post-decrement and pre-decrement operations.

The increment and decrement operators may be used in complex statements. Say, we have two variables '**x**' with a value of 15 and '**y**' with a value of 10. The execution breakup corresponding to some expressions are as follows:

Expression	Execution Breakup	Result
m = x++ * ++y;	1) ++y *(y is incremented)* 2) m = x * y *(x is multiplied with y and the value assigned to m)* 3) x++ *(x is incremented)*	m: 165, x: 16, y: 11
m = x++ + ++y;	1) ++y *(y is incremented)* 2) m = x + y *(x is added with y and the value assigned to m)* 3) x++ *(x is incremented)*	m: 26, x: 16, y: 11
m = x++ + ++y * 2;	1) ++y *(y is incremented)* 2) m = x + y * 2 *(y is multiplied by 2, added with x and the result assigned to m)* 3) x++ *(x is incremented)*	m: 37, x: 16, y: 11

Expression	Execution Breakup	Result
m = x-- + ++y * 2;	1) ++y *(y is incremented)* 2) m = x + y * 2 *(y is multiplied by 2, added with x and the result assigned to m)* 3) x-- *(x is decremented)*	m: 37, x: 14, y: 11
m = ++x + y-- * 2;	1) ++x *(x is incremented)* 2) m = x + y * 2 *(y is multiplied by 2, added with x and the result assigned to m)* 3) y-- *(y is decremented)*	m: 36, x: 16, y: 9

3.4 ASSIGNMENT OPERATORS

Assignment operators are used to assign the result of an expression to a variable. Apart from the usual assignment statement *'variable = expression;'*, C provides another kind of assignment statement in the following form:

var op= expression;

where 'var' is for variable and 'op' is for an arithmetic operator. The operator '**op=**' is called the *shorthand assignment operator*.

Consider the following examples:
index += 5;
index *= count – 2;

The first statement is similar to the following statement:
index = index + 5;

And the second statement is similar to the following statement:
index = index * (count – 2);

Shorthand assignment operator examples

Expression with shorthand operator	Similar expression with simple assignment operator
count -= 1;	count = count - 1;
count /= (j + 1);	count = count / (j + 1);
count %= j;	count = count % j;
count += k * 5;	count = count + (k * 5);
count *= k + 3;	count = count * (k + 3);

3.5 BITWISE OPERATORS

C is one of the few languages which allow manipulations at the bit level. We can do manipulations or comparisons at the bit level using the *bitwise operators*. Bitwise operators can be used only on '*char*' and '*int*' data types. There are five bitwise operators and they are:

Operator	Meaning
&	bitwise AND
|	bitwise INCLUSIVE OR (*OR*)
^	bitwise EXCLUSIVE OR (*XOR*)
~	bitwise NOT
<<	SHIFT LEFT
>>	SHIFT RIGHT

Now, lets describe all the above bitwise operators with some examples. Say we have two unsigned char variables, '**x**' with a value of *77* and '**y**' with a value of *55*. In binary format 'x' will be represented as '*01001101*' and 'y' will be represented as '*00110111*'. Now, lets explain what happens when we perform the above bitwise operations on these two variables.

- **& (bitwise AND)**: The bitwise 'AND' operator compares each bit of the first operand to the corresponding bit of the second operand. If both the bits are 1, the corresponding result bit is set to 1. Otherwise, the corresponding result bit is set to 0. In the following operation the value of '**m**' after the 'AND' operation will be 5.

unsigned char m = x & y;

77	0	1	0	0	1	1	0	1	x
55	0	0	1	1	0	1	1	1	y
5	0	0	0	0	0	1	0	1	m

- **| (bitwise INCLUSIVE OR)**: The bitwise 'INCLUSIVE OR' or simply '**OR**' operator compares each bit of the first operand to the corresponding bit of the second operand. If either bit is 1, the corresponding result bit is set to 1. Otherwise, the corresponding result bit is set to 0. In the following operation the value of '**m**' after the 'OR' operation will be 127.

unsigned char m = x | y;

77	0	1	0	0	1	1	0	1	x
55	0	0	1	1	0	1	1	1	y
127	0	1	1	1	1	1	1	1	m

- **^ (bitwise EXCLUSIVE OR)**: The bitwise 'EXCLUSIVE OR' or simply '**XOR**' operator compares each bit of the first operand to the corresponding bit of the second operand. If one bit is 0 and the other bit is 1, the corresponding result bit is set to 1. Otherwise, the corresponding result bit is set to 0. In the following operation the value of '**m**' after the 'EXCLUSIVE OR' operation will be 122.

unsigned char m = x ^ y;

77	0	1	0	0	1	1	0	1	x
55	0	0	1	1	0	1	1	1	y
122	0	1	1	1	1	0	1	0	m

- **~ (bitwise NOT):** The bitwise 'NOT' operator looks at the binary representation of the operand and does a bitwise negation operation on it. Any bit that is a 1 in the operand becomes 0 in the result and any bit that is a 0 becomes 1 in the result. When the ~ operator acts on an operand it returns a value of the same data type as the operand.

unsigned char m = ~x;

77	0	1	0	0	1	1	0	1	x
178	1	0	1	1	0	0	1	0	m

- **<< (SHIFT LEFT):** The bitwise 'LEFT SHIFT' operator shifts each bit in its left-hand operand to the left by the number of positions indicated by the right-hand operand. The left most bits *(numbering equal to the value of the second/right-hand operand)* are simply dropped-off in the result. For the number of bits shifted towards the left, equal number of 0s *(zeroes)* are inserted from the right side. In the following example, 3 left-most bits are dropped-off and 3 zeroes are inserted from the right-hand side in the final output in '*m*'.

unsigned char m = x << 3;

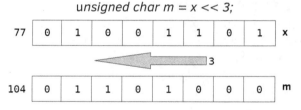

77	0	1	0	0	1	1	0	1	x
104	0	1	1	0	1	0	0	0	m

- **>> (SHIFT RIGHT):** The bitwise 'RIGHT SHIFT' operator shifts each bit in its left-hand operand to the right by the number of positions indicated by the right-hand operand. The right most bits *(numbering equal to the value of the second/right-hand operand)* are simply dropped-off in the result. For the number of bits shifted towards the right, equal number of 0s *(zeroes)* are inserted from the left side. In the following example, 2 right-most bits are dropped-off and 2 zeroes are inserted from the left-hand side in the final output in '*m*'.

unsigned char m = x >> 2;

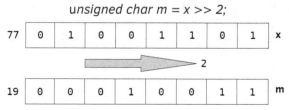

77	0	1	0	0	1	1	0	1	x
19	0	0	0	1	0	0	1	1	m

Bitwise operators can be part of some complex expressions like the ones given in the following table.

Expression	Simplified	Result
m = x | y >> 3;	x | (y >> 3);	m: 79, x: 77, y: 55
m = x | y & x ^ y;	x | ((y & x) ^ y);	m: 127, x: 77, y: 55
m = x++ | --y & x << 3;	1) --y *(y is decremented)*	m: 109, x: 78, y: 54
	2) m = x | (y & (x << 3));	
	3) x++ *(x is incremented)*	

3.6 RELATIONAL OPERATORS

The relational operators compare values to one another. When we decide to do certain operations depending on some conditions, these conditions are generally represented using relational operators. For example, we may compare the price of two products and decide to purchase the product with the lower price. This comparison may be done using the '<' or '>' relational operators. The expression represented using a relational operator is termed as a *relational expression*. One relational expression is generally composed of one relational operator and two operands *(values)* on both sides of the operator. The result of a relational expression is either *'true'* or *'false'* where false is denoted by '0' *(zero)* and true is non-zero. In C, true has the value of 1, but may be compiler specific. For example:

$$int\ x = 5;$$
$$int\ y = 10;$$

$x < y \rightarrow$ *Expression result is* **true**.
$x > y \rightarrow$ *Expression result is* **false**.

Different relational operators available in C are:

Operator	Meaning
<	Operand at the left of the operator is less than the right-hand operand
>	Left-hand operand is greater than the right-hand operand
<=	Left-hand operand is less than or equal to the right-hand operand
>=	Left-hand operand is greater than or equal to the right-hand operand
==	Left-hand operand is equal to the right-hand operand
!=	Left-hand operand is not equal to the right-hand operand

Multiple relational expressions may be combined using logical operators *(explained later)* to create one single expression.

Remember: In places where an expression requires a relational operator *(ex: within an if condition, conditional operator or loop condition)* but none has been specified, then by default the expression is compared for *inequality* with *0 (zero)*. So, the statement *'if (x)'* is the same as specifying *'if (x != 0)'*. We will learn more about *'if conditions'* and *'loop conditions'* in our later chapters.

Assume we have two variables x and y with values 5 and 10 respectively. On this assumption, the result of some relational expressions are given in the next table.

Expression	Result
x < y	true
x <= y	true
x != y	true
x == y	false
x > 3	true
x >= 7	false

3.7 LOGICAL OPERATORS

Logical operators are mainly used to control program flow and make decisions. There are three logical operators in C.

&&	logical **AND**
||	logical **OR**
!	logical **NOT**

Logical operators '&&' and '||' are used for combining multiple relational expressions into a single expression. The result of the individual relational expressions are combined to form a single overall result. Multiple conditions are evaluated to make a decision. An expression which combines two or more relational expressions is termed *logical expression* or *compound relational expression*. Like the relational expressions, logical expressions also yield the result as *'true'* or *'false'*.

- **&& (AND):** The '&&' operator combines two expressions as below.

    expression1 && expression2

    The logical AND operator *(&&)* returns true *(1)* if result of both the expressions *(expression1 and expression2)* are true *(1)* and returns false *(0)* otherwise.

    Logical AND is evaluated from left to right. The second expression is evaluated only if the result of the first expression evaluates to true *(non zero)*. This evaluation eliminates needless evaluation of the second expression when the result of the first expression is false. For two variables *x* and *y* with values 5 and 10 respectively, we can have the following expressions.

    Examples:

x < y && x != 2	→ Evaluates to true
x <= 5 && y >= 5	→ Evaluates to true
x > y && y == 10	→ Evaluates to false as expression1 is false.

- **|| (OR):** The '||' operator combines two expressions as below.

    expression1 || expression2

    The logical OR operator *(||)* returns true *(1)* if result of any of the expressions *(expression1 or expression2)* is true *(1)*, and returns false *(0)* if result of both the expressions are false *(0)*.

    Logical OR is evaluated from left to right. The second expression is evaluated only if the result of the first expression evaluates to false *(zero)*. This is simply because, if result of the first expression is true, the overall result of the entire logical expression also becomes true. This eliminates needless evaluation of the second expression when the result of the first expression is already true. For two variables *x* and *y* with values 5 and 10 respectively, we can have the following expressions.

Examples:

x < y || x != 5	→ Evaluates to true as expression1 is true.
x < 5 || y >= 5	→ Evaluates to true as expression2 is true.
x > y || y != 10	→ Evaluates to false as both expressions are false.

- **! (NOT):** The '!' operator performs logical negation on an expression. It is stated as:

!expression

If result of the expression is true *(1)*, NOT operator converts the overall result to false *(0)*. If result of the expression is false *(0)*, the overall result becomes *(1)*. For a variable *x* with value of 5, we can have the following expressions.

Examples:

!(x == 5)	→ Evaluates to false
!(x > 5)	→ Evaluates to true

3.8 CONDITIONAL (TERNARY) OPERATOR

The conditional operator pair (? :) takes three operands and so is also called *ternary operator*. It has the following syntax:

expression1 ? expression2 : expression3

- The expression1 is evaluated first.
- If the result of expression1 is *true (non zero)*, expression2 is evaluated.
- If the result of expression1 is *false (zero)*, expression3 is evaluated.

The result of the conditional operator is the result of whichever expression is evaluated — the second or the third. We should make sure that the data type of the result of expression2 and expression3 are the same. If not so, implicit type conversions occur which may not result in the desired output. Consider three variables *x, y and* z where 'x' and 'y' have values 5 and 10 respectively. We will assign the result of some conditional expressions to 'z'. Some examples are given below.

Expression	'z'	Explanation
z = (x > y) ? x : y;	10	As expression1 *'(x > y)'* is false, the result of expression3 *'y'* is assigned to 'z'.
z = (x < y) ? (x * 3) : (y * 5);	15	As expression1 is true, the result of expression2 *'(x * 3)'* is assigned to 'z'.
z = (x != y) ? 1 : 2;	1	As expression1 is true, the result of expression2 *'1'* is assigned to 'z'.
z = (x < y) ? (x > 0) ? x : 1 : (y > 0) ? y : 1;	5	Here, both expression2 and expression3 have inner expressions. As expression1 *'(x < y)'* is true, expression2 *'(x > 0) ? x : 1'* is evaluated and its result is assigned to 'z'. The result of expression2 is the value of 'x' as *'(x > 0)'* is true. The entire expression is similar to: z = (x < y) **?** ((x > 0) *? x : 1)* **:** ((y > 0) *? y : 1)*;

Expression	'z'	Explanation
		The entire expression actually tries to assign the smaller number out of 'x' and 'y' to 'z'. But, the value of 'z' cannot be lower than 1.

3.9 SPECIAL OPERATORS
There are four special operators in 'C' and they are:
- Comma operator (,)
- **sizeof** operator
- Pointer operators (**&** and *****)
- Member selection operators (. and →)

Here we will discuss only the comma (,) and sizeof operators. The pointer operators (& and *) and member selection operators (. and →) will be discussed in subsequent chapters.

3.9.1 COMMA OPERATOR
The comma operator links related expressions together. A comma separated list of expressions are evaluated from left to right and the value of the right-most expression is the final value of the combined expression.
Let us understand this with an example.
z = (x = 5, y = 10, x * y);

The expression within the first bracket is evaluated from left to right. First, 5 is assigned to 'x' and then 10 is assigned to 'y'. At last, 'x' is multiplied by 'y' and the result is assigned to 'z'. So, 50 *(5 * 10)* is ultimately assigned to 'z'. Since, comma operator has the lowest operator precedence i.e. it is the last one to be evaluated, the parentheses *(first brackets)* are necessary. If not done so, the assignment operator will take precedence and 'z' will acquire a value of 5 instead of 50.

3.9.2 sizeof OPERATOR
The sizeof is a compile time operator which means that the expression is evaluated during the compilation time. sizeof is also a 'C' keyword. When used with an operand, it returns the number of bytes the operand occupies in memory. The operand may be a variable, a constant or a data type. It can also be used to determine the total bytes used by arrays, structures and unions. Some examples of sizeof operator usage are:

z = sizeof(y);
z = sizeof(double);
z = sizeof(36L);

3.10 ARITHMETIC EXPRESSIONS
Arithmetic expressions are combination of variables, constants, operators and parentheses. The values contained within the variables are used for the arithmetic calculations. The parentheses are used for

prioritizing or sequencing the arithmetic operations. We can make operations with lower precedence executed before others by enclosing them in parentheses. The result of an arithmetic expression can be assigned to a variable using the assignment operator. When done so, the previous value of the variable is replaced by the newly assigned value. Assume we have two variables 'x' and 'y' with values 5 and 10. Some possible arithmetic expressions are:

$$z = x * 5 + y;$$
$$z = x * (5 + y);$$
$$z = x * 5 + (y*3);$$

The result of the second statement will be different from the first statement. The first bracket or parentheses in the second statement make the addition operation get performed before the product. So, when the first statement assigns 35 '(5 * 5) + 10' to 'z', the second statement assigns 75 '5 * (5 + 10)'. Notice that in the third statement we didn't specify any space within '(y*3)'. The space between operands and operators is optional and is recommended only for better readability.

Arithmetic expressions without parentheses are evaluated from left to right but, depends on the precedence of the operators. The precedence of the arithmetic operators are divided into two categories – **high precedence** and **low precedence**. The arithmetic operators with high precedence are * *(multiplication)*, / *(Division)* and % *(Modulus)*. All these three operators have the same precedence and are evaluated from left to right i.e. the operator on the left of an expression is evaluated first followed by the one on the right. The arithmetic operators with low precedence are + *(Addition)*, - *(Subtraction)*. These two operators have the same precedence and are evaluated from left to right. As stated earlier, the parentheses can be used to change the precedence or order of the evaluation. Lets look at one more example.

$$z = 15 + x * y / 2 \% 10 - 3;$$

The order of operations in the above example are:

Step count	Step	Result	
1	x * y	→ 50	[5 * 10]
2	50 / 2	→ 25	[*Result of #1* divided by 2]
3	25 % 10	→ 5	[*Result of #2* modulus 10]
4	15 + 5	→ 20	[15 plus *result of #3*]
5	20 – 3	→ 17	[*Result of #4* minus 3]
6	17 is assigned to z.		

While working with arithmetic expressions, we need to be careful regarding few things.
- While assigning real numbers to integer data type variables, the mantissa will be lost. So for example, trying to assign '6.75' to a variable 'z' of type 'int', only '6' will be assigned to 'z', as 'z' being an 'int' type is incapable of holding the mantissa.
- Result of an expression depends on the data type of the variables involved in the expression. This can be explained by a simple example. Assume, we have a variable 'x' of type **int** with value 15. The division of this variable by an integer constant or variable will yield a result as int, even if we assign the result to a float or double.

double z = x / 2;   → *'z' will be assigned a value of 7.*

To evaluate the expression in the data type of the target variable, we need to typecast the right-hand side variables to the data type of the target variable 'z'. We need to remember the precision rules as stated in **section 3.2**. All the below statements will assign 7.500000 to 'z'.

double z = (double) x / 2;
double z = x / (double) 2;
double z = (double) x / (double) 2;

- We should make sure that we do not divide by 0 *(zero)*. Division by 0, will make the program terminate abnormally. Care should be taken to test the denominator for 0 before doing any division.
- We should also be careful of overflow and underflow errors during arithmetic operations. We should make sure that the operands are of correct type and are capable of holding the result of the operation. Overflow and underflow errors generate wrong results. For more details on overflow and underflow errors please refer to **section 2.13**.
- We should be careful regarding the precedence and associativity of the operators involved in the expression. If ignored, we may get completely unexpected results.

3.11 TYPE CONVERSIONS

On many occasions we need to use variables or constants of mixed data types within arithmetic expressions. We may also need to assign a variable or constant of a different data type to another variable. We may also require to pass variable or constant of a different data type as argument to a function instead of the one the function accepts. On all these occasions, the data type of the source variable or constant needs to be converted to the data type of the target variable. Typecasting is a way to make a variable or constant of one type, such as an int, act like another type, such as a char, for one single operation. There are two ways in which we can do type conversions.

- **Implicit (Automatic) type conversion:** If one of the operand in an expression is of a 'lower' type *(lower capacity)* than the other, the lower type operand is automatically converted by the compiler to the 'higher' type *(higher capacity)* operand. This conversion is done automatically by the compiler and we need not specify anything explicitly. For the implicit conversion rules, please refer to **section 3.2**. The final result of the expression is converted to the type of the variable to which the result is getting assigned i.e. the variable on the left-hand side of the assignment operator. However, we should remember that conversion from real number *(float or double)* to integer *(char, short int, int, long int)* results in truncation of the mantissa. Also, conversion from a higher type to a lower type results in dropping of excess higher order bits resulting in reduced overall precision or capacity. Some examples of implicit type conversion are:

```
/* Header Files */
#include <stdio.h>

int main(void)
{
    /* Variable Declaration & Initialization */
    char    ch  = 'A';
    int     idx = 35;
```

```
    double val = 0;

    /* char is automatically converted to type int before the addition. */
    idx = idx + ch;

    /* int is automatically converted to double
       i.e. the data type of 10.5 before the addition. */
    val = idx + 10.5;

    /* 110.500000 will be printed. */
    printf("\nval: %lf.\n", val);

    return 0;
}
```

- **Explicit type conversion:** There are instances when we need to force a type conversion in a way which is different from what the automatic conversion would have achieved. This process is also called **type casting** and it is user defined. Here the user can type cast the result to convert it to a particular data type. This is better explained using an example. Say, in a class we need to find the ratio of the number of girls to the boys. Though, the number of girls and boys are whole integer values, we will need the ratio to be in decimals. When calculating the ratio, we will need to typecast the girl-number and boy-number to double to get the ratio in double.

```
/* Header Files */
#include <stdio.h>

int main(void)
{
    /* Variable Declaration & Initialization */
    unsigned int uiNumGirls = 26;
    unsigned int uiNumBoys  = 31;
    double       dblRatio   = 0;

    /* Both uiNumGirls and uiNumBoys are typecasted to
       double before the division. This results in the
       division operation to retain the fractional part. */
    dblRatio = (double)uiNumGirls / (double)uiNumBoys;

    /* 0.838710 will be printed. */
    printf("\nRatio: %lf.\n", dblRatio);

    return 0;
}
```

The general form of typecast is:

(data-type) expression;

The expression can be an expression, variable or constant. An expression should be typecasted before using its value in further arthmetic operations for getting correct results. Some examples of typecast are given in the next table.

Example	Behavior
int x = **(int)** 56.6;	56 is assigned to 'x' after truncation of the fractional part.
double x = **(int)** 37.5 / 6;	37.5 is converted to **int** resulting in its value as 37, which in turn is divided

47

Example	Behavior
	by the integer 6. The division is between two integers **(int)** and so yields the result in integer **(int)**. 37 is divided by 6 to get the result as 6 after truncating the fractional part. The final result of 6 is assigned to the variable of type **double**.
float x = **(float)** 37 / 6;	37 is converted to **float** resulting in its value as 37.000000, which in turn is divided by the integer 6. But, 6 is automatically *(implicitly)* converted to type **float** *(i.e. the higher type)* before the division is performed. The division is between two floating point values. The final result 6.166667 is assigned to the variable 'x' of type float.

3.12 OPERATOR PRECEDENCE AND ASSOCIATIVITY

Precedence determines the order of evaluation of the operators. Every operator has a precedence associated with it. Precedence determines how an expression involving more than one operator is evaluated. If an expression contains multiple operators, the operator with the higher precedence is evaluated first. The operators of the same level of precedence is either evaluated from left to right or right to left depending on the precedence level. This is called the **associativity** of an operator. *Associativity* is used when two operators of same precedence appear in an expression. When evaluating an arithmetic expression, we should be very careful regarding the precedence and associativity of the operators involved in the expression. Many a times, programmers either ignore and wrongly interpret the precedence and associativity resulting in incorrect results. Consider the following statement.

$$int\ x = 10 + 25 * 3 - 15 / 5;$$

In the above statement '*25 * 3*' is evaluated first followed by '*15 / 5*'. On doing so, our expression gets simplified to '*10 + 75 – 3*'. Now, as the '+' (addition) and '-' (subtraction) are at the same level of precedence, their associativity property comes into play resulting in the expression to be evaluated from left to right. So, '*10 + 75*' is evaluated first resulting in the final result of 82.

If we have confusion regarding the precedence and associativity of the operators, an easy way is to enclose the operations which need to be evaluated first within parentheses. We can also have nested parentheses i.e. one pair of parentheses stated within another. When done so, the innermost parentheses are evaluated first followed by the outer ones. Examples:

$$(x + (y – z)) / 2;$$
$$(x \% 5) – y + 10;$$
$$(x << 3) + y * z;$$

A complete list of the operators and their associativity are given in the next table.

Precedence	Operator	Description	Associativity
1	( )	Function call, and within arithmetic operations	Left-to-right
	[ ]	Array element reference	
	.	Structure or union member access	
	->	Structure or union member access using pointer	

Precedence	Operator	Description	Associativity
2	+	Unary plus	Right-to-left
	–	Unary minus	
	++	Increment	
	– –	Decrement	
	!	Logical NOT	
	~	Bitwise NOT	
	*	Pointer indirection (dereference)	
	&	Address-of	
	sizeof	Size-of	
	(*data type*)	Type cast	
3	*	Multiplication	Left-to-right
	/	Division	
	%	Modulus	
4	+	Addition	Left-to-right
	–	Subtraction	
5	<<	Bitwise LEFT SHIFT	Left-to-right
	>>	Bitwise RIGHT SHIFT	
6	<	Less than	Left-to-right
	<=	Less than or equal to	
	>	Greater than	
	>=	Greater than or equal to	
7	==	Relational equality	Left-to-right
	!=	Relational inequality	
8	&	Bitwise AND	Left-to-right
9	^	Bitwise XOR	Left-to-right
10	|	Bitwise OR	Left-to-right
11	&&	Logical AND	Left-to-right
12	||	Logical OR	Left-to-right
13	? :	Conditional expression (Ternary operator)	Right-to-left
14	=	Simple assignment	Right-to-left
	*=	Assignment by product	
	/=	Assignment by division	
	%=	Assignment by remainder (modulus)	
	+=	Assignment by addition	
	-=	Assignment by subtraction	
	&=	Assignment by bitwise AND	
	^=	Assignment by bitwise XOR	
	|=	Assignment by bitwise OR	
	<<=	Assignment by bitwise LEFT SHIFT	
	>>=	Assignment by bitwise RIGHT SHIFT	
15	,	Comma operator	Left-to-right

3.13 SAMPLE PROGRAMS

1. Swap the values of two variables using a temporary variable.

```
/* Header Files */
#include <stdio.h>

int main(void)
{
    /* Variable Declaration & Initialization */
    int iVar1 = 5;
    int iVar2 = 10;
    int iTemp = 0;

    /* Swap */
    iTemp = iVar1;
    iVar1 = iVar2;
    iVar2 = iTemp;

    /* Print the swapped values. */
    printf("After swap, iVar1: %d, iVar2: %d.\n", iVar1, iVar2);

    return 0;
}
```

Output:

```
        After swap, iVar1: 10, iVar2: 5.
```

2. Swap the values of two variables without using a temporary variable.

```
/* Header Files */
#include <stdio.h>

int main(void)
{
    /* Variable Declaration & Initialization */
    int iVar1 = 5;
    int iVar2 = 10;

    /* Swap */
    iVar1 += iVar2;
    iVar2  = iVar1 − iVar2;
    iVar1  = iVar1 − iVar2;

    /* Print the swapped values. */
    printf("iVar1: %d, iVar2: %d.\n", iVar1, iVar2);

    return 0;
}
```

Output:

```
        After swap, iVar1: 10, iVar2: 5.
```

3. Circular shift bits 3 places to the left. All bits are moved 3 places to the left and the highest 3 bits move to the lowest 3 places in the final result.
    How do we do it?

We first left-shift the data 3 places to the left, and then we 'OR' it with the highest 3-bits of the data. This internally gets done in 3 steps.

a) When we left-shift the data 3 places, the highest 3 bits drop-off and 0 (*zeroes*) get inserted in the lowest 3 bit positions. If our value is 187 which has a binary representation of '10111011', our left-shifted value becomes '11011000'.

b) To get the highest 3 bits to the lowest 3 positions we right-shift the data equal to 5 places (8 - 3) i.e. the number of bits in a byte minus the number of high order bits we want to put in the lower positions. When we right-shift the value '10111011' 5 places, it becomes '00000101'.

c) The result obtained in step **(a)** gets 'OR'ed to the result obtained in step **(b)** resulting in the final value of '11011101' (221).

```c
/* Header Files */
#include <stdio.h>

int main(void)
{
    /* Variable Declaration & Initialization */
    /* Binary representation of ch is 10111011.*/
    unsigned char ch      = 187;
    /* cShift refers to the number of places to shift.
       It should not be greater than 8. */
    unsigned char cShift = 3;

    /* Circular shift the bits 'cShift' places to the left.
       This can also be done in 3 separate steps as given below.
          unsigned char temp1 = ch << 3;
          unsigned char temp2 = ch >> (8 - 3);
          ch = temp1 | temp2;
       The above 3 statements will also achieve the same result. */
    ch = (ch << 3) | (ch >> (8 - 3));

    /* Print the shifted value. */
    printf("Circular shift of ch yields: %d.\n", ch);

    return 0;
}
```

Output:

```
Circular shift of ch yields: 221.
```

4. The price of a package of 25 chocolates is $14. If the chocolates are sold separately, an extra 6 cents are charged for every chocolate. Find the price of 65 such chocolates assuming that 50 chocolates will be sold in 2 packages and the rest 15 will be sold separately.

```c
/* Header Files */
#include <stdio.h>

/* Defined Values */
#define PACKAGEQTY      25
#define PACKAGEPRICE    14.0f
#define EXTRACHARGE     0.06f

int main(void)
{
    /* Variable Declaration & Initialization */
```

```
int     iNumChocToPurchase   = 65;
int     iCompletePackage     = 0;
int     iNumChocSoldSeparate = 0;
double dblRatePerChoc        = 0;
double dblFinalPrice         = 0;

/* Calculate the price per chocolate when sold separately. */
dblRatePerChoc = PACKAGEPRICE / PACKAGEQTY + EXTRACHARGE;

/* Calculate the number of complete packages we will get at the
   price of 'PACKAGEPRICE' for 'PACKAGEQTY' chocolates. */
iCompletePackage = iNumChocToPurchase / (int) PACKAGEQTY;

/* Calculate the number of chocolates which we need to purchase separately*/
iNumChocSoldSeparate = iNumChocToPurchase - iCompletePackage * PACKAGEQTY;

/* Now, calculate the final price for the total purchase. */
dblFinalPrice = iCompletePackage * PACKAGEPRICE + iNumChocSoldSeparate *
                dblRatePerChoc;

/* Print the final price. */
printf("Amount needed to purchase %d chocolates is $%.2lf.\n",
       iNumChocToPurchase, dblFinalPrice);

return 0;
}
```

Output:

```
Amount needed to purchase 65 chocolates is $37.30.
```

INPUT, OUTPUT AND FORMAT SPECIFIERS

[CHAPTER-4]

4.1 INTRODUCTION

As discussed in **section 1.3**, we can use the *'printf'* function to print results on the standard output device. Similarly, we have a function *'scanf'* for accepting inputs from the user. In C, all input and output operations are performed through function calls such as 'printf' and 'scanf'. These functions are collectively called **standard input and output functions** and are part of the C library. Every program which uses these standard input and output functions must include the header file *'stdio.h'* at the beginning of source file or header, using the following statement.

#include <stdio.h>

where *'stdio'* stands for **standard input and output.**

The statement *'#include <stdio.h>'* tells the compiler to search for a file named 'stdio.h' and place that entire file's contents at that location within the program. The content of the header file becomes part of the source code when it is compiled. Some modern intelligent compilers do not include the header file contents, if nothing *(functions, defines etc.)* from the header file is referenced within the program.

Another header file which we are going to discuss in this chapter is *'ctype.h'*. This header declares a set of functions to classify and transform individual characters.

4.2 READING INPUT

4.2.1 SIMPLE INPUT FUNCTIONS

There are multiple functions in C which can be used to read keyboard input. Each function is targeted towards a specific way of accepting the input. The simplest functions are the ones which accept a single character. There are three such functions.

- **int getch(void):** This function is specific to MS-DOS supporting compilers and is not available on most Unix and Linux targeted compilers. This function has been deprecated and is superseded by the function *'int _getch(void)'* which has the same behavior as *'getch'*. It waits for a keyboard input and returns the ASCII value of the character entered. The function does not echo the entered character to the console screen. Consider the following example usage.

  *char chVar = **getch()**;*

- **int getche(void):** Like *'getch'*, this function too is specific to MS-DOS supporting compilers and is not available on most Unix and Linux targeted compilers. This function has been deprecated due to some security concerns and is superseded by the function *'int _getche(void)'* which has the same behavior as *'getche'*. It waits for a keyboard input and returns the ASCII value of the character entered. The function echoes the entered character to the console screen. Consider an example usage.

char chVar;
*chVar = **getche**();*

- **int getchar(void):** This function gets a character *(an unsigned char)* from standard input *(stdin)* device, typically the keyboard. To indicate an error, it returns EOF *(-1)*. This function is available in all C compilers. The function has the following form of declaration and usage:

    Declaration → int getchar(void);
    Usage → Variable_Name = getchar();

Where *'Variable_Name'* is a variable generally of type *'char'*. When this statement is encountered, the compiler waits until a key is pressed. It returns the entered character which gets assigned to the variable *'Variable_Name'*. We may also have *'Variable_Name'* of *'int'* data-type, if we are looking to work with the ASCII value of the entered character.

'getchar' function can also be used to read a sequence of inputs from the user within a loop statement. We will know more about the loop statements in later chapters.

The 'getchar' function accepts any key available in the keyboard buffer including the RETURN (ENTER) key and the TAB key. Consider the following example usage.

char chVar = ' ';
printf("Please enter a character");
*chVar = **getchar**();*

Unlike the above functions which accept only a single input character, we can have an entire string *(including spaces within the string)* accepted as input using the *'gets'* function. The function takes the following form.

char * **gets**(char * buffer);

Where *'buffer'* is a character array which accepts the entered string. An array is a sequence of values of the same data type stored in contiguous memory locations. The function accepts the pointer to the buffer where the string needs to be stored. We will read about arrays and pointers in later chapters. We should **avoid** using this function as it does not check for buffer overflows and may write past the buffer. *This function has been removed starting from C11 and is replaced with a more secure variant **'gets_s'**.*

4.2.2 FORMATTED INPUT

Till now we learned about accepting only a specific type of keyboard input – either single character or a character string. In C, we can also accept formatted data from the keyboard. Formatted input refers to an input data formatted to a particular data type. Assume, we accept *four* types of input: 627, 52611.26, 'G' and "Football". These four data are of four different types. The value 627 is an integer and can be held in the data type *'int'*. The second value 52611.26 is a real number and must be held in the data types *'float'* or *'double'*. The third value 'G' is a single character and can be held in the data type *'char'*. The fourth value "Football" is a sequence of characters called a *string*. A NULL (ASCII value 0 *[zero]*) character marks the end of the string.

We can accept formatted data from the standard input device using the *'scanf'* function. The function is declared in the header file *'stdio.h'* and has the following form.

int scanf("format string", arg1, arg2, ... argn);

The *'format string'* specifies the data formats to which the input needs to be accepted. The argument list specify the memory address of the variables in which the accepted input needs to be stored. The number of arguments must equal the number of *format specifiers* in the *'format string'*. The format string may also contain spaces, tabs and new lines which are ignored. Spaces are used for better readability. In our next section, let us see discuss format specifiers.

4.3 FORMAT SPECIFIERS

Each *format specifier* is of the form:

% [flags] [field_width] [.precision] [length_modifier] conversion_character

where components in brackets [] are optional.

Format specifiers tell the compiler regarding the type of value to be read or printed. This can be explained using a simple example. If we want to print the value '1', the format specifier enables the compiler to understand whether we want to print the character '1' or the number 1. The character '1' has an ASCII value of 49 whereas if represented as a number it will simply be 1. Format specifiers must start with a percentage (%) operator.

'conversion_character' specifies the type of the value i.e. *int, char, float* etc. They can be:

Conversion character	Meaning
c	Single character.
d, i	Signed decimal integer.
u	Unsigned decimal integer.
o	Octal integer.
x, X	Hexadecimal integer.
f	Signed floating point value.
e, E	Signed floating point value in scientific notation.
g, G	Signed floating point or signed scientific notation, whichever is shorter.
s	A character string. A string is a sequence of characters ending in NULL.
p	Pointer address. Displays the argument as an address in hexadecimal digits.
n	Nothing is printed.
	The corresponding argument must be a pointer to a signed int.
	The number of characters written so far is stored in this pointed location.
%	A % followed by another % character will write a single % to the stream.

The *'flags'* are applicable for number values only. They can be:

Flag	Meaning
- (minus)	The output is left justified *(aligned)* in its field, not right justified which is the default.
+ (plus)	Signed numbers will always be printed with a leading sign (+ or -). The default is to print the '–' (minus) sign but not the '+' plus.

Flag	Meaning
space	Prepends a space for positive signed numeric types. This flag is ignored if the '+' flag exists. The default does not prepend anything in front of positive numbers.
0 (zero)	When the 'field_width' option is specified, prepends zeros for numeric types. The default prepends spaces.
#	Alternate form: For g and G types, trailing zeros are not removed. For f, e, E, g, G types, the output always contains a decimal point. For o, x, X types, the text 0, 0x, 0X, respectively, is prepended to non-zero numbers.

The '*field_width*' specifies a minimum number of characters to output. If the converted argument has fewer characters than the field width, it will be padded on the left *(or right, if left adjustment has been requested)* to make up the field width. The padding character is normally ' ' *(space)*, but can be '0' if the *zero* padding flag (0) is present. It does not cause truncation of oversized fields. It is typically used to pad fixed width fields as tabulated output. Consider the following example.

```
int   iValue     = 5;
char szName[ ] = "John";
printf("Value is %02d", iValue);
printf("Value is %2d", iValue);
printf("Name is %6s", szName);
```

The above three statements will print the following output in a single line *(we are showing in three separate lines for understandability and readability purposes)*:

```
Value is 05
Value is  5
Name is    John
```

The '*.precision*' field specifies the maximum limit on the output, depending on the particular formatting type. For floating point numeric types, it specifies the number of digits to the right of the decimal point that the output should be rounded to. For the string type, it limits the number of characters that should be printed, after which the string is truncated. Consider the following example.

```
float fltValue = 2.35435;
printf("Value is %.2f", fltValue);
```

The above statement will print:

```
Value is 2.35
```

'*length_modifier*' tells the compiler regarding the size or capacity of the data. For example the format specifier '%hu' signifies *short unsigned integer*. The different length modifiers are:

Length modifier	Meaning
h	The capacity of the number is limited to short. It can be used with d, i, u, o, x and X *conversion characters*.
l	The capacity of the number is extended to long. It can be used with d, i, u, o, x , X and f *conversion characters*. When specified with 'f', it signifies the data type '*double*'.

Length modifier	Meaning
ll	The capacity of the number is extended to long long. It can be used with d, i, u, o, x and X *conversion characters*.
L	Long double. It can be used with e, E, f, g and G *conversion characters*.

Some example usage of length modifiers are *'%hu'*, *'%hd'*, *'%lu'*, *'%ld'*, *'%lf'*, *'%llu'*, *'%lld'*, *'%Lf'* etc.

4.3.1 FORMATTED INPUT [EXAMPLES]

As we discussed, we can accept formatted input using the *'scanf'* function. For our understanding, let us take six variables of different data types. We will then accept values from the user into these variables in separate 'scanf' functions.

```
/* Header Files */
#include <stdio.h>

int main(void)
{
    char            chValue     = ' ';
    short           shValue     = 0;
    int             iValue      = 0;
    unsigned int    uValue      = 0;
    double          dblValue    = 0;
    char            szName[101] = "";

    printf("Please enter a single character [char]: ");
    scanf("%c", &chValue);

    printf("\nPlease enter a number between -32768 to +32767 [short signed int]: ");
    scanf("%hd", &shValue);

    printf("\nPlease enter a number between -2147483648 to +2147483647 "
           "[signed int]: ");
    scanf("%d", &iValue);

    printf("\nPlease enter a number between 0 to +4294967295 [unsigned int]: ");
    scanf("%u", &uValue);

    printf("\nPlease enter a real number [float]: ");
    scanf("%lf", &dblValue);

    printf("\nPlease enter a name within 100 characters [string]: ");
    scanf("%s", szName);

    printf("\n\nThe values entered are: %c, %hd, %d, %u, %lf and %s.", chValue,
           shValue, iValue, uValue, dblValue, szName);

    return 0;
}
```

4.3.2 FORMATTED INPUT [SECURITY ENHANCEMENT]

Before we move toward examples on formatted input, let us get acquainted with another function **'scanf_s'**. C11 introduced a more secure version *(scanf_s)* of the function 'scanf'. The function is very similar to 'scanf' except for one vital difference. Unlike 'scanf', 'scanf_s' requires the buffer size to be specified for all input parameters of type %c *(character input)* and %s *(string input)*. The buffer size in characters is passed as an additional parameter immediately following the argument *(pointer to the buffer or variable)* of type '%c' or '%s'. An example usage of the function is:

> *int iVal1;*
> *int iVal2;*
> *char ch;*
> *char str[10];*
> *scanf_s("%d %c %d %s", &iVal1, &ch, 1, &iVal2, str, 10);*

Not all compilers support the 'scanf_s' function and thus, we have used the function 'scanf' in all our examples.

4.4 GENERATING OUTPUT

4.4.1 SIMPLE OUTPUT FUNCTIONS

In previous sections, we have seen the various input functions available in C. Similarly, we have output functions which are classified into two types – Functions for non formatted output and functions for formatted output. Let us first discuss about the simpler functions for producing non formatted output.

- Similar to the input *'getchar'* function, we have an output function *'putchar'* which produces a single character on the standard output device *(stdout)*. This function is available in all C compilers. The function has the following form of declaration and usage:

> *Declaration →   int **putchar**(int character);*
> *Usage → **putchar**(Variable_Name);*

  Where *'Variable_Name'* is a variable generally of type *'char'*. Few example usage are given below.

> *char chVar = 'W';*
> *putchar(chVar);*
> *putchar('O');*
> *putchar(chVar);*
> *putchar('!');*
> *putchar('\n');*

  The above statements will print the following word on the screen:
  WOW!

- Like the *'gets'* input function we have the *'puts'* output function which produces a character string on the standard output device *(stdout)*. It also appends a newline character ('\n') at the end of the string. The function has the following form:

> *int **puts** (const char * str);*

  The function begins copying from the address specified *(str)* until it reaches the terminating

NULL character ('\0'). This terminating NULL character is not written to the output. We will read about variable addresses *(pointers)* in later chapters.

4.4.2 FORMATTED OUTPUT

We have been using the *'printf'* function in our various examples for printing captions and results. We should generate the output in such a way which is understandable to the user. We use the *'printf'* function not only to give instructions but also present the output. The *'printf'* function is declared in the header file *'stdio.h'* and has the following form:

int printf("format string", arg1, arg2, …. argn);

The function writes the C string pointed by the *'format string'* to the standard output *(stdout)*. If format includes format specifiers, the additional arguments following the format string are formatted and inserted in the resulting string replacing their respective specifiers. We can also include backslash character constants within the format string (refer **section 2.4.3**). The number of format specifiers in the format string should equal the count of the arguments following the format string. Also, the format specifiers should match the data type of the corresponding arguments. The format specifiers should follow the rules as stated in **section 4.3**. Consider the following code as an example.

```c
#include <stdio.h>

int main(void)
{
    printf("Characters:\t\t\t %c, %c \n", 'a', 65);
    printf("Decimals:\t\t\t %d, %ld \n", 2007, 83839394L);
    printf("Integer preceding with blanks:\t %10d \n", 2007);
    printf("Integer preceding with zeroes:\t %010d \n", 2007);
    printf("Width adjusted:\t\t\t %*d \n", 5, 100);
    printf("Different radices:\t\t %d, %x, %o, %#x, %#o \n", 2007, 2007, 2007, 2007,
            2007);
    printf("Floating point numbers:\t\t %4.2f, %+.0e, %E \n", 3.1416, 3.1416, 3.1416);
    printf("A string:\t\t\t %s \n", "C Language");

    return 0;
}
```

The above code will yield the following output:

```
Characters:                     a, A
Decimals:                       2007, 83839394
Integer preceding with blanks:        2007
Integer preceding with zeroes:  0000002007
Width adjusted:                    100
Different radices:              2007, 7d7, 3727, 0x7d7, 03727
Floating point numbers:         3.14, +3e+00, 3.141600E+00
A string:                       C Language
```

4.5 SAMPLE PROGRAMS

1. Accept two numbers from the user and calculate the average (mean) of the two.

```c
/* Header Files */
#include <stdio.h>

int main(void)
{
    /* Variable Declaration & Initialization */
    unsigned int uNumber1   = 0;
    unsigned int uNumber2   = 0;
    double       dblAverage = 0;

    /* Accept the first number. */
    printf("Enter the first number: ");
    scanf("%u", &uNumber1);

    /* Accept the second number. */
    printf("Enter the second number: ");
    scanf("%u", &uNumber2);

    /* Calculate the average. We are typecasting the numbers to a higher data type
       (double) because addition of the two numbers could create an overflow
       condition, if the entered numbers are of very high value. Also, typecasting
       helps us get the result in fraction which we intend to. */
    dblAverage = ((double)uNumber1 + (double)uNumber2) / 2;

    /* Print the result. */
    printf("\nThe average of the two numbers %u and %u is %.02lf.\n", uNumber1,
            uNumber2, dblAverage);

    return 0;
}
```

2. Accept the length of two sides (legs) of a right-angled triangle and calculate the hypotenuse using the Pythagorean theorem.

```c
/* Header Files */
#include <stdio.h>
#include <math.h>

int main(void)
{
    /* Variable Declaration & Initialization */
    double dblSide1     = 0;
    double dblSide2     = 0;
    double dblHypotenuse = 0;

    /* Accept the length of the first side. */
    printf("Enter the length of the first side: ");
    scanf("%lf", &dblSide1);

    /* Accept the length of the second side. */
    printf("Enter the length of the second side: ");
    scanf("%lf", &dblSide2);

    /* Calculate the hypotenuse. It can also be calculated as
       dblHypotenuse = sqrt(dblSide1 * dblSide1 + dblSide2 * dblSide2); */
    dblHypotenuse = hypot(dblSide1, dblSide2);

    /* Print the result. */
    printf("\nThe hypotenuse of the triangle is %.02lf.\n", dblHypotenuse);

    return 0;
}
```

In the above program, we have used the math function *'hypot'* to calculate the hypotenuse of the triangle. Instead of it, we could have also used the following statement to calculate the hypotenuse.

dblHypotenuse = sqrt(dblSide1 * dblSide1 + dblSide2 * dblSide2);

The *'hypot'* function takes the length of two sides of the triangle as *'double'* and returns the hypotenuse of the triangle also as *double*. The *'sqrt'* function takes a number as *double* and returns its square root value. Both these functions are declared in the header file *'math.h'* and so we have included that header at the start of our program.

3. Accept the horizontal and vertical sides of a rectangle and calculate its area and perimeter.

```c
/* Header Files */
#include <stdio.h>

int main(void)
{
    /* Variable Declaration & Initialization */
    double dblSideHorizontal = 0;
    double dblSideVertical   = 0;
    double dblArea           = 0;
    double dblPerimeter      = 0;

    /* Accept the length of the first side. */
    printf("Enter the length of the horizontal side [1 - 9999]: ");
    scanf("%lf", &dblSideHorizontal);

    /* Accept the length of the second side. */
    printf("Enter the length of the vertical side [1 - 9999]: ");
    scanf("%lf", &dblSideVertical);

    /* Calculate the area. */
    dblArea = dblSideHorizontal * dblSideVertical;

    /* Calculate the perimeter. */
    dblPerimeter = (dblSideHorizontal + dblSideVertical) * 2;

    /* Print the result. */
    printf("\nThe area of the rectangle is %.02lf and the perimeter is %.02lf.\n",
            dblArea, dblPerimeter);

    return 0;
}
```

ARRAYS

[CHAPTER-5]

5.1 INTRODUCTION

An array is a collection of data items, all of the same type, accessed using a common name. An array is used to store a collection of data, but, it is often more useful to think an array as a collection of variables of the same type. For example, we may define an integer *(int)* array with the name *'MathMark'* which stores the marks obtained in Mathematics by all the students of a specific class or standard. In the definition, the array name is followed by the array capacity within square brackets. Assuming we have 20 students in the class, the array will be defined as:

int MathMark[20];

The general form of an array declaration is:

Data-Type ArrayName[Dimension1-Size][Dimension2-Size]...;

An individual value within the array is accessed using the array name followed by the index number or subscript. In C, array indexes or subscripts start from 0 *(zero)* and continue to 1 less than the array capacity. So in our example, the indexes will start from 0 and continue till 19 *(20 – 1)*. The marks of the first student will be at the index location 0 and that of the last will be at index location 19. To store or access the marks obtained by the 15th student in the class, we need to use the following statements:

Store → *MathMark[14] = <Value>;*
Access → *MathMark[14]*

While the complete set of values is referred to as an array, the individual values within the array are called *elements*. Arrays can be of any data type. Arrays are stored in memory unless we persist them to disk using any of the file management functions which we will read in later chapters. As they are stored in memory, they will be lost when the program terminates unless we save the array contents to disk.

Arrays are created using contiguous memory locations. The lowest address corresponds to the first element of the array and the highest address belongs to the last element. A one-dimensional array will be represented as:

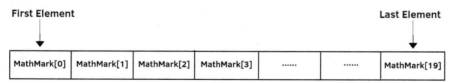

Assuming *'int'* takes 4 bytes and our array starts at an imaginary memory location of 100, the first element *(MathMark[0])* will be located at the memory location 100, followed by 104 for *'MathMark[1]'*, *108 for 'MathMark[2]'* and so on.

Arrays help us to write concise and efficient programs enabling us to store and access values within loops. An array can be of single or multi-dimension. A dimension is a direction in which you can vary the specification of an array's elements. A one-dimensional array is like a list whereas a two dimensional array is like a table. The C language places no limits on the number of dimensions in an array, though specific implementations may vary.

5.2 ONE-DIMENSIONAL ARRAYS

A one-dimensional array is like a list which has only one subscript and is also known as *single-subscripted array*. The example which we discussed in **section 5.1** is one-dimensional array. The general form of a one-dimensional array is:

Data-Type ArrayName[Array-Size];

The values are assigned to a one-dimensional array in the following manner:

MathMark[0] = 88;
MathMark[1] = 81;
MathMark[2] = 92;
.
.
.
MathMark[19] = 68;

Array elements can be used just like any other C variable. Any operation which can be performed on a variable of the same data type as that of the array, can also be performed on an array element. For example, if *'Numbers'* is an array of type *'int'* with capacity of 10 elements:

int iValue = Numbers[5] – 3;
Numbers[2] = Numbers[4] + Numbers[7];
*Numbers[0] = Numbers[3] * 3;*
*Numbers[3] = 6 * 8;*
Numbers[8] += 17;

C does not perform any bound checking on arrays. If care is not taken, we may overshoot the array index and thus try to access a memory location outside the array-size. This will result in a run time error and lead to program crash. So, we need to be careful and do bound checking before accessing any array element.

5.2.1 INITIALIZATION OF ONE-DIMENSIONAL ARRAYS

Just like oridinary variables, array elements can be initialized during declaration time. The general form of initialization of a one-dimensional array is:

Data-Type ArrayName[Array-Size] = { comma separated list of values };

Where the comma separated values are assigned to the array elements sequentially in the provided order. Say, if we specify 3 initialization values, then the first value gets assigned to the first array element; the second value gets assigned to the second array element; and the third value to the third array element. If the array-size is more than the number of values specified, the remaining elements will automatically be initialized to 0 *(zero)*.

int rgiNumbers[5] = { 62, 81, 23 };

In the above example, the value *62* is assigned to *'rgiNumbers[0]'*, *81* is assigned to *'rgiNumbers[1]'* and *23* is assigned to *'rgiNumbers[2]'*. The other two elements *'rgiNumbers[3]'* and *'rgiNumbers[4]'* are automatically assigned 0 *(zero)* by the compiler.

When we are initializing the array during declaration, the array-size becomes optional. If omitted, the size of the array equals the number of initialization values specified. So, if we have provided three comma separated values during initialization, the array will have three elements. Consider the following example.

float rgfltTotal[] = { 13.5, 16.7, 89, 107.6, 70.0 };

The above statement creates a float array of 5 elements, as we have provided 5 initialization values.

Initialization of arrays in C has two drawbacks.
1. We cannot initialize specific elements. Values are assigned sequentially from the first element.
2. Large number of array elements cannot be initialized in one go. We need to use separate loop statements to initialize the elements.

Character arrays can be initialized in the same way as below.

char rgchInitial[] = { 'S', 'T', 'A', 'R' };

Please note that the above statement declares an array called *'rgchInitial'* with 4 elements. It is **not** a **string** as the array does not end with a NULL character ('\0'). Lets read the next section to understand the reason.

5.2.2 STRINGS

In our earlier sections we have read about character *strings*. Strings are created using single dimension array of characters *(char/wchar_t)*. The NULL character *(ASCII value 0)* marks the end of the string. Each string is represented using a single one-dimensional array. The array-size of the character array determines the number of characters the string can hold including the terminating NULL character. So, the character array,

ANSI: char name[11];
Unicode: wchar_t name[11];

is capable of holding 11 characters. If *'name'* is to be used as a *string*, the last character needs to be a NULL character, which leaves only 10 elements starting from the beginning to be used for storing other characters. So, if we want to store the string "C LANGUAGE", it will be represented in the array as below:

'C'	' '	'L'	'A'	'N'	'G'	'U'	'A'	'G'	'E'	'\0'

Each character is stored in a separate array element with the last element having the '\0' *(NULL)* character. So, for strings we must leave one position for the NULL character and thus, calculate the array-size accordingly. Now, let us consider the following six character array declaration and initialization:

1. char rgchLang[] = { 'C', ' ', 'L', 'A', 'N', 'G', 'U', 'A', 'G', 'E' };
2. char rgchLang[10] = { 'C', ' ', 'L', 'A', 'N', 'G', 'U', 'A', 'G', 'E' };
3. char rgchLang[11] = { 'C', ' ', 'L', 'A', 'N', 'G', 'U', 'A', 'G', 'E' };
4. char rgchLang[11] = { 'C', ' ', 'L', 'A', 'N', 'G', 'U', 'A', 'G', 'E', '\0' };
5. char rgchLang[] = "C LANGUAGE";
6. char rgchLang[11] = "C LANGUAGE";

The first and second statements declare the array *'rgchLang'* to be of 10 elements. Both are **not strings** as both do not end with a NULL character. The third statement declares the array to be of size 11 elements, but has only the first 10 elements filled with the initialization values. As we have discussed in the previous section, the last element of the array is automatically initialized to 0 *(NULL)* because we have not specified any initialization value for that element. So, the array declared in the third statement is a string. The fourth statement too declares a string as we have specifically terminated the array with a NULL character during the initialization. The fifth and sixth statements also declare strings. When we initialize character arrays within *double quotes* as in the fifth and sixth statements, the compiler automatically terminates the array with a NULL character. In the fifth statement, the compiler calculates the required array-size to be of the initialization string's length plus a terminating NULL character. This makes it 11 in our example.

5.3 TWO-DIMENSIONAL ARRAYS

We may have situations where we need to store a table of values. If we need to store the marks of all the subjects of an entire class, a one-dimensional array will not serve the purpose. We will need a two-dimensional array which will help us represent the marks as a table, with each student in a row and mark in each individual subject in a column. A two dimensional array has the following general form:

Data-Type ArrayName[Total-Rows][Total-Columns];

The array elements are accessed as *'ArrayName[Row][Column]'*. While storing values, we generally store each row at a time i.e. one row is completed before moving to the next row. Similar to one-dimensional arrays, the row and column subscripts start from 0 *(zero)* and continue till *'Total-Rows – 1'* for rows and *'Total-Columns – 1'* for columns.

It is worth noting that C follows a **row-major** ordering for representing multi-dimensional arrays *(two-dimensional and higher)* unlike some languages like *'Fortran'* which follow a *column-major* ordering. Row-major order and column-major order are methods for storing multidimensional arrays in linear storage such as random access memory. In a row-major order, the consecutive elements of a row reside next to each other *(like [0][0], [0][1], [0][2], [1][0], [1][1], [1][2], [2][0], [2][1], [2][2], ...)*. Similarly in a column-major order, the consecutive elements of a column reside next to each other *(like [0][0], [1][0], [2][0], [0][1], [1][1], [2][1], [0][2], [1][2], [2][2], ...)*.

A two-dimensional array is logically represented as given in the next diagram.

Though it is worth knowing that in actual memory the two-dimensional array is represented in a linear contiguous order and not as a table as we see it. What we see in the above image is the logical representation and not the physical representation. In physical representation, array elements occur sequentially with all columns of each row appearing together. So, all columns of row 0 will come first followed by the columns of row 1 and so on. We need to be bothered about the logical representation only, as C internally converts the logical representation to physical representation and vice versa. If we are accessing the array elements using a pointer *(points to the memory location of the data)*, we may need to work as per the physical representation. We will study about pointers in our later chapters.

For our above example, we may have a table similar as below *(Total Marks in each subject:100)*.

	Mathematics	Physics	Chemistry	Biology
Student 1	78	85	80	71
Student 2	92	89	70	68
Student 3	67	72	84	81
Student 4	75	70	73	79
Student 5	71	67	64	68
Student 6	94	91	82	76
Student 7	83	77	67	71
Student 8	76	78	85	82
Student 9	88	73	83	78
Student 10	67	71	68	70

Now, let us write a program which accepts the above information from the user and stores them in an array. At the end, the program print the marks and the aggregate percentage obtained by a student.

```c
/* Header Files */
#include <stdio.h>

/* Defined Values */
#define TOTALSUBJECTS   4
#define TOTALSTUDENTS   10

int main(void)
{
    /* Variable Declaration & Initialization */
    int        iCounterStudents                        = 0;
    int        iCounterSubjects                        = 0;
    int        iAggregate                              = 0;
    int        rgiMarks[TOTALSTUDENTS][TOTALSUBJECTS]  = { 0 };
    const char rgszSubjects[TOTALSUBJECTS][12]         = { "Mathematics",
                                                           "Physics",
                                                           "Chemistry",
                                                           "Biology" };

    /* Accept the marks obtained by all the students. */
    while (iCounterStudents < TOTALSTUDENTS)
    {
        printf("Student #%02d\n===========\n", iCounterStudents + 1);
        iCounterSubjects = 0;

        while (iCounterSubjects < TOTALSUBJECTS)
        {
            printf("Enter the marks for %s: ", rgszSubjects[iCounterSubjects]);
            scanf("%d", &rgiMarks[iCounterStudents][iCounterSubjects]);
            iCounterSubjects++;
        }

        printf("\n");
        iCounterStudents++;
    }

    iCounterStudents = 0;
    iCounterSubjects = 0;

    /* Now, display the marks and the percentage obtained by all the students. */
    /* We will first print the headings and then the marks. */
    printf("\n\t\t\t\tSTUDENT MARKS\n\t\t\t\t*************\n\t\t");
    while (iCounterSubjects < TOTALSUBJECTS)
    {
        /* Make each subject column fixed width (11 chars) & left aligned. A tab is also
           inserted between two columns to provide proper separation between columns. */
        printf("%-11s\t", rgszSubjects[iCounterSubjects++]);
    }

    /* After the subject headings, print the heading for the percentage column. */
    printf("%%");

    /* Now, print the marks and the percentage obtained by the students. */
    while (iCounterStudents < TOTALSTUDENTS)
    {
        printf("\nStudent #%02d:\t", iCounterStudents + 1);
        iCounterSubjects = 0;
        iAggregate       = 0;

        while (iCounterSubjects < TOTALSUBJECTS)
        {
            printf("%02d        \t", rgiMarks[iCounterStudents][iCounterSubjects]);
```

```
                    /* Calculate the aggregate of all the subjects for the student. */
                    iAggregate += rgiMarks[iCounterStudents][iCounterSubjects];

                    /* Move to the next subject marks for the student. */
                    iCounterSubjects++;
          }

          /* Print the percentage obtained by this student. */
          printf("%02.02lf", (double) iAggregate / (double) TOTALSUBJECTS);
          /* Move to the next student. */
          iCounterStudents++;
    }

    printf("\n\n");

    return 0;
}
```

The program will generate the following output:

```
                         STUDENT MARKS
                         *************
                Mathematics    Physics        Chemistry      Biology       %
Student #01:    78             85             80             71            78.50
Student #02:    92             89             70             68            79.75
Student #03:    67             72             84             81            76.00
Student #04:    75             70             73             79            74.25
Student #05:    71             67             64             68            67.50
Student #06:    94             91             82             76            85.75
Student #07:    83             77             67             71            74.50
Student #08:    76             78             85             82            80.25
Student #09:    88             73             83             78            80.50
Student #10:    67             71             68             70            69.00
```

Now, let us understand what we are doing in the above program.
We have declared two counters *'iCounterStudents'* and *'iCounterSubjects'*. *'iCounterSubjects'* is incremented to help us move to the next subject when accepting or printing the marks. Similarly, *'iCounterStudents'* is incremented to help us move to the next student. We store the marks in the *'iCounterSubjects'* subject column for each student row. The marks obtained by each student are stored in the *'iCounterStudents'* row corresponding to the respective student.

We use a *while loop (iteration statements)* for accepting or printing the values. We will study about loops in our later chapters. For a brief understanding, loops help us execute a group of statements *(stated within the loop block)* repeatedly. *'while loops'* execute the group of statements enclosed within the while block *(marked by the opening and ending curly braces just following the while statement)* repeatedly till the *while condition* is true. The while condition is the expression following the while statement within the parentheses. In our program, the expressions like *'iCounterStudents < TOTALSTUDENTS'* and *'iCounterSubjects < TOTALSUBJECTS'* are the while conditions. An example of the while loop block in the above program is:

```
while (iCounterSubjects < TOTALSUBJECTS)
{
        printf("%-11s\t", rgszSubjects[iCounterSubjects++]);
}
```

For scenarios where we need to both increment a counter and also check for the loop condition, *'for loops' (explained in later chapters)* are better. But, for simplicity of understanding we have used the *while loops* over here.

In the first *while loop*, we are accepting the marks obtained by all the students of the class. We have used two while loops over here with one inside the other. The outer while block enumerates through all the students of the class. The inner while block accepts the marks obtained by a student in all the subjects. So in simple terms, the outer while block loops through all the students of the class and the inner while block loops through all the subjects for each student.

In the next while block we are printing the subject names as headings. Note, that we are looping through the string array *'rgszSubjects'* to print the subject names. A string array is actually a two dimensional character array with each row representing a string, and each column representing a single character of that string. We have declared the array as *'const'* as we do not expect the array's contents to change. We are printing the subject names in fixed length size of 11 characters and as left-aligned. This makes our output format remain consistent. We have separated each heading by a *'tab' ('\t')* character. Please refer to **section 2.4.3** and **4.3** for *special characters* and *format specifiers* respectively.

In the final while block we are printing the marks obtained by the students. Over here too, we are using two while blocks – one within another. As discussed earlier, the outer while block enumerates through all the students and the inner while block enumerates through all the subjects for a student. The inner while block also calculates the aggregate of all the marks obtained by each student, and the outer while block prints the aggregate percentage obtained by the student.

5.3.1 INITIALIZATION OF TWO-DIMENSIONAL ARRAYS

Like a one-dimensional array, a two-dimensional array may be initialized with a list of values *(enclosed in braces)* during its declaration. The general form of initialization of a two-dimensional array is:

Data-Type ArrayName[Total-Rows][Total-Columns] = *{ { comma separated list of values for Row 0 },*
{ comma separated list of values for Row 1 },

.
.
.

{ comma separated list of values for Row N } };

Where the comma separated values are assigned to the column elements of a row sequentially in the provided order.

int rgiNumbers[3][3] = *{ { 62, 81, 23 },*
{ 34, 98, 23 } };

In the above example, the value *62* is assigned to *'rgiNumbers[0][0]'*, *81* is assigned to *'rgiNumbers[0][1]'*, *23* is assigned to *'rgiNumbers[0][2]'*, *34* is assigned to *'rgiNumbers[1][0]'*, *98* is assigned to *'rgiNumbers[1][1]'* and *23* is assigned to *'rgiNumbers[1][2]'*. The other three elements *'rgiNumbers[2][0]'*, rgiNumbers[2][1]' and 'rgiNumbers[2][2]'* are automatically assigned 0 *(zero)* by the compiler.

When we are initializing the array during declaration, the total row count becomes optional. If omitted, the total row count becomes equal to the number of rows specified during the initialization. So, if we change our above example as below.

int rgiNumbers[][3] =   { { 62, 81, 23 },
                            { 34, 98, 23 } };

The array will now have **2 rows** and 3 columns.

5.3.2 STRING ARRAYS

We have read about strings in **section 5.2.2**. An array of strings is called a string array. As each string is represented in a one-dimensional array, an array of such strings is represented using a two-dimensional array. Each string within the array is stored in each row of the array. A string array is nothing but a two-dimensional character *(char/wchar_t)* array and is declared as:

ANSI string array: *char Array-Name[Total-Rows][Total-Columns];*
Unicode string array: *wchar_t Array-Name[Total-Rows][Total-Columns];*

The *'Total-Columns'* must be greater than or equal to the largest character string *(including the terminating NULL character)* within the entire array. Just like any other two-dimensional array, we can also initialize the string array during declaration.

char Names[5][11] =   { "John",
                          "Somshubhro",
                          "Mary" };

In the above declaration cum initialization, the first 3 rows of the array will have the strings *"John"*, *"Somshubhro"* and *"Mary"*. The remaining 2 rows will have 0 *(zero)* length *(blank - "")* strings.
If we are initializing the array during declaration, we may skip specifying the total row size of the array. In such a case the total row count becomes equal to the number of rows specified during the initialization. If we change our above example to:

char Names[][11] =   { "John",
                         "Somshubhro",
                         "Mary" };

We will now have **3 rows** in the array.

5.4 MULTI-DIMENSIONAL ARRAYS

C allows arrays of more than two dimensions. The exact limit depends on the compiler. The general form of a multi-dimensional array is:

Data-Type ArrayName[Size 1][Size 2][Size 3]....[Size N];

where *'Size n'* is the size of the nth dimension. Some examples of multi-dimensional arrays are:

int   rgiValues[10][7][5];
const float rgfltRates[5][3][2];

Remember: The **sizeof** operator we had discussed in **section 3.9** can also be used on arrays. When the *sizeof* operator is passed an array, it returns the total memory *(in bytes)* used by the array. Consider the following integer array:

$$int\ rgiValues[10][7][5];$$

The array will have '10 * 7 * 5' elements and will occupy '10 * 7 * 5 * sizeof(int)' bytes of memory. Assuming *'int'* occupies 4 bytes, the sizeof operator will return '10 * 7 * 5 * 4' as the total memory size consumed by the array.

Within our program, we can calculate the number of elements of an array using the sizeof operator as: *'sizeof(rgiValues)/sizeof(int)'*. The expression will return the total number of elements in all dimensions of the array *(10 * 7 * 5)*.

The expression *'sizeof(rgiValues)/sizeof(rgiValues[0])'* will return the array size in the first dimension of the array i.e. 10 in our case.

We can define a macro which will return the number of elements in a **single dimension array** as:

$$\#define\ ARRAYSIZE(x)\qquad sizeof(x)/sizeof(x[0])$$

We can use the macro as below:
int rgiMarks[30];
int iNumElements = ARRAYSIZE(rgiMarks);   /* Will return 30 */

5.5 COMPOUND LITERALS

Compound literals were introduced since C99. They allow creation of unnamed object of a specified type in-place. They are used when a variable of type array, struct or union would be needed only once. The data type of the object is specified by the *'cast'* and value of the object is assigned using an initializer list following the cast. Compound literals give us a constant-like notation for arrays, structs and unions. It can be used anywhere an object with the same type of the compound literal can be used. The general form of a compound literal is:

$$(Type)\ \{\ Initializer\text{-}list\ \}$$

where, 'Type' is the valid data type of the object or an array of specified/unknown size and 'Initializer-list' is the list of values to be assigned to the object. Compound literals are mainly used when passing variables to functions without the need to declare the variables beforehand. Some example use of compound literals are:

printf("The value is %d.", (int) { 19 });	Prints the value 19.
int iVal = (int) { 1 };	Assigns the value 1 to 'iVal'.
double *pdblVals = (double[2]) { 5.2, 0.8 };	Creates a *double* array of 2 elements and assigns its starting address to the pointer 'pdblVals'.
int iVal = (int) { 5 } + (int) { 7 };	'iVal' is assigned the value 12.
int *piVals = (int []) { 5, 7, 3 };	Creates an *integer* array of 3 elements and

	assigns its starting address to the pointer 'piVals'.
const char *pszName = (const char[]) { "Tutan" };	Creates a *const string* and assigns its starting address to the pointer 'pszName'.
const char *pszVals = (const char[]) { 'a', 'b' };	Creates a *character* array of 2 elements and assigns its starting address to the pointer 'pszVals'.

We will read about pointers a little later in our chapter on 'Pointers'.

5.6 SAMPLE PROGRAMS

1. Accept numbers from the user and sort the given numbers in ascending order.

```c
/* Header Files */
#include <stdio.h>

/* Defined Values */
#define MAX_NUMBERS    10

int main(void)
{
    /* Variable Declaration & Initialization */
    int rgiNumbers[MAX_NUMBERS] = { 0 };
    int iCounter1              = 0;
    int iCounter2              = 0;
    int iMinimum               = 0;
    int iSwap                  = 0;

    /* Accept the numbers from the user. */
    while (iCounter1 < MAX_NUMBERS)
    {
        printf("Enter the number: ");
        scanf("%d", &rgiNumbers[iCounter1]);
        iCounter1++;
    }

    /* Now, sort the numbers. We go till second last element. We do not iterate till the last
       element because before we start iterating the second last element, all elements till that
       element are already sorted and have values less than or equal to the second last and the
       last elements. Only the second last and last elements need sorting between themselves
       which is done during the second last iteration itself i.e. if the last element is found
       to have a value less than the second last element, their values are swapped. */
    iCounter1 = 0;
    while (iCounter1 < MAX_NUMBERS - 1)
    {
        /* We start assuming that we have no elements with value less than this element. If
           we find any, we will mark that as minimum. */
        iMinimum  = iCounter1;
        iCounter2 = iCounter1 + 1;

        /* All elements before 'iCounter1' are already sorted and have values less than
           or equal to the elements which are yet to be sorted. Now, try to find the
           next minimum value within the remaining unsorted elements.*/
```

```
    while (iCounter2 < MAX_NUMBERS)
    {
        if (rgiNumbers[iCounter2] < rgiNumbers[iMinimum])
        {
            /* We found a new minimum value. */
            iMinimum = iCounter2;
        }

        /* Increase the inner counter. */
        iCounter2++;
    }

    /* Swap the 'iCounter1' element's content with the element with the least value
       within the unsorted elements. If 'iCounter1' and 'iMinimum' are the same, we
       will have no swapping and it will remain the same. */
    iSwap                 = rgiNumbers[iMinimum];
    rgiNumbers[iMinimum]  = rgiNumbers[iCounter1];
    rgiNumbers[iCounter1] = iSwap;

    /* Increase the outer counter. */
    iCounter1++;
}

/* Print the sorted sequence. */
printf("\n\nSorted list: ");
iCounter1 = 0;
while (iCounter1 < MAX_NUMBERS)
{
    printf("%d%s", rgiNumbers[iCounter1++],
                ((MAX_NUMBERS - 1) == iCounter1) ? "\n\n" : ", ");
}

    return 0;
}
```

We are doing selection sort in our program. The selection sort algorithm sorts an array by repeatedly finding the minimum element *(considering ascending order)* from the unsorted part of the array and adding it to the sorted part. The algorithm maintains two imaginary sub-arrays within a given array.

- The sub-array which is already sorted at the left of the array.
- Remaining sub-array in the right which is unsorted.

In every iteration of selection sort, the minimum element *(considering ascending order)* from the unsorted sub-array is picked and swapped with the initial element in the unsorted sub-array. Initially, the sorted sub-array is empty and the unsorted sub-array is the entire input list. The algorithm proceeds by finding the smallest *(or largest, depending on sorting order)* element in the unsorted sub-array, swapping it with the leftmost unsorted element say 'A'. We then continue the process from the element following this element 'A' i.e. from 'A + 1'. Assume we have the array as 5, 7, 8, 2. In our first iteration, the entire array is unsorted. The minimum value '2' within the array is found and swapped with '5' resulting in the array becoming 2, 7, 8, 5. Now in our next iteration, we start from '7' and swap it with the next minimum value '5' resulting in the array becoming 2, 5, 8, 7. Now, start from '8' and find the next minimum value i.e. '7'. We swap '7' and '8' resulting in the array becoming 2, 5, 7, 8, which is the sorted array.

2. Accept a string from the user and reverse the string in-place i.e. within the same array.

```c
#include <stdio.h>

#define MAX_STRING  100

int main(void)
{
    /* Variable declaration and initialization. */
    char szName[MAX_STRING + 1] = { 0 };
    char chSwap                 = 0;
    int  iCounter1              = 0;
    int  iCounter2              = 0;

    /* Accept the string from the user. */
    printf("Enter a string within %d characters: ", MAX_STRING);
    scanf("%s", szName);

    /* Make 'iCounter2' move to the end of the string. */
    while (szName[iCounter2] != '\0')
    {
        iCounter2++;
    }

    /* Decrement 'iCounter2' to make it point to the last NON NULL character. */
    iCounter2 = (0 < iCounter2) ? (iCounter2 - 1) : 0;

    /* Now, reverse the string. */
    while (iCounter1 < iCounter2)
    {
        /* Swap the element values. */
        chSwap              = szName[iCounter1];
        szName[iCounter1] = szName[iCounter2];
        szName[iCounter2] = chSwap;

        /* Update the counters. */
        iCounter1++;
        iCounter2--;
    }

    /* Print the reversed string. */
    printf("\nThe reversed string is: %s.\n\n", szName);

    return 0;
}
```

For reversing the string we need to start from both ends of the string/array. We will move 'iCounter1' from the beginning of the array and 'iCounter2' from the end. We will keep swapping the 'iCounter1' and 'iCounter2' element values. We will move 'iCounter1' forward and 'iCounter2' backwards after each swap. We will keep moving till 'iCounter1' is less than 'iCounter2', because by the time they cross, we have already reversed the entire string. Assuming our string to be "ABCDE", 'iCounter1' will initially point to 'A' and 'iCounter2' will point to 'E'. When they are swapped our string becomes "EBCDA". Now, 'iCounter1' is incremented and 'iCounter2' is decremented, making 'iCounter1' point to 'B' and 'iCounter2' point to 'D'. After swapping, the string now becomes "EDCBA". Again, 'iCounter1' is incremented and 'iCounter2' is decremented. Their values become equal and we stop. We get the reversed string as 'EDCBA'.

For making 'iCounter2' point to the end of the string, we need to increment 'iCounter2' till it finds the terminating NULL ('\0') character. 'iCounter2' will then be decremented by 1 to point to the last NON NULL character in the string.

3. Accept 10 numbers from the user and calculate the *'mean'* and *'standard deviation'* of the numbers. *'Mean'* means the average of the numbers. *'standard deviation'* is a measure that is used to quantify the amount of variation or dispersion of a set of data values. A low standard deviation indicates that the values tend to be close to the mean of the set, while a high standard deviation indicates that the values are spread out over a wider range. For a finite set of numbers, the standard deviation is found by taking the square root of the average of the squared deviations of the values from their average value. The *'deviation'* is obtained by squaring the difference between the value and the mean. The average of these deviations is obtained to get the *'variance'*. The square root of the variance is the standard deviation.

```c
/* Header Files */
#include <stdio.h>
#include <math.h>

/* Defined Values */
#define MAX_NUMBERS 10

int main(void)
{
    /* Variable declaration and initialization. */
    int    rgiNumbers[MAX_NUMBERS] = { 0 };
    int    iCounter               = 0;
    double dblMean                = 0;
    double dblTotalDeviation      = 0;
    double dblStandardDeviation   = 0;

    /* Accept the numbers from the user. */
    while (iCounter < MAX_NUMBERS)
    {
        printf("Enter the number: ");
        scanf("%d", &rgiNumbers[iCounter]);
        iCounter++;
    }

    /* Calculate the mean. We increment the counter in a single statement
       as the addition. As we have done a post-increment, the counter will be
       incremented after the addition is performed. */
    iCounter = 0;
    while (iCounter < MAX_NUMBERS)
    {
        dblMean = dblMean + rgiNumbers[iCounter++];
    }
    dblMean = dblMean / MAX_NUMBERS;

    /* Calculate the total deviation. */
    iCounter = 0;
    while (iCounter < MAX_NUMBERS)
    {
        dblTotalDeviation += pow(rgiNumbers[iCounter] - dblMean, 2);
        iCounter++;
    }
```

```
        /* Calculate the standard deviation. */
        dblStandardDeviation = sqrt(dblTotalDeviation / MAX_NUMBERS);

        /* Print the results. */
        printf("\nThe mean is %.06lf and the standard deviation is %.06lf.\n",
                dblMean, dblStandardDeviation);

        return 0;
}
```

We have used two math functions *'pow'* and *'sqrt'* in our program. These functions are builtin functions and are declared in the header file 'math.h'. So, we have included the header file 'math.h' in our program.

The 'pow' function finds the power of a provided base value. It takes two arguments, where the first argument is the base value whose power is to be found and the second argument is the exponent of the power. It returns the power as a *'double'*. It has the following declaration:

double pow (double base, double exponent);

The 'sqrt' function finds the square root of the provided argument value. It returns the square root as a *'double'*. It has the following declaration:

double sqrt (double argValue);

4. Write a program which accepts numbers from the user and stores them in a 3-dimensional array. It then prints the array and the sum of all the entered numbers.

```
#include <stdio.h>

/* Defined Values */
#define SIZEX    2
#define SIZEY    3
#define SIZEZ    4

int main(void)
{
    /* Variable declaration and initialization. */
    int   rgiNumbers[SIZEX][SIZEY][SIZEZ] = { 0 };
    int   i                               = 0;
    int   j                               = 0;
    int   k                               = 0;
    long  lSum                            = 0;

    /* Accept the numbers from the user. */
    while (i < SIZEX)
    {
        j = 0;
        while (j < SIZEY)
        {
            k = 0;
            while (k < SIZEZ)
            {
                printf("Enter rgiNumbers[%d][%d][%d]: ", i, j, k);
                scanf("%d", &rgiNumbers[i][j][k]);
                k++;
            }

            j++;
        }
```

```
        i++;
    }

    /* Print the numbers and calculate the sum. */
    i = 0;
    while (i < SIZEX)
    {
        j = 0;
        while (j < SIZEY)
        {
            k = 0;
            while (k < SIZEZ)
            {
                printf("\nrgiNumbers[%d][%d][%d]: %d", i, j, k, rgiNumbers[i][j][k]);
                lSum = lSum + rgiNumbers[i][j][k];
                k++;
            }

            j++;
        }

        i++;
    }

    /* Now, print the sum. */
    printf("\nThe sum of all the numbers is: %ld.\n\n", lSum);

    return 0;
}
```

There will be a total of SIZEX x SIZEY x SIZEZ (2 x 3 x 4 = 24) numbers accepted from the user.

CONDITIONAL STATEMENTS AND BRANCHING

[CHAPTER-6]

6.1 INTRODUCTION

Programs do not always execute statements sequentially in the order in which they appear. Situations may arise where we may have to change the order of execution of statements depending on certain conditions. We can incorporate decision making ability depending on conditions within our C programs. These kind of statements are called **decision control statements** and they are:

- **if, if-else, if-else ladder** and **nested if** statements
- **switch** statement
- **Conditional** or **Ternary** operator statement
- **goto** statement

6.2 DECISION CONTROL USING if STATEMENT

'**if**' statement is followed by an expression which evaluates a condition, and if the result of the condition check is true *(non-zero)*, it performs the operations stated within the 'if' block. The 'if' block is the group of statements specified between the opening and closing curly brace pair just following the 'if' statement. 'if' statements take the following form:

> **if** *(test condition)*
> *{*
> *   Statements to execute if condition check is true.*
> *}*

The 'if' statement can be visualized as the **decision block** *(diamond)* within a flowchart.

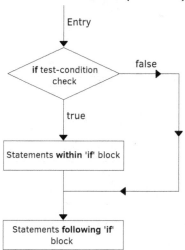

In most computer Languages including C, *'true'* means a *non-zero* value and *'false'* means a value of *zero.*

If the test-condition expression requires a relational operator but none has been specified, then by default the expression is compared for *inequality* with *0 (zero)*. Consider the following examples:

> if *(x)*
> {
>   printf("x is **not equal** to 0.");
> }

> if *(1)*
> {
>   printf("This statement will **always** be printed.");
> }

> if *(0)*
> {
>   printf("This statement will **never** get printed.");
> }

There can be multiple statements within the 'if' block. If the test-condition is *true*, the statements within the 'if' block will be executed and if the test-condition is *false,* they will be skipped and the execution will jump to the statements following the 'if' block. When the test-condition is true, both the statements within the 'if' block and the statements following the 'if' block are executed in sequence.

If the number of statements within the *'if'* block is limited to one, then the curly brace pair bounding the 'if' block becomes optional. So, we may have something like this:

> if *(x < 0)*
>   printf("The value of x is negative.");

Let us write a C program which accepts the rate and quantity to be purchased of an item and calculates the total amount to be paid by the customer. It also gives a discount of 5% to a regular customer.

```c
/* Header Files */
#include <stdio.h>
#include <ctype.h>

/* Defined Values */
#define DISCOUNT_RATE    5

int main(void)
{
    /* Variable declaration and initialization. */
    unsigned int uQuantity  = 0;
    double       dblRate     = 0;
    double       dblAmount   = 0;
    char         chDiscount = 0;
```

```
    printf("Enter the quantity of the item to be purchased: ");
    scanf("%u", &uQuantity);

    printf("\nEnter the rate of the item to be purchased: ");
    scanf("%lf", &dblRate);

    while (toupper(chDiscount) != 'Y' && toupper(chDiscount) != 'N')
    {
        printf("\nApply discount (y/n): ");
        chDiscount = getchar();
    }

    dblAmount = uQuantity * dblRate;

    if (toupper(chDiscount) == 'Y')
    {
        /* Apply discount. */
        dblAmount = dblAmount * ((double)(100 - DISCOUNT_RATE) / (double)100);
    }

    printf("\n\nThe total amount due from the customer is %.02lf.\n\n", dblAmount);

    return 0;
}
```

In the above program we have used a C library function *'toupper'*. The function accepts a character and returns its uppercase value. If the provided character is already uppercase, the same is returned. It has the following form:

int toupper (int c);

6.3 DECISION CONTROL USING if-else STATEMENT

The **if-else** statement extends the *'if'* statement for providing the ability to perform a set of operations when the *'if'* condition is **not** met. It has the following form:

> **if** *(test condition)*
> *{*
>   *Statements to execute if the condition check is true.*
> *}*
> **else**
> *{*
>   *Statements to execute if the condition check is false.*
> *}*

If the result of the test-condition check is *'true'*, the statements within the *'if'* block are executed and if it is *'false'*, the statements within the *'else'* block are executed. So, either the *if-block* or the *else-block* is executed but not both. The **if-else** control can be visualized as the next flowchart:

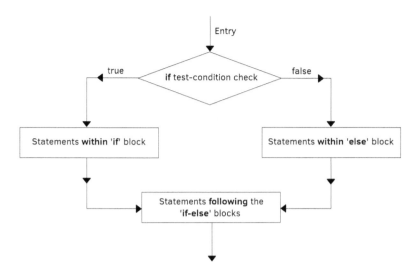

If the number of statements within the *'if'* block or the *'else'* block is limited to one, then the curly brace pair bounding the block becomes optional. But, it is **recommended** that we use curly braces as it improves readability and is considered a good programming practice. So, we may have:

> *if (x < 0)*
> > *printf("The value of x is negative.");*
>
> *else*
> > *printf("The value of x is positive.");*

Let us write a C program which checks whether a given number is odd or even.

```c
/* Header Files */
#include <stdio.h>

int main(void)
{
    /* Variable declaration and initialization. */
    unsigned int uNumber = 0;

    printf("Enter the number: ");
    scanf("%u", &uNumber);

    if (uNumber % 2 == 0)
    {
        /* The number is divisible by 2 i.e. it leaves a
           remainder of 0 when divided by 2. So, it is even. */
        printf("\nThe number is even.\n\n");
    }
    else
    {
        /* The number is odd. */
        printf("\nThe number is odd.\n\n");
    }

    return 0;
}
```

6.4 DECISION CONTROL USING if-else LADDER STATEMENTS

We may have situations where we need to check multiple conditions and perform operations depending on the condition which comes *true*. The *'if-else'* ladder statements allow us to do just that. The test conditions are checked one after the other till a condition comes true, upon which the control moves within the condition block which has come true. It has the following form:

> **if** *(test condition 1)*
> *{*
>   *Statements to execute if the condition check 1 is true.*
> *}*
> **else if** *(test condition 2)*
> *{*
>   *Statements to execute if the condition check 2 is true.*
> *}*
> **else if** *(test condition 3)*
> *{*
>   *Statements to execute if the condition check 3 is true.*
> *}*
> ....
> ....
> ....
> ....
> **else if** *(test condition N)*
> *{*
>   *Statements to execute if the condition check N is true.*
> *}*
> **else**
> *{*
>   *Statements to execute if all the above condition checks are false.*
> *}*

The *'if-else'* ladder can be visualized as the next flowchart:

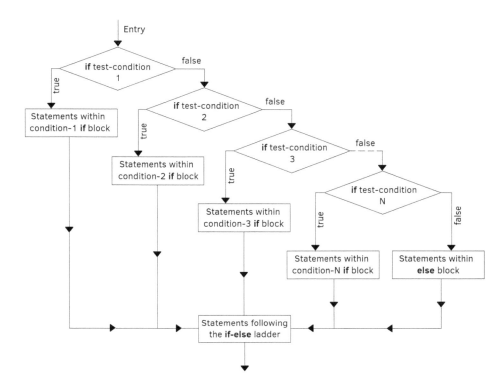

The *'test condition 1'* is checked for validity and if *'false'*, the program checks *'test condition 2'*. If that too is *'false'*, the program checks *'test condition 3'*. This continues till a condition is found to be *'true'*. When a satisfied condition is found, the control moves within the block corresponding to the condition, and all statements corresponding to that block are executed. Thereafter, all test condition checks following the satisfied condition are skipped and control moves to the statements following the *'if-else'* ladder. If the *'test condition 1'* is found to be *'true'*, the statements corresponding to *'test condition 1'* are executed and then the control jumps to the statement following the *'if-else'* ladder, skipping rest of the condition checks. If none of the test condition checks satisfy, the control moves directly within the *'else'* block of the *'if-else'* ladder. If we do not have any *'else'* block, the control jumps to the statement following the *'if-else'* ladder.

Let us write a C program which accepts the sides of a triangle from the user. It first checks whether the provided dimensions can form a triangle. If they form a triangle, it checks whether the triangle is an equilateral triangle or an isosceles triangle or a scalene.

```c
/* Header Files */
#include <stdio.h>

int main(void)
{
    /* Variable declaration and initialization. */
    double dblSide1 = 0;
    double dblSide2 = 0;
    double dblSide3 = 0;
```

```
    /* Accept the dimensions from the user. */
    printf("Enter the length of the first side: ");
    scanf("%lf", &dblSide1);

    printf("Enter the length of the second side: ");
    scanf("%lf", &dblSide2);

    printf("Enter the length of the third side: ");
    scanf("%lf", &dblSide3);

    if (dblSide1 <= 0 || dblSide2 <= 0 || dblSide3 <= 0)
    {
        /* In a triangle no side can be of zero length. */
        printf("\nThe provided dimensions do not form a triangle.\n\n");
    }
    else if ((dblSide1 + dblSide2) <= dblSide3 ||
             (dblSide1 + dblSide3) <= dblSide2 ||
             (dblSide2 + dblSide3) <= dblSide1)
    {
        /* In a triangle the addition of the length of any
           two sides is always greater than the third. */
        printf("\nThe provided dimensions do not form a triangle.\n\n");
    }
    else if (dblSide1 == dblSide2 && dblSide2 == dblSide3)
    {
        /* A triangle is equilateral, if all its sides are equal in length. */
        printf("\nThe triangle is an equilateral triangle.\n\n");
    }
    else if (dblSide1 == dblSide2 || dblSide1 == dblSide3 || dblSide2 == dblSide3)
    {
        /* A triangle is isosceles, if any of its two sides are equal. */
        printf("\nThe triangle is an isosceles triangle.\n\n");
    }
    else
    {
        /* A triangle with all unequal sides is called scalene. */
        printf("\nThe triangle is scalene.\n\n");
    }

    return 0;
}
```

6.5 DECISION CONTROL USING NESTED if STATEMENTS

What if we need to make more decisions within an *'if'* or *'else'* block itself. In such cases we can use more *'if'* control statements within an existing *'if'* block. As a matter of fact, we may use any kind of valid C control statements within an *'if'* or *'else'* block including other *'if-else'* statements. When *'if-else'* statements are nested within outer *'if-else'* statements, we call them nested *'if'* statements.

```
if (test condition 1)
{
    if (test condition 2)
    {
        Statements;
    }
    else
    {
```

```
            Statements;
        }
    }
    else
    {
        if (test condition 3)
        {
            Statements;
        }
        else
        {
            Statements;
        }
    }
```

Let us write a C program which accepts three numbers from the user and finds the greatest of the three numbers.

```c
/* Header Files */
#include <stdio.h>

int main(void)
{
    /* Variable declaration and initialization. */
    int iValue1 = 0;
    int iValue2 = 0;
    int iValue3 = 0;

    printf("Enter the first value: ");
    scanf("%d", &iValue1);

    printf("Enter the second value: ");
    scanf("%d", &iValue2);

    printf("Enter the third value: ");
    scanf("%d", &iValue3);

    if (iValue1 >= iValue2)
    {
        if (iValue1 >= iValue3)
        {
            printf("\nThe largest number is %d.\n\n", iValue1);
        }
        else
        {
            printf("\nThe largest number is %d.\n\n", iValue3);
        }
    }
    else
    {
        if (iValue2 >= iValue3)
        {
            printf("\nThe largest number is %d.\n\n", iValue2);
        }
```

```
        else
        {
            printf("\nThe largest number is %d.\n\n", iValue3);
        }
    }

    return 0;
}
```

6.6 DECISION CONTROL USING switch STATEMENT

When we need to make decisions depending on many possible values of a variable or expression, we can use *'if-else'* ladders for the purpose. But if the possible alternatives are many, we will end up with a long list of statements, making our program not only complex but unreadable. For such situations, C provides the **'switch'** statement. The *'switch'* statement tests the value of a variable or expression against a list of **'case'** values. When a match is found, a block of statements corresponding to the matching case is executed. The general form of a *'switch'* statement is given below:

> **switch** *(expression)*
> {
>   **case** value1:
>   *Statements to be executed when the result of expression is value1.*
>   **break**;
>   **case** value2:
>   *Statements to be executed when the result of expression is value2.*
>   **break**;
>   ....
>   ....
>   **default**:
>   *Statements to be executed when the result of expression does not match*
>   *any of the above values.*
>   **break**;
> }

The result of the *'expression'* must be an integer or a character value. The **'case'** values *'value1'*, *'value2'*, ... are constants or constant expressions *(resulting in an integer result)* and are called *'case labels'*. Each of these values must be unique within the **'switch'** statement. There can be 0 *(zero)* or more statements corresponding to a *case label*. There is no need to include braces around these statements, though it is a good practice to use braces when there are multiple statements. Every *case label* must end with a colon (:).

When the *'switch'* block is encountered, the result of the *expression* is compared sequentially against the *'case'* values. If a match is found, the block of statements corresponding to the matching *case label* is executed. The **'break'** statement at the end of each *case label* block causes an exit from the *'switch'* statement and the control jumps to the statement following the *'switch'*. If the *'break'* statement is not provided or missed, the control will thereupon move to the next *case label,* and the block corresponding to that *case label* will also get executed. The control does not break out of the *'switch'* until a *'break'* statement is found or the end of the *'switch'* statement is encountered.

The **'default'** is an optional *label*. It is executed when the value of the expression does not match any of the *case* values. If not present, no action takes places and the control moves to the statement following the *'switch'* block.

Now it is time for us to understand the *'switch'* statement with the help of a program.

A local footwear shop has a reward system for all its customers depending on the amount of purchase made by them during a year. The customers are divided into six categories ranging from category 0 to 5. Category 1 to 5 are for repeat customers who made purchases ranging from $100 to $1000 during the year. First time customers or customers who made purchases of less than $100 are placed under category-0. All customers are provided a certain percentage of discount depending on the category to which the customer belongs. The discount is calculated on the marked price and are as follows:

Category	Discount Percentage
Category-0	2-4
Category-1	7
Category-2	9
Category-3	11
Category-4	14
Category-5	15

The discount percentage of category-0 customers vary between 2 to 4 depending on the current purchase amount. A discount of 2% is provided for purchase amount of within $20, 3% for purchases between $21 to $60 and 4% for purchases above $60. Category-5 customers not only get the discount percentage assigned to them but also the discount percentage assigned for category-0 customers. So, for a purchase amount of $80, a category-5 customer will get a discount of (*15+4*) 19% and for a purchase amount of $15, the customer will get a discount of (*15+2*) 17%.

The program accepts the marked price of the total purchase made by a customer and the category of the customer. It then calculates the net amount payable by the customer after applying the discount.

```c
/* Header Files */
#include <stdio.h>

/* Defined Values */
#define CATEGORY_0_DISC1     2
#define CATEGORY_0_DISC2     3
#define CATEGORY_0_DISC3     4
#define CATEGORY_1_DISCOUNT 7
#define CATEGORY_2_DISCOUNT 9
#define CATEGORY_3_DISCOUNT 11
#define CATEGORY_4_DISCOUNT 14
#define CATEGORY_5_DISCOUNT 15

int main(void)
{
    /* Variable declaration and initialization. */
```

```
double          dblMarkedAmount   = 0;
double          dblNetBillAmount  = 0;
unsigned int uDiscount            = 0;
unsigned int uCategory            = 10;

while (uCategory > 5)
{
    /* Keep asking for the category unless the user enters a valid one. */
    printf("Enter the customer's category: ");
    scanf("%u", &uCategory);
}

printf("Enter the total marked price of the items purchased: ");
scanf("%lf", &dblMarkedAmount);

switch (uCategory)
{
    case 1:
        uDiscount = CATEGORY_1_DISCOUNT;
        break;
    case 2:
        uDiscount = CATEGORY_2_DISCOUNT;
        break;
    case 3:
        uDiscount = CATEGORY_3_DISCOUNT;
        break;
    case 4:
        uDiscount = CATEGORY_4_DISCOUNT;
        break;
    case 5:
        uDiscount = CATEGORY_5_DISCOUNT;
        /* Deliberately falling through as category-5 customers also get the
            discount offered to the category-0 customers. So, avoided using the
            break statement which makes us fall through to the next case label. */
    case 0:
    {
        if (dblMarkedAmount <= 20)
        {
            uDiscount = uDiscount + CATEGORY_0_DISC1;
        }
        else if (dblMarkedAmount <= 60)
        {
            uDiscount = uDiscount + CATEGORY_0_DISC2;
        }
        else
        {
            /* For purchases made above $60. */
            uDiscount = uDiscount + CATEGORY_0_DISC3;
        }

        break;
    }
    default:
        break;
}

dblNetBillAmount = dblMarkedAmount * ((double)(100 - uDiscount) / (double)100);

printf("\nThe total bill amount for the customer is $%.02lf.\n", dblNetBillAmount);

return 0;
}
```

If the user enters a wrong category, we ask for the category again. We keep doing so until the user enters a valid category *(0-5)*. As, *'uCategory'* is of type *'unsigned int'*, it can never have a value of less than 0 *(zero)*. Even if the user enters a value of less than 0 *(zero)*, it is wrapped around and will produce a value greater than 5.

Note, for the *case label 5*, we did not use a **break** statement. This is because category-5 customers also get the discount available to category-0 customers. So, we have allowed the control to fall through to the *case label 0*.

While calculating the net amount, we have typecasted the discount to *double,* as we need to avoid the integer round-off.

6.7 DECISION CONTROL USING CONDITIONAL (TERNARY) OPERATOR

We have read about the conditional operator in **section 3.8**. We will carry on our discussion from there. We can nest conditional statements where one conditional statement is within another. This can be explained using a sample program.

Let us write a program which accepts three numbers from the user and prints the greatest number.

```c
/* Header Files */
#include <stdio.h>
int main(void)
{
    /* Variable declaration and initialization. */
    int iValue1   = 0;
    int iValue2   = 0;
    int iValue3   = 0;
    int iMaxValue = 0;

    printf("Enter the first number: ");
    scanf("%d", &iValue1);

    printf("Enter the second number: ");
    scanf("%d", &iValue2);

    printf("Enter the third number: ");
    scanf("%d", &iValue3);

    /* Get the largest number within iMaxValue. */
    iMaxValue = (iValue1 >= iValue2)
            ? (iValue1 >= iValue3) ? iValue1 : iValue3
            : (iValue2 >= iValue3) ? iValue2 : iValue3;

    printf("\nThe largest number is %d.\n\n", iMaxValue);

    return 0;
}
```

In the program we are using nested conditional operator statements to find the largest of the three values. *'(iValue1 >= iValue2)'* is the first *(outer)* conditional comparison, and if it is *'true'* the expression *'(iValue1 >= iValue3) ? iValue1 : iValue3'* is evaluated. If it is *'false'*, the expression *'(iValue2 >=*

iValue3) ? iValue2 : iValue3' is evaluated.

If the inner conditional comparison *'(iValue1 >= iValue3)'* is *'true'* we get *'iValue1'* else *'iValue3'*.
If the inner conditional comparison *'(iValue2 >= iValue3)'* is *'true'* we get *'iValue2'* else *'iValue3'*.

6.8 DECISION CONTROL USING goto STATEMENT

All the previous decision control statements we discussed control the execution flow depending on certain specified conditions. Like many other languages, C also supports the unconditional jump statement **'goto'**. *'goto'* statement allows us to jump from one location to another within the same function of a program.

The *'goto'* requires a *label* to be defined within the function in which the *'goto'* statement is used. The *label* identifies the location to which the jump is to be made. The *label* is any valid variable name and is followed by a colon. The label is placed immediately before the statement where the control needs to be transferred upon a *goto* call. The *goto* statement can be of the following forms:

```
goto label;                    label:
...........                    statement;
...........                    ...........
...........                    ...........
label:                         ...........
statement;                     goto label;
```

Forward Jump   Backward Jump

Whenever the control reaches the *goto* statement, the control jumps to the statement immediately following the *label*. When the *label* is placed after a *goto* statement, all statements appearing between the *goto* call and the label will be skipped. This is called **forward jump**. On the other hand, if the *label* is placed before the *goto* statement, then we may have a loop kind of situation where all the statements between the *label* and the *goto* call are executed repeatedly. This is called **backward jump**.

Using a *goto* statement we can make the control jump out of a control block (like *if, switch, while, for* statements), but cannot make it to jump into a control block. The *goto label* is generally used at the end of a function and *goto* calls to this *label* is made to skip operations when further processing within the function is not desired *(such as when an essential condition is not met)*.

Though in some cases *'goto'* comes in real handy but, for most occasions the use of *'goto'* should be avoided. The biggest drawbacks of the *'goto'* statement are:
- It reduces the readability of the program as the jump location can be far off from the *goto* statement and we need to keep searching for the *goto label* within the entire function.
- It becomes difficult to trace or track the control flow of the program, making the program logic difficult to understand.
- It is error prone to code using *goto* as it alters the sequential flow of logic and can make unintended statements to be executed. On the other hand, it can also lead to required

statements getting missed from execution. If care is not taken, we may get into an *infinite* loop when using backward jump.

'goto' statements should only be used in situations where the use of structured solutions are far more complex to be implemented.

Let us write a program which determines whether a specified year is a leap year or not. *A year is a leap year if it is divisible by 4 and is not divisible by 100, or it is divisible by 400.*

```c
/* Header Files */
#include <stdio.h>

int main(void)
{
    /* Variable declaration and initialization. */
    int iYear = 0;

ACCEPTYEAR:
    printf("Enter the year to check (Enter 1582 or less to stop): ");
    scanf("%d", &iYear);

    if (iYear <= 1582)
    {
        /* Stop the program. */
        goto STOP;
    }

    if (iYear % 4 == 0 && iYear % 100 != 0)
    {
        /* The year is divisible by 4 but not 100. So, it is a leap year. */
        printf("The year %d is a leap year.\n\n", iYear);
    }
    else if (iYear % 400 == 0)
    {
        /* The year is divisible by 400. So, it is a leap year. */
        printf("The year %d is a leap year.\n\n", iYear);
    }
    else
    {
        printf("The year %d is not a leap year.\n\n", iYear);
    }

    /* Accept the next year to be checked for a leap year. */
    goto ACCEPTYEAR;

STOP:
    printf("\nStopping execution...\n\n");

    return 0;
}
```

In the program, we have two *goto* statements and *labels*. When the user enters a year *1582* or less, we stop the program. We have used the statement *'goto STOP'* for doing so. When the statement *'goto ACCEPTYEAR'* is hit, the program jumps to the *label 'ACCEPTYEAR'*. This makes the program ask the user to enter the next year to check.

6.9 SAMPLE PROGRAMS

1. We are provided with the length of two sides of a triangle and the angle between these two sides. We need to find the length of the third side. We can keep the following in mind when writing the program:
    ○   The angle between two sides of a triangle must be less than 180 degrees.
    ○   Assume '*a*', '*b*' and '*c*' are the three sides of a triangle, with '*a*' being the unknown side. '*A*' is the angle *(in degrees)* between the sides '*b*' and '*c*'.

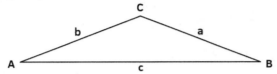

On these assumptions, the length of the side '*a*' is calculated as:

$$\sqrt{b^2 + c^2 - 2bc\ cosA}$$

```c
/* Header Files */
#include <stdio.h>
#include <math.h>

/* Defined Values */
#define PI 3.141592

int main(void)
{
    /* Variable declaration and initialization. */
    double dblSide1  = 0;
    double dblSide2  = 0;
    double dblSide3  = 0;
    double dblAngle  = 0;
    double dblRadian = 0;
    double dblCosine = 0;

    printf("Enter the first side of the traingle: ");
    scanf("%lf", &dblSide1);

    printf("Enter the second side of the triangle: ");
    scanf("%lf", &dblSide2);

    printf("Enter the angle between the two sides: ");
    scanf("%lf", &dblAngle);

    if (dblSide1 == 0 || dblSide2 == 0)
    {
        printf("\nThe length of a side cannot be 0.\n");
        goto STOP;
    }
    else if (dblAngle >= 180)
    {
        printf("\nThe angle must be less than 180 (degrees).\n");
        goto STOP;
    }
```

```
    /* We have accepted the angle in degrees but cos function in C accepts
       the angle is radians. So, we need to convert the degrees to radians. */
    dblRadian = (dblAngle * PI) / 180;

    dblCosine = (dblSide1 * dblSide1) + (dblSide2 * dblSide2) -
                (2 * dblSide1 * dblSide2 * cos(dblRadian));
    if (dblCosine < 0)
    {
        /* We take only the positive square root. */
        dblCosine = -dblCosine;
    }

    dblSide3 = sqrt(dblCosine);
    printf("\nThe length of the third side is %.02lf.\n", dblSide3);
STOP:
    printf("\nStopping program...\n\n");

    return 0;
}
```

In our program we have used two math functions *'cos'* and *'sqrt'*. So, we have included the header file *'math.h'*. The *'cos'* function returns the *cosine* of an angle. The function accepts the angle in *radian*. As the angle specified by the user is in degrees, we needed to convert it to *radian*, so that we can pass it to the *'cos'* function. The *'cos'* function has the following declaration:

double cos(double)

The *'sqrt'* function returns the square root of a number and has the following declaration:

double sqrt(double);

2. In our next program we try to find all the *roots* of a *quadratic equation*. A *quadratic equation* is of the form:

ax2 + bx + c = 0

Our program will accept the values of '*a*', '*b*' and '*c*' from the user and then find the *roots* of the equation using the following formula:

$$\frac{-b \pm \sqrt{b^2 - 4ac}}{2a}$$

The program will try to find the *roots* in two steps. In the first step, it will try to find the *discriminant* which is:

$b^2 - 4ac$

When we look at the formula to find the *roots* of the equation, we notice that the *discriminant* is the same value which appears under the square root.

In the second step we find the roots of the *quadratic equation* depending on the value of the *discriminant*.

- If the *discriminant* is positive, there are two real *roots* of the *quadratic equation*.
- If the *discriminant* is 0 *(zero)*, there are two real *roots* with equal value and are calculated as '*-b/2a*'.

- If the *discriminant* is negative, there are two complex roots, as the square root of a negative number is a complex number. We will not go into the details of complex numbers over here. As for a quick understanding a complex number is a number that can be expressed in the form *'a + bi'*, where *'a'* and *'b'* are real numbers and *'i'* is an imaginary unit. The square of *'i' (imaginary unit)* is *-1*. We have two parts in a complex number: *'a'* is the real part and *'b'* is the imaginary part. So, the roots of the equation in this case will be

$$\frac{-b}{2a} + \frac{\sqrt{|\,\text{Discriminant}\,|}}{2a}\,i \qquad \frac{-b}{2a} - \frac{\sqrt{|\,\text{Discriminant}\,|}}{2a}\,i$$

where,

$$|\,\text{Discriminant}\,|$$

is the modulus or absolute value of the *discriminant*.

```c
/* Header Files */
#include <stdio.h>
#include <math.h>

int main(void)
{
    /* Variable declaration and initialization. */
    double a              = 0;
    double b              = 0;
    double c              = 0;
    double dblDiscriminant = 0;
    double dblImaginary   = 0;
    double dblRoot1       = 0;
    double dblRoot2       = 0;

    /* Accept the numbers from the user. */

ACCEPTA:
    printf("Enter the value of a: ");
    scanf("%lf", &a);

    if (a == 0)
    {
        /* The value of 'a' cannot be 0. If it is 0, the equation becomes
           linear and does not remain quadratic. */

        printf("a cannot be 0. Please re-enter.\n");
        goto ACCEPTA;
    }

    printf("Enter the value of b: ");
    scanf("%lf", &b);

    printf("Enter the value of c: ");
    scanf("%lf", &c);

    dblDiscriminant = (b * b) - (4 * a * c);

    if (dblDiscriminant > 0)
    {
        dblRoot1 = (-b + sqrt(dblDiscriminant)) / (2 * a);
        dblRoot2 = (-b - sqrt(dblDiscriminant)) / (2 * a);
```

```c
    printf("\nThere are two distinct and real roots, and they are "
            "%.02lf and %.02lf.\n", dblRoot1, dblRoot2);
}
else if (dblDiscriminant == 0)
{
    dblRoot1 = dblRoot2 = -b / (2 * a);

    printf("\nThere are two equal and real roots with the value %.02lf.\n", dblRoot1);
}
else
{
    /* The discriminant is negative. We need to use the absolute value of
       discriminant when finding its square root. As the discriminant is
       negative, we are adding a '-' sign in front to make it positive. */
    dblRoot1 = dblRoot2 = -b / (2 * a);
    dblImaginary = sqrt(-dblDiscriminant) / (2 * a);

    printf("\nThere are two distinct and complex roots, and they are "
            "%.02lf + %.02lfi and %.02lf - %.02lfi.\n",
            dblRoot1, dblImaginary, dblRoot2, dblImaginary);
}

    return 0;
}
```

CONDITIONAL STATEMENTS WITH LOOPS

[CHAPTER-7]

7.1 INTRODUCTION

Loops help us execute a group of statements repeatedly till a condition called the *loop condition* is met. In our previous chapter we have read the use of *goto* statements to simulate a *loop*. But, it is very impractical and inconvenient to implement a loop using *goto*. Moreover, it is prone to errors due to the inherent disadvantages of the *goto* statement.

C language provides us with three kinds of *loop constructs* and they are:
- The **while** loop
- The **do while** loop
- The **for** loop

Every *program loop* consists of two components, one is the *body of the loop* consisting of the group of statements which needs to be executed repeatedly, and the other being the *control condition.* The *control condition* is a test condition which determines how long the loop is repeated. The loop is executed repeatedly till the *test condition* is *true*. Depending on the location of the *control condition* in the loop, a loop construct can be classified as *entry-controlled loop* or *exit-controlled loop.* In the entry-controlled loop, the control conditions are tested before the start of the loop. If the conditions are satisfied the loop is executed, else it is skipped. In the exit-controlled loop, the control conditions are tested at the end of the body of the loop. So, the body of the loop is executed at-least once and the first execution is unconditional. The flowcharts corresponding to the entry-controlled loop and the exit-controlled loops are given below.

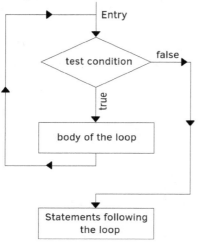

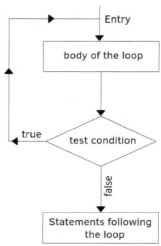

Entry-Controlled Loop   **Exit-Controlled Loop**

When working with *loops* we should be careful regarding the *control condition*. The control condition should achieve the exact number of loop executions as the logic desires. If the loop runs less or more than the desired number, we may get invalid results and even a program crash *(in case working with pointers or array indices)*. Also if the control condition is never reached, we will get into an *infinite loop* resulting in the body of the loop getting executed infinitely. So, when working with a loop we should always do a dry run *(with a pen and paper)* using some dummy data before doing the actual execution. The dummy data helps us understand the desired number of loop repetitions that will yield the required result. It also helps us determine the correct control condition that will provide that number of repetitions. As a simple example, if we want a loop to be executed *5 times* and we start our counter *'i'* from *0 (zero)*, should we execute the control condition till *'i < 5'* or *'i <= 5'* ? The correct answer is *'i < 5'* , which can easily be evaluated using a dry run. So when writing a loop, we need to take care of the following:

1. Declaring the counter of the correct data type and initializing it to a proper value.
2. Determine the number of times the body of the loop needs to be executed.
3. Provide the correct control condition which achieves the #2 point.
4. Write the body of the loop which gives us the desired result.
5. Increment the counter.

7.2 THE while LOOP

We have used the *while* loop in our previous chapters. It is the simplest of all the loop constructs in C. The while loop is an entry-controlled loop and has the following form:

while *(test condition)*
{
    body of the loop
}

Before the loop is entered, the test condition is evaluated and if *true*, the body of the loop gets executed. After the body of the loop is executed, the test condition is again evaluated and if *true*, the body is executed again. This continues until the test condition becomes *false* and the control moves to the statement following the loop.

The body of the loop may contain any number of statements. But for program readability, it is desirable to limit the number of statements to the number of lines visible at a time *(does not require scrolling)* in the editor or IDE *(Integrated Development Environment)*. We can do so by moving groups of statements to separate *user-defined functions*. We will learn about user-defined functions in our later chapters.

The braces of the while loop are required only when we have more than one statement in the loop body. In case we have only one statement, the braces become optional. Though it is considered a good programming practice to use the braces on all occasions for better program readability.

In our first example, we try to reverse the digits of a given number. For example, if the entered number is 12345, the program will produce the reverse as 54321.

```c
/* Header Files */
#include <stdio.h>

int main(void)
{
    /* Variable declaration and initialization. */
    unsigned int uNumber  = 0;
    unsigned int uReverse = 0;

    /* Accept a number from the user. */
    printf("Enter a positive number: ");
    scanf("%u", &uNumber);

    /* Reverse the number. */
    while (uNumber > 0)
    {
        /* Advance the place value of all digits in uReverse by one place
            and put the next digit from uNumber at the unit's place. */
        uReverse = uReverse * 10 + uNumber % 10;
        uNumber  = uNumber / 10;
    }

    /* Print the result. */
    printf("\nThe reverse of the number is %u.\n\n", uReverse);

    return 0;
}
```

We keep iterating till *'uNumber'* is greater than 0 *(zero)*, which means we have reversed all the digits and nothing is left to be reversed.

If the test-condition expression requires a relational operator but none has been specified, then by default the expression is compared for *inequality* with 0 *(zero)*. In our above example, we could have also achieved the same result if we had used the statement *'while (uNumber)'* which would have been equivalent to using *'while (uNumber != 0)'*.

7.3 THE do while LOOP

The **while** loop is an *entry-controlled loop* as it checks the test condition before executing the *loop body*. The body of the loop may not get executed even once, if the test condition is not met at the very first attempt.

We may need situations where we need to execute the body of the loop at-least once irrespective of whether the condition is met or not. Such situations demand the use of an *exit-controlled loop.* For the exit-controlled conditions, C language provides the loop construct **'do while'**. It has the following form:

> **do**
> {
>   *body of the loop*
> } **while** *(test condition);*

Unlike other loop constructs, the *'do while'* construct has a semi-colon at the end of the test condition.

The program executes the body of the loop and then proceeds to test the control condition. If *true*, it executes the body of the loop again. This continues until the *test condition* becomes *false,* upon which the control goes to the statement following the loop block.

Now let us write a program that accepts numbers from the user and calculates their sum. It keeps accepting the numbers until the user enters *0 (zero)* as the number. Even if the user does not want to run the program, we need to accept the number at-least once when the user gets the chance to enter *0 (zero)* to stop the program. This desires the use of an exit-controlled loop.

```c
/* Header Files */
#include <stdio.h>

int main(void)
{
    /* Variable declaration and initialization. */
    int   iNumber = 0;
    long  lSum    = 0;

    /* We have to accept atleast one number from the user. If it is 0 (zero) we stop. */
    do
    {
        /* Accept the number. */
        printf("Enter a number: ");
        scanf("%d", &iNumber);

        lSum += iNumber;

    } while (0 != iNumber);

    /* Print the result. */
    printf("\nThe sum of all the numbers is %ld.\n\n", lSum);

    return 0;
}
```

7.4 THE for LOOP

Similar to the **while** loop, the **for** loop is also an *entry-controlled* loop but provides a more concise and convenient loop structure. It has the following form:

> **for** (*initialization* ; *test condition* ; *increment or decrement*)
> {
>   *body of the loop*
> }

The **for** loop consists of the following components:
- The initialization of the control variables are done in the *initialization* section of the statement. The *initialization* section may optionally contain initialization of other variables used within the *for* loop too, but is mostly used for the control variables. Initialization is done by assignment of initial *(starting)* values to the variables using assignment statements *(example: iCount=idx=0)*. We can initialize multiple variables, with each initialization being separated from the other by a comma. As an example while counting the sum of all numbers starting from *5 (and continuing*

till 10) we could be initializing the variables as: *iNumber = 5, lSum = 0.* The *initialization* section is executed *only once* and is done **before** any other portion of the loop gets executed.

- After the initialization section, the *test condition* is evaluated and if *true*, the *body of the loop* gets executed. Unlike the *initialization* section, the *test condition* is evaluated at the start of each iteration, and this continues until the *test condition* becomes *false.* The body of the loop keeps getting executed again and again until the test condition becomes *false,* upon which the control goes to the statement following the *for* loop.
- After the *test condition* is evaluated, the *body of the loop* gets executed.
- After executing the *body of the loop,* the control comes to the *'increment or decrement'* section of the *for* statement. Here, the control variable is incremented or decremented depending on the program logic *(example: i++ or idx = idx − 1 or a = a + 2).* We can increment or decrement multiple variables, with each increment or decrement being separated from the other by a comma *(example: i++, j--).*

Let us write a small C program which uses two variables. It initializes the first variable to *1* and the second to *100.* It prints the value of the first variable from *1 to 100* and the second variable from *100 to 1.* We loop till the first variable is less than 101 and the second variable is greater than 0. If any of the condition is *false,* we break out of the loop.

```c
/* Header Files */
#include <stdio.h>

int main(void)
{
    /* Variable declaration and initialization. */
    int  iNumber1 = 0;
    int  iNumber2 = 0;

    /* iNumber1 starts from 1 and is incremented till it is less than or equal to 100.
       So, it prints the number from 1 to 100 and as soon as it crosses 100, the test
       condition becomes false. iNumber2 starts from 100 and is decremented till it is
       greater than 0. So, it prints the number from 100 to 1, and as soon as it
       reaches 0, the test condition becomes false. */
    for (iNumber1 = 1, iNumber2 = 100; iNumber1 <= 100 && iNumber2 > 0; iNumber1++, iNumber2--)
    {
        printf("iNumber1: %d, iNumber2: %d.\n", iNumber1, iNumber2);
    }

    return 0;
}
```

The loop in our program gets executed 100 times, printing the number *'iNumber1'* from 1 to 100 and the number *'iNumber2'* from 100 to 1. The variable *'iNumber1'* is initialized to 1 and the variable *'iNumber2'* is initialized to 100 before starting the loop. The test condition *'iNumber1 <= 100 && iNumber2 > 0'* is evaluated before moving to the *loop body.* As both the conditions in the test condition are joined by the *logical AND (&&) operator,* both need to be *true* for the entire *test condition* to be *true.* After the body of the loop is executed, the *increment or decrement* section *'iNumber1++, iNumber2--'* of the **for** statement gets executed. Thereupon the *test condition* is evaluated again, and if *true* the *body of the loop* gets executed once more. This continues until the test condition evaluates to *false.*

As the **for** loop is an entry-controlled loop, the body of the loop may never get executed if the test condition is evaluated to *false* at the very beginning of the loop itself.

In our next program, we will try to find all the factors of a given number. The factors will include 1 and the number itself. There will be no factors *(except the number itself)* which will be greater than the half of the given number. So, we iterate till we are less than or equal to the half of the number *'uNumber / 2'*.

```c
#include <stdio.h>

int main(void)
{
    /* Variable declaration and initialization. */
    unsigned int uNumber  = 0;
    unsigned int uReverse = 0;

    /* Accept a number from the user. */
    printf("Enter a positive number: ");
    scanf("%u", &uNumber);

    /* Find factors. */
    printf("\nThe factors of the number are:\n");
    for (unsigned int i = 1; i <= uNumber / 2; i++)
    {
        if (0 == uNumber % I)
        {
            printf("%u, ", i);
        }
    }

    /* Now print the number entered by the user as that is also a factor. */
    printf("%u\n\n", uNumber);

    return 0;
}
```

The **for** statement has the following features:

1. As discussed earlier, the initialization section may initialize multiple variables separated by commas *(example: iNumber = 1, lSum = 0)*. If both the variables need to be initialized to the same value we could do something like *'lSum = iNumber = 0'*.
2. As we had discussed, the increment or decrement section may also contain more than one expression that are separated by commas *(example: iNumber1++, iNumber2 = iNumber2 – 2)*.
3. Just like other loop constructs, the test condition may contain multiple conditions joined together using the logical operators.
4. If any section within the *for* statement is not required, it may be omitted. However, the semi-colons separating the sections must remain. If the *test condition* is omitted, we may get into an *infinite* loop, until broken using a **break** or a **goto** statement. We will read about **break** a little later in this chapter. We may have something like below:

    > *int i = 0;*
    > **for** *(; i < 50;)*
    > *{*
    >   *printf("The value of i is %d. \n", i++);*
    > *}*

5. If the *body of the loop* has only one statement, we may omit the *braces* of the *for* loop. Consider the next example:

    for *(i = 0; i < 50; i++)*
    printf("The value of i is %d.\n", i);

6. We may have a **for** statement without any *body of the loop*. The statement may just increment a variable until it reaches a specific value. These are useful when working with arrays, such as situations where we need to search for an element with a specific value within the array. Consider the below example where we have an integer array *'rgiValues'* of 100 elements. The array is filled with values and we need to find the first element with a value of 0.

    for *(idx = 0; idx < 100 && rgiValues[idx] != 0; idx++);*

    We come out of the loop when *'idx'* reaches 100 *(means we did not find any element with a value of 0)* or we find an element with the value 0. Such statements without any *body of the loop* need to be ended with a semi-colon.

7.5 NESTED LOOPS

What if we need to use another loop inside an outer loop. In such cases we can use more *loop* control statements within an existing *loop* block. As a matter of fact, we may use any kind of valid C control statements within a *loop* block including other *loop* statements. When *loop* statements are nested within outer *loop* statements, we call them nested *loop* statements. They take the following form:

```
while (test condition)
{
    while (test condition)
    {
        --------
        --------
        for (initialization; test condition; increment or decrement)
        {
            --------
            --------
        }
        --------
        --------
    }

    do
    {
        ---------
        ---------
    } while(test condition);
    ---------
    ---------
}
```

Nested loops are useful in situations where we need to do further iterations within an existing loop. Accepting or printing values in multi-dimensional arrays are examples in which we will require nested loop constructs, where each loop will work with a particular dimension of the array. The outermost loop will work with the first dimension, the first inner loop will work with the second dimension, the second inner loop will work with the third dimension and so on.

```
for (i = 0; i < first dimension length; i++)
{
    for (j = 0; j < second dimension length; j++)
    {
        for (k = 0; k < third dimension length; k++)
        {
            ---------
            ---------
            ---------
        }
    }
}
```

Let us write a program which accepts the element values of two matrices from the user. It then prints the sum of these two matrices.

```c
/* Header Files */
#include <stdio.h>

/* Defined Values */
#define MATRIX_ROWS 3
#define MATRIX_COLS 4

int main(void)
{
    /* Variable declaration and initialization. */
    int rgiMatrix1[MATRIX_ROWS][MATRIX_COLS] = { 0 };
    int rgiMatrix2[MATRIX_ROWS][MATRIX_COLS] = { 0 };
    int iRow                                 = 0;
    int iCol                                 = 0;

    /* Accept the first matrix from the user. */
    printf("Enter the elements of the first matrix:\n");
    for (iRow = 0; iRow < MATRIX_ROWS; iRow++)
    {
        for (iCol = 0; iCol < MATRIX_COLS; iCol++)
        {
            printf("Element [%02d][%02d]: ", iRow, iCol);
            scanf("%d", &rgiMatrix1[iRow][iCol]);
        }
    }

    /* Accept the second matrix from the user. */
    printf("\nEnter the elements of the second matrix:\n");
    for (iRow = 0; iRow < MATRIX_ROWS; iRow++)
    {
        for (iCol = 0; iCol < MATRIX_COLS; iCol++)
        {
```

103

```
            printf("Element [%02d][%02d]: ", iRow, iCol);
            scanf("%d", &rgiMatrix2[iRow][iCol]);
        }
    }

    /* Add the two matrices and print the result. */
    printf("\nThe sum of the two matrices is:");
    for (iRow = 0; iRow < MATRIX_ROWS; iRow++)
    {
        printf("\n");
        for (iCol = 0; iCol < MATRIX_COLS; iCol++)
        {
            printf("%9d", rgiMatrix1[iRow][iCol] + rgiMatrix2[iRow][iCol]);
        }
    }

    printf("\n\n");

    return 0;
}
```

7.6 JUMPING WITHIN LOOPS

The group of statements within a *loop* is repeated until the *test condition* becomes *false.* When executing a *loop,* it sometimes becomes necessary to break out of the *loop* or skip a part of the loop when certain condition occurs. Consider an example where we are searching for a particular value within an array of 50 elements. We need to loop though the entire array in search of the element with the given value. This will require us to loop through all the 50 elements of the array. But, we need to terminate the search as soon as we find the desired value. In such a case we will require to break out of the loop when the value is found.

7.6.1 THE break STATEMENT

The **break** statement is a C keyword and when used within a *loop,* the control comes out of the innermost loop containing the *break* statement. We have seen the use of *break* in *switch* statement which makes the control break out of the innermost *switch* block. Similarly, when the *break* statement is used within a *loop (while, do while or for),* the control breaks out of the innermost *loop* and goes to the statement immediately following the *loop.* In case of nested *loops,* when the *break* statement is encountered in an inner *loop,* the control comes out of the *loop* which directly encloses the *break* statement.

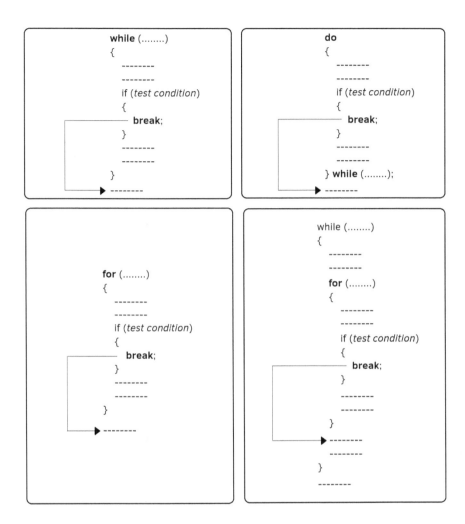

We can achieve the same functionality of **break** statement using the **goto** statement. For that we need to define a *label* outside the *loop* and use the *goto* statement to jump to that *label*. When using nested *loops* we can use a single *goto* statement to jump out of multiple *loops*, unlike the *break* statement which breaks out of the innermost *loop* only. But, it is recommended that we avoid using the *goto* statement as a means to *break* out of a *loop* in situations where the *break* statement can be used. The *break* statement is **not** prone to the disadvantages inherent to the *goto* statement *(drawbacks mentioned in **section 6.8**)*. Some example usage of *goto* statement to break out of *loops* are:

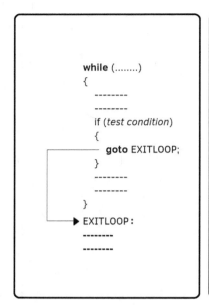

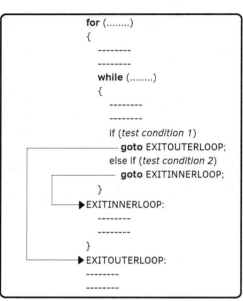

In our example we accept an array of integers from the user. We search the array for the first occurrence of a negative number within the array. If found, we print its location.

```c
/* Header Files */
#include <stdio.h>

/* Defined Values */
#define ARRAY_MAX_ELEMENT 20

int main(void)
{
    /* Variable declaration and initialization. */
    int rgiNumbers[ARRAY_MAX_ELEMENT] = { 0 };
    int iCounter                      = 0;

    /* Accept the array from the user. */
    for (; iCounter < ARRAY_MAX_ELEMENT; iCounter++)
    {
        printf("Enter array element [%02d]: ", iCounter);
        scanf("%d", &rgiNumbers[iCounter]);
    }

    /* Search for the first negative number within the array. */
    for (iCounter = 0; iCounter < ARRAY_MAX_ELEMENT; iCounter++)
    {
        if (rgiNumbers[iCounter] < 0)
        {
            /* We found it. No need to continue any more. */
            break;
        }
    }

    if (iCounter == ARRAY_MAX_ELEMENT)
    {
        /* We reached the end of the array. */
```

```
        printf("There are no negative numbers within the array.\n\n");
    }
    else
    {
        printf("The first negative number is at the index location %d.\n\n", iCounter);
    }

    return 0;
}
```

7.6.2 THE continue STATEMENT

Just like the **break** statement, **continue** is also a C keyword and is used to skip a portion of the loop. But, unlike the *break* statement which makes the control break out of the *loop,* the *continue* statement makes the control jump to the next *iteration* by skipping any statements in-between. Whenever it is encountered, the control directly jumps to the beginning of the *loop* for the next iteration, skipping the statements following the *continue* statement in the current iteration. For the **for** loop, *continue* statement causes the *increment* and *test condition* of the *loop* to execute. For the **while** and **do while** *loops, continue* statement causes the control to pass to the *test condition*.

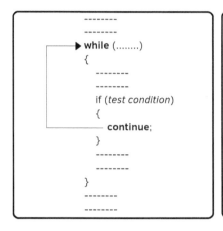
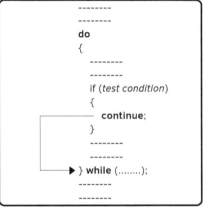

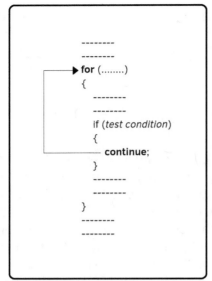 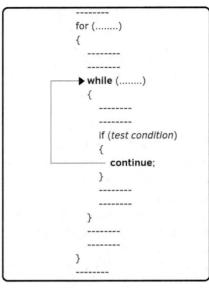

We can achieve the same functionality of **continue** statement using **goto**. For that we need to define a *label* inside the *loop* and just after the *loop* statement. Consider the following example:

```
while (...........)
{
    LOOP:
    ----------

    ----------

    if (test condition)
    {
        goto LOOP;
    }
    ---------
}
```

In our next program we will generate a pyramid of stars. It will accept the number of rows of the pyramid from the user subject to a maximum rows of 30. The program will keep printing the pyramids until the user enters 0 (zero) as the number of rows to print. It will print a similar pattern for each user input:

```
         *
        ***
       *****
      *******
     *********
    ***********
   *************
```

To keep symmetry, the number of stars in each row has to be two more than the previous row, with each extra star extending on both sides of the previous row. So if the top of the pyramid has one star, we will have odd number of stars in every row of the pyramid *(1, 3, 5, ...)*. The number of stars in each row is one less than the twice of the row number i.e. if the row number is 'a', the number of stars in this row will be '2a - 1'. For each row, spaces will be inserted at the beginning to help the stars align to the middle of the pyramid.

```c
/* Header Files */
#include <stdio.h>

/* Defined values */
#define MAX_ROWS    30

int main(void)
{
    /* Variable declaration and initialization. */
    unsigned int uRows   = 0;
    unsigned int uCurRow = 0;
    unsigned int idx     = 0;
    unsigned int uSpaces = 0;
    unsigned int uStars  = 0;

    do
    {
        /* Accept the number of rows to print. */
        printf("Enter the number of rows of the pyramid: ");
        scanf("%u", &uRows);

        if (0 == uRows)
        {
            break;
        }
        else if (uRows > MAX_ROWS)
        {
            printf("Please enter a row count within %d.\n\n", MAX_ROWS);
            continue;
        }

        printf("\nThe pyramid of stars:\n");
        /* Print each row at every iteration. */
        for (uCurRow = 1; uCurRow <= uRows; uCurRow++)
        {
            /* Print the preceding spaces so as the stars appear
               at the middle of the next row to come. */
            uSpaces = uRows - uCurRow;
            for (idx = 1; idx <= uSpaces; idx++)
                printf(" ");

            /* Now print the stars. */
            uStars = 2 * uCurRow - 1;
            for (idx = 1; idx <= uStars; idx++)
                printf("*");

            /* Move to the next row. */
            printf("\n");
        }

        printf("\n\n");

    } while (0 != uRows);

    return 0;
}
```

7.7 CONCISE TEST CONDITIONS

Just like **if** conditions, in *loops* too, if the test-condition expression requires a relational operator but none has been specified, then by default the expression is compared for *inequality* with 0 *(zero)*. We need not make explicit comparisons with 0 *(zero)*. Consider the following:

while *(expression != 0)*
is equivalent to using
while *(expression)*

AND

while *(expression == 0)*
is equivalent to using
while *(!expression)*

Example:
while *(x != 0 && y % 2 == 0)* is same as
while *(x && ! (y % 2))*

for (x = 10; x != 0; x--) is same as
for (x = 10; x; x--)

7.8 SAMPLE PROGRAMS

1. Let us write a C program which will show the multiplication tables of numbers. The program will accept two numbers from the user. Multiplication tables of all numbers starting from the first given number to the second will be printed. The program uses nested **for** loops where the first *for* loop iterates through the numbers whose multiplication tables are shown. The second *for* loop shows the multiplication table corresponding to each number.

```c
/* Header Files */
#include <stdio.h>

int main(void)
{
    /* Variable declaration and initialization. */
    unsigned int uNumber    = 0;
    unsigned int uEndNumber = 0;
    unsigned int uMultiply  = 0;

    /* Accept the number from which to start showing the multiplication tables.
       The number must be between 1 and 99. If less than 1 or greater than 99,
       we ask the user to again enter the number. */
    while (uNumber < 1 || uNumber > 99)
    {
        printf("The number from which to start the multiplication tables (1-99): ");
```

```
    scanf("%u", &uNumber);
}

/* Accept the number up to which the multiplication tables need to be shown.
   The number must be between 1 and 99. If less than 1 or greater than 99,
   we ask the user to again enter the number. The number must also be greater
   than or equal to the number from which to start. */
while (uEndNumber < 1 || uEndNumber > 99 || uEndNumber < uNumber)
{
    printf("The last number till which multiplication tables to show (1-99): ");
    scanf("%u", &uEndNumber);
}

/* Loop through all the numbers and show their multiplication table. Each
   multiplication table is shown in each row with each product being shown
   separated from the other by a comma. To properly show the results, we
   are left-aligning our output and using a fixed length 4-character output
   with space as the padding character. */
printf("\nThe multiplication table of the numbers are:");
for (; uNumber <= uEndNumber; uNumber++)
{
    printf("\n%2u: ", uNumber);

    /* Show the multiplication table of uNumber. */
    for (uMultiply = 1; uMultiply <= 10; uMultiply++)
    {
        if (uMultiply < 10)
        {
            printf("%4u, ", uNumber * uMultiply);
        }
        else
        {
            printf("%4u", uNumber * uMultiply);
        }
    }
}

printf("\n\n");

return 0;
}
```

2. In our next program we will accept a number from the user and determine whether the number is prime or composite. We will keep accepting numbers from the user until the user enters 0 (zero) as the number.

    To check whether a number is prime or not, we need to check for the number's divisibility till the square root of the number. If a number n is not a prime *(i.e. a composite)*, it can be factored into two factors 'A' and 'B' as below:
    N = A * B;
    where 'A' and 'B' are whole numbers. If both 'A' and 'B' were greater than the square root of 'N', then 'A * B' would have been greater than 'N'. So, both 'A' and 'B' together cannot be greater than 'N'. If say the number 'A' is greater than the square root of 'N', then 'B' must be less than the square root of 'N'. So, if we check for divisibility of 'N' till the square root of 'N', then we must have also checked its divisibility by 'B'. If it is divisible, 'N' is not a prime and is a composite. So, checking its divisibility by 'A' becomes a non-requirement.

```c
/* Header Files */
#include <stdio.h>
#include <math.h>

int main(void)
{
    /* Variable declaration and initialization. */
    unsigned int  uNumber    = 0;
    unsigned int  uMaxFactor = 0;
    unsigned int  uFactor    = 0;
    unsigned char IsPrime     = 0;

    do
    {
        /* Accept the number which needs to be checked for prime. */
        printf("Enter the number to check for prime: ");
        scanf("%u", &uNumber);

        if (0 == uNumber)
        {
            /* The user does not want to continue. */
            break;
        }
        else if (1 == uNumber)
        {
            printf("The number '1' is neither a prime nor composite.\n\n");
            continue;
        }

        uMaxFactor = (unsigned int) sqrt((double) uNumber);
        for (IsPrime = 1, uFactor = 2; uFactor <= uMaxFactor; uFactor++)
        {
            if (0 == (uNumber % uFactor))
            {
                /* The number is divisible by uFactor. So, it is not a prime.
                   Break out of this inner loop. */
                IsPrime = 0;
                break;
            }
        }

        if (IsPrime) /* It is the same as 'if (IsPrime != 0)'. */
        {
            printf("The number '%u' is a prime number.\n\n", uNumber);
        }
        else
        {
            printf("The number '%u' is a composite number.\n\n", uNumber);
        }

    } while (0 != uNumber);

    printf("\n\n");

    return 0;
}
```

3. Let us write a program which accepts two positive numbers from the user and finds the HCF and LCM of the two numbers. To find the HCF of the two numbers, we use the Euclidean algorithm. Here, we continuously replace the larger of the two numbers by its remainder when divided by

the smaller of the two numbers. This is repeated until the remainder comes as 0 *(zero)*, upon which the last divisor *(for which the remainder came as 0 [zero])* is the HCF. The LCM is calculated as the product of the two numbers divided by their HCF.

```c
/* Header Files */
#include <stdio.h>

int main(void)
{
    /* Variable declaration and initialization. */
    unsigned int  uNumber1 = 0;
    unsigned int  uNumber2 = 0;
    unsigned int  uModulo1 = 0;
    unsigned int  uModulo2 = 0;
    unsigned int  uHCF     = 0;
    unsigned long uLCM     = 0;

    do
    {
        /* Accept the first number. */
        printf("Enter the first number: ");
        scanf("%u", &uNumber1);

    } while (0 == uNumber1);

    do
    {
        /* Accept the second number. */
        printf("Enter the second number: ");
        scanf("%u", &uNumber2);

    } while (0 == uNumber2);

    /* Find the HCF using the Euclidean algorithm. */
    uModulo1 = uNumber1;
    uModulo2 = uNumber2;
    while (uModulo1 != 0 && uModulo2 != 0)
    {
        if (uModulo1 > uModulo2)
        {
            uModulo1 = uModulo1 % uModulo2;
        }
        else
        {
            uModulo2 = uModulo2 % uModulo1;
        }
    }

    if (0 == uModulo1)
    {
        uHCF = uModulo2;
    }
    else
    {
        uHCF = uModulo1;
    }

    /* Calculate the LCM. The LCM is calculated as the product of the
       two numbers divided by their HCF. */
    uLCM = (uNumber1 * uNumber2) / uHCF;

    /* Print the results. */
```

```
        printf("\nThe HCF of the numbers is %u and LCM is %lu.\n\n", uHCF, uLCM);

        return 0;
}
```

4. Let us write a program which accepts a positive number and prints its binary representation. To do this, we need to loop through each bit of the number from left to right, determine if the bit is 0 or 1, and print its value. We keep doing so until we have printed all the bits.

```
/* Header Files */
#include <stdio.h>

int main(void)
{
    /* Variable declaration and initialization. */
    unsigned int uNumber = 0;
    int          idx     = 0;
    unsigned int uBit    = 0;

    /* Accept the number from the user. */
    printf("Enter the number: ");
    scanf("%u", &uNumber);

    printf("The binary equivalent of the number is:\n");
    for (idx = (sizeof(uNumber) * 8) - 1; idx >= 0; idx--)
    {
        /* We are evaluating each bit of the number one by one starting from
            the most significant bit (MSB) (i.e. the left-most bit) and
            continuing towards the right. At every iteration, we are doing a
            right-shift of the current bit in such a manner so that it becomes
            the least significant bit (LSB) (i.e. the right-most bit).
            |MSB|0|1|0|1|1|0|......|LSB|.
            We are then doing a bitwise AND of it with 1 which gives 1 if the
            LSB is 1, else gives 0. So, in effect we are just trying to find
            whether the current bit is 1 or 0 and printing it accordingly.
            Remember: The value of uNumber does not change due to the shift or
            bitwise AND, as it is not the LValue (i.e. it does not appear at
            the left of the assignment operator). So, its original value is
            retained and does not change as nothing gets assigned to it.
        */
        uBit = (uNumber >> idx) & 1;
        printf("%u", uBit);
    }

    printf("\n\n");

    return 0;
}
```

5. In the next example we will accept a number from the user and find its factorial.

```
/* Header Files */
#include <stdio.h>

int main(void)
{
    /* Variable declaration and initialization. */
    unsigned short uNumber    = 0;
    unsigned short uCounter   = 0;
    unsigned long  uFactorial = 0;
```

```c
    /* Accept the number from the user. */
    printf("Enter the number: ");
    scanf("%hu", &uNumber);

    /* Generate the factorial. */
    for (uFactorial = 1, uCounter = uNumber; uCounter > 1; uCounter--)
    {
        uFactorial *= uCounter;
    }

    /* Print the result. */
    printf("\nThe factorial of %hu is %u.\n\n", uNumber, uFactorial);

    return 0;
}
```

6. Let us write a program which prints the Fibonacci series.

```c
/* Header Files */
#include <stdio.h>

/* Defined Values */
#define MAX_NUM_COUNT    47

int main(void)
{
    /* Variable declaration and initialization. */
    unsigned int    uNumber1 = 0;
    unsigned int    uNumber2 = 1;
    unsigned int    uTemp    = 0;
    unsigned short  uCount   = 0;

ACCEPTCOUNT:
    /* Accept the count of the Fibonacci numbers to print. */
    printf("Enter the count of Fibonacci numbers: ");
    scanf("%hu", &uCount);

    if (uCount < 1 || uCount > MAX_NUM_COUNT)
    {
        /* At count 47, we get the largest number that can be held
           in an 'unsigned int' variable, after which we will start
           witnessing an overflow and the value will roll over. */
        printf("Please enter a count between 1-47\n\n");
        goto ACCEPTCOUNT;
    }

    /* Print the numbers. */
    printf("\nThe Fibonacci numbers are:\n");
    for (; uCount > 0; uCount--)
    {
        printf("%u, ", uNumber2);
        uTemp    = uNumber2;
        uNumber2 += uNumber1;
        uNumber1  = uTemp;
    }

    printf("\n\n");

    return 0;
}
```

POINTERS

[CHAPTER-8]

8.1 INTRODUCTION

C is one of the very few languages which allow direct access to memory locations. With this C brings one of the powerful features of assembly languages right into a high-level language. In other words C provides the convenience of a high-level language with the power of an assembly language. We access the memory locations of variables and functions using **pointers**. Pointers can be very confusing in the beginning but, is a very powerful feature which comes really handy. To be able to code well in C, we must have a very good understanding of **pointers**.

The entire computer memory is divided into memory cells where each cell is capable of holding 1 *byte* of data. Each such memory cell is assigned an *address* by the operating system. This address helps the operating system know where to store the data or from where to fetch the data. Each such memory cell has a numeric address and the maximum size of this address depends on the computer architecture and the operating system. Many a times we hear about 32-bit/64-bit processor and operating system. In a 32-bit *(4 bytes)* system, the address is a numeric value which can be stored in *4 bytes* (a maximum address value of 4,29,49,67,295 or 0xFFFFFFFF). So, if the first memory location has an address of 1, the last one will have an address of 4,29,49,67,295 *(0xFFFFFFFF)*. Similarly in a 64-bit system, the address is stored in *8 bytes* (a maximum address value of 1,84,46,74,40,73,70,95,51,615 or 0xFFFFFFFFFFFFFFFF).

Every variable in a program is assigned a memory location in which the value of the variable is stored. The size of the memory space *(i.e. the number of consecutive memory cells the variable occupies)* depends on the data type of the variable. The address of the variable refers to the starting address of the memory location which is assigned for the variable. Consider the following example:

int iValue = 978562;

Assuming **int** takes 4-bytes, the data will be stored in 4 consecutive memory cells with each cell capable of holding 1 byte of data. Let us assume that the system has chosen the address *100* as the starting location for this variable. On these assumptions, the variable may be stored as shown in the following diagram *(the order of the bytes depend on the computer architecture)*:

Bits:	10000010	11101110	00001110	00000000
Values:	130	238	14	0
Memory Addresses:	100	101	102	103

The first memory byte holds the value *130*, the second byte holds *238*, the third holds *14* and the fourth holds *0*. The four bytes collectively hold *978562* as a single value for the entire variable. If the variable is assigned a starting memory location of *100* the four bytes belonging to the variable will have addresses of *100*, *101*, *102* and *103* respectively. During execution, the system assigns the address *100* corresponding to the variable name '*iValue*'. We may access the value using its variable name '*iValue*' or its address '*100*'. Since the memory addresses are just numbers, they can be assigned to variables and these variables can be used for later direct access of the memory locations. Say in our above example, we may have a variable called '*ptr*' which is assigned the memory location of the variable '*iValue*' which in our case is *100*. So, '*ptr*' will have the value 100 assigned to it. Later on, we may use this variable '*ptr*' to directly access and manipulate the value contained in '*iValue*'. Variables like '*ptr*' are called **pointers**. In other words, pointers are variables that contain the memory addresses of other variables or functions within our program.

Pointers can be used to directly access the memory locations and read or write values to that location. As a pointer points to the memory location of a variable or function, thus their name. Since pointers are also variables, they too occupy a memory location and have an address of their own. As pointers have memory addresses, we may declare pointers which point to other pointers as well *(pointer to pointer)*. We will come to this a little later in this chapter. For now let us understand this concept using a simple diagram.

Variable Name	Value	Memory Address
iValue	978562 ◀	100
ptr	100	656

We have the variable '*iValue*' which holds the value *978562* and is located at the *(starting)* memory address *100*. The pointer '*ptr*' is another variable which has the value *100* *(the memory address of iValue)* and is itself located at the memory address *656*.

Some of the advantages of using pointers are:
* They increase the execution speed of the program as we have direct access to the memory locations.
* A pointer helps us to access and manipulate variables which are defined outside the function.
* Pointers are more efficient and convenient to use when dealing with arrays and character strings.
* Pointers help us to allocate memory dynamically during execution. This helps us to allocate memory when needed and thus, reduces memory wastage. In simple words, it reduces the memory needed for a program to run. We will learn about dynamic memory allocation in our later chapters.
* It is almost impossible to work with some data structures like linked lists, trees etc. without the help of pointers.
* In many cases, pointers reduce the length and complexity of a program.

Some of the disadvantages of using pointers are:
- If pointers are not used carefully, we may end up accessing and manipulating wrong memory locations leading to program crashes.
- C does not check the validity of a pointer location and allows us free use of the location. Pointer arithmetic involves calculation of locations using pointers. If we are wrong in our calculations, C will not stop us and we may overrun or under run our memory location leading to incorrect results.
- If dynamically allocated memory is not freed properly, it may result in memory leak.
- Pointer syntax is complex and a little difficult to master, especially pointer to pointer. We may generate wrong results if we use wrong pointer syntax.

8.2 DECLARING, INITIALIZING AND ASSIGNING POINTERS

Like every other variable in C, pointers too belong to specific data types. Pointer variables need to be declared as pointers and their data type needs to be specified during declaration. This enables C to know that these variables are going to be used as pointers and the kind of data they will be pointing to. The data type of a pointer enables the compiler to determine the operations that will be allowed on the pointer variable. The declaration of a pointer variable takes the following form:

*Data-Type *pointer_name;*

The above statement tells the compiler three things:
- The asterisk (*) tells the compiler that this variable *(pointer_name)* is a pointer.
- *pointer_name* will point to a variable of type *Data-Type*.
- Just like any other variable, the *pointer_name* is assigned a memory location with a memory address of its own. The size of the memory space assigned to the pointer depends on the computer architecture. In a 32-bit system, it will use 32 bits *(4 bytes)* of space and in a 64-bit system, it will use 64 bits *(8 bytes)*.

Examples:

int **ptr1* → *ptr1* is a pointer variable which will point to an integer *(int)* variable.
float **ptr2* → *ptr2* is a pointer variable which will point to a floating point *(float)* variable.
char **ptr3* → *ptr3* is a pointer variable which will point to a character *(char)* variable.

We may declare a pointer of **void** data type. This tells the compiler that this pointer is capable of pointing to a variable of any data type. As the data type of variable pointed by this pointer is unspecified, many operations on this pointer variable are restricted. For example, we have to typecast this variable to a specific data type before performing any arithmetic, assignment or increment operations. void pointers are used in situations where we are not sure regarding the type of data this variable will point to when we are writing the code. An example declaration of a void pointer is:

void *ptr;

The memory address of a variable is only known during the execution of the program and is not known to us during writing of the code. So C provides us with an operator (**&**) which is called the '*address of*' operator. We have seen it being used in functions like '*scanf*' in our previous chapters. When the operator **&** immediately precedes a variable in a statement, it returns the address of that variable.

Consider the following example:

> *int iValue = 56;*
> *int *ptr;*
> *ptr = &iValue;*

In the above statements, we are declaring a pointer *'ptr'* of type **int** and assigning the address of the integer variable *'iValue'* to it. The statement *'ptr = &iValue'* assigns the address of the variable *'iValue'* to the pointer *'ptr'*. If the address of the variable *'iValue'* is *100*, that address is assigned to the pointer *'ptr'*. The **&** operator can be used with a simple variable or an array element. Consider the following example which uses an array element:

> *int rgValues[] = {1, 2, 3, 4, 5, 6, 7, 8, 9, 10};*
> *int *ptr;*
> *ptr = &rgValues[3];*

Assuming **int** takes 4 bytes of memory space, if *'rgValues[0]'* starts from the address *100*, the 4th element *(rgValues[3])* will be located at the memory address *112 (100 + 3 * 4)*. So in our case *112* will be assigned to the pointer *'ptr'*.

Some of the invalid usage of the **&** operator may be:
- *int rgValues[] = {1, 2, 3, 4, 5, 6, 7, 8, 9, 10};*
  int *ptr;
  ptr = &rgValues;

  Array names themselves point to the starting address of the array and thus, they cannot be used with the **&** operator. To get the starting address, we may do any of the following valid operations:
  - *ptr = rgValues;*
  - *ptr = &rgValues[0];*

- *int *ptr;*
  ptr = &56;

  Address of a constant cannot be retrieved using the **&** operator.

Just like any other variable, pointer variables can also be initialized during their declaration itself. Pointer variables can also be initialized to **NULL** *(ASCII values 0)* signifying that they are currently not pointing to any memory location. As a matter of fact, we may assign **NULL** to a pointer variable at any moment within our program, upon which it signifies that the pointer from thereon does not point to any memory location. Consider the following example:

> *int iValue = 475;*
> *int *ptr1 = &iValue;*
> *int *ptr2 = NULL;*

```
    if (NULL == ptr2)
    {
        ptr2 = ptr1;
    }
```

As we can see in the above example, a pointer can also be compared with equality or inequality with **NULL**. The first pointer *'ptr1'* is assigned the address of the variable *'iValue'* during its declaration itself. As the *'iValue'* variable is an integer *(int)*, the pointer *'ptr1'* is also of integer type. The pointer *'ptr2'* is declared and initialized to NULL. Within our **if** condition, we are checking whether *'ptr2'* is NULL *(does not point to any valid memory location)*, and if so, we are assigning the value of *'ptr1'* to *'ptr2'*. The assignment makes *'ptr2'* contain the address of *'iValue'* and thus, thereupon both *'ptr1'* and *'ptr2'* point to *'iValue'*.

Remember: Before a pointer is initialized or assigned an address, it should not be used as it contains a garbage value. So, it is always a good practice to initialize a pointer to **NULL** during its declaration. We must ensure that the pointer points to the corresponding type of data before performing any operation using the pointer.

8.3 ACCESSING A VARIABLE USING ITS POINTER

Once a pointer has been assigned the address of a variable, the value of the variable can be accessed using the pointer. This is done with the help of the *indirection* operator * *(asterisk)*. Using this operator, we can not only access the value of a variable *(which the pointer is pointing to)* but also change it. Consider the following example:

```
1.  int   iValue   = 728;
2.  int   iNumber = 0;
3.  int *ptr       = NULL;
4.  ptr       = &iValue;
5.  iNumber = *ptr;
6.  *ptr      = *ptr + 10;
7.  (*ptr)++;
8.  iNumber++;
```

In our above example, we are declaring two integer variables and a pointer. Let us find out what happens in rest of the statements.

- In statement 4, we are assigning the address of the variable *'iValue'* to the pointer *'ptr'*.
- In statement 5, we are using the indirection operator * to retrieve the integer value contained in the memory location pointed by the pointer *'ptr'*. As *'ptr'* is pointing to *'iValue'*, the * operator returns the value stored in *'iValue'*. This value is assigned to the variable *'iNumber'*. Using *'*ptr'* is equivalent to using *'iValue'* itself.
- In statement 6, on the right hand side, we are accessing the value of *'iValue'* and adding 10 to it. We are then assigning the value back to the location where *'ptr'* is pointing to. So in effect, we are updating *'iValue'* with this new value. Note, the use of the indirection operator * does not update the pointer but, the value in the memory location pointed by the pointer. The pointer keeps pointing to the same memory location as before.
- In statement 7, we are **not** incrementing or changing the pointer but, the value in the memory location pointed by the pointer, which in our case is *'iValue'*. So, *'iValue'* gets incremented after

this statement. But, *a statement like *(ptr++) or *ptr++ would have incremented the memory address pointed by the pointer and tried to access the value contained in that address. In our case, it may generate a run-time error as that memory address does not belong to us or may be invalid.*

- In statement 8, we are simply incrementing the value of *'iNumber'*. Incrementing this variable does not have any effect on the pointer or the location pointed by it.

Let us now write a small program which adds two numbers and prints the result. It will do all the operations using pointers.

```c
/* Header Files */
#include <stdio.h>

int main(void)
{
    /* Variable Declaration & Initialization */
    int    iNumber1 = 0;
    int    iNumber2 = 0;
    long   lSum     = 0;
    int   *pNumber1 = &iNumber1;
    int   *pNumber2 = &iNumber2;
    long  *pSum     = &lSum;

    /* Accept the numbers from the user. */
    printf("Enter the first number: ");
    scanf("%d", pNumber1);

    printf("Enter the second number: ");
    scanf("%d", pNumber2);

    *pSum = *pNumber1 + *pNumber2;

    printf("\nThe sum of the two numbers is %ld.\n\n", *pSum);

    return 0;
}
```

8.4 ARRAY OF POINTERS AND POINTER TO AN ARRAY

8.4.1 ARRAY OF POINTERS

Array of pointers is very similar to declaring array of any other type. Each element of such an array is capable of pointing to the memory address of a variable which is of the same data type as the pointer. The general form for declaring an array of pointers is:

Data-Type *array_name[Dimension1-Size][Dimension2-Size]....;

We assign the address of a variable to an element of *(a single dimensional)* array of pointers in the following way:

array_name[element-index] = &variable_name;

Let us explain this with a simple example. We assume a single-dimensional array of integer pointers *'ptr'* with size of *5* elements. So, it is capable of pointing to *5* integer variables. We declare the array and assign the address of variables *'iValue1'*, *'iValue2'* and *'iValue3'* to the first three elements of the array as below:

> *int *ptr[5];*
> *ptr[0] = &iValue1;*
> *ptr[1] = &iValue2;*
> *ptr[2] = &iValue3;*

Have a look at the below diagram which shows five variables with memory addresses of 100, 112, 116, 6752 and 6756 respectively. The elements of the array point to the addresses of these variables.

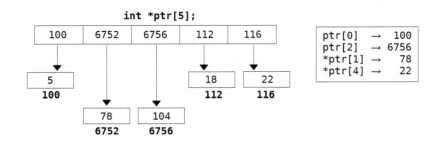

We can access the value contained in the location pointed by an element of the array using the *indirection* operator ***** *(asterisk)* as below:

> **array_name[array-index]*

8.4.2 POINTER TO AN ARRAY

Pointer to an array is a single pointer variable which is capable of pointing to an entire array. The declaration of the pointer must include the size of the array to which it will point. The general form of declaring pointer to a single dimension of an array is:

> *Data-Type (*pointer_name)[Array-Dimension-Size];*

This kind of pointers point to an entire dimension of an array. The array must be of the same data type as the pointer. If the array is a single-dimensional array, the pointer points to the entire array. In case of a two-dimensional array, the pointer will point to an entire row of the array. If incremented, the pointer points to the next row. The general form of assigning the address of an array to such a pointer is:

pointer_name = &array_name;	When *'pointer_name'* has the same number of dimensions as the array *'array_name'*.

Example [One-dimensional]:
```
int rgiValues[5]     = { 1, 2, 3, 4, 5 };
int (*prgValues)[5] = &rgiValues;
```

pointer_name = &array_name[0];	When *'pointer_name'* points to an entire row of a two dimensional array *'array_name'* i.e. it points to only a single dimension of the array.

Example [Pointer points to Row-0 of the array]:
```
int rgiMatrix[3][4] = { { 1, 2, 3, 4 },
                        { 5, 6, 7, 8 },
                        { 9, 10, 11, 12 } };
int (*pMatrix)[4]   = &rgiMatrix[0];
```

We can access *(read and assign)* an element of the array pointed by such a pointer as below:

Read → *Variable_Name = (*pointer_name)[column-index];*

Assign → *(*pointer_name)[column-index] = Value;*

Another way to access an element of the array is to add the column index of the element with the pointer value. This makes it point to the required element. Thereupon, we may use the indirection operator ***** *(asterisk)* to get or set the value of the element.

Memory Address → **pointer_name + column-index*

Element Value → **(*pointer_name + column-index)*

Let us understand the above using a diagram. Assume we have an integer array *'rgiValues'* of *8* elements and a pointer *'ptr'* which points to this array.

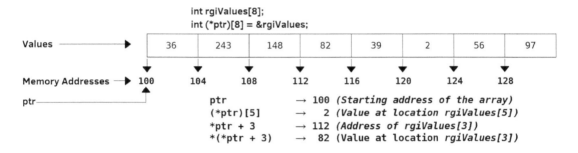

```
int rgiValues[8];
int (*ptr)[8] = &rgiValues;
```

| Values | 36 | 243 | 148 | 82 | 39 | 2 | 56 | 97 |

Memory Addresses → 100   104   108   112   116   120   124   128

ptr

```
ptr          → 100 (Starting address of the array)
(*ptr)[5]    →   2 (Value at location rgiValues[5])
*ptr + 3     → 112 (Address of rgiValues[3])
*(*ptr + 3)  →  82 (Value at location rgiValues[3])
```

Let us write a program in which we are going to use an array of pointers to the elements of an integer array. We will print the element values using their respective pointers.

```c
/* Header Files */
#include <stdio.h>

/* Defined Values */
#define NUM_COUNT    5

int main(void)
{
    /* Variable declaration and initialization. */
    int  idx                 = 0;
    int  iNumbers[NUM_COUNT] = { 1, 2, 3, 4, 5 };
    int *pNumbers[NUM_COUNT];

    /* Assign the address of the elements to the pointers. */
    for (idx = 0; idx < NUM_COUNT; idx++)
    {
        pNumbers[idx] = &iNumbers[idx];
    }

    /* Now, print the numbers. */
    printf("The numbers are: ");
    for (idx = 0; idx < NUM_COUNT;)
    {
        printf("%d", *pNumbers[idx++]);
```

```
        if (idx < NUM_COUNT)
        {
            /* Do not print ',' after the last element. */
            printf(", ");
        }
    }
    printf("\n\n");

    return 0;
}
```

Let us write another program which utilizes array of pointers. But this time around, these pointers will point to character strings. String is an array of characters where the last element is a NULL character *(ASCII value 0)*. The NULL value marks the end of the string. We will declare an array of pointers and initialize its elements to point to the string constants. We will then print these strings using the pointers.

```
/* Header Files */
#include <stdio.h>

/* Defined Values */
#define MAX_CITIES     10

int main(void)
{
    /* Variable declaration and initialization. */
    int         idx                 = 0;
    const char *pCities[MAX_CITIES] = { "New Delhi",
                                        "Washington, D.C.",
                                        "London",
                                        "Moscow",
                                        "Tokyo",
                                        "Ottawa",
                                        "Canberra",
                                        "Gaborone",
                                        "Nairobi",
                                        "Brasilia"
                                      };

    printf("The list of cities are:\n");
    for (idx = 0; idx < MAX_CITIES; idx++)
    {
        printf("%s\n", pCities[idx]);
    }

    printf("\n");

    return 0;
}
```

8.5 POINTER ARITHMETIC

Pointers can be incremented and decremented just like any other variable. We can also add or subtract a number from a pointer to directly point to a specific memory location. We can also subtract one pointer from another giving us the number of items between the two pointer locations.

The result of such pointer arithmetic depends on the data type of the pointer involved in the expression.

When a character pointer is incremented, it will point to the next memory byte address as *'char'* data takes one byte space. Whereas when a float pointer is incremented, it will shift by four memory bytes as *'float'* uses 4 bytes of memory. This comes in real handy when we are working with contiguous memory locations like an array. We may declare a pointer which points to the elements of an array. The pointer is incremented or decremented for accessing the array elements, and we need not bother about the memory size of each element of the array. When incremented, the pointer automatically jumps to the next element of the array irrespective of the memory space used by each array element.

Remember: If we use the **sizeof** operator with a pointer argument, the operator returns the size of the pointer i.e. the total memory used by the pointer itself. It does **not** return the size of the variable pointed by the pointer. The size of a pointer depends on the architecture of the program, and will be 4 bytes for a 32-bit program and 8 bytes for a 64-bit program.

We can typecast the memory address of a data type to a pointer of another data type. We need to use explicit typecast for the purpose. Consider the below example:

```
unsigned int uValue = 16649;
char        *pLetter = (char *) &uValue;
pLetter++;
printf("\nThe second byte is the letter %c.\n\n", *pLetter);
```

In the above example, we are assigning the address of the *'unsigned int'* variable to a *'char'* pointer. As the data type of the pointer is different from the data type of the variable, we have to explicitly typecast the variable's address to the pointer's data type before assigning. After the address has been typecast-ed to the *'char'* pointer, incrementing the pointer will make it point to the next memory byte address. Though we have assigned the address of an *'unsigned int'* variable *(which takes 4 or 8 bytes of memory depending on the compiler and architecture)* to the pointer, yet, incrementing the pointer will shift the pointer by only *1* byte as the pointer is of *'char'* data type *(which takes 1 byte of memory)*. In our above example, the pointer will point to the second byte within the variable which contains the value *65*. Hence, the *'printf'* statement will print the character 'A' which corresponds to the ASCII value *65*.

To understand pointer arithmetic better, let us have a look at the following three scenarios.
1. In the first scenario, we have a character array *'rgVals[8]'* and two character pointers *'ptr1'* and *'ptr2'*. *'ptr1'* points to the first element of the array and *'ptr2'* points to the last element. We assume that the array starts from the memory location *100*. On these assumptions, we evaluate the result of various pointer arithmetic operations.
2. In the second scenario, we have an integer array *'rgVals[8]'* and two integer pointers *'ptr1'* and *'ptr2'*. *'ptr1'* points to the first element of the array and *'ptr2'* points to the last element. We assume that **'int'** takes 4 bytes of memory and our array starts from the memory location *100*.
3. In our last scenario, we have an array *'rgVals[8]'* of **double** data type and two pointers *'ptr1'* and *'ptr2'* of the data type **double**. *'ptr1'* points to the first element of the array and *'ptr2'* points to the last element. We assume that the array starts from the memory location *100*. All results are calculated assuming *'ptr1'* is pointing to address *100* and *'ptr2'* is pointing to the address *156*.

char rgVals[8] Values →	'I'	' '	'L'	'o'	'v'	'e'	' '	'C'

Memory addresses →	100	101	102	103	104	105	106	107

rgVals → 100
ptr1 → 100
ptr2 → 107

ptr1++	→ 101	&rgVals[3]	→ 103	ptr2--	→ 106
ptr1 + 3	→ 103	rgVals + 2	→ 102	ptr2 - 3	→ 104
ptr1 - rgVals	→ 0	ptr2 - rgVals	→ 7	ptr2 - ptr1	→ 7

int rgVals[8] Values →	10	34	23	38	5	98	2	7

Memory addresses →	100	104	108	112	116	120	124	128

rgVals → 100
ptr1 → 100
ptr2 → 128

ptr1++	→ 104	&rgVals[3]	→ 112	ptr2--	→ 124
ptr1 + 3	→ 112	rgVals + 2	→ 108	ptr2 - 3	→ 116
ptr1 - rgVals	→ 0	ptr2 - rgVals	→ 7	ptr2 - ptr1	→ 7

double rgVals[8] Values →	12.3	1.5	34.1	76.5	3.2	98.3	15.9	7.1

Memory addresses →	100	108	116	124	132	140	148	156

rgVals → 100
ptr1 → 100
ptr2 → 156

ptr1++	→ 108	&rgVals[3]	→ 124	ptr2--	→ 148
ptr1 + 3	→ 124	rgVals + 2	→ 116	ptr2 - 3	→ 132
ptr1 - rgVals	→ 0	ptr2 - rgVals	→ 7	ptr2 - ptr1	→ 7

In the above diagram we can see that addition and subtraction from a pointer moves the pointer depending on the data type of the pointer. If it is of type *'char'* it moves by 1 byte and if its *'double'* it moves by 8 bytes. We also notice that the name of the array is actually a *const* pointer to the starting address of the array and the address of an element of the array can be obtained using the element index as '&array[element index]'.

When we have a pointer pointing to a multidimensional array, we need to keep in mind that in memory a multidimensional array is represented sequentially. For example, in case of a two-dimensional array all the columns of row-0 come first, then all the columns of row-1, then row-2 and so on. All the columns for a row appear together and then the columns of the next row. So in effect the entire two-dimensional array appears sequentially in the actual physical memory. Assuming we have a two-dimensional array called *'rgiValues'* which has 3 rows and 4 columns and is declared as:

```
int rgiValues[3][4] = { { 7, 14, 2, 6 },
                        { 11, 28, 5, 25 },
                        { 43, 8, 30, 72 } };
```

The above array will be represented as the below diagram in actual physical memory.

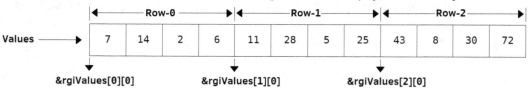

When we are using a pointer to a single element of the multi-dimensional array, the pointer arithmetic depends on the physical representation. Say, the pointer is currently pointing to the element at row-0, column-0 of a two-dimensional array and we want it to point to the element at row-1, column-0. To move the pointer to this new location, we need to add the total column-count of the array to the pointer. Adding the column-count moves the pointer to same column of the next row. When we are at the last column of a row and do an increment of the pointer, the pointer moves to the first column of the next row.

When we are using a row-pointer *(a pointer pointing to an entire row of the array) [refer section 8.4.2]*, incrementing the pointer makes it point to the next row of the array. Adding a count with the pointer advances the pointer by the number of rows equal to the count *(pointer_name + count)*. For example, if we add *2* with the pointer, the pointer advances by *2* rows. Instead of advancing the pointer or adding a count to it, we may also use the index of the row to directly make the pointer point to the required row *(pointer_name[row-index])*. Now as we are pointing to the starting address of the required row, we may just add the column index to point to the required column within the row. We may then use the indirection operator * *(asterisk)* to get the value stored at that location. Assuming the pointer is pointing to the first row *(Row-0)*, we may do any of the following to get the address and value of an element within the two-dimensional array.

Memory Address	Value
(pointer_name + row-index) + column-index	*(*(pointer_name + row-index) + column-index)*
pointer_name[row-index] + column-index	*(pointer_name[row-index] + column-index)*

If the *'pointer_name'* is incremented to point to the required row of the two-dimensional array, we may use the following syntax to get the value at a specific *'column-index'* corresponding to the row.

*(*pointer_name)[column-index]*

Now, let us understand the above using a diagram. Assume, we have a two-dimensional integer array of *4* rows and *5* columns *([4][5] array)*. We have a pointer *'ptr1'* which points to a single element of the array and a pointer *'ptr2'* which points to an entire row of the array. The integer data type takes *4* bytes of memory space and the array starts from the imaginary memory location *100*. So, the two pointers are declared as:

*int *ptr1 = &array_name[0][0];*
*int (*ptr2)[5] = &array_name[0];*

	Column-0	Column-1	Column-2	Column-3	Column-4
	↓	↓	↓	↓	↓
	[0][0]	[0][1]	[0][2]	[0][3]	[0][4]
Row-0 →	1	2	3	4	5
Memory Address →	100	104	108	112	116
	[1][0]	[1][1]	[1][2]	[1][3]	[1][4]
Row-1 →	6	7	8	9	10
Memory Address →	120	124	128	132	136
	[2][0]	[2][1]	[2][2]	[2][3]	[2][4]
Row-2 →	11	12	13	14	15
Memory Address →	140	144	148	152	156
	[3][0]	[3][1]	[3][2]	[3][3]	[3][4]
Row-3 →	16	17	18	19	20
Memory Address →	160	164	168	172	176

As per the above diagram, various pointer operations on *'ptr1'* and *'ptr2'* will yield the following results:

Operation	Result	Explanation
ptr1 + 3	112	Address of element [0][3] as 'ptr1' is pointer to a single element / variable and not a row
ptr1 + 5	120	Address of element [1][0], due to sequential representation in actual physical memory
ptr1 + 17	168	Address of element [3][2]
*(ptr1 + 5)	6	Value of element [1][0]
ptr1++	104	Increments 'ptr1' to point to the next element '[0][1]'
ptr2 + 2	140	Address of Row-2 (*3rd row of the array, as 'ptr2' points to an entire row*)
*ptr2 + 2	108	Address of element [0][2] (*3rd column of row to which 'ptr2' is pointing*)
*(*ptr2 + 2)	3	Value of the element [0][2]
*(ptr2 + 3)	160	Address of element [3][0]. It is same as specifying '*(ptr2 + 3) + 0'
*(ptr2 + 3) + 2	168	Address of element [3][2] (*3rd column of the row pointed by 'ptr2 + 3'*)
((ptr2 + 3) + 2)	18	Value of element [3][2]
ptr2[2] + 3	152	Address of element [2][3]
*(ptr2[2] + 3)	14	Value of element [2][3]
(*ptr2)[2]	3	Value of element [0][2]. (*3rd column of the row pointed by 'ptr2'*)

In our next example, we will accept an array of numbers from the user. We will then calculate the sum and mean of all the numbers. To understand pointers better, we will accept and enumerate the array elements using a pointer.

```c
/* Header Files */
#include <stdio.h>

int main(void)
{
    /* Variable Declaration & Initialization */
    int    rgiNumbers[MAX_NUMBERS] = { 0 };
    int    *ptr1                   = NULL;
    long   lSum                    = 0;
    double dblMean                 = 0;

    /* Accept the numbers from the user. */
    for (ptr1 = rgiNumbers; (ptr1 - rgiNumbers) < MAX_NUMBERS; ptr1++)
    {
        printf("Enter the number: ");
        scanf("%d", ptr1);

        lSum = lSum + *ptr1;
    }

    dblMean = (double)lSum / (double)MAX_NUMBERS;
    printf("\nThe mean of the numbers is %.02lf.\n\n", dblMean);

    return 0;
}
```

In our next program we will have two matrices and two pointers. Each pointer will point to an entire row of a matrix. We will use these two pointers to subtract one matrix from another and print the result.

```c
/* Header Files */
#include <stdio.h>

/* Defined Values */
#define NUM_ROWS 5
#define NUM_COLS 4

int main(void)
{
    /* Variable Declaration & Initialization */
    int   rgiMatrix1[NUM_ROWS][NUM_COLS] = { { 3, 6, 9, 12 },
                                             { 15, 18, 21, 24 },
                                             { 27, 30, 33, 36 },
                                             { 39, 42, 45, 48 },
                                             { 51, 54, 57, 60 } };

    int   rgiMatrix2[NUM_ROWS][NUM_COLS] = { { 2, 4, 6, 8 },
                                             { 10, 12, 14, 16 },
                                             { 18, 20, 22, 24 },
                                             { 26, 28, 30, 32 },
                                             { 34, 36, 38, 40 } };
    int   (*pMatrix1)[NUM_COLS]          = &rgiMatrix1[0];
    int   (*pMatrix2)[NUM_COLS]          = &rgiMatrix2[0];
    int   iRow                           = 0;
    int   iCol                           = 0;
    long  lDifference                    = 0;

    printf("The difference of the matrices is:\n");
```

```
for (; iRow < NUM_ROWS; iRow++, pMatrix1++, pMatrix2++)
{
    for (iCol = 0; iCol < NUM_COLS; )
    {
        lDifference = (*pMatrix1)[iCol] - (*pMatrix2)[iCol];
        /* Instead, we can also do the following: */
        /* lDifference = *(*pMatrix1 + iCol) - *(*pMatrix2 + iCol); */
        printf("%2ld", lDifference);
        if (++iCol < NUM_COLS)
        {
            printf(", ");
        }
    }

    printf("\n");
}

printf("\n");

return 0;
}
```

From the above discussions we know that pointers can take part in various kinds of arithmetic expressions. Some more examples are:

*iValue += *ptr1;*
*iValue = *ptr1 * *ptr2;*
*iValue = *ptr1 / *ptr2;*
**ptr2 += *ptr1;*
ptr1 += 3;
ptr1++;
ptr2 = ptr1 + 2;

Notice in the second statement above, we have used a space between the two consecutive asterisk (*****). This is required for the compiler to understand that the first * is for multiplication and the second one is the indirection operator. If the space is not given, the compiler will confuse it with a pointer to pointer expression *(we will learn about pointer to pointer a little later)*. Similarly in the third statement, we have used a space between the forward slash (**/**) and the asterisk (*****). Absence of a space between these two will make the compiler assume it as the start of a comment section which starts with the character pair '**/***'.

There are few kinds of arithmetic expressions which cannot be used with pointers. Some arithmetic expressions involving pointer variables are not allowed as they are outright meaningless to be performed. Addition of two pointers and pointers involved in multiplication or division are some of the disallowed operations involving pointers. Assuming two pointers *'ptr1'* and *'ptr2'*, some examples of **invalid use** of pointers in expressions are:

*ptr1 * 3;*
*ptr1 * ptr2;*
ptr1 / 2;
ptr1 / ptr2;
ptr1 + ptr2;

In addition to the arithmetic operations, pointers can also take part in expressions involving relational operators. These expressions are really useful when we are working with pointers to array elements. Expressions like *'ptr1 < ptr2'*, *'ptr2 >= ptr1'*, *'ptr1 != ptr2'*, *'ptr1 == ptr2'*, *'ptr1 != NULL'* and *'ptr2 == NULL'* are valid expressions involving pointers. As discussed in **section 7.7**, the last two expressions *'ptr1 != NULL'* and *'ptr2 == NULL'* may also be written as *'ptr1'* and *'!ptr2'* respectively.

8.6 POINTER TO ANOTHER POINTER

Just like pointers point to the memory addresses of other variables, they can also point to the memory locations of other pointers. We have learned in **section 8.2** that pointers are also variables which occupy memory space and have an address of their own. We can declare another pointer which points to this memory address. In other words the second pointer will have the address of the first pointer as its value. The syntax for declaring a pointer to another pointer is:

*Data-Type **pointer_name;*

Notice, we have two asterisk (*****) in the declaration of a pointer to pointer. The number of asterisk in the declaration is proportional to the level of the pointer. This means that a pointer to a simple variable will have a single asterisk, a pointer to another pointer will have two asterisks, and a pointer to a pointer which again points to another pointer will have three asterisks and so on. We rarely require pointers with more than two levels which we will explore in this section.

Variable Name	Value	Memory Address
iValue	978562	100
pointer_name1	100	656
pointer_name2	656	3936

In the above image, we can see a pointer *'pointer_name1'* is pointing to the variable *'iValue'* and contains the memory address of *'iValue'* as its value. Similarly, a pointer *'pointer_name2'* is pointing to the pointer variable *'pointer_name1'* and contains the memory address of *'pointer_name1'* as its value.

Similar to other variables, the *'address of'* operator (**&**) is used to assign the address of a pointer to another pointer.

pointer_name2 = &pointer_name1;

The *indirection* operator (*****) is used with *'pointer_name2'* to retrieve the value stored in *'pointer_name1'*. Using a single indirection operator will get us the value stored in *'pointer_name1'* which as per our above diagram will be the value *100 (the address of iValue)*. To get the value stored in *'iValue'*, we have to use two indirection operators with *'pointer_name2'*.

Expression	Value	Explanation
pointer_name1	100	Address of iValue *(The value stored in pointer_name1)*.
*pointer_name1	978562	Value stored in iValue.
pointer_name2	656	Address of pointer_name1 *(The value stored in pointer_name2)*.
*pointer_name2	100	Address of iValue *(The value stored in pointer_name1)*.
**pointer_name2	978562	Value stored in iValue.

So each indirection operator gets the value stored in the location specified at the right side of the operator. When we are specifying *'*pointer_name2'*, it retrieves the value stored in the address location pointed by *'pointer_name2'*. The address location pointed by *'pointer_name2'* is 656 *(the address of pointer_name1)*. The value stored in this location i.e. at *'pointer_name1'* is 100 *(the address of iValue1)*. So, *'*pointer_name2'* returns the value 100.

When we are specifying *'**pointer_name2'*, it retrieves the value stored in the address location pointed by *'*pointer_name2'*. From our previous finding, *'*pointer_name2'* is 100. This makes *'**pointer_name2'* give us the value stored in the address location 100 *(the value stored in 'iValue')*. So, *'**pointer_name2'* returns the value 978562.

In our next program we will have an integer array of *10* elements. We will declare a pointer *'ptr1'* which points to the first element of the array. We will have another pointer *'ptr2'* which points to the first pointer *'ptr1'*. We will then calculate the sum of all the elements of the array by using the second pointer *'ptr2'*. We will increment the first pointer *'ptr1'* until it crosses the address of the last element of the array. To make matters more complicated, we will do the increment and the addition using the pointer *'ptr2'*. This is a very cryptic way of solving a very simple problem. We are just doing it to get a better understanding of the concept of *pointer to another pointer*.

```
/* Header Files */
#include <stdio.h>

int main(void)
{
    /* Variable declaration and initialization. */
    int    rgiValues[10] = { 7, 72, 83, 20, 37, 6, 10, 26, 9, 57 };
    int   *ptr1          = &rgiValues[0];
    int  **ptr2          = &ptr1;
    int    iSum          = 0;

    /* We are incrementing the value at the location pointed by ptr2. As ptr2 is pointing
       to ptr1, we are essentially incrementing ptr1 to point to the next element. We are
       not changing ptr2 in any way. We are incrementing ptr1 until it points to an address
       greater than the last element of the array which is 'rgiValues[9]'. *ptr2 refers
       to the value at the location pointed by ptr2, which in other words is ptr1. */
    for (; *ptr2 <= &rgiValues[9]; (*ptr2)++)
    {
        iSum += **ptr2;
    }

    /* Print the sum. */
    printf("The sum of the elements is %d.\n\n", iSum);

    return 0;
}
```

Output
The sum of the elements is 327.

8.7 SAMPLE PROGRAMS

1. In our next program we will left-rotate an array. The number of places the element values will be rotated is user specified. So, if the array is {'A', 'B', 'C', 'D', 'E'} and we left-rotate 3 places, the array will become {'D', 'E', 'A', 'B', 'C'}.

```c
/* Header Files */
#include <stdio.h>

/* Defined Values */
/* ARRAY_SIZE must be greater than 1. */
#define ARRAY_SIZE    10

int main(void)
{
    /* Variable declaration and initialization. */
    char   rgValues[ARRAY_SIZE] = { 0 };
    char  *ptrCur               = NULL;
    char   chFirst              = '\0';
    int    iNumRotation         = 0;
    int    iCurRotation         = 0;

    /* Accept all the characters from the user.
       To understand pointers better, instead of an index counter,
       we are using a pointer to loop through the array elements. */
    for (ptrCur = rgValues; ptrCur < (rgValues + ARRAY_SIZE); ptrCur++)
    {
        printf("Enter the element rgValues[%d]: ", (ptrCur - rgValues));
        scanf("%c", ptrCur);
    }

    printf("\n");
    while (iNumRotation <= 0 || iNumRotation >= ARRAY_SIZE)
    {
        printf("Enter the number of places to rotate: ");
        scanf("%d", &iNumRotation);
    }

    /* Print the array before the rotation.
       To understand pointers better, instead of an index counter,
       we are using a pointer to loop through the array elements. */
    printf("\n\nThe array before the rotation is:\n");
    for (ptrCur = rgValues; ptrCur < (rgValues + ARRAY_SIZE); ptrCur++)
    {
        printf("%c", *ptrCur);
        if (ptrCur < (rgValues + (ARRAY_SIZE - 1)))
        {
            /* We do not print the comma after the last element. */
            printf(", ");
        }
    }

    /* Rotate the array. For each rotation shift all the
       array elements one place to the left. */
```

```c
for (iCurRotation = 0; iCurRotation < iNumRotation; iCurRotation++)
{
    /* Save the first array element, before it is overwritten. */
    chFirst = rgValues[0];

    /* Shift all the array elements one place to the left. */
    for (ptrCur = rgValues; (ptrCur + 1) < (rgValues + ARRAY_SIZE); ptrCur++)
    {
        *ptrCur = *(ptrCur + 1);
    }

    /* The first array element becomes the last element after each rotation. */
    *(rgValues + ARRAY_SIZE - 1) = chFirst;
}

/* Print the array after the rotation. */
printf("\n\nThe array after the rotation is:\n");
for (ptrCur = rgValues; ptrCur < (rgValues + ARRAY_SIZE); ptrCur++)
{
    printf("%c", *ptrCur);
    if (ptrCur < (rgValues + (ARRAY_SIZE − 1)))
    {
        /* We do not print the comma after the last element. */
        printf(", ");
    }
}

printf("\n\n");

return 0;
}
```

2. In our next program we will do selection sort on an array of numbers. The selection sort algorithm sorts an array by repeatedly finding the minimum element *(considering ascending order)* from unsorted part and putting it at the beginning. The algorithm maintains two imaginary sub-arrays within a given array – The sub-array which is already sorted at the left of the array, and remaining sub-array in the right which is unsorted.

In every iteration of selection sort, the minimum element *(considering ascending order)* from the unsorted sub-array is picked and swapped with the initial element in the unsorted sub-array. Initially, the sorted sub-array is empty and the unsorted sub-array is the entire input list. The algorithm proceeds by finding the smallest *(or largest, in case descending sort order)* element in the unsorted sub-array, swapping it with the leftmost unsorted element say 'A'. We then continue the process from the element after this element 'A' i.e. from 'A + 1'. Assume we have the array as 5, 7, 8, 2. In our first iteration, the entire array is unsorted. The minimum value '2' within the array is found and swapped with '5' resulting in the array becoming 2, 7, 8, 5. Now in our next iteration, we start from '7' and try to find the next minimum value. We find '5' which is swapped with the value '7' resulting in the array becoming 2, 5, 8, 7. Now, start from '8' and try to find the next minimum, which is '7'. We swap '7' and '8' resulting in the array becoming 2, 5, 7, 8, the sorted array.

```c
/* Header Files */
#include <stdio.h>

/* Defined Values */
```

```c
#define MAX_NUMBERS    10

int main(void)
{
    /* Variable Declaration & Initialization */
    int  rgiNumbers[MAX_NUMBERS] = { 0 };
    int *ptr1                    = NULL;
    int *ptr2                    = NULL;
    int *pMinimum                = NULL;
    int  iSwap                   = 0;

    /* Accept the numbers from the user. */
    for (ptr1 = rgiNumbers; (ptr1 - rgiNumbers) < MAX_NUMBERS; ptr1++)
    {
        printf("Enter the number: ");
        scanf("%d", ptr1);
    }

    /* Now, sort the numbers. We go till second last element. We do not iterate till the last
       element because when we are iterating the second last element, all elements till that
       element are already sorted and have values less than or equal to the second last and the
       last elements. Only the second last and last elements need sorting between themselves
       which is done during the second last iteration itself i.e. if the last element is found
       to have a value less than the second last element, their values are swapped. */
    for (ptr1 = rgiNumbers; (ptr1 - rgiNumbers) < (MAX_NUMBERS - 1); ptr1++)
    {
        /* We start assuming that we have no elements with value less than this element. If
           we find any, we will mark that as minimum. */
        pMinimum = ptr1;

        /* All elements before 'ptr1' are already sorted and have values less than
           or equal to the elements which are yet to be sorted. Now, try to find the
           next minimum value within the remaining unsorted elements.*/
        for (ptr2 = ptr1 + 1; (ptr2 - rgiNumbers) < MAX_NUMBERS; ptr2++)
        {
            if (*ptr2 < *pMinimum)
            {
                /* We found a new minimum value. */
                pMinimum = ptr2;
            }
        }

        /* Swap the 'ptr1' element's content with the element with the least value
           within the unsorted elements. If 'pMinimum' is the same as 'ptr1' i.e.
           'ptr1' is the minimum, we do not need to swap. */
        if (ptr1 != pMinimum)
        {
            iSwap = *pMinimum;
            *pMinimum = *ptr1;
            *ptr1 = iSwap;
        }
    }

    /* Print the sorted sequence. We do not print the comma after the last number.*/
    printf("\n\nSorted list: ");
    for (ptr1 = rgiNumbers; (ptr1 - rgiNumbers) < MAX_NUMBERS; ptr1++)
    {
        printf("%d%s", *ptr1, ((MAX_NUMBERS - 1) == (ptr1 - rgiNumbers)) ? "\n" : ", ");
    }

    return 0;
}
```

3. In our next example, we will accept an array of numbers from the user. We will then calculate the sum and mean of all the numbers. To understand pointers better, we will accept and enumerate the array elements using a pointer.

```c
/* Header Files */
#include <stdio.h>

/* Defined Values */
#define MAX_NUMBERS    10

int main(void)
{
    /* Variable Declaration & Initialization */
    int    rgiNumbers[MAX_NUMBERS] = { 0 };
    int    *ptr1                   = NULL;
    long   lSum                    = 0;
    double dblMean                 = 0;

    /* Accept the numbers from the user. */
    for (ptr1 = rgiNumbers; (ptr1 - rgiNumbers) < MAX_NUMBERS; ptr1++)
    {
        printf("Enter the number: ");
        scanf("%d", ptr1);

        lSum = lSum + *ptr1;
    }

    dblMean = (double)lSum / (double)MAX_NUMBERS;
    printf("\nThe mean of the numbers is %.02lf.\n\n", dblMean);

    return 0;
}
```

4. Let us write a program which declares and initializes an array. It accepts a number from the user and a location within the array. It inserts the number in the location specified by the user. We need to move all elements on the right of the specified location by one place to make space for the new number. The number at the last element within the array is simply dropped off.

```c
/* Header Files */
#include <stdio.h>

/* Defined Values */
#define MAX_NUMBERS    10

int main(void)
{
    /* Variable Declaration & Initialization */
    int    rgiNumbers[MAX_NUMBERS] = { 1, 2, 3, 4, 5, 6, 7, 8, 9, 10 };
    int    *ptrLoc                 = NULL;
    int    *ptrMove                = NULL;
    int    iNewNumber              = 0;
    int    iLocation               = -1;

    /* Accept the number to insert. */
    printf("Enter the number to insert: ");
    scanf("%d", &iNewNumber);
```

```
/* Accept the location where to insert this number within the array. */
while (iLocation < 0 || iLocation >= MAX_NUMBERS)
{
    printf("Enter its location (0-%d): ", MAX_NUMBERS - 1);
    scanf("%d", &iLocation);
}

/* Starting from the array end to the specified location, move all
   the elements one place to the right. The last array element has
   nowhere to go and so, gets overwritten by the previous element. */

/* Locate the position where we will do the insert. */
ptrLoc = rgiNumbers + iLocation;

/* Move all the elements to the right by one place. */
ptrMove = rgiNumbers + (MAX_NUMBERS - 1);
for (; ptrMove > ptrLoc; ptrMove--)
{
    *ptrMove = *(ptrMove - 1);
}

*ptrLoc = iNewNumber;

/* Now, print the array. We do not print the comma after the last number. */
printf("\n\nRevised array: ");
for (ptrMove = rgiNumbers; (ptrMove - rgiNumbers) < MAX_NUMBERS; ptrMove++)
{
    printf("%d%s", *ptrMove,
            ((MAX_NUMBERS - 1) == (ptrMove - rgiNumbers)) ? "\n\n" : ", ");
}

return 0;
}
```

CHARACTER STRING OPERATIONS

[CHAPTER-9]

9.1 INTRODUCTION

We have read about strings in our previous chapters. To reiterate, string is an array of characters defined between double quotation marks. A '\0' (NULL) character *(ASCII value 0)* marks the end of the string. A character array or constant which does not end with the NULL character is not a string but is simply an array of characters. Consider the following examples:

    1. char szString1[] = "String 1";
    2. char szString2[20] = "String 2";
    3. const char *pszString3 = "String 3";
    4. char szString4[] = { 'S', 't', 'r', 'i', 'n', 'g', ' ', '4', '\0' };
    5. char szString5[20] = { 'S', 't', 'r', 'i', 'n', 'g', ' ', '5', '\0' };
    6. char szString6[20] = { 65, 66, 67, 68, 69, 0 };
    7. char rgArray1[] = { 'N', 'o', 't', ' ', 'a', ' ', 's', 't', 'r', 'i', 'n', 'g', '1' };
    8. char rgArray2[20] = { 'N', 'o', 't', ' ', 'a', ' ', 's', 't', 'r', 'i', 'n', 'g', '2' };
    9. char rgArray3[20] = { 65, 66, 67, 68, 69 };
    10. **static** char szString7[20] = { 65, 66, 67, 68, 69 };

Let us have a look at what happens in the above examples.

The first example declares a character array of 9 elements and initializes it to the string *'String 1'*. The first element contains the character *'S'*, the second element contains the character *'t'*, the third contains the character *'r'* and so on. The last element contains the character '\0' *(NULL)*. We have enclosed the term *"String 1"* within double quotes indicating to the compiler that it needs to be treated as a string, and so should end with the '\0' *(NULL)* character. During compilation, the compiler automatically calculates the number of elements needed to store the data *(specified on the right)* including the terminating '\0' *(NULL)* character. The compiler sets the size of the character array *'szString1'* as per this calculated size. As the string on the right *"String 1"* has 8 characters, the compiler sets the size of the character array *'szString1'* to 9, where the first 8 elements will contain the 8 specified characters and the last element will have the terminating '\0' *(NULL)* character.

The second example is very similar to the first, except for the fact that the character array *'szString2'* contains *20* elements instead of the *9* for *'szString1'*. This is because we have explicitly stated the size of the array *'szString2'* to be of *20* elements. So in this case, the compiler does not automatically assign the array size by calculating the size requirement.

The third example declares a string *"String 3"* in the memory. As a string is nothing but a character array ending with the '\0' *(NULL)* character, the program allocates a character array somewhere in memory and assigns the string *"String 3"* to it. This array ends with the '\0' *(NULL)* character. The program declares a character pointer *'pszString3'* and assigns the starting address of the array to it. We can then use this pointer to access this string within our program. As we have declared the pointer *'pszString3'* as a constant *(using the keyword **const**),* the pointer cannot be changed anywhere within the program. It can only be read or accessed, but cannot be modified. As the pointer is the only way for us to access the string, modifying this pointer will make the string constant inaccessible. So, we have declared the pointer as a **const**.

In our fourth example, we are not initializing the array using a string literal *(specified within double quotes)* as in the previous cases. We are specifying the individual characters to be stored in each of the array elements. So, the compiler does not automatically append a '\0' *(NULL)* character at the end of the array. So, we are explicitly specifying a '\0' character as the last value during the initialization. The compiler automatically calculates the required size of the array equal to the number of specified values during the initialization which is 9 *(including the ending '\0' character)*. As we have specified a '\0' at the end, the array *'szString4'* has a string *"String 4"* as its content.

The fifth example is very similar to the fourth, except for the fact that the character array *'szString5'* contains *20* elements instead of the *9* for *'szString**4**'*. This is because we have explicitly stated the size of the array *'szString5'* to be of *20* elements.

The sixth example is again very similar to the fifth. The only difference is that we have initialized the array elements by directly using ASCII values instead of characters. The array *'szString6'* will have the string *"ABCDE"* as the ASCII value *65* refers to the character *'A'*, the value *66* refers to the character *'B'* and so on. We have specified 0 at the end which is the ASCII value of the '\0' *(NULL)* character.

In our seventh example the array *'rgArray1'* does **not** have a string as its content. We have neither initialized it using a string literal *(specified within double quotes)* nor we have specified a '\0' character at the end during initialization. The array *'rgArray1'* will have 13 elements i.e. the number of values specified during the initialization. It will have no element left for the terminating '\0' character.

The next example is similar to the seventh except for the fact that the array contains 20 elements instead of 13. This is because we have explicitly specified 20 as the array size.

The ninth example too is very similar to the eighth. The only difference is that we have initialized the array elements by directly using ASCII values of the characters. This array too does not contain a string as it does not end with a '\0' character.

Our last example is an interesting one. We have used the storage qualified **static** for the array *'szString7'*. From our previous understanding in **section 2.9**, we know that uninitialized static variables are automatically initialized to the value 0. So in this case too, all our uninitialized array elements will have the value 0. We have 20 elements in our array and we are initializing the first 5 elements ASCII values 65, 66, 67, 68 and 69 corresponding to the characters 'A', 'B', 'C', 'D', 'E' respectively. As the array is declared as static, the rest 15 uninitialized elements will automatically be initialized to the value 0. So, this makes our array contain the string *"ABCDE"* as its content.

The common operations performed on character strings are:
- Reading and writing strings
- Copying one string to another
- Combining strings
- Comparing two strings for equality
- Extracting a sub-string (portion) from a larger string
- Converting a string with numeric characters to an *int*, *float* or *double* data type

9.2 UNICODE CHARACTERS

As we have read in **section 2.2**, a new character representation called Unicode is defined which is capable of representing characters from most of the World languages, unlike ASCII which is capable of representing only English characters. Till now, we have read about ASCII character representation in our earlier chapters. In this chapter we will study a bit about working with Unicode characters.

The first 128 characters of ASCII are also present in Unicode. So, the first 128 symbols are the same in ASCII and Unicode. Unicode can be implemented by different character encoding mechanisms. Character encoding means the representation of a character in digital format. The Unicode standard defines UTF-8, UCS-2, UTF-16, UTF-32 and many other character encodings.

UTF-8 encoding uses one byte for the first 128 characters, and up to 4 bytes for other characters. So, it is a variable size encoding scheme which varies depending on the character used. The first 128 characters of UTF-8 are the same as ASCII and are represented using 1 byte which makes ASCII and UTF-8 same for these 128 characters.

UCS-2, a precursor of UTF-16 simply uses two bytes *(16 bits)* for each character but can only encode 65,536 characters. UCS-2 is widely used across software and is also the one supported by many operating systems and C compilers. As it represents only 65,536 characters, not all World language characters can be accommodated in it. UTF-16 extends UCS-2, by using the same 16-bit encoding as UCS-2 for most languages, and a 4-byte encoding for others.

UTF-32 *(also referred to as UCS-4)* uses four bytes for each character. Like UCS-2, the number of bytes per character is fixed. UTF-32 is capable of representing all World characters. However, because each character uses four bytes, UTF-32 uses significantly more memory than other encoding mechanisms and so, and is not widely used.

ASCII characters are represented internally using 7 bits. ASCII was very limited in capability and could support only 128 characters. This was sufficient for the English language but, could not represent most other world languages. Another standard **ANSI** was developed which used all of the 8 bits of a byte. For compatibility purposes, the first 128 characters of ANSI was the same as ASCII. Due to the use of 1 extra bit, ANSI supported different code pages which allowed it to represent various character sets as defined by different vendors. Each vendor could define a specific code page to support a certain language and use that code page within its programs. A Code Page *(also referred to as Character Set or*

Encoding) is a table of values where each character has been assigned a numerical representation and that numerical value is used to identify that character. ANSI too faced a big limitation. Due to the use of different code pages across different vendors, there was no standard which defined all of them. So, a program written for one computer may not work properly when executed on another computer. Also, ANSI still could not support most world languages.

Unicode was defined to overcome all the limitations of ASCII and ANSI. Due to the use of multiple bytes to represent one character, it extended the reach of Unicode by many folds. Unicode is no longer limited like ASCII and ANSI and could represent almost all world languages. Unlike ANSI, Unicode is controlled by a single standard which allows the programs written for Unicode to be easily ported from one computer to another.

As Unicode uses multiple bytes to represent one character, characters encoded using any of the Unicode encodings are called **wide characters**. This is because of the availability of a wide range of values to represent the characters.

Another type of characters called **multi-byte characters** are defined by the use of one or more bytes for a single character *(typically 1 or 2 bytes)*. Single byte characters are a special cases for multi-byte character set and many multi-byte character set define ASCII as a subset of them.

As ASCII characters are represented in C using the data type *'char'*, a new type *'wchar_t'* is defined which represents a Unicode character. Unlike the data type *'char'* whose size is 1 byte across compilers, the size of *'wchar_t'* varies between compilers depending on the encoding mechanism used internally by the compilers. *'wchar_t'* has a minimum size of 1 byte and can go up to 4 bytes, with 2 bytes as the most widely used across compilers.

We have seen that ASCII character constants are represented within single quotes ('A', '1', 'z', '#', ...) and ASCII string constants are represented within double quotes ("C Language", "Tania", ...). In case of Unicode, we prefix a **L** before the character or string constant. So, the character 'A' will be written as **L**'A' and the string "C Language" will be written as **L**"C Language" in Unicode. Some example usage are:

```
wchar_t wchValue = L'w';
wchar_t wchValue = 65;       /* The ASCII value of 'A' */
wchar_t wchValue = L'5';
wchar_t wszName[] = L"Tania";
wchar_t wszName[20] = L"C Language";
wchar_t wszName[3] = { L'W', L'e', L'\0' };   /* The string "We" */
wchar_t *pwszName = L"Williamson";
```

9.3 ACCEPTING STRINGS FROM USER

We have read about input and output operations on strings in **chapters 4 and 5**. From these chapters we know the behavior of the functions *'getchar'*, *'scanf'* and *'gets'*.

'scanf' function is used to receive formatted input from the user. Character strings are accepted using

the *'%s'* format specifier. Example:

> *char szName[20] = { 0 };*
> *scanf("%s", szName);*

When we are accepting strings using the 'scanf' function, the **&** *(ampersand)* sign is not required before the variable name. We will read more about this in our chapter on pointers. 'scanf' automatically terminates the string that is read using a **'\0'** *(NULL)* character. So when declaring the size of the array, we should be careful in accounting for this NULL character at the end.

The problem with 'scanf' function is that it does not check overflow conditions i.e. if the user has entered a string larger than what our array can hold. To address this, we need to use the field width **(please read section 4.3)** when accepting the input, as given below:

> *scanf("%19s", szName);*

The above statement will only read *19 characters* into the string *'szName'*, though it will keep accepting from the user until it encounters any white space *(space, tab, carriage return, new line)*. So, even if we enter a string of 30 characters long, the function will copy only the first 19 characters into the string and terminate it with a **'\0'** *(NULL)* character, dropping rest of the 11 characters.

More secured version of 'scanf' has been created and are supported by some of the latest compilers. The function 'scanf_s' is similar to 'scanf' except that we need to specify the array/buffer length too, when we are accepting a string input. The function has the following declaration:

> *int scanf_s(const char * format, ...);*

This protects the program from overflow conditions even when no field width is specified. The buffer length is required only when a string or character value is accepted as input. For other variables, no length needs to be specified. The buffer length should include the space for the terminating NULL character. We may also specify the field width. If no field width is specified, and the string read is too big to fit in the array buffer, nothing is written to that buffer. Consider the following example:

> *char szName[20] = { 0 };*
> *scanf_s("%s", szName, 20);*

Providing a hard-coded value *(20 in our above example)* is never recommended and must be avoided. If in the future, we change the array length to something else and forget to do the same within the 'scanf_s' function, the program may generate errors or even crash. To avoid this, we may do three things:

- Define a symbolic name using the *'#define'* statement and use that name *(in place of the hard-coded value)* in both the places. Changing the value within the '#define' statement will have the effect in both the places at one go. Consider the following example:

> *#define MAX_SIZE 20*
> *char szName[MAX_SIZE] = { 0 };*
> *scanf_s("%s", szName, MAX_SIZE);*

- Rather than specifying the hard-coded value of *20* in the 'scanf_s' function, we can specify the array length by making the compiler compute it during compile time. It is done using the macro '*_countof*'.

      char szName[20] = { 0 };
      scanf_s("%s", szName, _countof(szName));

- If the compiler with which we are working does not support the '*_countof*' macro, we can define a macro which does the same as what '*_countof*' does. Refer to **section 2.10** for information on defining macros.

      #define ARRAYSIZE(x)   sizeof(x) / sizeof(x[0])
      char szName[20] = { 0 };
      scanf_s("%s", szName, ARRAYSIZE(szName));

  The macro **call** *'ARRAYSIZE(szName)'* is replaced by the expression corresponding to the macro and it becomes *'sizeof(szName) / sizeof(szName[0])'*. The macro calculates the number of elements in the array *'szName'*. It divides the size *(memory usage)* of the entire array *'sizeof(szName)'* by the size *(memory usage)* of one single element of the array *'sizeof(szName[0])'*. So, in effect we get the total number of elements within the array.

Another problem with 'scanf' function when working with character strings is that it terminates its input on the first white space *(space, tab, carriage returns, new line)* it encounters. So, when we type "David Miller" as its input, 'scanf' will only accept "David" as the input, because of the presence of a *space* between the words *"David"* and *"Miller"*. To accept both the words, we may use two character arrays within the 'scanf' function.

      char szFirstname[11] = { 0 };
      char szLastname[11] = { 0 };
      scanf("%s %s", szFirstName, szLastName);

The above example will work only when we are sure that there will be two separate words to be entered. For all other scenarios, the above example will fail. So, wherever a string *(to be accepted)* may contain white spaces in between, we should avoid using the 'scanf' function and rely on another input function **'fgets'** with *'stdin'* as the input stream.

All the above input methods display the text entered by the user. This is not suitable for situations where we are looking to accept secret information like password. We can use the **'getch'** function for accepting such information. We will accept one character at a time within a loop. A sample program is given below.

Program for accepting a password from the user:

```
/* Header Files */
#include <stdio.h>
#include <conio.h>

/* Defined Values */
```

```
#define MAX_PASS     20

int main(void)
{
    /* Variable declaration and initialization. */
    char szPassword[MAX_PASS + 1] = { 0 }; /* One extra for NULL. */
    int  idx                      = 0;

    /* Accept the password in a loop. */
    printf("Enter the password: ");
    while (idx < MAX_PASS)
    {
        szPassword[idx] = getch();
        if (szPassword[idx] == '\n' || szPassword[idx] == '\r')
        {
            break;
        }

        idx++;
    }

    /* The terminating '\0' character to make it a string. */
    szPassword[idx] = '\0';

    return 0;
}
```

The program accepts the entire password within a loop. It keeps accepting till the number of characters entered is less than the array length. If the *<Return> (Enter)* key is hit, it breaks out from the *'while'* loop.

9.4 PRINTING STRINGS TO CONSOLE

We have read about formatted output using the *'printf'* function in the **section 4.4.2**. Here we will go through some more examples of formatted output of strings. We know character strings are printed using the *'%s'* format specifier. We should remember that the strings must be *'\0' (NULL)* terminated.

We may use flags, field width and precision along with the conversion character as specified in **section 4.3**. In the following example, the field width is 6 and the precision is 4.

printf("%6.4s", "Jupiter");

Some of the rules which apply when printing a string using the format specifiers are:
- The number of characters printed is equal to the precision specified or the length of the string whichever is lower.
- We can left-align the printed text by specifying a '-' *(minus)* sign to the immediate right of the '%' sign.
- If the printed text is right-aligned *(the default)*, *spaces* equal to the difference between the field width and the precision is printed on the left side of the printed text. So, in the above example 2 spaces will be printed to the left of the word *"Jupi"*.
- If the printed text is left-aligned, *spaces* equal to the difference between the field width and the precision is printed on the right side of the printed text. So, in the above example 2 spaces will be printed to the right of the word *"Jupi"*, if it was made left-aligned.
- If no precision is specified and the specified field width is less than the length of the string then

the entire string is printed.
- If the precision is specified as 0 *(zero)*, nothing is printed.

Let us write a program which prints the words "C Language" using various format specifiers.

```c
/* Header Files */
#include <stdio.h>

int main(void)
{
    /* Variable declaration and initialization. */
    char szName[] = "C Language";

    printf("************\n");
    printf("%s\n", szName);
    printf("%12s\n", szName);
    printf("%-12s\n", szName);
    printf("%12.6s\n", szName);
    printf("%-12.6s\n", szName);
    printf("%.0s\n", szName);
    printf("%.6s\n", szName);
    printf("%12.0s\n", szName);
    printf("************\n\n");

    return 0;
}
```

Output:

```
************
C Language
  C Language
C Language
        C Lang
C Lang

C Lang

************
```

9.5 ARITHMETIC OPERATIONS WITH CHARACTERS

We can perform arithmetic operations with characters in the same way we do with integers. Whenever a character appears in an arithmetic expression, it is converted to an integer value depending on the character representation we are using. If we are using ASCII, the character is converted to its equivalent ASCII value before performing the arithmetic operation. If we are using Unicode, the character is converted to its equivalent Unicode value. Consider the following expressions:

Expression	Explanation
int iValue = 'A';	The ASCII value of *'A'* i.e. *65* is assigned to the variable *'iValue'*.
int iValue = 'Z' - 'A' + 1;	The ASCII value of *'A'* is subtracted from the ASCII value of *'Z'* resulting in the value 25 *(90 – 65)*. 1 is then added with 25 to get

Expression	Explanation
	26, which is assigned to *'iValue'*.

char ch = 'B';
if (ch >= 'A' and ch <= 'Z')
  printf("It is UPPERCASE.");
else
  printf("It is lowercase.");
	Prints the string *"It is UPPERCASE."*.

9.6 ARITHMETIC OPERATIONS WITH STRINGS

Unlike single characters which can take part in arithmetic operations, strings being arrays cannot take part in arithmetic operations. Neither two strings can be concatenated together by simply adding them together nor they can be compared for equality. Consider some of the following invalid usages:

```
char szString1[] = "I Love ";
char szString2[] = "C Language";
char szString3[50] = szString1 + szString2;     /* INVALID */
```
```
char szString1[] = "A String";
char szString2[] = "A String";
if (szString1 == szString2)     /* INVALID */
   printf("The strings are equal");
```
```
char szString1[] = "A String";
char szString2[] = "A String";
if (szString1 > szString2)     /* INVALID */
   printf("szString1 is greater than szString2");
```

In the above examples, the statements in **bold** are invalid. We **cannot** concatenate two strings together by simply adding them. We need to use specific functions for the purpose which we will discuss later in this chapter. In the second example, we are comparing two strings for equality using the relational operator '**==**'. We cannot compare two strings using any of the relational operators like '==', '!=', '>', '<'. We have specific functions for the purpose which we are going to read a little later in this chapter.

9.7 STRING PROCESSING FUNCTIONS

Most standard string processing functions are declared in the header file **'string.h'** for the ANSI version and **'wchar.h'** for the wide character version. So when using any of the following functions, we must include the respective header file within our program.

9.7.1 GENERAL STRING PROCESSING FUNCTIONS

- **ANSI** → size_t **strlen**(const char *str);
  Wide Character → size_t **wcslen**(const wchar_t *wstr);

- ○ Returns the length of the string *'str'* provided as an argument to the function. It accepts the pointer to the string and returns the number of characters in the string excluding the terminating '\0' *(NULL)* character. The return type is *'size_t'* which is a type-defined type and is compiler dependent. It must always be of unsigned integer type. Usually it is 'unsigned int' in 32-bit programs and 'unsigned _int64' in 64-bit programs. The length of the string is calculated as the number of characters from the start of the string to the terminating '\0' *(NULL)* character *(excluding the terminating '\0' (NULL) character itself in the count)*. Usage example:

char szLanguage[] = "C Language"; size_t cchLen = **strlen**(szLanguage);   /* Returns 10 */
wchar_t szLanguage[] = L"C Language"; size_t cchLen = **wcslen**(szLanguage);   /* Returns 10 */

- **ANSI** → char * **strcpy**(char *destination, const char *source);
  Wide Character → wchar_t * **wcscpy**(wchar_t *destination, const wchar_t *source);
  - ○ Copies the string pointed by *'source'* into the array pointed by *'destination'*, including the terminating '\0' *(NULL)* character. To avoid overflows, we must ensure that the *'destination'* array is able to contain all the characters in the *'source'* string, including the terminating '\0' *(NULL)* character. If it is not large enough, **strcpy/wcscpy** will write past the *'destination'* array and will cause a program crash. The function returns the starting address of the *'destination'* array. Usage example:

char szString1[] = "C Language"; char szString2[11]; **strcpy**(szString2, szString1);
wchar_t szString1[] = L"C Language"; wchar_t szString2[11]; **wcscpy**(szString2, szString1);

- **ANSI** → char * **strcat**(char *destination, const char *source);
  Wide Character → wchar_t * **wcscat**(wchar_t *destination, const wchar_t *source);
  - ○ Appends a copy of the *'source'* string to the *'destination'* string. The terminating '\0' *(NULL)* character in *'destination'* is overwritten by the first character of *'source'*, and a '\0' *(NULL)* character is included at the end of the new string formed by the concatenation of both the strings in *'destination'*. To avoid overflows, we must ensure that the *'destination'* array is able to contain all the characters after the concatenation, including the terminating '\0' *(NULL)* character. If it is not large enough, **strcat/wcscat** will write past the *'destination'* array and will cause a program crash. The function returns the starting address of the *'destination'* array. Usage example:

char szString1[] = "C Language"; char szString2[20] = "I Love "; **strcat**(szString2, szString1);
wchar_t szString1[] = L"C Language";

```
wchar_t szString2[20] = L"I Love ";
wcscat(szString2, szString1);
```

- **ANSI** → int **strcmp**(const char *str1, const char *str2);
  Wide Character → int **wcscmp**(const wchar_t *str1, const wchar_t *str2);
  - ○ Compares the string 'str1' to the string 'str2'. The function starts comparing the two strings from the first character of each string. It continues comparing a character in *'str1'* with the same indexed character in *'str2'*, until they differ or a terminating '\0' *(NULL)* character is reached in any of the two strings. It basically does a binary value comparison between the characters of the two strings and returns a value depending on the difference of the binary values for the first occurrence of non-identical characters in *'str1'* and *'str2'*. It returns a value indicating the difference between the strings:

Less than 0	The first character that does not match has a lower value in 'str1' than in 'str2'.
0 *(Zero)*	Contents of both the strings are equal.
Greater than 0	The first character that does not match has a greater value in 'str1' than in 'str2'.

Usage example:

```
char szString1[15] = "I am a string";
char szString2[18] = "I Am A String";
int iCompare = strcmp(szString1, szString2);
printf("The result of the comparison is %d", iCompare);
```
```
wchar_t szString1[15] = L"I am a string";
wchar_t szString2[18] = L"I Am A String";
int iCompare = wcscmp(szString1, szString2);
wprintf(L"The result of the comparison is %d", iCompare);
```

- **ANSI** → int **stricmp**(const char *str1, const char *str2);
  Wide Character → int **wcsicmp**(const wchar_t *str1, const wchar_t *str2);
  - ○ This function is not standard C function. It is provided by many modern C compilers and may be quite useful. This function is very similar to 'strcmp/wcscmp' except for the fact that it performs a case-insensitive comparison between the two input strings. So, the uppercase character 'A' is treated as same as the lowercase character 'a'. This function will return 0 *(indicating equality)*, if it is provided with the two strings *"I AM A STRING"* and *"I am a string"* as its arguments.

- **ANSI** → const char * **strchr**(const char *str, int iChar);
  Wide Character → const wchar_t * **wcschr**(const wchar_t *str, int iChar);
  - ○ The function searches the string *'str'* for the first occurrence of the character whose binary value is equal to *'iChar'*. It returns a pointer to the location in *'str'*, where it found the character *'iChar'*. If the character is not found, the function returns NULL. Usage example:

```
/* Find all occurrences of the character 'a' within the string. */
char szString[] = "Abra Cadabra";
char *pchr = NULL;

pchr = strchr(szString, 'a');
while (pchr != NULL)
{
    printf ("Found at location %d\n", pchr - szString);
    pchr = strchr(pchr + 1, 'a');   /* Find the next occurrence within the string */
}
```

```
/* Find all occurrences of the wide character 'a' within the string. */
wchar_t szString[] = L"Abra Cadabra";
wchar_t *pchr = NULL;

pchr = wcschr(szString, L'a');
while (pchr != NULL)
{
    wprintf (L"Found at location %d\n", pchr - szString);
    pchr = wcschr(pchr + 1, L'a');   /* Find the next occurrence within the string */
}
```

- **ANSI → const char * strrchr(const char *str, int iChar);**
  Wide Character → const wchar_t * wcsrchr(const wchar_t *str, int iChar);
  - This function is very similar to 'strchr/wcschr'. The only difference is that it performs a reverse search of the character *'iChar'* in the string *'str'* and hence the extra 'r' within the function name. It starts searching for the character from the end of the string pointed by *'str'*. So, in effect it finds the last occurrence of the character *'iChar'* within the string *'str'* and returns a pointer to its location in *'str'*. The function returns NULL, if the character is not found within the string.

- **ANSI → const char * strstr(const char *str1, const char *str2);**
  Wide Character → const wchar_t * wcsstr(const wchar_t *str1, const wchar_t *str2);
  - The function searches the string 'str1' for any occurence of a string similar to *'str2'* and returns a pointer to the first occurrence of *'str2'* in *'str1'*. If *'str1'* is the string *"I am a long long string"* and *'str2'* is the string *"long"*, the function will return a pointer to the first *"long"* within *'str1'*. So, it will return the address of the location *'str1[7]'*. If *'str2'* is not found in *'str1'*, the function returns NULL. Usage example:

    ```
    char str1[] = "I am a long long string";
    char *pstr = strstr(str1, "long");
    ```

    ```
    wchar_t str1[] = L"I am a long long string";
    wchar_t *pstr = wcsstr(str1, L"long");
    ```

- **ANSI** → char * **strtok**(char *str, const char *szDelims);
  Wide Character → wchar_t * **wcstok**(wchar_t *str, const wchar_t *szDelims);
  - ○ A sequence of calls to this function returns pointers to tokens within *'str'*, which are sequences of contiguous characters separated by any of the characters specified within *'szDelims'*. A token is a sequence of contiguous characters appearing between two delimiters. During the first call to this function, we need to provide a string as an argument for *'str'*, whose first character is used as the starting location to scan for tokens. In subsequent calls, we specify NULL as the argument for *'str'*. The function uses the position right after the end of the last found token as the new starting location for the search for the next token. If *'str'* is the string *"C: A programming language"*, and *'szDelims'* is specified as " :", the function will return tokens as *"C"*, *"A"*, *"programming"* and *"language"*. Usage example:

```
char str[] = "C: A programming language";
char *pstr = NULL;

pstr = strtok(str, " :");
while(pstr != NULL)
{
    printf("%s\n", pstr);
    pstr = strtok(NULL, " :");
}
```
```
wchar_t str[] = L"C: A programming language";
wchar_t *pstr = NULL;

pstr = wcstok(str, L" :");
while(pstr != NULL)
{
    wprintf(L"%s\n", pstr);
    pstr = wcstok(NULL, L" :");
}
```

- **ANSI** → const char * **strpbrk**(const char *str1, const char *str2);
  Wide Character → const wchar_t * **wcspbrk**(const wchar_t *str1, const wchar_t *str2);
  - ○ The function searches *'str1'* and returns a pointer to the first occurrence in *'str1'* of any of the characters that are part of *'str2'*. If no matches are found, the function returns NULL. Usage example:

```
char str[] = "I Love C programming language";
char *pChr = NULL;

pChr = strpbrk(str, "aeiouAEIOU");
while (pChr != NULL)
{
    printf("%c ", *pChr);
```

```
    pChr = strpbrk(pChr + 1, "aeiouAEIOU");
}
```

```
wchar_t str[] = L"I Love C programming language";
wchar_t *pChr = NULL;

pChr = wcspbrk(str, L"aeiouAEIOU");
while (pChr != NULL)
{
    wprintf(L"%c ", *pChr);
    pChr = wcspbrk(pChr + 1, L"aeiouAEIOU");
}
```

- **ANSI** → size_t **strcspn**(const char *str1, const char *str2);
  Wide Character → size_t **wcscspn**(const wchar_t *str1, const wchar_t *str2);
  - The function returns the index within *'str1'* of the first occurrence of any of the characters that are part of *'str2'*. The function will return the length of *'str1'* if none of the characters of *'str2'* are found in *'str1'*. Usage example:

  ```
  char str[] = "It takes 2 to tango";
  size_t idx = strcspn(str, "0123456789");
  ```

  ```
  wchar_t str[] = L"It takes 2 to tango";
  size_t idx = wcscspn(str, L"0123456789");
  ```

- **ANSI** → size_t **strspn**(const char *str1, const char *str2);
  Wide Character → size_t **wcsspn**(const wchar_t *str1, const wchar_t *str2);
  - The function returns the index of the first character in the string 'str1', that does not belong to any of the characters in 'str2'. Usage example:

  ```
  char str[] = "2 C or not to see";
  size_t idx = strspn(str, "0123456789");
  ```

  ```
  wchar_t str[] = L"2 C or not to see";
  size_t idx = wcsspn(str, L"0123456789");
  ```

- **ANSI** → char * **strerror**(int errnum);
  Wide Character → wchar_t * **_wcserror**(int errnum);
  - Interprets the value of a C function error code given in *'errnum'* and returns a string with a message that describes the error condition.

- **ANSI** → char * **strncpy**(char *dest, const char *src, size_t cchCopy);
  Wide Character → wchar_t * **wcsncpy**(wchar_t *dest, const wchar_t *src, size_t cchCopy);
  - This function is very similar to 'strcpy/wcscpy' except for the fact that it copies a maximum of *'cchCopy'* characters from *'src'* to *'dest'*. It stops the copy process when it reaches the '\0' character in *'src'* or it has already copied *'cchCopy'* number of characters, whichever condition comes first.

- **ANSI** → char * **strncat**(char *dest, const char *src, size_t cchAppend);
  Wide Character → wchar_t * **wcsncat**(wchar_t *dest, const wchar_t *src, size_t cchAppend);
  - ○ This function is very similar to 'strcat/wcscat' except for the fact that it appends a maximum of *'cchAppend'* characters from *'src'* to *'dest'*. It stops the process when it reaches the '\0' character in *'src'* or it has already appended *'cchAppend'* number of characters, whichever condition comes first.

- **ANSI** → int **strncmp**(const char *str1, const char *str2, size_t cchCompare);
  Wide Character → int **wcsncmp**(const wchar_t *str1, const wchar_t *str2, size_t cchCompare);
  - ○ This function is very similar to 'strcmp/wcscmp' except for the fact that it compares a maximum of *'cchCompare'* characters. It stops comparing if it finds a '\0' character in either *'str1'* or *'str2'*, or it has already compared *'cchCompare'* number of characters.

- **ANSI** → int **strnicmp**(const char *str1, const char *str2, size_t cchCompare);
  Wide Character → int **wcsnicmp**(const wchar_t *str1, const wchar_t *str2, size_t cchCompare);
  - ○ Just like 'stricmp/wcsicmp', this function is not standard C function. This function is provided by many modern C compilers and may be quite useful. This function is very similar to 'stricmp/wcsicmp' except for the fact that it compares a maximum of *'cchCompare'* characters. It stops comparing if it finds a '\0' character in either *'str1'* or *'str2'*, or it has already compared *'cchCompare'* number of characters.

9.7.2 MEMORY COPY AND COMPARISON FUNCTIONS

Apart from the string processing functions, **'string.h'** has declarations for some binary data processing functions too. They are:
- void * **memcpy**(void *dest, const void *src, size_t cBytes);
  - ○ Copies a total of *'cBytes'* bytes from the location pointed to by *'src'* directly to the memory block pointed to by *'dest'*. The data type of *'dest'* and *'src'* may differ and is irrelevant for the function. The result is a binary copy of the data from *'src'* to *'dest'*. The *'src'* and *'dest'* buffers must not overlap. The function does not check for any terminating '\0' *(NULL)* character in *'src'*. As the function does not check the availability of *'cBytes'* data in *'src'* or an adequate available buffer size in *'dest'*, we must ensure that *'src'* has atleast *'cBytes'* bytes of data to be read and *'dest'* has atleast *'cBytes'* bytes of available buffer. If not so, this function will read past the actual data in *'src'* or write past the available buffer in *'dest'*, causing a program crash due to overflow. Usage example:
    char szElemSym[15] = { 'H', '\0', '\0', 'H', 'e', '\0', 'L', 'i', '\0', 'B', 'e', '\0', 'B', '\0', '\0' };
    char rgElementSymbols[5][3];

    memcpy(rgElementSymbols, szElemSym, 15);

- void * **memmove**(void *dest, const void *src, size_t cBytes);
  - ○ **'memmove'** is very similar to 'memcpy' except for the fact that in case of **'memmove'** the 'src' and 'dest' buffers can overlap. This added flexibility makes **'memmove'** work a little

slower than 'memcpy'.

- int **memcmp**(const void *ptr1, const void *ptr2, size_t cBytes);
  - ○ The function compares the first *'cBytes'* bytes of the block of memory pointed by *'ptr1'* to the first *'cBytes'* bytes pointed by *'ptr2'*. It performs binary comparison of the data. The function returns 0 *(Zero)* if they all match, greater than 0 *(Zero)* if the first non-identical bytes have a greater value in *'ptr1'*, and less than 0 *(Zero)* if the first non-identical bytes have a greater value in *'ptr2'*. Unlike 'strcmp', this function does not stop comparing after finding a '\0' character. Usage example:
    char szElemSym[15] = { 'H', '\0', '\0', 'H', 'e', '\0', 'L', 'i', '\0', 'B', 'e', '\0', 'B', '\0', '\0' };
    char rgElementSymbols[5][3];
    int iCompare = 0;

    memcpy(rgElementSymbols, szElemSym, 15);
    szElemSym[4] = 'E';
    iCompare = **memcmp**(szElemSym, rgElementSymbols, 15);

- const void * **memchr**(const void *ptr, int iValue, size_t cBytes);
  - ○ The function searches within the first *'cBytes'* bytes of the block of memory pointed by *'ptr'* for the first occurrence of *'iValue'*, and returns a pointer to the location in *'ptr'* where it found the value. If the function does not find the value, it returns NULL. Usage example:
    char *pch = NULL;
    char szString[] = "I Love to see C";
    pch = (char *) **memchr**(szString, 's', strlen(szString));
    if (pch)
        printf ("Found at index %d.\n", pch – szString);
    else
        printf ("Not found.\n");

- void * **memset**(void *ptr, int iValue, size_t cBytes);
  - ○ The function sets the first *'cBytes'* bytes of the block of memory pointed by *'ptr'* to the value *'iValue'*. Usage example:
    char szString[] = "I Love to see C";
    memset(szString, '*', 9);

9.7.3 SINGLE CHARACTER PROCESSING FUNCTIONS

Apart from the above functions declared in **'string.h'**, there are some single-character handling functions which may be very handy when writing programs. These functions are declared in the header file **'ctype.h'** for the ANSI version and **'wctype.h'** for the wide character version. All of these functions accept an integer argument which is the binary equivalent of the character to process. The wide character version of the functions use a user-defined type called **'wint_t'**. This type varies between compilers and is generally of the type 'int'. They also return an integer as their result.

Function	Description
int **tolower**(int ch); wint_t **towlower**(wint_t ch);	Returns the lowercase equivalent of the given character *'ch'*. If no such conversion is possible, the function returns *'ch'* itself. The function returns the value as 'int/wint_t' which can be casted to 'char/wchar_t'.
int **toupper**(int ch); wint_t **towupper**(wint_t ch);	Returns the UPPERCASE equivalent of the given character *'ch'*. If no such conversion is possible, the function returns the *'ch'* itself. The function returns the value as 'int/wint_t' which can be casted to 'char/wchar_t'.
int **isalpha**(int ch); int **iswalpha**(wint_t ch);	Checks whether *'ch'* is an alphabet. It returns a non-zero value if *'ch'* is an alphabetic character, else returns 0 *(Zero)*.
int **isdigit**(int ch); int **iswdigit**(wint_t ch);	Checks whether *'ch'* is a decimal digit character. It returns a non-zero value if *'ch'* is indeed a decimal digit character, else returns 0 *(Zero)*.
int **isalnum**(int ch); int **iswalnum**(wint_t ch);	Checks whether *'ch'* is either a decimal digit or an alphabet. It returns a non-zero value if *'ch'* is an alphanumeric character, else returns 0 *(Zero)*.
int **isupper**(int ch); int **iswupper**(wint_t ch);	Checks whether *'ch'* is an UPPERCASE alphabet. It returns a non-zero value if *'ch'* is an uppercase alphabetic character, else returns 0 *(Zero)*.
int **islower**(int ch); int **iswlower**(wint_t ch);	Checks whether *'ch'* is a lowercase alphabet. It returns a non-zero value if *'ch'* is a lowercase alphabetic character, else returns 0 *(Zero)*.
int **isspace**(int ch); int **iswspace**(wint_t ch);	Checks whether *'ch'* is a white space character. White space characters are: ' ' *(Space, ASCII value: 32)*, '**\t**' *(Horizontal tab, ASCII value: 9)*, '**\n**' *(Newline, ASCII value: 10)*, '**\v**' *(Vertical tab, ASCII value: 11)*, '**\f**' *(Form feed, ASCII value: 12)*, '**\r**' *(Carriage return, ASCII value: 13)*. It returns a non-zero value if *'ch'* is a white space character, else returns 0 *(Zero)*.
int **isprint**(int ch); int **iswprint**(wint_t ch);	Checks whether *'ch'* is a printable character. Printable characters are the ones which have ASCII values between 32 to 126 (included). It returns a non-zero value if *'ch'* is a printable character, else returns 0 *(Zero)*.
int **iscntrl**(int ch); int **iswcntrl**(wint_t ch);	Checks whether *'ch'* is a control character. This function returns the opposite of the function **'isprint'**. A control character is a character that is not printed on a display. It returns a non-zero value if *'ch'* is a control character, else returns 0 *(Zero)*.
int **ispunct**(int ch); int **iswpunct**(wint_t ch);	Checks whether *'ch'* is a punctuation character. Punctuation characters are all printable characters which are neither alphanumeric nor space. It returns a non-zero value if *'ch'* is a punctuation character, else returns 0 *(Zero)*.
int **isxdigit**(int ch); int **iswxdigit**(wint_t ch);	Checks whether *'ch'* is a hexadecimal character. Hexadecimal characters are: [0-9], [a-f] and [A-F]. It returns a non-zero value if *'ch'* is a hexadecimal character, else returns 0 *(Zero)*.
int **isgraph**(int ch); int **iswgraph**(wint_t ch);	Checks whether *'ch'* has a graphical representation. A character can be graphically represented if it is a printable character except the character ' ' *(Space)*. It returns a non-zero value if *'ch'* is a graphical character, else returns 0 *(Zero)*.

9.7.4 STRING CONVERSION FUNCTIONS

What happens if we have a number stored in a string and we need to convert that to a numeral. For operations like these we have the string conversion functions, which help in converting data to and from string. These functions are defined in the header file **'stdlib.h'** and have wide character equivalents.

- **ANSI** → double **atof**(const char *str);
  Wide Character → double **_wtof**(const wchar_t *str);
  - Converts the string *'str'* to a double and returns the value. The function discards as many whitespace characters in front of the string. It then starts converting from the first non whitespace character and continues until it finds a character which does not fit into a floating point number. Usage example:

char szValue[] = "3.141592";
double dblValue = **atof**(szValue);
wchar_t szValue[] = L"3.141592";
double dblValue = **_wtof**(szValue);

- **ANSI** → int **atoi**(const char *str);
  Wide Character → int **_wtoi**(const wchar_t *str);
  - Converts the string *'str'* to an integer and returns the value. The function discards as many whitespace characters in front of the string. It then starts converting from the first non whitespace character *(supports an optional plus or minus sign at the start)* and continues until it finds a character which is not a digit [0-9]. Usage example:

char szValue[] = "12345";
int iValue = **atoi**(szValue);
wchar_t szValue[] = L"12345";
int iValue = **_wtoi**(szValue);

- **ANSI** → long int **atol**(const char *str);
  Wide Character → long int **_wtol**(const wchar_t *str);
  - Converts the string *'str'* to a long integer and returns the value. Usage example:

char szValue[] = "12345";
long lValue = **atol**(szValue);
wchar_t szValue[] = L"12345";
long lValue = **_wtol**(szValue);

- **ANSI** → double **strtod**(const char *str, char **endptr);
  Wide Character → double **wcstod**(const wchar_t *str, wchar_t **endptr);
  - Converts the string *'str'* to a double and returns the value. If *'endptr'* is not NULL, the function sets the value of *'endptr'* to point to the first character after the number. Usage example:

```
char szValues[] = "67.34    84.583";
char *pEnd = NULL;
double dblValue1 = strtod(szValues, &pEnd);
double dblValue2 = strtod(pEnd, NULL);
```

```
wchar_t szValues[] = L"67.34    84.583";
wchar_t *pEnd = NULL;
double dblValue1 = wcstod(szValues, &pEnd);
double dblValue2 = wcstod(pEnd, NULL);
```

- **ANSI →** long int **strtol**(const char *str, char **endptr, int base);
  Wide Character → long int **wcstol**(const wchar_t *str, wchar_t **endptr, int base);
  - ○ Converts the string 'str' to a long int and returns the value. If 'endptr' is not NULL, the function sets the value of 'endptr' to point to the first character after the number. If 'base' is between 2 and 36, it is used as the base of the number. If 'base' is 0 *(Zero)*, the initial characters of the string pointed to by 'str' are used to determine the base. If the first character is '0' *(Zero)* and the second character is not 'x' or 'X', the string is interpreted as an octal integer. If the first character is '0' *(Zero)* and the second character is 'x' or 'X', the string is interpreted as a hexadecimal integer. If the first character is '1' to '9', the string is interpreted as a decimal integer. Usage example:

```
char szNumbers[] = "2007 51a1b1 100010010110 0x5A41C8";
char *pEnd = NULL;
long lValue1 = strtol(szNumbers, &pEnd, 10);
long lValue2 = strtol(pEnd, &pEnd, 16);
long lValue3 = strtol(pEnd, &pEnd, 2);
long lValue4 = strtol(pEnd, NULL, 0);
```

```
wchar_t szNumbers[] = L"2007 51a1b1 100010010110 0x5A41C8";
wchar_t *pEnd = NULL;
long lValue1 = wcstol(szNumbers, &pEnd, 10);
long lValue2 = wcstol(pEnd, &pEnd, 16);
long lValue3 = wcstol(pEnd, &pEnd, 2);
long lValue4 = wcstol(pEnd, NULL, 0);
```

- **ANSI →** unsigned long int **strtoul**(const char *str, char **endptr, int base);
  Wide Character → unsigned long int **wcstoul**(const wchar_t *str, wchar_t **endptr, int base);
  - ○ This function is similar to 'strtol/wcstol' except for the fact that it interprets an unsigned long integer and returns the value.

Apart from the above functions, there are few functions which are available from C99 or later. These functions were created to support higher precision and value. They are:
- **ANSI →** _int64 **_atoi64**(const char *str);
  Wide Character → _int64 **_wtoi64**(const wchar_t *str);
  - ○ Converts the string *'str'* to a 64-bit integer and returns the value. Usage example:

```
char szValue[] = "123456789";
_int64 iValue = _atoi64(szValue);
```

```
wchar_t szValue[] = L"123456789";
_int64 iValue = _wtoi64(szValue);
```

- **ANSI** → long long int **atoll**(const char *str);
  Wide Character → long long int **_wtoll**(const wchar_t *str);
  - Converts the string *'str'* to a long long integer and returns the value. Usage example:

  ```
  char szValue[] = "1234567890123";
  long long llValue = atoll(szValue);
  ```

  ```
  wchar_t szValue[] = L"1234567890123";
  long long llValue = _wtoll(szValue);
  ```

- **ANSI** → float **strtof**(const char *str, char **endptr);
  Wide Character → float **wcstof**(const wchar_t *str, wchar_t **endptr);
  - This function is similar to 'strtod/wcstod' except for the fact that it converts the string to a single precision floating point value and returns that value.

- **ANSI** → long double **strtold**(const char *str, char **endptr);
  Wide Character → long double **wcstold**(const wchar_t *str, wchar_t **endptr);
  - This function is similar to 'strtod/wcstod' except for the fact that it converts the string to a long double value and returns that value.

- **ANSI** → long long **strtoll**(const char *str, char **endptr, int base);
  Wide Character → long long **wcstoll**(const wchar_t *str, wchar_t **endptr, int base);
  - This function is similar to 'strtol/wcstol' except for the fact that it converts the string to a long long integer value and returns that value.

- **ANSI** → unsigned long long **strtoull**(const char *str, char **endptr, int base);
  Wide Character → unsigned long long **wcstoull**(const wchar_t *str, wchar_t **endptr, int base);
  - This function is similar to 'strtol/wcstol' except for the fact that it converts the string to an unsigned long long integer value and returns that value.

Till now we have read about string conversion functions which convert a string to only one type of data, be it an integer, a float or a double. The conversion produces the data corresponding to only a single type. They also generate only a single value as their output. What if a string consists of multiple values corresponding to a single or multiple data type? Is there a function which will enable us to extract multiple values from a single string at one go? The function **'sscanf'** is the function which will enable us to do just that. This function is declared in the header file **'stdio.h'** and has the following declaration:

ANSI → int **sscanf**(const char *str, const char *format, ...);
Wide Character → int **swscanf**(const wchar_t *str, const wchar_t *format, ...);
Just like the 'scanf' function, this function too accepts variable number of arguments denoted by '...'.

The function reads data from *'str'* and stores them in the parameter list *(called additional arguments)* provided to the function after the parameter *'format'*. We need to provide addresses of the variables in which we want the formatted output to be stored. The format of the desired generated output needs to be specified in the *'format'* string and their data type must match with the data type of the variables specified in additional arguments section. The number of additional arguments must be at-least the number of format specifiers specified in *'format'*. This function is very similar to the **'scanf'** function which we have already studied (refer **section 4.2.2**). The only difference is that rather than reading the input from the standard input device *(example: console)*, this function reads the input from the provided string *'str'*. Usage example:

```c
/* Header Files */
#include <stdio.h>

int main(void)
{
    /* Variable Declaration & Initialization */
    char   szValues1[]  = "20 is the age of Matt Jones";
    char   szValues2[]  = "Canada 6217 N 3.141592";
    char   szValues3[] = "360;1.414213;S;Tutan";
    int    iResult      = 0;
    char   szOutput[50] = { 0 };
    int    iOutput      = 0;
    char   chOutput     = 0;
    float  fltOutput    = 0;

    iResult = sscanf(szValues1, "%50s", szOutput);
    iResult = sscanf(szValues1, "%d", &iOutput);
    iResult = sscanf(szValues1, "%c", &chOutput);
    iResult = sscanf(szValues1, "%f", &fltOutput);

    /* Print the values. */
    printf("szOutput: %s, iOutput: %d, chOutput: %c, fltOutput: %f\n",
            szOutput, iOutput, chOutput, fltOutput);

    memset(szOutput, 0, sizeof(szOutput));
    fltOutput = 0;
    iOutput   = chOutput = 0;

    /* Now, lets get all values at one go. */
    iResult = sscanf(szValues2, "%6s %d %c %f", szOutput, &iOutput, &chOutput, &fltOutput);

    /* Print the values. */
    printf("szOutput: %s, iOutput: %d, chOutput: %c, fltOutput: %f\n",
            szOutput, iOutput, chOutput, fltOutput);

    memset(szOutput, 0, sizeof(szOutput));
    fltOutput = 0;
    iOutput   = chOutput = 0;

    /* Now, lets get all values again. */
    iResult = sscanf(szValues3, "%d;%f;%c;%s", &iOutput, &fltOutput, &chOutput, szOutput);

    /* Print the values. */
    printf("szOutput: %s, iOutput: %d, chOutput: %c, fltOutput: %f\n",
            szOutput, iOutput, chOutput, fltOutput);

    return 0;
}
```

The above functions help us to convert a string type to values of other data types. Is there a way to do the just opposite i.e. convert values of other data types to a string? We can use the **'sprintf'** function to do just that. This function too is declared in the header file **'stdio.h'** and has the following declaration:

ANSI → int **sprintf**(char *str, const char *format, ...);

Wide Character → int **swprintf**(wchar_t *str, const wchar_t *format, ...);

Just like the 'printf' function, this function too accepts variable number of arguments. The function sets the string 'str' with the values specified in additional arguments. We need to provide the list of values/variables in the additional argument section. The format specifiers corresponding to the values in the argument list need to be specified in the 'format' string and their data type must match with the data type of the values/variables. The number of additional arguments must be same as the number of format specifiers specified in 'format'. The function composes a string with the same text that would be printed if 'format' was used on the **'printf'** function. The only difference is that rather than producing the output to the standard output device *(example: console)*, this function generates the output in the provided string 'str'. The size of the buffer in 'str' should be large enough to contain the entire resulting string. A terminating '\0' *(NULL)* character is automatically appended at the end of the string. Usage example:

```c
/* Header Files */
#include <stdio.h>

int main(void)
{
    /* Variable Declaration & Initialization */
    char  szOutput[80] = { 0 };
    int   iResult      = 0;
    char  szInput[]    = "Gingerbread";
    int   iInput       = 2739;
    char  chInput      = 'K';
    float fltInput     = 3.141592;

    sprintf(szOutput, "%s", szInput);
    printf("szOutput: %s\n", szOutput);

    sprintf(szOutput, "%d", iInput);
    printf("szOutput: %s\n", szOutput);

    sprintf(szOutput, "%c", chInput);
    printf("szOutput: %s\n", szOutput);

    sprintf(szOutput, "%f", fltInput);
    printf("szOutput: %s\n", szOutput);

    memset(szOutput, 0, sizeof(szOutput));

    sprintf(szOutput, "%s, %d, %c, %f", szInput, iInput, chInput, fltInput);
    printf("szOutput: %s\n", szOutput);

    memset(szOutput, 0, sizeof(szOutput));

    sprintf(szOutput, "%s, %d, %c, %f\n", "New York", 112, 65, 1.73205);
    printf("szOutput: %s", szOutput);

    return 0;
}
```

9.8 SAMPLE PROGRAMS

1. Write a C program which reverses an existing string.

```c
/* Header Files */
#include <stdio.h>

int main(void)
{
    /* Variable Declaration & Initialization */
    char szName[] = "Sarah Taylor";
    char *ptr1    = NULL;
    char *ptr2    = NULL;
    char  ch      = 0;

    /* Move the second pointer to the end of the string. */
    for (ptr2 = szName; '\0' != *ptr2; ptr2++);

    /* Keep swapping element values, until the pointers cross each other.
       When the pointers cross, it will mean we have a reversed string.
       'ptr2' has moved up to the NULL character. We don't want the NULL
       character to be reversed. So, move one place back before continuing. */
    for (ptr1 = szName, ptr2--; ptr1 < ptr2; ptr1++, ptr2--)
    {
        ch    = *ptr2;
        *ptr2 = *ptr1;
        *ptr1 = ch;
    }

    /* Print the reversed string. */
    printf("The reversed string is %s.\n\n", szName);

    return 0;
}
```

2. Let us write a program which finds the frequency of occurrence of a given character within a string. The program will do a case in-sensitive search for the character.

```c
/* Header Files */
#include <stdio.h>
#include <ctype.h>

/* Defined Values */
/* Maximum string length including the NULL character. */
#define MAX_STRING_LEN      201

int main(void)
{
    /* Variable Declaration & Initialization */
    char szString[MAX_STRING_LEN] = { 0 };
    int  idx                      = 0;
    int  iCount                   = 0;
    char chToFind                 = 0;

    /* Accept a string from the user. */
    printf("Enter the string: ");
```

```
    gets_s(szString, MAX_STRING_LEN);

    /* Accept the character to find. */
    printf("Enter the character to find: ");
    scanf("%c", &chToFind);

    for (idx = 0; szString[idx] != '\0'; idx++)
    {
        if (toupper(szString[idx]) == toupper(chToFind))
        {
            iCount++;
        }
    }

    /* Print the result. */
    printf("\nThe character '%c' appears %d times within the string '%s'.\n\n",
           chToFind, iCount, szString);

    return 0;
}
```

3. Let us write a program which accepts a string and a character from the user. The program will remove all occurrence of the given character within the string.

```
/* Header Files */
#include <stdio.h>

/* Defined Values */
/* Maximum string length including the NULL character. */
#define MAX_STRING_LEN      201

int main(void)
{
    /* Variable Declaration & Initialization */
    char szString[MAX_STRING_LEN] = { 0 };
    int  idx1                     = 0;
    int  idx2                     = 0;
    char chToRemove               = 0;

    /* Accept a string from the user. */
    printf("Enter the string: ");
    gets_s(szString, MAX_STRING_LEN);

    /* Accept the character to remove. */
    printf("Enter the character to remove: ");
    scanf("%c", &chToRemove);

    /* Remove the character. */
    for (; szString[idx2] != '\0'; idx2++)
    {
        if (szString[idx2] != chToRemove)
        {
            szString[idx1++] = szString[idx2];
        }
    }

    /* Set the terminating NULL character. */
    szString[idx1] = '\0';

    /* Print the result. */
```

```
    printf("\nThe modified string is %s.\n\n", szString);

    return 0;
}
```

4. In our next program we will accept two wide character strings from the user and concatenate one string to another. We will do so without using the C library functions.

```
/* Header Files */
#include <stdio.h>

/* Defined Values */
/* Maximum string length including the NULL character. */
#define MAX_STRING_LEN      201

int main(void)
{
    /* Variable Declaration & Initialization */
    wchar_t wszString1[MAX_STRING_LEN * 2] = { 0 };
    wchar_t wszString2[MAX_STRING_LEN]     = { 0 };
    int   idx1                             = 0;
    int   idx2                             = 0;

    /* Accept the first string from the user. */
    wprintf(L"Enter the first string (no space): ");
    wscanf(L"%200s", wszString1);

    /* Accept the second string from the user. */
    wprintf(L"Enter the second string to concatenate (no space): ");
    wscanf(L"%200s", wszString2);

    /* Go to the end of the first string. */
    for (; wszString1[idx1] != L'\0'; idx1++);

    /* Concatenate the strings. */
    while (idx1 < (MAX_STRING_LEN * 2 - 1) && wszString2[idx2] != L'\0')
    {
        wszString1[idx1++] = wszString2[idx2++];
    }

    wszString1[idx1] = L'\0';

    /* Print the result. */
    wprintf(L"\nThe concatenated string is %s.\n\n", wszString1);

    return 0;
}
```

5. Let us write a program which will accept a wide character string from the user. The program will then count the number of vowels, consonants, digits and spaces within the string.

```
/* Header Files */
#include <stdio.h>
#include <ctype.h>

/* Defined Values */
```

```c
/* Maximum string length including the NULL character. */
#define MAX_STRING_LEN      201

int main(void)
{
    /* Variable Declaration & Initialization */
    wchar_t wszString[MAX_STRING_LEN] = { 0 };
    wchar_t wch                 = 0;
    int     idx                 = 0;
    int     iVowels             = 0;
    int     iConsonants         = 0;
    int     iDigits             = 0;
    int     iSpaces             = 0;

    /* Accept the string from the user. */
    wprintf(L"Enter the string: ");
    fgetws(wszString, MAX_STRING_LEN, stdin);

    /* Count the characters. */
    for (; wszString[idx] != L'\0'; idx++)
    {
        wch = towupper(wszString[idx]);
        if (L'A' == wch || L'E' == wch || L'I' == wch ||
            L'O' == wch || L'U' == wch)
        {
            iVowels++;
        }
        else if (wch >= L'A' && wch <= L'Z')
        {
            iConsonants++;
        }
        else if (wszString[idx] >= L'0' && wszString[idx] <= L'9')
        {
            iDigits++;
        }
        else if (wszString[idx] == L' ')
        {
            iSpaces++;
        }
    }

    /* Print the results. */
    wprintf(L"\nThere are %d vowels, %d consonants, %d digits and %d spaces.\n\n",
            iVowels, iConsonants, iDigits, iSpaces);

    return 0;
}
```

STRUCTURES AND UNIONS

[CHAPTER-10]

10.1 INTRODUCTION

We have seen the use of arrays to represent a group of items which belong to the same data type (ex: char or int). But, is there a way to represent a group of items belonging to different data types using a single name? C supports such a user-defined data type called a **'structure'**. A structure is a collection of logically related fields belonging to same or different data type. For example, we may use a structure to represent the details of each student in a class. The structure may contain the student's registration number, name, roll number and marks. We may have the registration number and roll number as of integer data type, the name as of string *(character array)*, and the marks as integer array. We may have all these fields declared together within a structure and give the structure a name. So, structures help us organize multiple logically related fields together in a more meaningful way. Another concept called **'unions'** is a similar concept to structure but differs in memory/storage usage. We will discuss about unions a little later in this chapter. For now, let us concentrate on structures.

10.2 DEFINING A STRUCTURE

When we define a structure, we specify the format and composition of the structure on which the structure variables will be based. The structure variables are variables which are of the structure data type and contain values as per the structure definition. Assume we are having a grocery shop where we are using a structure to store the details of each grocery item. We need to store details like item name, item code, item rate and quantity in stock. We will define the structure as:

```
struct Item_Details
{
    unsigned int uCode;
    char szName[100];
    float fltRate;
    double dblQty;
};
```

The above structure has the fields *'uCode'*, *'szName'*, *'fltRate'* and *'dblQty'*. The fields of a structure are called structure *elements* or *members*. Each structure member may be of a different data type and may also be an array or even of another structure type. *'Item_Details'* is the name of the structure and is also called the *structure tag*. The structure tag is subsequently used in the program to declare variables belonging to the structure type. We can declare structure variables corresponding to our structure in the following manner:

```
struct Item_Details Item1;
struct Item_Details Item2, Item3, Item4;
```

The general format of defining a structure is as follows:

struct tag_name
{
    Data-Type member1;
    Data-Type member2;
    Data-Type member3;
    .
    .
    .
};

And the general format for declaring the structure variables is:

struct tag_name *Value1, Value2, Value3;*

As we can see that while specifying the structure type *(also during declaration of the structure variables)*, we need to specify the term *'struct'* followed by its *tag name*. This may be a bit inconvenient and we may want an easier way for specifying the structure type. For this, we may type-define the structure to a name, and use that name in places wherever the structure type needs to be specified.

typedef struct tag_name
{
    Data-Type member1;
    Data-Type member2;
    Data-Type member3;
    .
    .
    .
}***tag_alias;***

The type-defined name helps us to avoid typing the term *'struct'*, making our code appear a little cleaner. It also helps us to achieve the same functionality using a little less keystrokes. But, using the alias name has some disadvantages too. A type-defined name hides the actual type, i.e. by looking at the code we cannot understand whether the alias belongs to a structure, an enum or of any other data type. Once type-defined, we may use the alias name to declare variables belonging to the structure type.

tag_alias Value1;

We may also define the structure and declare the structure variables at one go. Consider the following example *(Please note that in this case, we are not using the typedef keyword)*:

struct *Item_Details*
{
    unsigned int uCode;
    char szName[100];
    float fltRate;
    double dblQty;
} *Item1, Item2, Item3;*

The above statement defines the format of the structure and also declares three variables *'Item1'*, *'Item2' and 'Item3'* belonging to the structure type. We may also define a structure without a tag_name when we declare the variables corresponding to the structure as in the above case *(i.e. during structure definition itself)*. We may use the already declared variables in our program, but will not be able to declare any more variables later on in our program, as the structure does not possess any name. This kind of structures are called name-less structures and are not recommended to be used.

We can summarize the following related to a structure:
- We must provide a semi-colon at the end of each member declaration.
- The structure definition must also end with a semi-colon.
- The structure definition must be enclosed within parenthesis.
- The data type of each member may be different and may even be an array, union or another structure type. We may also have pointers as members of a structure.
- We may type-define the structure to have an alias name. We may then use the alias name in places where the structure type needs to be specified.
- We may declare variables of the structure during the structure definition itself.
- Starting from C11, we may create a name-less structure i.e. a structure without a tag-name, when we declare the structure variables during the structure definition itself.

Every variable of the structure type contain the same format as defined in the structure tag and are the ones which actually carry the data. The memory allocation of the structure is as per the defined format. For our structure *'Item_Details'*, the memory space corresponding to the structure variables will have *'uCode'* appearing first followed by the character array *'szName'*, the float variable *'fltRate'* and ending with the double *'dblQty'*. All the members of the structure will appear consecutively in memory and in the order as specified within the structure definition. Though the members appear consecutively, it will be wrong to assume that the next member will appear immediately at the next memory location after the end of the previous member. For performance reasons, some compilers align the structure members on specific byte boundaries like 4 bytes, 8 bytes, 16 bytes etc. Assume that the members are aligned on 8 bytes boundaries and our first member *'uCode'* starts from the memory location 96 and takes 4 bytes of memory. Our next member *'szName'* will start from the memory location 104 *(**not** 100)* as the members are aligned on 8 bytes boundaries. We do not need to bother about byte boundaries as it is automatically managed by the compiler and we access the structure members using their names.

10.3 ACCESSING MEMBERS

The members of a structure can be accessed using the *dot operator* '.' which is also called the *member operator* or the *period operator*. The usage of a structure member is very similar to a simple variable of the same type, except that it needs to be used in conjunction with the structure variable and separated from the structure variable by the *dot operator*.

$$Item1.uCode$$
$$Item1.fltRate$$
$$Item2.szName$$

We can not only access the members of the structure but also assign values to them in the same manner as we do with other variables of the same data type. Consider the following statements:

> struct Item_Details Item1;
> Item1.uCode = 1;
> Item1.dblQty = 106.50;
> strcpy(Item1.szName, "Vanilla ice cream");
> scanf("%f", &Item1.fltRate);
> printf("Total amount of %s is %lf.", Item1.szName, Item1.dblQty * Item1.fltRate);

Let us understand the discussed concepts using a simple program. Here we will accept the item details within a loop and continue doing so till the user wants to. We will then print the accepted values.

```c
/* Header Files */
#include <stdio.h>
#include <ctype.h>

/* Defined Values */
#define ARRAYLEN(x)     sizeof(x)/sizeof(x[0])

/* Structure Definition */
struct Item_Details
{
    unsigned int uCode;
    char         szName[100];
    float        fltRate;
    double       dblQty;
};

int main(void)
{
    /* Variable Declaration & Initialization */
    struct Item_Details Item;
    size_t              cchLen    = 0;
    char                chContinue = 'y';

    while ('Y' == toupper(chContinue))
    {
        /* Initialize the structure variable with 0s. */
        memset(&Item, 0, sizeof(Item));

        /* Accept the item details. */
        printf("Enter the item code: ");
        scanf("%u", &Item.uCode);

        /* When we use 'fgets' function with 'stdin' as input stream, it
           accepts the string from the standard input device ex. Console.
           We will read more about 'fgets' function in our chapter on
           file management. Here we are avoiding 'scanf' function as it
           does not accept spaces within an input string. Using of 'gets'
           function should be avoided as it does not check for buffer overflows,
           and will write past the buffer if provided with a long string.*/
        printf("Enter the item name: ");
        fgets(Item.szName, ARRAYLEN(Item.szName), stdin);

        /* Get rid of the new line character as 'fgets' function retains
           the new line character in the input string. */
```

167

```
        cchLen = strlen(Item.szName);
        if (0 < cchLen && '\n' == Item.szName[cchLen − 1])
        {
            Item.szName[cchLen - 1] = '\0';
        }

        printf("Enter the item rate: ");
        scanf("%f", &Item.fltRate);

        printf("Enter the item quantity: ");
        scanf("%lf", &Item.dblQty);

        /* Print the accepted values. */
        printf("\n\nThe item details are:");
        printf("\nItem code: %u", Item.uCode);
        printf("\nItem name: %s", Item.szName);
        printf("\nItem rate: %.02f", Item.fltRate);
        printf("\nItem quantity: %.02lf", Item.dblQty);
        printf("\nTotal amount: %.02lf\n\n", Item.dblQty * Item.fltRate);

        /* Check if user wants to continue. */
        printf("Continue ('Y' to continue)? ");
        chContinue = getchar();

        printf("\n\n");
    }

    return 0;
}
```

10.4 STRUCTURE INITIALIZATION

A structure is initialized a little differently than other variables. Unlike simple variables, initializing a structure involves initializing all its member variables. Thus, initialization of structure has a different format than other variables. Structure variables can be initialized during structure definition or during variable declaration. Have a look at some examples:

struct Item_Details
{
    unsigned int uCode;
    char szName[100];
    float fltRate;
    double dblQty;
} Item1 = { 10, "Dark Chocolate", 5.00, 50.00 };

In the example, 10 gets assigned to 'uCode', the string "Dark Chocolate" gets assigned to 'szName', 5.00 gets assigned to 'fltRate' and 50.00 gets assigned to 'dblQty'. All these values are assigned to the members of the structure variable 'Item1'. There is a one-to-one mapping between the values specified within the curly braces and the structure members. The order of the values should match the order of the structure members to which they are to be assigned. Structure variables can also be initialized as:
struct Item_Details Item2 = { 11, "Brown bread", 1.50, 20.00 };
static **struct** Item_Details Item3 = { 12, "Darjeeling Tea", 12.50, 20.50 };

We may also initialize one structure variable from another structure variable in the same way we do with other variables.

```
struct Item_Details Item2 = { 11, "Brown bread", 1.50, 20.00 };
struct Item_Details Item3 = Item2;
static struct Item_Details Item4 = Item3;
```

As it is evident from the above examples, when one structure variable is assigned to another structure variable a byte-by-byte copy occurs from the variable on the right to the variable on the left. So, all members of the left-side variable get the same values as the members of the right-side variable. In the above example, when *Item2* gets assigned to *Item3*, the members of *Item3* also get the same values as the *Item2* members. So, *'uCode'* gets the value *11*, *'szName'* gets the string *"Brown bread"*, *'fltRate'* gets the value *1.50* and *'dblQty'* gets the value *20.00*.

If we want to initialize all the members of a structure variable to a same value, we may do so as below:
```
struct Item_Details Item2 = { 0 };
```

The above statement initializes all members of the structure variable to the value 0.

10.5 ARRAY OF STRUCTURE

We can declare array of structures in the same way as we do for other data types. Let us understand this using a simple program. In this program, we declare an array of structures consisting of 10 elements. Each structure element accepts and holds the marks details of a single student of a class. It then prints the marks and also the average marks received by each of the students.

```
#include <stdio.h>

/* Defined Values */
#define MAX_STUDENTS    10

/* Structure Definition */
struct Student_Marks
{
    int iMathematics;
    int iChemistry;
    int iPhysics;
    int iBiology;
};

int main(void)
{
    /* Variable Declaration & Initialization */
    struct Student_Marks rgMarks[MAX_STUDENTS] = { 0 };
    int             idx                 = 0;
    int             iAggregate          = 0;

    for (; idx < MAX_STUDENTS; idx++)
    {
        printf("Student #%02d:\n=============\n", idx + 1);
        printf("Enter the marks obtained in Mathematics: ");
```

```
            scanf("%d", &rgMarks[idx].iMathematics);

            printf("Enter the marks obtained in Chemistry: ");
            scanf("%d", &rgMarks[idx].iChemistry);

            printf("Enter the marks obtained in Physics: ");
            scanf("%d", &rgMarks[idx].iPhysics);

            printf("Enter the marks obtained in Biology: ");
            scanf("%d", &rgMarks[idx].iBiology);
            printf("\n");
    }

    printf("\n\n");

    /* We will first print the headings and then the marks. */
    printf("\n\t\t\t\tSTUDENT MARKS\n\t\t\t\t*************\n\t\t");

    /* Make each subject column fixed width (11 chars) & left aligned. A tab is also
        inserted between two columns to provide proper separation between columns. */
    printf("Mathematics\tChemistry \tPhysics    \tBiology    \tAverage\n");

    /* Now, print the marks and the percentage obtained by the students. */
    for (idx = 0; idx < MAX_STUDENTS; idx++)
    {
        printf("\nStudent #%02d:\t", idx + 1);

        printf("%02d          \t", rgMarks[idx].iMathematics);
        printf("%02d          \t", rgMarks[idx].iChemistry);
        printf("%02d          \t", rgMarks[idx].iPhysics);
        printf("%02d          \t", rgMarks[idx].iBiology);

        /* Calculate the aggregate of all the subjects for the student. */
        iAggregate = rgMarks[idx].iMathematics + rgMarks[idx].iChemistry +
                    rgMarks[idx].iPhysics + rgMarks[idx].iBiology;

        /* Print the percentage obtained by this student. */
        printf("%02.02lf", (double) iAggregate / (double) 4);
    }

    printf("\n\n");

    return 0;
}
```

Sample output:

```
                              STUDENT MARKS
                              *************
                Mathematics   Chemistry      Physics       Biology       Average

Student #01:    76            68             72            70            71.50
Student #02:    67            62             69            70            67.00
Student #03:    84            87             82            84            84.25
Student #04:    77            81             78            75            77.75
Student #05:    91            85             81            84            85.25
Student #06:    58            66             63            67            63.50
Student #07:    75            72             77            73            74.25
Student #08:    61            64             69            59            63.25
Student #09:    73            71             69            68            70.25
Student #10:    74            86             72            78            77.50
```

In the above program we have declared an array *'rgMarks'* of the structure *'Student_Marks'*. The array has 10 elements and each element holds the marks details corresponding to a single student. An element of the array of a structure is accessed in the same way as any other array element.

rgMarks[4]	The 4th element of the array.
rgMarks[4].iPhysics	The 'iPhysics' member of the 4th element of the array.

10.6 POINTER TO STRUCTURE

If we have a pointer to a structure variable, the method of accessing its member element is a bit different. When used with a pointer variable, a member is accessed using the *arrow operator* **(–>)**. The *arrow operator* is formed using a minus sign followed by a greater than sign. Consider the below example which implements the above program *(only the main() function shown)* using a pointer.

```c
int main(void)
{
    /* Variable Declaration & Initialization */
    struct Student_Marks  rgMarks[MAX_STUDENTS] = { 0 };
    struct Student_Marks *pMarks                = NULL;
    int                   iAggregate            = 0;

    for (pMarks = rgMarks; (pMarks - rgMarks) < MAX_STUDENTS; pMarks++)
    {
        printf("Student #%02d:\n=============\n", (pMarks - rgMarks) + 1);
        printf("Enter the marks obtained in Mathematics: ");
        scanf("%d", &pMarks->iMathematics);

        printf("Enter the marks obtained in Chemistry: ");
        scanf("%d", &pMarks->iChemistry);

        printf("Enter the marks obtained in Physics: ");
        scanf("%d", &pMarks->iPhysics);

        printf("Enter the marks obtained in Biology: ");
        scanf("%d", &pMarks->iBiology);
        printf("\n");
    }

    printf("\n\n");

    /* We will first print the headings and then the marks. */
    printf("\n\t\t\t\tSTUDENT MARKS\n\t\t\t\t*************\n\t\t");

    /* Make each subject column fixed width (11 chars) & left aligned. A tab is also
       inserted between two columns to provide proper separation between columns. */
    printf("Mathematics\tChemistry \tPhysics    \tBiology    \tAverage\n");

    /* Now, print the marks and the percentage obtained by the students. */
    for (pMarks = rgMarks; (pMarks - rgMarks) < MAX_STUDENTS; pMarks++)
    {
        printf("\nStudent #%02d:\t", (pMarks - rgMarks) + 1);

        printf("%02d          \t", pMarks->iMathematics);
        printf("%02d          \t", pMarks->iChemistry);
        printf("%02d          \t", pMarks->iPhysics);
        printf("%02d          \t", pMarks->iBiology);
```

```
        /* Calculate the aggregate of all the subjects for the student. */
        iAggregate = pMarks->iMathematics + pMarks->iChemistry +
                     pMarks->iPhysics + pMarks->iBiology;

        /* Print the percentage obtained by this student. */
        printf("%02.02lf", (double) iAggregate / (double) 4);
    }

    printf("\n\n");

    return 0;
}
```

In the above program we have declared a pointer *'pMarks'* of the structure *'Student_Marks'*. The statement *'pMarks = rgMarks'* assigns the address of the 0th element of the array to the pointer *'pMarks'*. This statement is equivalent to using the statement *'pMarks = &rgMarks[0]'*. As per pointer arithmetic, incrementing *'pMarks',* makes the pointer point to the next element of the array. Similarly, decrementing its value makes it point to the previous element. Subtracting one pointer from another gives the number of elements between the two pointers. So the expression *'pMarks – rgMarks'* gives the number of elements between the element pointed by *'pMarks'* and start of the array. A member of an element of the array is accessed as below:

pMarks->iMathematics
pMarks->iChemistry
pMarks->iPhysics
pMarks->iBiology

We can also use the following syntax to access a member of the element pointed by the pointer.

*(*pMarks).iMathematics*
*(*pMarks).iChemistry*
*(*pMarks).iPhysics*
*(*pMarks).iBiology*

The above four statements initially dereference the pointer *'(*pMarks)'* and then use the dot operator to access the structure member. The parentheses around *'*pMarks'* is important as the dot operator has higher precedence than the pointer indirection operator **(*)**.

While using the operators **'->'** and **'.'**, we must be careful regarding their precedence. They have one of the highest precedence of all the operators (refer **section 3.12**). Consider few examples:

(++pMarks)->iPhysics	Increments *'pMarks'* first and then accesses the value of *'iPhysics'*.
++pMarks->iPhysics	Increments *'iPhysics'* corresponding to the element pointed by *'pMarks'*.
pMarks++->iPhysics	Accesses *'iPhysics'* and then increments *'pMarks'*.

10.7 NESTED STRUCTURES

When a structure variable is declared within another structure, it is called nesting of structures. Nested structures can be of two types:

1. **Externally defined nested structures:** When a structure variable is declared *(as a member)* within another structure but, the definition of the former structure is outside the latter. Some examples of such nested structures are:

```
struct Struct1
{
    int iValue1;
};

struct Struct2
{
    struct Struct1 firstStruct;
    int iValue2;
};
```

In our example, the structure *'Struct1'* is defined outside *'Struct2'* but, is declared as a member of *'Struct2'* using the variable *'firstStruct'*. If we declare a variable *'secondStruct'* of type *'Struct2'*, we may access the *'Struct1'* member *'iValue1'* as *'secondStruct.firstStruct.iValue1'*.

2. **Embedded nested structures:** When one structure is defined within another structure, it is called an embedded nested structure. Have a look at the below example:

```
struct Struct1
{
    struct Struct2
    {
        int iValue2;
    };
    int iValue1;
};
```

The structure *'Struct2'* is defined within *'Struct1'* which makes it an embedded nested structure. If we declare a variable *'firstStruct'* of type *'Struct1'*, we may access the *'Struct2'* member *'iValue2'* as *'firstStruct.iValue2'*. We can access *'iValue2'* directly as a member of *'firstStruct'* because *'Struct2'* is embedded nested and no structure variable of *'Struct2'* is declared within *'Struct1'*. Consider another example:

```
struct Struct1
{
    struct Struct2
    {
        int iValue2;
    }secondStruct;

    int iValue1;
};
```

In the previous example, if we declare a variable *'firstStruct'* of type *'Struct1'*, we may access *'Struct2'* member *'iValue2'* as *'firstStruct.secondStruct.iValue2'*. This is because we have now declared a variable *'secondStruct'* of type *'Struct2'*. This variable is declared within *'Struct1'*.

Starting from C11, we may create anonymous structures and unions. Given below are two such examples:

struct Struct1
{
  int iValue1;
  struct
  {
    int iValue2;
    int iValue3;
  };
};
	struct Struct1
	{
	  int iValue1;
	  struct
	  {
	    int iValue2;
	    int iValue3;
	  }*secondStruct*;
	};

Let us now write a program which accepts the student details of a class. The program will define a structure called *'Student_Profile'* which contains the profile *(registration number, name and address)* of a student. The program will define another structure called *'Student_Marks'* which will hold the marks obtained by each student of the class. Both *'Student_Profile'* and *'Student_Marks'* will be nested within another structure *'Student_Details'*.

```c
/* Header Files */
#include <stdio.h>

/* Defined Values */
#define MAX_STUDENTS    10

/* Structure Definitions */
struct Student_Profile
{
    int  iRegistration;
    char szName[50];
};

struct Student_Details
{
    int iRoll;

    struct Student_Profile Profile;

    struct Student_Marks
    {
        int iMathematics;
        int iChemistry;
        int iPhysics;
        int iBiology;
    }Marks;
};

int main(void)
```

```
{
    /* Variable Declaration & Initialization */
    struct Student_Details rgDetails[MAX_STUDENTS] = { 0 };
    int                    idx                     = 0;

    for (; idx < MAX_STUDENTS; idx++)
    {
        printf("Student #%02d:\n=============\n", idx + 1);
        printf("Enter the student's registration number: ");
        scanf("%d", &rgDetails[idx].Profile.iRegistration);

        printf("Enter the student's name: ");
        gets_s(rgDetails[idx].Profile.szName, 50);

        printf("Enter the student's roll number: ");
        scanf("%d", &rgDetails[idx].iRoll);

        printf("Enter the marks obtained in Mathematics: ");
        scanf("%d", &rgDetails[idx].Marks.iMathematics);

        printf("Enter the marks obtained in Chemistry: ");
        scanf("%d", &rgDetails[idx].Marks.iChemistry);

        printf("Enter the marks obtained in Physics: ");
        scanf("%d", &rgDetails[idx].Marks.iPhysics);

        printf("Enter the marks obtained in Biology: ");
        scanf("%d", &rgDetails[idx].Marks.iBiology);
        printf("\n");
    }

    printf("\n\n");

    /* We will first print the headings and then the marks. */
    printf("\n\t\t\tSTUDENT MARKS\n\t\t\t*************\n");

    /* Now, print the marks by the students. */
    for (idx = 0; idx < MAX_STUDENTS; idx++)
    {
        printf("\n\nRegistration: %d", rgDetails[idx].Profile.iRegistration);
        printf("\nName         : %s\t", rgDetails[idx].Profile.szName);

        printf("\nRoll Number : %03d", rgDetails[idx].iRoll);

        printf("\nMathematics : %02d", rgDetails[idx].Marks.iMathematics);
        printf("\nChemistry   : %02d", rgDetails[idx].Marks.iChemistry);
        printf("\nPhysics     : %02d", rgDetails[idx].Marks.iPhysics);
        printf("\nBiology     : %02d", rgDetails[idx].Marks.iBiology);
    }

    printf("\n\n");

    return 0;
}
```

10.8 BIT FIELDS

A *'char'* data type takes 1 byte, a *'short'* takes 2 bytes and an *'int'* takes 2, 4 or 8 bytes depending on the compiler. In situations where we do not require an entire byte for a structure member, we may use a *bit field*. This saves memory space and we can accommodate more data by using less memory. The general form of bit field definition is:

```
struct tag-name
{
    Data-Type field1: bit-length;
    Data-Type field2: bit-length;
    ....
    ....
    Data-Type fieldN: bit-length;
};
```

The size of a bit field can vary from 1 bit to the total bit-length of the data type if it had no bit-field specified. So, a *'short int'* data type can have bit-field length of 1 bit to a maximum of 16 bits which is the size of a *'short int'* data type. A signed bit field should have at-least 2 bits *(1 extra bit for the sign)*. The maximum value that can be stored in a bit field depends on the bit-field length. If the bit-field length is specified as 'n', the maximum value that can be stored in the field is 2^{n-1}.

The internal representation of the bits vary depending on the machine. They may be stored from left to right, or from right to left depending on the machine architecture.

The points worth noting regarding bit-fields are:
- The first bit-field starts from a word boundary.
- The address of a bit-field member cannot be accessed as they may not start at a byte boundary. This means that we cannot do pointer operations on a bit-field or use the *'scanf'* function to read value into a bit-field.
- A special unnamed bit field of size 0 *(zero)* is used to force alignment on to next boundary. This makes the next member always starts from a byte boundary.
- We cannot have an array of bit fields.
- The bit-field length of a field cannot be more than the number of bits in the specified data-type. It has to have a minimum length of 1. Signed bit-fields must have a minimum length of 2.
- We should be careful in assigning values in the range which a bit-field can hold. The behavior due to assignment of out of range values is compiler specific.
- Consecutive bit-fields of same data-type share the bits and though the sum of all the bits may not be an exact multiple of the data-type size *(ex: 8 bits for char, 16 bits for short int)*, all these fields together will occupy a size equal to a multiple of the data-type size in bytes.

In our next program we will pick the current date-time from the system. We use the C function **'time'** to get the current time. The function accepts a pointer to a variable of type *'time_t'*. *'time_t'* is generally a type-defined name of any integer data type. The function populates this variable with a value which is equal to the number of seconds elapsed since *00:00 hours, Jan 1, 1970 UTC*. The value returned in the *'time_t'* variable is passed to another C function called **'localtime'**. This function in turn returns a *'tm'* structure pointer. This returned structure variable has a global scope which allows its value to be retained even after the function has ended. The variable's value can be changed in any subsequent call to functions **'gmtime'** or *'localtime'*. *'gmtime'* is a similar function like *'localtime'* except that it returns the time in UTC. The *'tm'* structure has the following members:

Member	Data Type	Description	Range
tm_sec	int	Seconds passed after the last minute	0-59
tm_min	int	Minutes passed after the last hour	0-59
tm_hour	int	Hours passed since midnight	0-23
tm_mday	int	Day of the month	1-31
tm_mon	int	Months since January	0-11
tm_year	int	Years since 1900	
tm_wday	int	Days since Sunday i.e. weekday	0-6
tm_yday	int	Days since January 1 of the year	0-365
tm_isdst	int	Daylight Saving Time flag. It is greater than 0 *(zero)* if Daylight Saving Time is in effect, 0 *(zero)* if Daylight Saving Time is not in effect, and less than 0 *(zero)* if the information is unavailable.	

After getting the current time, we assign the values to our structure with the bit-fields. Do notice, in our structure we have defined an unnamed field with 0 *(zero)* bits. This field forces the alignment on to the next boundary. So, the time related field *(uHour)* starts from the next boundary. So, all the date related fields *(uYear, uMonth and uDate)* together occupy starting 21 bits *(of unsigned int)* leaving rest of the bits unused. If the *'unsigned int'* data type occupies 32 bits *(4 bytes)* of memory, the rest 11 bits remain unused. If 'unsigned int' occupies 16 bits *(2 bytes)* of memory, 2 consecutive unsigned int locations *(totalling 4 bytes)* will be used. The first 'unsigned int' will be fully used and 5 bits from the next one will be used. The rest 11 bits from the second 'unsigned int' will remain unused. The time field *(uHour)* will start from a fresh byte boundary.

After assigning the values to our structure variable, we print the values. In the *'printf'* function, we use the format specifier of the data type of the bit-fields for printing their values.

```
/* Header Files */
#include <stdio.h>
#include <time.h>

/* Structure Definitions */
struct DateTime
{
    unsigned uYear    : 12;
    unsigned uMonth   : 4;
    unsigned uDate    : 5;
    unsigned          : 0;
    unsigned uHour    : 5;
    unsigned uMinute  : 6;
    unsigned uSecond  : 6;
};

int main(void)
{
    /* Variable Declaration & Initialization */
    struct DateTime datetime = { 0 };
    struct tm       *pCurTime = { 0 };
    time_t          itime    = 0;

    time(&itime);
    pCurTime = localtime(&itime);
```

```
if (pCurTime)
{
    datetime.uYear = pCurTime->tm_year + 1900;
    datetime.uMonth = pCurTime->tm_mon + 1;
    datetime.uDate = pCurTime->tm_mday;
    datetime.uHour = pCurTime->tm_hour;
    datetime.uMinute = pCurTime->tm_min;
    datetime.uSecond = pCurTime->tm_sec;
}

printf("Size: %u\n\n", sizeof(datetime));

printf("Todays date : %u/%u/%u\n", datetime.uYear, datetime.uMonth,
        datetime.uDate);
printf("Current time: %u:%u:%u\n\n", datetime.uHour, datetime.uMinute,
        datetime.uSecond);

return 0;
}
```

10.9 UNIONS

Unions are a concept borrowed from structures. As they are very similar to structures, their syntax is also similar to structures. The way a union's member is accessed, its initialization, arrays of unions, pointers to unions etc. are all very similar to structures. The major distinction between structures and unions is in terms of memory usage. In structures, each member has its own separate storage location, whereas all the members of a union are assigned the same memory location. This implies that although a union may have multiple members of different data types, we may use *(store and read)* only one member at a time. The memory used by a union is equal to the size of its biggest member i.e. the member which occupies the highest amount of storage. The general form of a union is as follows:

union tag_name
{
    Data-Type member1;
    Data-Type member2;
    Data-Type member3;

    .

    .
};

We may type-define union in the same way we do with structures. We may also declare union variables in the same way we do for structure variables. Consider the below example of a union:

union Values
{
    char   chVal;
    short   iVal;
    double dblVal;
    char   szName[10];
};

The union *'Values'* has four members. We can use only one member at a time as all members occupy the same memory location. The size of the union is equal to its largest member, which in our case is *'szName'* occupying 10 bytes of storage. So, the storage allocation of the members of the union will be:

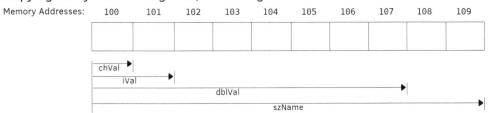

We can use the same syntax as that of structures while accessing union members. For example, if we declare a variable *'MyValues'* of the above union type, we may access its members as:

> **union** *Values MyValues;*
> *MyValues.chVal = 'A';*
> *strcpy(MyValues.szName, "Jones");*

While accessing a member, we should make sure that we are accessing the member whose value is currently stored. Union allocates a memory space which can be used by any one of its members at a time. When a different member is assigned a value, the new value supersedes the value stored in the previous member. The following group of statements will produce *erroneous* output as we are accessing a member which is different from the one which currently contains the value.

> **union** *Values MyValues;*
> *MyValues.iVal = 793;*
> *strcpy(MyValues.szName, "Hanna");*
> *printf("Value is %d.", MyValues.iVal);*

A union may be nested inside another structure or union. A structure may also be nested inside a union.

In our next program we will calculate the perimeter of different geometrical shapes. We will define a union which will hold the dimensions needed to calculate the perimeter of the shape.

```c
#include <stdio.h>

union Dimensions
{
    struct Rectangle
    {
        int x;
        int y;

    }rect;

    struct Square
    {
        int x;

    }square;
```

```c
    struct Circle
    {
        float fltRadius;

    }circle;
};

int main(void)
{
    union Dimensions dim;
    int    iOption   = 0;
    const double PI = 3.141592;

    while (4 != iOption)
    {
        printf("\n1. Rectangle\n2. Square\n3. Circle\n4. Exit\n\n");

        iOption = 0;
        while (iOption < 1 || iOption > 4)
        {
            printf("Enter the option: ");
            scanf("%d", &iOption);
        }

        if (4 == iOption)
        {
            break;
        }

        switch (iOption)
        {
        case 1:
            printf("\n\nEnter the length of the rectangle: ");
            scanf("%d", &dim.rect.x);
            printf("Enter the width of the rectangle: ");
            scanf("%d", &dim.rect.y);

            printf("\nThe perimeter of the rectangle is: %d.\n",
                2 * (dim.rect.x + dim.rect.y));

            break;

        case 2:
            printf("\n\nEnter the length of the sides of the square: ");
            scanf("%d", &dim.square.x);

            printf("\nThe perimeter of the square is: %d.\n", 4 * dim.square.x);

            break;

        case 3:
            printf("\n\nEnter the radius of the circle: ");
            scanf("%f", &dim.circle.fltRadius);

            printf("\nThe perimeter of the circle is: %lf.\n",
                (2 * PI * dim.circle.fltRadius));

            break;
        }
    }

    return 0;
}
```

10.10 COMPOUND LITERALS

We have read about compound literals in the chapter on arrays. Here we will see some examples of compound literals using structures and unions.

```c
#include <stdio.h>

typedef struct _POINT
{
    int x;
    int y;

} POINT;

typedef union _LENGTH
{
    float fltMeter;
    float fltCM;

}LENGTH;

int main(void)
{
    // Creates a _POINT structure object with x = 20 and y = 30.
    // Assigns it to the structure variable 'p'.
    POINT  p       = (struct _POINT) { 20, 30 };

    // Creates a _POINT structure object with x = 150 and y = 50.
    // Assigns its address to the pointer 'ptr1'.
    POINT *ptr1    = &(POINT) { 150, 50 };

    // Creates a _POINT structure object with x = 32 and y = 64.
    // Assigns it's x member's value to 'iLocX'.
    int    iLocX   = (POINT) { 32, 64 }.x;

    // Creates a _POINT structure object with x = 32 and y = 64.
    // Assigns its y member's value to 'iLocY'.
    int    iLocY   = (&(POINT) { 32, 64 })->y;

    // Creates a _LENGTH union object with its fields containing value 70.
    // Assigns it to the variable 'len'.
    LENGTH  len    = (LENGTH) { 70 };

    // Creates a _LENGTH union object with its fields containing value 50.
    // Assigns its address to the pointer 'ptr2'.
    LENGTH *ptr2   = &(union _LENGTH) { 50 };

    // Creates a _LENGTH union object with its fields containing value 70.
    // Assigns the value of its member 'fltMeter' to variable 'fltMtr'.
    float   fltMtr = (union _LENGTH) { 70 }.fltMeter;

    // Creates a _LENGTH union object with its fields containing value 70.
    // Assigns the value of its member 'fltCM' to variable 'fltCM'.
    float   fltCM  = (&(LENGTH) { 70 })->fltCM;

    return 0;
}
```

10.11 ALIGNING ADDRESSES

When we declare variables or structure members, they may be assigned any valid and available memory address. One *'char'* variable may be assigned an address of 1757 while the next one may be assigned 2240. Programs may have a requirement to align certain variable addresses to the multiples of a constant *(power of 2)*. This requirement becomes more significant for structure members when we want the members to start at the same relative address to each other, irrespective of the machine architecture. For example, we may want all consecutive integer members of a structure to start at a relative address of 8 bytes from its previous member, irrespective of whether an integer takes 2 bytes, 4 bytes or 8 bytes.

A new keyword '**_Alignas**' has been introduced from C11 which modifies the alignment requirement of a variable being declared. The variable is aligned to the specified type or integer constant value. The type specifier is prepended to a variable declaration and may take the following form:

_Alignas(integer constant)

Or

_Alignas(type)

The '*_Alignas*' type specifier cannot be used for declaring bit fields, register variables and function parameters. If an *integer constant* is specified, the declared variable will have its alignment requirement set to the integer constant. If *type* is specified, the variable will have its alignment requirement similar to that of the given type.

This keyword is also available as a macro '**alignas**' which is declared in the header file '**stdalign.h**'.

Examples:

// All the below variables are aligned to 8 bytes.
_Alignas(8) int a, b, c;

// All the below variables are aligned to 2 bytes.
_Alignas(2) char x, y, z;

struct _MYSTRUCT
{
    alignas(8) int iVar1, iVar2;
    alignas(8) double dblVar1, dblVar2;
};

USER DEFINED FUNCTIONS

[CHAPTER-11]

11.1 INTRODUCTION

In our previous chapters, we have used many system functions which help us achieve certain specific functionalities. We also defined the **'main'** function in all our programs which forms the entry point of the program. As discussed earlier, a function is a group of statements which perform certain specific tasks. A C program is divided into functions and a function is called from other functions to make it perform the required tasks. Dividing a program into multiple functions has the following advantages:

1. **Functions improve program readability and understanding:** It is much easier to understand a program if it is broken down into multiple pieces and the functionality of each piece is understood separately. It also improves the readability as we may be looking at functions entirely contained within a single screen in the IDE, rather than functions which require a lot of scrolling.

2. **Increase in code flexibility:** As a function is generally short and does specific tasks, making changes to it becomes easy till its input, output and basic functionality remains the same. Also, there is less chance of regression when fixing bugs within a function.

3. **Increase in code re-usability:** Shifting a specific task to a function helps us to avoid writing the same piece of code again and again. If a bug is found in a group of statements repeated across multiple locations, we will require to make the fixes across all such locations. If the repeatative code is shifted to a function, we will then need to make the fix only within the function. Writing the same code again and again increases program complexity and must be avoided.

4. **Functions achieve procedural abstraction:** Once a function is written and tested, it serves as a black box for the caller functions. All that a programmer *(when writing the caller functions)* needs to know for invoking a function is its name and the parameters that it expects.

5. **Simplifies program development:** When working on a big project, a program may be divided between multiple programmers with each programmer assigned to implement a specific functionality using a group of functions. This enables us to implement the project in parallel.

6. **Program testing becomes easy:** Each function may be tested separately without the need for the entire program to be ready for testing. The function may be provided dummy inputs and the actual output verified against expected output. Also when a bug is found, we need to concentrate only on the faulty function.

7. **Code sharing becomes easy:** A function written for one program may be used by other programs too. This is another form of code re-usability.

C functions may be classified into two categories viz. *Library* functions (refer **section 1.2**) and *user-defined* functions. **'printf'** and **'scanf'** are examples of library functions and **'main'** is an example of user-defined function. The main distinction between these two categories is that library functions come bundled with the compiler and do not require to be written by the programmer, whereas user-defined functions have to be developed by the programmer at the time of writing the program.

Before writing a program, we should always create a design layout of the entire program by dividing it into functions with proper understanding regarding a function's task, the kind of output it will generate and the list of inputs it will accept. We should try to move any functionality which may appear in multiple places to functions.

An example of a program structure broken up into multiple modules using functions is shown below:

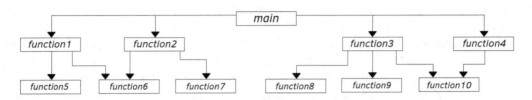

In the above figure, the function **'main'** calls the four functions *'function1'*, *'function2'*, *'function3'* and *'function4'* for getting its work done. *'function1'* in turn calls the two functions *'function5'* and *'function6'*. *'function2'* calls the functions *'function6'* and *'function7'* to get some of its tasks get done by them. Similarly, *'function3'* calls the functions *'function8'*, *'function9'* and *'function10'* to get some of its work done. The function *'function4'* too calls the function *'function10'*. We can see that the function *'function6'* gets called by two functions *'function1'* and *'function2'* respectively to help them perform their work. Similarly, *'function10'* gets called by the two functions *'function3'* and *'function4'*.

11.2 THE STRUCTURE OF A C FUNCTION
Every C function have the following form:

> *Return-Data-Type* **function-Name**(*Comma separated argument list*)
> **{**
>
>   Local Variable Declarations;
>
>   Executable statement 1;
>   Executable statement 2;
>   ......
>   ......
>
>   **return** *value/expression*;
> **}**

Some of the parts of a function are optional and may be skipped.

11.2.1 FUNCTION NAME
Every function is recognized by a name. Naming a function is similar to naming any other C identifier (refer **section 1.6**). A function name must be unique across the program and is case-sensitive. We

should be careful to avoid naming a function with the same name as a library function.

11.2.2 FUNCTION RETURN TYPE AND VALUES

How does a function let its caller know the result of its operation? The called function can return only one value to its caller indicating the result of its operation. If it has multiple values to return, it can do so using pointers as arguments to the function. It can also return multiple values to the caller by enclosing all of them within a structure variable and returning it. A function can return a value using the **return** statement. The return statement can be written as any one of the below:

- return;
- return (value/expression);

The first *'return'* statement does not return a value and is simply used to return the control back to the calling function. When a *'return'* is encountered, all successive statements within the function is ignored and the control is immediately transferred to the calling function. As for the second *'return'* statement, it immediately returns the value or the result of the expression following the *'return'* statement to the caller. The type of value returned by the *'return'* statement must match the return data type specified in the function declaration *(before the function name)*.

int sum(int x, int y)
{
   return (x + y);
}
	long Sum(int x, int y)
	{
	   long lSum = (long) x + (long) y;
	   return lSum;
	}
		int CheckValue(int x)
		{
		   if (x <= 0)
		      return 0;
		   else
		      return 1;
		}

A function may return nothing, in which case **'void'** is specified as the return type of the function. In such a case, we need not specify any *'return'* statement for returning control from the called function to the caller. If any premature return of control is needed *(when we do not want to execute successive/later statements based on a condition check)*, we may use the first *'return'* statement *(i.e. the 'return' statement without any accompanying value/expression)*.

```
void IsZero(int x)
{
    if (x == 0)
    {
        printf("x is zero");
        return;
    }
    printf("x is not zero");
}
```

When we return a variable from a function, we actually return the value contained within the variable. Similarly when we return a pointer from a function, we are actually returning the memory address held in the pointer variable and not the variable itself. Care must be taken so that we do not return address of any local variable *(variables declared within a function)* of the called function, because when a function returns, all local variables of the function cease to exist *(except static or dynamically allocated variables)*. So, if the caller function tries to access the returned memory address, it will cause a memory violation error.

11.2.3 FUNCTION ARGUMENTS

The argument variables or parameter variables receive values from the calling function, thus providing a means to pass data from the calling function to the called function. The argument or parameter list contains a list of variable declarations separated by commas.

An argument or parameter is the data which is taken as input by a function. There are two types of arguments or parameters. The arguments which are passed in the function call are known as **actual arguments** or **actual parameters**. The arguments which are received by the called function are known as **formal arguments** or **formal parameters**.

```
int sum(int argX, int argY)
{
    return (argX + argY);
}

int main(void)
{
    int x = 36, y = 64;
    sum(x, y);
    return 0;
}
```

In the above program, the *'x'* and *'y'* specified within the call to the function *'sum'* are the actual arguments *(parameters)*. The variables *'argX'* and *'argY'* specified within the function *'sum'* are the formal arguments *(parameters)*. There is a one to one mapping between the actual arguments and the formal arguments. The values contained in the actual arguments are assigned to the formal arguments when the control comes within the called function.

The argument list of a function is also optional. In such a case, we may specify **'void'** as the argument or leave it empty.

If the formal argument list is left empty, the function is assumed to accept an unspecified number of arguments. So, all calls to the function become valid *(called with or without any arguments)*. Remember, the parentheses *(first brackets)* around the argument list is required even if there are no arguments present.

If *'void'* is specified as the formal argument *(refer to the main function in the last example)*, the function is believed to be taking no arguments. So if you call this function with any arguments, the compiler will raise an error.

Based on the arguments and return values, functions can be categorized into four types. They are:
- Function without arguments and without return value.
- Function without arguments but with return value.
- Function with arguments and also with return value.
- Function with arguments but without return value.

11.2.4 FUNCTION BODY

The body of a function is enclosed within the opening and closing curly braces. If we are working with ANSI C, the local function level variables are declared at the start of a function just after the opening curly braces for the function. In case of C99 or later, we can declare the variables anywhere in the function before their use, though it is a good practice to declare the variables at the start of the function to improve readability.

All variables declared within the function exist only till the control within the function remains. As soon as a function returns, these variables lose their existence. These variables will be re-declared in the next call to the function. There are few exceptions. A variable declared as **'static'** remains into existence and retains its value even when the function exits. This variable will not be re-declared *(or re-initialized)* and will continue with its previous value during the next call to the function. Dynamically allocated memory space *(if not freed)* also remains into existence even when the function exits. We will read more about them in our chapter on *'Dynamic Memory Allocation'*. Though any pointer variable *(if not declared as static)* pointing to such dynamically allocated memory ceases to exist, the allocated memory space if not freed, stays. If we return the address of the allocated memory to the caller function, the caller may still access this memory location once the called function has ended.

11.2.5 EXAMPLE PROGRAMS

In our first multi-function program, we will keep it simple. We will declare two variables *'x'* and *'y'* in **'main'**, initialize them and then pass them as actual parameters to another function *'PrintValues'*. *'PrintValues'* declares two integer variables *'ParamX'* and *'ParamY'* as its formal parameters. There is a one to one mapping between the actual parameters and the formal parameters. So, the values of the variables *'x'* and *'y'* are assigned to the formal parameters *'ParamX'* and *'ParamY'* within *'PrintValues'*. *'PrintValues'* gets the values in the variables *'ParamX'* and *'ParamY'* and prints their values.

```c
#include <stdio.h>

void PrintValues(int ParamX,
                 int ParamY)
{
    printf("\nThe two numbers are %d and %d.", ParamX, ParamY);
}

int main(void)
{
    /* Variable Declaration & Initialization */
    int x    = 50;
    int y    = 500;
```

```
    PrintValues(x, y);

    return 0;
}
```

The function *'PrintValues'* is an example of a function accepting arguments but having no return values.

In our next program, we will pass two values *44* and *55* from **'main'** to another function *'sum'*. The function *'sum'* will add the two numbers and return the sum of the numbers to the caller function *'main'*. The function *'main'* will accept the return value in the variable *'iSum'* and print the value. We will have another function called *'Multiply'* which does not accept any arguments. It just multiplies two values and prints the result.

```c
#include <stdio.h>

int Sum(int ParamX,
        int ParamY)
{
    return (ParamX + ParamY);
}

int Multiply(void)
{
    int iValue = 25 * 5;
    printf("The multiplication result is %d.\n", iValue);
}

int main(void)
{
    /* Variable Declaration & Initialization */
    int iSum = 0;

    iSum = Sum(45, 55);
    Multiply();
    printf("The sum of the two numbers is %d.\n\n", iSum);

    return 0;
}
```

The output of the above program will be:
The multiplication result is 125.
The sum of the two numbers is 99.

11.3 FUNCTION VARIABLES: SCOPE AND LIFETIME

The scope and lifetime of a variable depends on its storage class **(refer section 2.9)**. The scope of a variable determines the parts of the program a variable is available for use. The variables can also be categorized depending on the place of their declaration. When a variable is declared within a function, it is referred as a **local variable**. This variable is available to be accessed and used only within the function in which it is declared. The lifetime of such a variable depends on the storage class specified for the variable. When a variable is declared outside every function, it has a global scope and is available to be accessed and used by every function within the source file *(the '.c' file in which it is declared)* of the program. Such a variable is called a **global variable** and the lifetime of such a variable is equal to the entire program lifetime.

11.3.1 AUTOMATIC VARIABLES

Automatic variables are the ones which are declared within a function and need to be created when a function is called. They are automatically destroyed when the function exits. All variables declared within a function and without any specified storage class are automatic variables. A variable may also be specified as automatic by specifying the **'auto'** keyword in front of its declaration. The *'auto'* keyword makes the storage class of the declared variable as automatic. Automatic variables are also referred as **local** or **internal** variables. Following are the examples of automatic variables:

```
int main(void)
{
    int iValue = 0;
    auto int iSum;
    char szName[100];
    double dblPrice;

    ........
    ........
}
```

The scope of automatic variables may further be limited to *code blocks* in which they are declared. Code blocks are group of statements defined within a set of braces. Consider the below example:

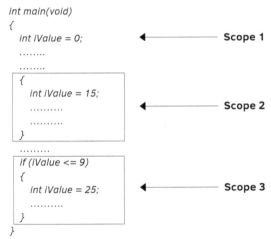

In the previous diagram, we can see that three variables with the same name *'iValue'* have been declared but in three different scopes. The variable in scope-1 has its lifetime for the entire **'main'** function. The second *'iValue'* has its lifetime only in scope-2. Similarly, the third *'iValue'* has its lifetime only in scope-3. The scope of a variable is determined by the innermost curly brace *(parenthesis)* pair enclosing the variable. Also, a scope-local variable has higher precedence. So, if we try to access *'iValue'* within scope-2, the *'iValue'* declared in scope-2 will be used rather than the one declared in scope-1. So, printing the value of the variable will print 15. But, the variable declared within scope-2 loses its existence once the control exits scope-2. So, the condition check *'if (iValue <= 9)'* will do the comparison based on the value of the variable declared in scope-1 which has its existence for the entire *'main'* function. But once the control enters the scope-3, the variable declared within scope-3 starts getting used. **If** we had **not** declared any variable with the same name *'iValue' (as declared in scope-1)* within scope-3 then, accessing *'iValue' (within scope-3)* would have meant using the variable declared in scope-1.

Prior to C99, all local variables must be declared at the start of the block *(scope)* within which it is declared. Starting from C99, a variable may be declared anywhere within a block, even at the point of its usage. Consider the below example:

```
int main(void)
{
    int iVal1 = 0;
    int iVal2 = 0;
    printf("Enter value 1: ");
    scanf("%d", &iVal1);
    printf("Enter value 2: ");
    scanf("%d", &iVal2);
    int iSum = iVal1 + iVal2;
    printf("Sum of the values is: %d.\n\n", iSum);
    return 0;
}
```

11.3.2 GLOBAL AND EXTERNAL VARIABLES

Variables that are defined outside every function have a lifetime equal to the entire program. These variables are alive during the entire program execution. Such variables are called **global variables**. Unlike local variables, global variables can be accessed by every function in the program.

```
int iValue;

void PrintValue(void)
{
    iValue++;
    printf("The value within PrintValue is %d.\n", iValue);
}

int main(void)
{
    iValue = 32;
    printf("The value within main is %d.\n", iValue);
    PrintValue();
    return 0;
}
```

In the above program, the variable *'iValue'* is a global variable and is available to both *'PrintValue'* and *'main'* functions. The output of the program will be:

The value within main is 32.
The value within PrintValue is 33.

The values stored in global variables can be accessed and changed by any function within the program. When a function changes a global variable's value, subsequent functions will start using the new value. So if there is uncontrolled usage of a global variable within a program, the correctness of the value stored within it cannot be guaranteed. This may lead to incorrect results. Due to this behavior, we should try to avoid using global variables as much as possible. For communication between functions, we should rely more on function arguments *(parameters)*. We should use global variables only in scenarios where a value is used by multiple functions and argument passing between them is not viable or possible. We must make sure that the value of this variable is modified in as few places as possible, though there are minimal or no risks involved for reading such a variable's value.

Global variables must be declared before they are used within a program. Within the source code file, if a function tries to access a global variable which has been declared below it, the compiler will raise an error. In other words a global variable is visible only from the point of its declaration to the end of the source code file. Consider the below example:

```
void PrintValue(void)
{
    iValue++;
    printf("The value within PrintValue is %d. \n", iValue);
}

int iValue;
int main(void)
{
    iValue = 32;
    printf("The value within main is %d. \n", iValue);
    PrintValue();
    return 0;
}
```

We have modified our previous program and moved the 'iValue' declaration from above the 'PrintValue' function to below it. For this change, our program will stop compiling. This is because when 'PrintValue' function accesses 'iValue', the variable 'iValue' is still undefined to the compiler. When the compiler starts compiling from top of the source file, it compiles the 'PrintValue' function before coming to the declaration of 'iValue'. As a result, at that stage, the variable 'iValue' is still unknown to the compiler.

Unlike local variables, global variables are automatically initialized to 0 *(zero)* by the compiler. Hence, we can start using the global variables without explicitly initializing them.

Now, let us understand the working of global variables using a small program. In the program we have two global variables 'g_dblRate' corresponding to the rate of an item and 'g_iQuantity' corresponding to its quantity. Given these two values, we will calculate total cost of the item.

```c
#include <stdio.h>

/* Global Variables */
double g_dblRate;
int    g_iQuantity;

double CalculateCost(void)
{
    return g_dblRate * g_iQuantity;
}

void SetRate(void)
{
    g_dblRate = 56.90;
}

void AddQuantity(int iQuantity)
{
    g_iQuantity += iQuantity;
}

int main(void)
{
    g_iQuantity = 50;
    SetRate();
    printf("Total cost of the item: %.02lf.\n", CalculateCost());

    AddQuantity(20);
    printf("Total cost after 20 additional quantities: %.02lf.\n", CalculateCost());

    return 0;
}
```

Before explaining *external variables*, let us discuss a bit about multi-file programs. Till now we have assumed that all our functions *(including main)* reside within a single source code file. But, this rarely happens in an actual project environment. On most occasions there will be multiple programmers working on a single project and each programmer will be in-charge of a single source code file. This helps in parallel development of the project, resulting into faster deliveries. All the source code files are compiled separately and then linked together to form a single executable program.

In a multi-file environment, we may need to share a variable within our program. A global variable declared in one source file *(say source1.c)* may need to be accessed or even modified in another source file *(say source2.c)*. But, there is one complexity in achieving this. When the source file 'source2.c' is compiled, the compiler does not find a declaration of the variable *(as the variable is declared in source1.c)* and thus, raises an error. To help compiler know that such a variable is declared in another source file, we use the keyword **'extern'**. *'extern'* is derived from the word *'external'* implying that the variable is declared external of the source file in which it is getting referenced. The variable is mentioned as *'extern'* in the source file in which it is referenced but not declared. When we mention the variable as *'extern'*, the compiler understands that there is a variable declared with that name and of the specified data type in some other source file. This variable will be evaluated for existence during link time rather than compilation time. Let us understand the working with a simple example. Suppose, we have two source files *'source1.c'* and *'source2.c'*. *'g_iCounter'* is a global variable declared in the file *'source1.c'*. Functions within *'source2.c'* also need access to this variable and thus, this variable is declared in *'source2.c'* using the keyword *'extern'* making the variable available to all the functions in the source file *'source2.c'*. If the variable is needed only in a few functions within *'source2.c'*, the *'extern'* declaration can be specified at the function level, within the functions requiring the use of the variable. So, we can have two possible ways of using the *'extern'* specifier within *'source2.c'*– at the global level and at the function level. Both these possibilities are shown in the below table.

Scenario	source1.c	source2.c

1	**int g_iCounter;**
	
	int main(void)
	{
	   ....
	   ....
	   return 0;
	}
	
	void func1(void)
	{
	   g_iCounter++;
	   ....
	   ....
	}
		extern int g_iCounter;
		
		void func2(void)
		{
		   g_iCounter++;
		   ....
		   ....
		}
		
		int func3(void)
		{
		   g_iCounter++;
		   ....
		   ....
		   return 1;
		}

2	**int g_iCounter;**
	
	int main(void)
	{
	   ....
	   ....
	   return 0;
	}
	
	void func1(void)
	{
	   g_iCounter++;
	   ....
	   ....
	}
		void func2(void)
		{
		   extern int g_iCounter;
		   g_iCounter++;
		   ....
		   ....
		}
		
		int func3(void)
		{
		   ....
		   ....
		   return 1;
		}

11.3.3 STATIC VARIABLES

Though we have discussed earlier *(section 11.2.4)* about **static** variables, we will look into them again a little more deeply. Continuing from where we left off in that para, the value of static variables persist till the end of the program. A variable is declared as static using the keyword '*static*':

> **static** *int iValue;*
> **static** *double dblValue;*
> **static** *char szName[100];*

A static variable may be declared locally or globally. When declared locally *(inside a function)*, the scope of the variable lies within the function and cannot be accessed outside it. But, when the function is called again, the value of the variable continues from where it was left off in the previous call to the function. The variable is declared and initialized only during the first call to the function. On all later calls to the function, the variable continues to exist and is not declared or initialized again. We could be using a static variable to count the number of calls made to the function *(possibly during recursion which we will discuss a little later)*. A global static variable is declared globally i.e. external to all the functions within a source file. That variable is available across all the functions. But, there is a catch. A global static variable is **only** available to the functions within the source file *('.c' file)* in which it is declared. It is not available to functions of other source files within the program. This is a major difference between a static global variable and a simple global variable.

We can also make a function as static. In such a case, the function becomes visible only to other functions within the same source file in which it is defined. That function cannot be accessed by functions in other source files within the program. We declare a function as static by using the keyword '*static*' in front of the function declaration as below:

> **static** int Func(void);

Now, let us illustrate the use of a static variable using a small program. In the below program, we will count the number of times a function gets called and print that count.

```c
#include <stdio.h>

void Func(void)
{
    static int s_iCallCount = 0;

    s_iCallCount++;
    printf("Func called %d times.\n", s_iCallCount);
}

int main(void)
{
    int iCounter = 0;

    for (; iCounter < 5; iCounter++)
        Func();

    printf("\n");
    return 0;
}
```

Output:
Func called 1 times.
Func called 2 times.
Func called 3 times.
Func called 4 times.
Func called 5 times.

The function 'Func' is called by the 'main' function 5 times and on each occassion, the function 'Func' increments the static counter 's_iCallCount' by 1. The variable gets declared and initialized during the first call to the function. On all subsequent calls, it does **not** get declared or initialized again. The function 'Func' then prints the call count. We have initialized the variable 's_iCallCount' with a value of 0 *(zero)*. One important thing to remember is that static variables *(like global variables)* are automatically initialized to 0 *(zero)*, if they are not explicitly initialized. We could have skipped the initialization of the variable 's_iCallCount' within our program, in which case it would have been implicitly initialized to 0.

11.3.4 REGISTER VARIABLES

In some processor intensive operations *(ex: doing several calculations within a time bound period)*, we cannot afford to store and retrieve the values of the variables from main memory to processor registers. Doing store and retrieve repeatedly may affect performance of the operation. In such cases, we may use **register** variables which as the name suggests are stored in the processor registers *(provided free register space is available)*. Register variables are *auto* by nature but are stored in registers instead of main memory. Register memory is much faster than main memory, and since all processing is done using these registers, storing the values in registers improves the performance. We should be careful when using register variables as register memory is very limited and varies between computer architectures. We should limit our usage to the minimum and must avoid using register variables wherever it is not a necessity. When using register variables, we must remember that availability of register space is not guaranteed and our variables may automatically be shifted to main memory if register memory is unavailable. We declare register variables within our functions as below:

register Data-Type Variable-Name;

Although, there is no limitation in C regarding the data type of variables that can be placed in registers, many C compilers restrict the data type to be of int and char. Register variables can only be declared within functions or code-blocks and cannot be global or external.

11.4 FUNCTIONS WITH POINTER ARGUMENTS

Functions can accept any type of valid data type as their arguments. They can accept simple variables, structures, unions, arrays and also pointers. Accepting pointers enables a C program to operate faster and also use less memory. This can be explained with a simple example. Assume, we have two functions *'func1'* and *'func2'*, where *'func1'* calls *'func2'*. The program has a structure called *'MyStruct'* which is passed as argument to *'func2'*. So, we may code the two functions in any of the two ways stated in the next table:

Method 1	Method 2

void func2(**struct MyStruct arg**)
{
  ……..
  ……..
}
 	
void func1(void)
{
  struct MyStruct ms;
  ……..
  ……..
  func2(ms);
}
	void func2(**const struct MyStruct *pArg**)
	{
	  ……..
	  ……..
	}
	
	void func1(void)
	{
	  struct MyStruct ms;
	  ……..
	  ……..
	  func2(&ms);
	}

In the first method we are declaring a variable 'ms' of type 'MyStruct'. We are passing the structure variable as an argument to the call to 'func2'. In 'func2', we declare another variable 'arg' of type 'MyStruct' as the formal parameter or argument. Now when we pass the actual argument 'ms' in the function call to 'func2', the contents of the variable 'ms' are assigned to the formal argument 'arg'. So, what we have is an assignment of the values of 'ms' to the variable 'arg'. **Remember:** *These two variables are completely separate variables and changes to one will not affect the others' values.* Hence in method-1, we have two separate structure variables and the value of one gets assigned to the other.

In the second method we have a little variation. The function 'func2' instead of declaring a structure variable, declares a pointer 'pArg' of type 'MyStruct'. The function 'func1' calls 'func2' with the address of the variable 'ms' as the actual argument. So instead of the contents of 'ms' getting passed to 'func2', the address of 'ms' gets assigned to the pointer 'pArg' of the function 'func2'. This makes 'pArg' point to the same memory location of the variable 'ms'. In method-2, rather than two separate variables containing the same values, we have one variable 'ms' in function 'func1', and a pointer 'pArg' in 'func2' pointing to this variable's location. So in case of method-2, we not only save the time required for assigning an entire structure content to another, but also we save memory space as we do not have separate structure variables but just a pointer to the same memory location.

It should be noted that we have made the 'pArg' pointer in method-2 as constant *(using the const keyword)*. If we had not done so, any changes made to the structure variable in 'func2' using the pointer 'pArg' would have affected the value contained in 'ms' of function 'func1'. This is because 'pArg' is pointing to the same memory location as 'ms' and any changes done using 'pArg' would have affected the contents of 'ms'. *Making 'pArg'* **const** *prevents function 'func2' from making any changes to the values of the structure.*

Whether we should pass the value or the address of a variable to another function depends on the requirements of the program and must be judged on a case by case basis. Generally for simple data-type variables, we pass their values if we do not want or require the called function to make any changes to the variable's values. If the called function needs to make changes to the values contained in the actual arguments, we pass their addresses. For data-types such as structures, we generally pass their addresses to improve the calling efficiency. If we do not want the called function to be making any changes to the values, we mark the formal parameters as **const**.

In our next program, apart from *'main'*, we will have two more functions. One function will accept two numbers and another will print the numbers.

The first function *'AcceptNumbers'* will accept the address of two integer variables. *'AcceptNumbers'* will declare two integer pointers as its formal parameters. The caller *(main)* function will pass the address of two integer variables when calling *'AcceptNumbers'*. The parameters *'px'* and *'py'* *(in AcceptNumbers)* are declared as pointers which are assigned the addresses of the two variables *'x'* and *'y'* respectively, when the function call is made. We pass these same addresses to *'scanf'*, and *'scanf'* fills these memory locations with the values accepted from the user. So in effect, the values are stored in the variables *'x'* and *'y'* belonging to the function *'main'*.

We now pass the values in *'x'* and *'y'* to the function *'PrintValues'*. *'PrintValues'* declares two integer variables *'argX'* and *'argY'* which are assigned the values of *'x'* and *'y'* respectively. Note that, changing the values of *'argX'* and *'argY'* within *'PrintValues'* will have no effect on the values contained in *'x'* and *'y'* within the *'main'* function. This is because we have only assigned the values of *'x'* and *'y'* to *'argX'* and *'argY'* respectively, and not their addresses. So, *'argX'* and *'argY'* only get a copy of the values contained in *'x'* and *'y'*.

After printing the two numbers, *'PrintNumbers'* adds the numbers and returns their sum as an integer *(int)*. The *'main'* function accepts the sum of the two numbers *(returned by 'PrintNumbers')* in the variable *'iSum'* and prints its value.

```c
#include <stdio.h>

void AcceptNumbers(int *px,
                   int *py)
{
    /* Check if the caller function has sent us valid addresses. */
    if (px == NULL || py == NULL)
    {
        return;
    }

    printf("Enter the first value: ");
    scanf("%d", px);

    printf("Enter the second value: ");
    scanf("%d", py);
}

int PrintNumbers(int argX,
                 int argY)
{
    printf("\nThe two numbers are %d and %d.", argX, argY);
    return (argX + argY);
}
```

```
int main(void)
{
    /* Variable Declaration & Initialization */
    int x    = 0;
    int y    = 0;
    int iSum = 0;

    AcceptNumbers(&x, &y);
    iSum = PrintNumbers(x, y);
    printf("\nThe sum of the two numbers is %d.\n\n", iSum);

    return 0;
}
```

11.4.1 FUNCTION POINTER AS ARGUMENT

Just like any variable, a function also has a specific address of its own. This is the starting address of the location where the function's binary code is loaded in memory for execution. Similar to a variable, we can pass the address of a function to another function. Within the called function we declare a pointer as the formal argument, which accepts the address of the function. This helps in scenarios where we want the called function to call another function *(say func3)* for further processing. The other function that needs to be called varies depending on the logic. We will explain this with a simple program.

```
#include <stdio.h>

/* Define a function type pointer and give it a name. */
typedef double (*PFNCALCROUTINE)(double, double);


/* Function for adding to numbers. */
double sum(double x, double y)
{
    return x + y;
}

/* Function to find the difference between two numbers. */
double subtract(double x, double y)
{
    return x - y;
}

/* Function to find the product of two numbers. */
double multiply(double x, double y)
{
    return x * y;
}

/* Function to divide one number by another. */
double divide(double x, double y)
{
    return x / y;
}

/* The intermediary function which calls any function which accepts two arguments
   of type double and returns a double value. It calls the function pointed by
   the function pointer 'pfn' with the arguments 'x' and 'y'. 'Calculate' returns
   the same value returned by the function pointed by 'pfn'. */
```

```
double Calculate(double       x,
                 double       y,
                 PFNCALCROUTINE pfn)
{
    if (pfn)
        return pfn(x, y);
    return 0;
}

int main(void)
{
    double dblNum1 = 0;
    double dblNum2 = 0;

    printf("Enter the first number: ");
    scanf("%lf", &dblNum1);

    printf("Enter the second number: ");
    scanf("%lf", &dblNum2);

    /* Call the function 'Calculate' with the appropriate function pointer. 'Calculate'
       will call the function using the provided function pointer. */
    printf("\nThe sum of the numbers is %lf.", Calculate(dblNum1, dblNum2, &sum));
    printf("\nThe difference of the numbers is %lf.", Calculate(dblNum1, dblNum2, &subtract));
    printf("\nThe product of the numbers is %lf.", Calculate(dblNum1, dblNum2, &multiply));
    printf("\nThe division of the numbers is %lf.\n\n", Calculate(dblNum1, dblNum2, &divide));

    return 0;
}
```

In our above program we are telling the compiler that we will have functions which will accept two arguments of type *'double'*. Such functions will also return a value of type *'double'*. We are type defining pointers of such function types as *'PFNCALCROUTINE'*. We are defining four worker functions *'sum'*, *'subtract'*, *'multiply'* and *'divide'* which perform the actual operations *(calculations in this case)*. The function *'Calculate'* is an intermediary function which is responsible for calling these worker functions and getting the job done by them. Whatever is returned by the worker function is in turn returned by *'Calculate'*. Within the function *'main'*, we are actually calling the function *'Calculate'* and passing it the address of the worker function which is responsible for performing the actual calculation. *'Calculate'* in turn calls the function pointed by the function pointer *'pfn'*.

11.5 FUNCTIONS WITH ARRAY ARGUMENTS

Till now we have discussed passing single valued arguments to functions. If we have array arguments to pass to another function, we may pass the address of the starting location of the arrays. The called function then works directly on the memory location of the array. If we do not want the called function to be making changes to the array, we mark the formal parameter of the called function as **'const'**.

The called function works using the pointer to the starting location of the array, but, how does it know the size of the array? If it does not know the size of the array, it may easily overshoot the array index or try to access an element which does not exist. We can prevent this using two mechanisms. In the first mechanism, the called function may always accept a fixed size array by declaring a pointer to the entire array *(refer section 'Pointer to an array' of section 8.4)*. This will prevent any caller function from passing an array of a different size other than the one specified as the formal argument of the called function. In the second mechanism, we could pass the address to the first element of the array i.e. the starting location of the array. We also pass another argument with the array size *(number of elements in the array)*. This will make the called function work according to the count of elements in the array. Consider the below example explaining the two mechanisms.

```c
#include <stdio.h>

#define MAX_ELEMENTS    10

void AcceptNumbers(int *prgValues,
                   int  iNumElements)
{
    int iCounter = 0;

    if (!prgValues)
    {
        return;
    }

    for (; iCounter < iNumElements; iCounter++)
    {
        printf("Enter the number: ");
        scanf("%d", &prgValues[iCounter]);
    }
}

void PrintNumbers(const int *prgValues,
                  int        iNumElements)
{
    int iCounter = 0;

    if (!prgValues)
    {
        return;
    }

    printf("\nThe numbers are: ");
    for (; iCounter < iNumElements; iCounter++)
    {
        printf("%d", prgValues[iCounter]);
        if ((iCounter + 1) != iNumElements)
            printf(", ");   /* We do not want a comma after the last number. */
    }
}

double FindAverage(const int (*prgValues)[MAX_ELEMENTS])
{
    int iCounter = 0;
    int iSum     = 0;

    if (!prgValues)
    {
        return 0;
    }

    for (; iCounter < MAX_ELEMENTS; iCounter++)
    {
        iSum += (*prgValues)[iCounter];
    }

    return (double)iSum / MAX_ELEMENTS;
```

```
}

int main(void)
{
    int irgValues[MAX_ELEMENTS] = { 0 };

    AcceptNumbers(irgValues, MAX_ELEMENTS);
    PrintNumbers(irgValues, MAX_ELEMENTS);
    printf("\n\nThe average of the numbers is %.02lf.\n\n", FindAverage(&irgValues));

    return 0;
}
```

In the pointer *'prgValues'*, the function *'AcceptNumbers'* accepts the address of the starting location of the array. It also accepts the element count of the array. The function fills the elements of the array with the values accepted from the user. The number of values accepted depends on the element count of the array which it received from the caller in *'iNumElements'*. If we are building functions which are flexible and are **not** targeted towards arrays with some specific number of elements, we need the functions to behave like this. The arguments of function *'PrintNumbers'* are very similar to *'AcceptNumbers'* except that we are declaring the pointer to be of type **'const'**. This prevents the function from making any changes to the element values.

The function *'FindAverage'* is a little different in its prototype or declaration. Rather than declaring a pointer to the first element of the array as argument, it declares a pointer to the entire array. This enables it to specify the number of elements *(MAX_ELEMENTS in our case)* it expects within the array. So, any caller function trying to specify an array of a different size *(other than MAX_ELEMENTS)* will generate a compilation error. This makes the function targeted specifically for arrays with MAX_ELEMENTS number of elements and saves ourselves from specifying the element count as a separate parameter to the function.

11.6 FORWARD DECLARATION OF FUNCTIONS

When a source file is compiled by the compiler, every function prototype *(signature)* i.e. its name, arguments and return type is added to its function dictionary. The compiler compiles the program from top to bottom and proceeds downwards by adding each function signature to the dictionary. When it encounters a function call, it searches its dictionary for the function signature and if it finds one, it continues compiling. If it does not find the required function signature, it raises an error and may stop the compilation. So if in our source file, we have a function call specified before the function's definition, the compiler *(mainly single-pass compilers)* will fail to find the function signature in its dictionary and will raise an error. We may encounter situations where it becomes necessary to define a function a little later. For such situations, we may take the help of forward declarations. In forward declarations, we specify the function prototype or signature of a function before the first call to the function is made within the source file. The definition or body of the function may come later within the source file. When this is done, the compiler understands that the function is defined somewhere else within the program and adds the signature to its dictionary. The check for the function definition is postponed to link time. Hence, calls to the function before its definition will not raise an error. The function prototype is specified as:

Return-Data-Type Function_Name(List of arguments);

Let us understand this with a very simple example:

```c
#include <stdio.h>

/* Forward Declaration. The call to the 'StandardDeviation' function
   is made before the function is defined. When the compiler encounters
   the call (in the function 'main'), it still does not have the function
   signature in its function list. This lets the compiler know what the
   function accepts as arguments and what it is supposed to return. */
double StandardDeviation(const int *, int);

int main(void)
{
    int irgValues[10] = { 78, 26, 8, 17, 190, 3, 710, 62, 10, 82 };

    printf("Standard Deviation of the numbers is %lf.\n\n",
            StandardDeviation(irgValues, 10));

    return 0;
}

double StandardDeviation(const int *prgValues,
                                int  iNumElements)
{
    int    iCounter     = 0;
    double dblSum       = 0;
    double dblMean      = 0;
    double dblDiff      = 0;
    double dblVariance = 0;

    if (!prgValues || iNumElements <= 1)
    {
        return 0;
    }

    /* Find the sum of all the numbers. */
    for (; iCounter < iNumElements; iCounter++)
    {
        dblSum += prgValues[iCounter];
    }

    /* Now, find the mean. */
    dblMean = dblSum / iNumElements;

    /* Find the sum of the squared deviation from the mean. */
    for (iCounter = 0; iCounter < iNumElements; iCounter++)
    {
        dblDiff = prgValues[iCounter] – dblMean;
        dblVariance = dblVariance + dblDiff * dblDiff;
    }

    /* The variance... */
    dblVariance = dblVariance / (iNumElements – 1);

    /* Return the standard deviation. */
    return sqrt(dblVariance);
}
```

In the above program, we are finding the sample standard deviation of an array of 10 numbers. We have defined the 'StandardDeviation' function after the function 'main' where the call to the 'StandardDeviation' function is made. So, we have specified the signature of the function 'StandardDeviation' prior to the function 'main' to let the compiler add the function signature to its dictionary before the call to the function is made within the 'main' function. The sample standard deviation of a group of numbers $(x_1, x_2, x_3, ..., x_n)$ is given as:

$$S.D = \sqrt{\frac{\sum_{i=1}^{n} (x_i - \bar{x})^2}{n-1}}$$

where, $\bar{x}$ is the mean of all the numbers. We first find the mean of all the numbers. Next, we find the square of the difference of each number from the mean. We also find the summation of all these squares and divide the summation by '$n - 1$'. What we now have is the variance, and the square root of the variance is the standard deviation.

11.7 VARIABLE NUMBER OF ARGUMENTS

We have extensively used the C standard function 'printf', which accepts variable number of arguments. If we want a similar function of our own which accepts an indeterminate number of arguments, how do we achieve it? Assume we define a function which accepts any number of integer values and returns the average of the values. We can achieve this using a function which accepts variable number of arguments. Variable number of arguments is denoted by the use of ellipse (given as '...'). The ellipse must be the last argument of the function and the function must have at-least one argument preceding the ellipse.

We can read the arguments using a set of macros ('va_start', 'va_arg' and 'va_end'). A macro is a fragment of code specified using the '#define' statement, which has been given a name. Wherever the name is used, it is replaced by the contents of the macro following the defined name. Consider the below macro:

```
#define ARRAY_SIZE(x)    sizeof(x)/sizeof(x[0])
```

The above macro calculates the number of elements in an array. We call the macro with an array name as below:

```
int rgValues[10] = { 0 };
int iNumElements = ARRAY_SIZE(rgValues);
```

The macro divides the total size of the array by the size of the first element of the array returning the number of elements in the array. Wherever the macro name is specified, it is replaced by the code following the macro name (i.e. 'sizeof(x)/sizeof(x[0])'), where 'x' is replaced by the value or variable specified in the macro call ('rgValues' in our case).

The three macros 'va_start', 'va_arg' and 'va_end' have the following signatures:
void **va_start**(va_list arg_ptr, prev_param);
type **va_arg**(va_list arg_ptr, type);
void **va_end**(va_list arg_ptr);

where 'va_list' is a character pointer which is made to point to the next argument in the variable list. 'va_start' initializes the 'arg_ptr' to point to the first argument in the variable number of argument list. 'va_arg' makes 'arg_ptr' point to the next argument in the variable number of argument list. It also returns the current argument pointed by 'arg_ptr' after formatting it to the data type specified as the second argument to the macro. 'va_end' must be specified after we have completed processing our variable arguments list.

The prototype or signature of a function which accepts variable number of arguments is as below:

Return-Data-Type function_name(Fixed Arguments, ...);

Now, let us understand the use of variable number of arguments using a small program. We will write a function which accepts an indeterminate number of integer values. These values are specified after an argument *'iArgCount'*. *'iArgCount'* specifies the count of the variable number of arguments specified in the call to the function. The function finds the average of all the specified values.

```c
#include <stdio.h>
#include <stdarg.h>

double FindAverage(int iArgCount, …)
{
    va_list valist = NULL;
    double  dblSum = 0;
    int     idx    = 0;

    /* Initializes 'valist' to have the first optional argument specified
       after 'iArgCount'. As the second argument, we pass the preceding
       argument to the ellipse to our function. */
    va_start(valist, iArgCount);

    /* Access all the variable number of arguments one at a time. */
    for (idx = 0; idx < iArgCount; idx++)
    {
        /* After the call, 'valist' is set to the next argument in the
           list. 'va_arg' returns the current content in 'valist' formatted
           to the data-type specified in the second argument. */
        dblSum += va_arg(valist, int);
    }

    /* Clean memory reserved for 'valist'. */
    va_end(valist);

    return dblSum / iArgCount;
}

int main(void)
{
    /* The first argument '5' to 'FindAverage' is the count of the variable
       number of arguments following this argument. */
    printf("The average of the numbers is %lf.\n\n",
            FindAverage(5, 2, 4, 6, 8, 10));

    return 0;
}
```

We are including the header file *'stdarg.h'* as the macros *'va_start'*, *'va_arg'* and *'va_end'* are defined in this header file.

11.8 RECURSION

Think about a group of statements that needs repeated execution. The first thing that comes to our mind is to use looping constructs. What if, the group of statements almost spans the entire function. For such situations, we may use *recursion* where a function calls itself.

When a function calls itself, the new instance of the function executes in a manner as if a fresh new call is made to the function. This means that all the non-static variables of the function start afresh for the *new call* and are again re-declared and re-initialized for **that** call instance. The previous call instance *(which made the new call)* continues carrying its own set of variable values. In simple terms, each called instance of the function carries its own set of variable values distinct from the other instances. Each called instance starts executing from the first statement of the function. A simple example of recursion is given here under:

```c
#include <stdio.h>

#define TRIANGLE_HEIGHT    10

void RightTriangle(int iMaxStars)
{
    /* For every called instance of the function, we have a separate value of iCounter */
    int iCounter = 0;

    /* Print the stars up to a count of iMaxStars.
       In this function, we are printing our line first before asking the next
       call to the function to print the next line. So, 1 star is printed first,
       followed by the line with 2 stars, then the line with the 3 stars and so
       on. The line with 10 stars is printed last, giving us an impression of a
       right-angled triangle. */
    for (; iCounter < iMaxStars; iCounter++)
    {
        printf("*");
    }

    /* Make the next set of stars come in the next line. */
    printf("\n");

    /* After printing the 10th line of stars, we stop calling the function again.
       This is the exit criteria which makes the recursion stop and the function
       instances start exiting with the last function instance stopping/exiting
       first followed by the previous-last and so on. */
    if (iMaxStars < TRIANGLE_HEIGHT)
        RightTriangle(iMaxStars + 1);
}

void InvertedRightTriangle(int iMaxStars)
{
    int iCounter = 0;

    /* Before printing our own line, we ask the next function instance to draw
       its line. That instance again does the same. This continues until we are
       at the instance which needs to draw the longest line with 10 stars. We
       do not call further and print our line with 10 stars. We then print a
```

```
      newline and then exit this instance. For the previous instance, the
      recursive call to 'InvertedRightTriangle' ends and it prints its own line
      with 9 stars. It too prints a newline and exits. This continues till the
      first instance has printed its line with 1 star and exits. So, in this
      mechanism, the last instance prints its line first, followed by the
      previous-last and so on. The first instance prints its line the last. */
    if (iMaxStars < TRIANGLE_HEIGHT)
        InvertedRightTriangle(iMaxStars + 1);

    for (; iCounter < iMaxStars; iCounter++)
    {
        printf("*");
    }

    printf("\n");
}

int main(void)
{
    RightTriangle(1);
    InvertedRightTriangle(1);

    return 0;
}
```

The output of the above program will be:

```
*
**
***
****
*****
******
*******
********
*********
**********
**********
*********
********
*******
******
*****
****
***
**
*
```

It is important to remember that recursion operates in LIFO mechanism i.e. Last In First Out. This means that the function instance which was invoked the last, is the first one to complete its execution *(end)*. The first instance to be invoked is the last one to end.

Recursion is used to solve problems where we need to apply the same solution successively to subsets of the same problem. This means the bigger problem is broken up into multiple subsets with each subset being a similar representation of the bigger problem. When writing a recursive function we need to be careful in placing a proper *exit criteria* which effectively ends the recursion. If we miss the exit criteria, the recursion will continue indefinitely until we run out of memory. We should also be careful regarding the positioning and correctness of the exit criteria, without which we will generate incorrect results. *Exit criteria* determines the moment when we stop calling ourselves further, which effectively starts the end of the recursion. If the exit criteria is not met, the recursion continues. The recursion starts wrapping up when the exit criteria is hit. In our above program the condition check *'if (iMaxStars < TRIANGLE_HEIGHT)'* acts as the exit criteria. If the condition is fulfilled we continue the recursion, and we stop when the condition is not met. We may also call it the *recursion criteria*, as we continue the recursion depending on the condition being met.

Look carefully at the positioning of the *recursion criteria* in our above program. The *recursion criteria* is placed differently in the functions *'RightTriangle'* and *'InvertedRightTriangle'*. This makes the two functions behave differently, where the former generates an upside right-angled triangle and the latter generates a downward right-angled triangle. The function *'RightTriangle'* draws its own line first and then calls itself recursively. This makes the line with 1-star being drawn first, followed by line with 2-stars and so on. The function *'InvertedRightTriangle'* calls itself recursively before drawing its own line. This makes the last called instance to draw its line with 10-stars first, followed by the call which draws the line with 9-stars and so on.

Recursion can be of two types: *Direct recursion* and *indirect recursion*. Our above program is an example of direct recursion where the function directly calls itself. In case of indirect recursion, the function calls another function which in turn calls this function. As for example, *function f1* calls *function f2* which in turn calls the *function f1,* and this continues recursively. Indirect recursion is also called *mutual recursion,* as two or more functions are calling each other creating a recursive behavior.

11.9 INLINE FUNCTIONS

Every function call involves some processing and memory overheads. In a time critical operation, saving such overheads may help achieve better performance. C99 introduced a new type of function which may be considered as a combination of a function and a macro. These functions are qualified using the keyword '**inline**'. The general format of such a function is:

     inline Return-Data-Type **function-Name(***Comma separated argument list***)**

     {

        FUNCTION BODY

     }

The inline keyword instructs the compiler to insert the function code at the location of each function call. Every call to the inline function is replaced by the body of the function itself, and thus saving the overhead of a function call. Though an inline function reduces function call overhead, it suffers from many disadvantages:

- It increases program size and wastes memory space. As every call to the function is replaced by the function body itself, the compiled program size increases, because the same piece of code gets copied to multiple locations.
- The inline function's body becomes exposed to the caller functions.

- Using inline function increases the compilation time of the program as the function body is copied to multiple function call locations.
- inline functions increase the caller function's stack size. If we have a large inline function, the memory requirement of all its caller functions will increase tremendously.

inline functions should be used on a case by case basis. Also, it is preferable to limit the size of inline functions to few lines only.

11.10 COMPOUND LITERALS AS FUNCTION ARGUMENTS

We learned about compound literals in the chapters on *'arrays'* and *'structures and unions'*. We can pass compound literals as arguments to functions in the same way as we do with other variables. Assume we have a structure and four functions with the following declarations:

```
typedef struct _POINT
{
    int x;
    int y;

} POINT;

void Function1(POINT *pPoint);
void Function2(struct _POINT Point);
void Function3(int *prgVals);
void Function4(int rgVals[3]);
```

We may call the above functions in the following ways:
```
Function1(&(struct _POINT) { 50, 25 });
Function2((POINT) {10, 20});
Function3((int[4]) { 5, 9, 4, 2 });
Function4((int[3]) { 2, 1, 9 });
```

11.11 NON RETURNING FUNCTIONS

When a function completes its execution, the control returns back to the function's point of invocation *(call)* i.e. to the caller function. The next statement to be executed will be the one following the function call within the caller function. Starting from C11, we may declare a function to be non returning using the '**_Noreturn**' function specifier. Making a function non returning informs the compiler that the control will not return back to the function's point of invocation. A compiler may raise an error if such a function tries to return the control back to the caller function. An example of such a function is:

```
_Noreturn void Stop(int i)
{
    exit(i);
}

int main(void)
{
    printf("Stopping now...\n");
    Stop(2);
    printf("This statement will never get printed.\n");
    return 0;
}
```

11.12 SAMPLE PROGRAMS

1. Our next program will print a geometric progression. We will accept the starting number for the sequence and the common ratio. We will print a maximum of 10 numbers in the sequence.

    We are using recursion where the function *'PrintGP'* is calling itself to get the next number in sequence printed. The recursion continues until we have printed all the 10 numbers. The exit condition of the recursion is whether we have reached the 10 numbers, upon which we start coming out of the recursion. We have declared a global variable *'g_iNumCount'* which keeps a count of the numbers we have printed.

```c
/* Header Files */
#include <stdio.h>

/* Defined Values */
#define MAX_NUMBERS 10

/* Global variables */
int g_iNumCount;

void PrintGP(long int iCurNum, int iCommonRatio)
{
    /* Variable Declaration & Initialization */
    long int iNextNum = 0;

    /* Print the current number in sequence. */
    printf("%d ", iCurNum);
    g_iNumCount++;

    /* Have we already printed all the numbers. If so, do not
       print any more and start coming out of the recursion. */
    if (g_iNumCount < MAX_NUMBERS)
    {
        /* Find the next number in sequence and ask the next
           recursive call to 'PrintGP' to print that number. */
        iNextNum = iCurNum * iCommonRatio;
        PrintGP(iNextNum, iCommonRatio);
    }
}

int main(void)
{
    /* Variable Declaration & Initialization */
    int iStartNum    = 0;
    int iCommonRatio = 0;

    printf("Enter the starting number for the geometric sequence: ");
    scanf("%d", &iStartNum);

GETCOMMONRATIO:
    /* Refrain from giving a large number as we may overflow.
       To save ourselves from overflowing, we may have to provide
       checks on the value of common ratio and also use Int64. */
    printf("Enter the common ratio: ");
    scanf("%d", &iCommonRatio);
```

```
    if (iCommonRatio <= 0)
    {
        goto GETCOMMONRATIO;
    }

    g_iNumCount = 0;

    printf("\n\nThe Geometric sequence is:\n");
    PrintGP(iStartNum, iCommonRatio);
    printf("\n\n");

    return 0;
}
```

2. In our next program we will touch on the subject of compound interest for bank deposits. Compound interest is that interest which is added back to the principal sum so that the interest is earned on that added interest during the next compounding period. The shorter the compounding period the higher will be the maturity amount.

   Compounding frequency is the frequency at which the interest is calculated *(ex. every month, every quarter, every twelve months)*. A monthly compounding *(compound frequency of 12)* will earn a higher maturity amount than a half-yearly compounding *(compound frequency of 2)*, as the interest on interest is calculated much more frequently.

   The formula for calculating maturity amount based on compound interest is:
   $$A = P * (1 + r / n)^{(n * t)}$$
   Where:
   $A \rightarrow$ *The amount receivable including interest after the maturity period.*
   $P \rightarrow$ *The principal investment amount (the initial deposit).*
   $r \rightarrow$ *The annual rate of interest.*
   $n \rightarrow$ *The number of times the interest is compounded per year.*
   $t \rightarrow$ *The period of interest.*

   The amount of interest earned is calculated as 'I = A - P'.
   In the program we will accept the principal investment amount, annual rate of interest, compounding frequency and the period of investment. We will then calculate the total maturity amount and the total interest earned.

```c
#include <stdio.h>

/* Structure Definition */
typedef struct _CMPDINT
{
    double dblPrincipal;
    float  fltInterestRate;
    int    iCompoundFrequency;
    float  fltPeriod;
    double dblMaturityAmount;

}CMPDINT;
```

```c
CMPDINT GetValues(void)
{
    /* Variable Declaration & Initialization */
    CMPDINT cmpdint = { 0 };

    printf("Enter the principal investment amount: ");
    scanf("%lf", &cmpdint.dblPrincipal);

    printf("Enter the annual rate of interest: ");
    scanf("%f", &cmpdint.fltInterestRate);

    while (cmpdint.iCompoundFrequency > 12 || cmpdint.iCompoundFrequency < 1)
    {
        printf("Enter the compound frequency (1 - 12): ");
        scanf("%d", &cmpdint.iCompoundFrequency);
    }

    printf("Enter the period of interest (in years): ");
    scanf("%f", &cmpdint.fltPeriod);

    return cmpdint;
}

void CalculateMaturity(CMPDINT *pcmpdint)
{
    /* Variable Declaration & Initialization */
    double dblRate   = 0;
    double dblPeriod = 0;

    if (pcmpdint)
    {
        /* fltInterestRate is in percentage. Convert to decimals. */
        dblRate = (double) pcmpdint->fltInterestRate / 100;

        dblRate   = 1 + (dblRate / pcmpdint->iCompoundFrequency);
        dblPeriod = pcmpdint->iCompoundFrequency * (double) pcmpdint->fltPeriod;

        pcmpdint->dblMaturityAmount = pcmpdint->dblPrincipal * pow(dblRate, dblPeriod);
    }
}

int main(void)
{
    /* Variable Declaration & Initialization */
    CMPDINT cmpdint = { 0 };

    cmpdint = GetValues();
    CalculateMaturity(&cmpdint);

    printf("\nThe maturity value is %lf and the total interest if %lf.\n\n",
            cmpdint.dblMaturityAmount, cmpdint.dblMaturityAmount - cmpdint.dblPrincipal);

    return 0;
}
```

3. In our next program we will try to find whether a given number is a Narcissistic number. A Narcissistic number is a number that is equal to the sum of each of its digits raised to the power of the number of digits in the number. For example: '$153 = 1^3 + 5^3 + 3^3$, is a Narcissistic number.

```c
/* Header Files */
#include <stdio.h>

/* Function which counts the number of digits in a number. */
int CountDigits(int iNumber)
{
    /* Variable Declaration & Initialization */
    int iNumDigits = 0;

    while (iNumber > 0)
    {
        iNumber = iNumber / 10;
        iNumDigits++;
    }

    return iNumDigits;
}

/* Function which determines if a number is Narcissistic or not. */
int IsNarcissistic(int iNumber)
{
    /* Variable Declaration & Initialization */
    int iNumDigits    = 0;
    int iModulus      = 0;
    int iSum          = 0;
    int iTemp         = iNumber;
    int fNarcissistic = 0;

    /* Count the number of digits in the number. */
    iNumDigits = CountDigits(iNumber);

    /* Calculate through all the digits of the number. */
    while (iTemp > 0)
    {
        iModulus = iTemp % 10;
        iTemp    = iTemp / 10;

        iSum = iSum + (int) pow(iModulus, iNumDigits);
    }

    if (iSum == iNumber)
    {
        fNarcissistic = 1;
    }

    return fNarcissistic;
}

int main(void)
{
    /* Variable Declaration & Initialization */
    int iNumber = 0;

    printf("Enter the number to check: ");
    scanf("%d", &iNumber);

    if (0 != IsNarcissistic(iNumber))
    {
        printf("\nThe number %d is a Narcissistic number.\n\n",
                iNumber);
    }
```

```
    else
    {
        printf("\nThe number %d is not a Narcissistic number.\n\n",
                iNumber);
    }

    return 0;
}
```

4. The **Tower of Hanoi** *(also called the Tower of Brahma or Lucas Tower)* is a mathematical puzzle. It consists of three pegs and a number of disks of different sizes, which can slide onto any of the pegs. The puzzle starts with the disks in ascending order of size stacked on one peg with the smallest at the top, thus creating a conical shape.

    The objective of the puzzle is to move the entire stack to another peg, obeying the following rules:
    - Only one disk can be moved at a time.
    - In each move we can take the topmost disk from one of the stacks and place it on top of another stack.
    - No disk may be placed on top of a smaller disk.

    Assume we label the pegs as *'PegA'*, *'PegB'* and *'PegC'*, and we have *'n'* disks stacked on *'PegA'* with *'1'* being the smallest and *'n'* being the largest disk. We want to move the disks from *'PegA'* to *'PegC'* by using *'PegB'* as an intermediary/auxiliary peg.

    We break down the problem into smaller sub-problems and solve the sub-problems individually. This makes the larger problem getting solved automatically. If we work with just 3 disks, what will we do? We will do the following 7 steps:
    1. Transfer the smallest disk *'1'* from *'PegA'* to *'PegC'*.
    2. Transfer the disk *'2'* from *'PegA'* to *'PegB'*.
    3. Transfer the disk *'1'* from *'PegC'* to *'PegB'*.
    4. Transfer the disk *'3'* from *'PegA'* to *'PegC'*.
    5. Transfer the disk *'1'* from *'PegB'* to *'PegA'*.
    6. Transfer the disk *'2'* from *'PegB'* to *'PegC'*.
    7. Transfer the disk *'1'* from *'PegA'* to *'PegC'*.

    For a total of 'n' disks, there will be a minimum of (2^n - 1) transfers required to achieve the result.

    For every disk *'m'*, the general mechanism for solving the problem is:
    1. Move *(m − 1)* disks from source to auxiliary, by the same general solving procedure.
    2. Move the disk *'m'* from the source to the target peg.
    3. Move the *(m − 1)* disks that we have just placed on the auxiliary, from the auxiliary to the target peg by the same general solving procedure.

When working with m^{th} disk, the above three steps are repeated recursively for each of the disks till '$m - 1$', starting from the smallest disk to the largest.

Now let us implement a Tower of Hanoi using three structure variables. Each structure variable will be a logical or computer representation of a single peg in the Tower of Hanoi. The structure on which these variables will be based will have three members:

1. The first member will be a string which will identify the structure variable to the peg in the Tower of Hanoi. This will be done using a name assigned to it (ex: PegA, PegB).
2. The second member will be an array of integers which will hold the values aka. disks stacked on that peg. The larger the number the bigger the disk size. So as per the rules, the numbers will appear in descending order within the array.
3. The third member will hold the number of values aka. disks currently stored on the peg represented by this structure variable.

Notice that during the first recursive call, the current auxiliary peg becomes the target. In the second recursive call, the current auxiliary becomes the source.

```c
#include <stdio.h>

/* Defined Values */
#define MAX_DISKS    4

/* Structure Definition and global variables */
struct HanoiPeg
{
    char szName[20];
    int  rgiDisks[MAX_DISKS];
    int  iCurNum;
}
g_Src    = { "PegA", { 0 }, 0 },
g_Aux    = { "PegB", { 0 }, 0 },
g_Target = { "PegC", { 0 }, 0 };

void TowerOfHanoi(int                  n,
                  struct HanoiPeg *pSrc,
                  struct HanoiPeg *pTarget,
                  struct HanoiPeg *pAux)
{
    /* Variable Declaration & Initialization */
    int idx = 0;

    if (n > 0)
    {
        /* Move all smaller disks from source to auxillary
           and then from auxillary to target. */
        TowerOfHanoi(n - 1, pSrc, pAux, pTarget);

        pSrc->rgiDisks[--pSrc->iCurNum]       = 0;
        pTarget->rgiDisks[pTarget->iCurNum++] = n;

        /* Print our progress. */
        printf("\n#############################################");

        printf("\nMoving disk %d from %s to %s", n, pSrc->szName, pTarget->szName);
```

```c
    /* Over here the source may not be PegA, auxillary may not be PegB and
       the target may not be PegC. But, when printing we need to keep the
       order PegA, then PegB and then PegC for better readability. */
    printf("\nPeg %s: ", g_Src.szName);
    for (idx = 0; idx < g_Src.iCurNum; idx++)
        printf("%d ", g_Src.rgiDisks[idx]);

    printf("\nPeg %s: ", g_Aux.szName);
    for (idx = 0; idx < g_Aux.iCurNum; idx++)
        printf("%d ", g_Aux.rgiDisks[idx]);

    printf("\nPeg %s: ", g_Target.szName);
    for (idx = 0; idx < g_Target.iCurNum; idx++)
        printf("%d ", g_Target.rgiDisks[idx]);

    printf("\n###############################################\n");

    /* Move all smaller disks from source to auxillary
       and then from auxillary to target. */
    TowerOfHanoi(n - 1, pAux, pTarget, pSrc);
    }
}

int main(void)
{
    /* Variable Declaration & Initialization */
    int idx       = 0;
    int lDiskNum = MAX_DISKS;

    for (; idx < MAX_DISKS; idx++, IdiskNum--)
    {
        g_Src.rgiDisks[idx] = IdiskNum;
    }

    g_Src.iCurNum = MAX_DISKS;
    TowerOfHanoi(MAX_DISKS, &g_Src, &g_Target, &g_Aux);

    printf("\n");
    return 0;
}
```

FILE MANAGEMENT

[CHAPTER-12]

12.1 INTRODUCTION

Till now we have been working with console oriented input and output of data to a program. Our programs accept input from the user, processes them and shows the output on the screen. This works for data which is limited in size and does not require to be referenced later. What happens if we require the processed data to be available at a later time. Do we input the raw data and run the program to process the data again? If we had the option to store the processed data, we would not have required to enter the raw data again and could have referenced the stored data during our later use. This is where storing the data on disks comes in handy. The processed data is stored in files which are saved to disks. On a later use, the program just reads the data from the file and shows it to the user. This fulfills the following two purposes:

1. We do not need to input the entire data again to the program. Saving in files helps eliminate this cumbersome operation.
2. The program does not need to do the entire processing again. It just needs to read the already processed data from the files and show to the user.

The various file operations supported by C are:
- Creating a new file.
- Opening an existing file.
- Writing to a file.
- Reading a file.
- Modifying a file.
- Overwriting or clearing a file.
- Closing a file.

We can open and operate on a file in two different formats – Textual and Binary. In textual format the text and characters are stored one character a time. But, numbers are stored as strings of characters. Even if the number *637283* occupies 4 bytes of memory, when transferred to the disk in textual format, would occupy 6 bytes, with each digit as a separate character. So, each data item is stored as an ASCII or Unicode character *(depending on the C function used)*. In case of binary format, the exact memory representation of the data is written to disk. So, *637283* will use 4 bytes when using binary format.

We may use many of the C library functions to perform the file operations, and they are:

Function Name	Function Description
fopen	Creates a new file or opens an existing file.
fclose	Closes a file.
fseek	Sets the position to a desired byte location within the file. The next read or write operation begins from this location.

Function Name	Function Description
ftell	Returns the current position within the file *(in terms of bytes from the start of the file)*.
rewind	Sets the position to the beginning of the file. The next read or write operation begins from the start of the file.
getw	Reads an integer value from a file.
putw	Writes an integer value to a file.
ANSI → getc *Wide Character* → fgetwc	Reads a character from a file.
ANSI → putc *Wide Character* → fputwc	Writes a character to a file.
ANSI → fgets *Wide Character* → fgetws	Reads a character string from a file. Reads until a new line character or end of file is reached *(whichever comes first)*.
ANSI → fputs *Wide Character* → fputws	Writes a character string to a file. Writes until the NULL character, but does not write the NULL character itself to the file.
ANSI → fprintf *Wide Character* → fwprintf	Writes a set of formatted data values to a file. Similar to *'printf'*, except that it can write to the specified output stream which may be a file.
ANSI → fscanf *Wide Character* → fwscanf	Reads a set of formatted data values from a file. Similar to *'scanf'*, except that it can read from the specified input stream which may be a file.

12.2 CREATING AND OPENING FILE

A file in secondary storage is identified by its name and is accessed using its file path. For creating or opening a file, we must specify the path to the file. The path may be the full path to the file or simply the filename. When only the filename is specified, the file is assumed to be in the current working directory. For creating or opening a file, we may use the 'C' function *'fopen'*. To the function, we must specify a filename or file path which satisfies the operating system's file naming and path conventions. The function returns a pointer to a data structure called **'FILE'**. The function has the following prototype:

FILE * fopen(*"file path", "mode"*);

As the name suggests, *'file path'* is a character string representing the path to the file to create or open. It may also be a filename in which case the file is assumed to be in the current working directory. The parameter *'mode'* suggests the purpose of opening the file and may be the following:

r   Opens the file for reading only. If the file does not exist, the function fails and returns NULL. After opening, the file read-position is stationed at the beginning of the file.

w   Opens the file for writing only. If the file does not exist, a new file is created. If the file already exists, it is overwritten and no data exists in the file after opening. After opening, the file write-position is stationed at the beginning of the file.

a   Opens the file only for appending *(adding)* data. If the file does not exist, a new file is created. If the file already exists, it is opened *(**not** overwritten)* and the file write-location is stationed at the end of the file for appending data to it.

r+   Opens the file for both reading and writing. If the file does not exist, a new file is created. If the file already exists, it is opened and the file write-location is stationed at the start of the file. Previous data may be overwritten, if needed.

w+   Same as **'w'** except that the file is opened for both reading and writing.

a+   Same as **'a'** except that the file is opened for both reading and writing.

Additionally, we have the option to specify the format *(i.e. Textual or Binary)* when opening the file. The default format is textual. If we want to open a file in binary format, we have to specify an additional flag **'b'** in the *mode* parameter of *'fopen'*. If **'b'** is not specified, the file is opened for textual operation. Starting from C11, another flag **'x'** may be specified in the mode parameter. This flag forces the function to create a new file rather than overwrite any existing file. If a file with the same name already exists, the function *'fopen'* **fails,** rather than opening the file. If we use **'x'**, we can be sure that we will not clobber an existing file. Some usage examples of *'fopen'* are given below:

Variable Declaration:	FILE *fp = NULL;
Function Usage Examples:	**1.** fp = fopen("c:\\data\\myfile.dat", "r");
	2. fp = fopen("c:\\data\\myfile.dat", "a");
	3. fp = fopen("c:\\data\\myfile.dat", "r+");
	4. fp = fopen("c:\\data\\myfile.dat", "w+");
	5. fp = fopen("c:\\data\\myfile.dat", "ab");
	6. fp = fopen("c:\\data\\myfile.dat", "r+b");
	7. fp = fopen("myfile.dat", "wb");

The function *'fopen'* returns a pointer to a **'FILE'** data structure. This data structure holds all information regarding the opened file. The returned pointer is subsequently used for all operations on the opened file.

We can open and use multiple files at the same time. The maximum number of files that can be opened depends on the operating system restrictions.

By default, text files opened using *'fopen'* store data in ANSI format. If we want the files to store the characters in some other encoding like 'UTF-8' or 'UTF-16', we need to specify some additional attributes within the *'mode'* parameter. If the *'mode'* string contains the additional sequence **',ccs=encoding'**, *'encoding'* is taken as the type of encoding desired for storing the data in the file. Two example specifications with UTF-8 and 'UTF-16' encoding are given below:

FILE *fp = fopen("myfile.dat", "r+, *ccs=UTF-8*");

FILE *fp = fopen("myfile.dat", "a, *ccs=UTF-16LE*");

12.3 CLOSING A FILE

A file must be closed when all operations on the file have completed. When we write data to a file, the data may not get immediately written physically to the disk. The data may remain in the memory and get flushed *(written)* to the disk on an opportune time *(may be a size or time threshold)*. When a file is closed, all data related to it get flushed to the disk and the file pointer gets invalidated. Keeping too many open files may also slow down the system. So, we should avoid keeping files unnecessarily open and should close them when we are done working with them. We can close an already open file using the function *'fclose'*. It has the following prototype:

fclose(*file-pointer*);

Given below is a small example where we open two files, one in read mode and another in write mode. We then close the two files after their use.

> *FILE *fp1 = NULL;*
> *FILE *fp2 = NULL;*
> *fp1 = fopen("File1.txt", "r");*
> *fp2 = fopen("File2.txt", "w");*
> *.....*
> *.....*
> *fclose(fp1);*
> *fclose(fp2);*

12.4 WRITING-TO AND READING-FROM A TEXTUAL FILE

Before using any of the file operation functions we must open the file using the *'fopen'* function. The *'FILE'* pointer returned by the *'fopen'* function is specified as a parameter to all the file operation functions to identify the file to work with.

12.4.1 WRITING AND READING SINGLE CHARACTERS

We can use the **'fputc'** *(ANSI)* and **'fputwc'** *(Wide Character)* functions to write single character to a file. The functions have the following prototypes:

> ANSI → int **fputc**(int iCharacter, FILE *fp);
> Wide Character → wint_t **fputwc**(wchar_t iCharacter, FILE *fp);

The character identified by *'iCharacter'* is written at the current file position, which is then automatically advanced by one character. Both the functions are similar except that the later writes Unicode character instead of ANSI to the file. The file position is the byte position where the read or write operation will occur next. The file pointer *'fp'* identifies the file we are working with.

We wrote the character to the file. But, how do we read the character? We can use the functions **'fgetc'** *(ANSI)* or **'fgetwc'** *(Wide Character)* for the purpose. The functions have the following prototypes:

> ANSI → int **fgetc**(FILE *fp);
> Wide Character → wint_t **fgetwc**(FILE *fp);

Both the functions return the character at the current file position. The file position is then advanced by one character after the read. The function *'fgetwc'* returns Unicode character instead of ANSI. If we are at the end of the file *(i.e. no more data is available to be read)* the functions return EOF, and sets the end of file indicator for the file stream.

Now, let us understand the above functions using a simple program. In the program we will write all the characters corresponding to ASCII value *33* and higher *(till ASCII value 126)*. We will then reopen the file, read all the characters from the file and print them to the console.

```c
#include <stdio.h>

int main(void)
{
    /* Variable Declaration & Initialization. */
    FILE *fp         = NULL;
    int   iCharacter = 0;

    do
    {
        /* Create a new file for writing. */
        fp = fopen("Characters", "w");
        if (!fp)
        {
            printf("Failed to create the file.");
            break;
        }

        /* Write all the characters one by one within a loop. */
        for (iCharacter = 33; iCharacter < 127; iCharacter++)
        {
            fputc(iCharacter, fp);
        }

        /* Close the file. */
        fclose(fp);
        fp = NULL;

        /* Reopen the same file, but now for reading. */
        fp = fopen("Characters", "r");
        if (!fp)
        {
            printf("Failed to open the file.");
            break;
        }

        printf("The characters are: ");
        do
        {
            iCharacter = fgetc(fp);
            if (EOF != iCharacter)
            {
                printf("%c, ", iCharacter);
            }

        } while (EOF != iCharacter);

    } while (0);

    if (fp)
    {
        fclose(fp);
        fp = NULL;
    }

    printf("\n\n");
    return 0;
}
```

At first glance the above program seems to be doing something funny. We have used a do-while loop where the loop's exit criteria is **'0 != 0'** *[while (0)]*. This means that the condition will never get fulfilled and the loop will not go into an iteration. So, the body of the loop will always get executed only once *(being a do-while construct)*. So, why use a loop? We are using the loop just to enable us to stop the execution at any moment when some condition is not fulfilled. This achieves somewhat similar functionality of 'goto' statements eliminating some of its disadvantages. This also gets rid of multiple nested 'if-else' constructs which reduce program readability. Consider the 'if' block starting with **'if (! fp)'** within the loop body. This means, if the file pointer is NULL i.e. the file failed to open, we do not continue with the program, break out of the loop and exit the function.

12.4.2 WRITING AND READING INTEGERS

The previous functions we studied enable us to write and read characters. For writing an integer to a file we may use the function **'putw'** which has the following prototype:

int putw(int iValue, FILE *fp);

The function writes an integer value specified in *'iValue'* to the file identified by *'fp'*. After writing, the function advances the file position past the written integer value.

For reading an integer value, we may use the function **'getw'** which has the following prototype:

int getw(FILE *fp);

The function reads an integer value from the file and returns it. After reading the value, the function advances the file position past the integer value that was read. If the function reaches end of file, it returns EOF.

12.4.3 WRITING AND READING STRINGS

If we need to write entire strings to a file, it is inconvenient to be doing so using *'putc'* within a loop construct. We need a function which accepts an entire string from us and writes that to the file. This simplifies our programming by getting rid of unnecessary loop constructs. For writing an entire string to a file we may use the **'fputs'** *(ANSI)* or **'fputws'** *(Wide Character)* functions.

ANSI → int fputs(const char *pStr, FILE *fp);
Wide Character → int fputws(const wchar_t *pStr, FILE *fp);

The functions copy from the address pointed by *'pStr'* until they reach the terminating NULL character (`'\0'`). Both the functions are identical in behavior except that *'fputws'* writes a Unicode string to the file. The terminating NULL character is not written to the file. The file position is advanced by the number of characters written to the file. In case of an error the functions return EOF.

To read entire strings from a file, we may use the functions **'fgets'** *(ANSI)* or **'fgetws'** *(Wide Character)*. Both the functions keep reading the file until end of the specified buffer, a newline character or end of file is reached. The functions have the following prototypes:

ANSI → char * fgets(char *pStr, int iNumChars, FILE *fp);
Wide Character → wchar_t * fgetws(wchar_t *pStr, int iNumChars, FILE *fp);

We provide a buffer *(an array)* to both the functions which is then filled with the read string. We must make sure that the array is large enough to hold an entire string to be read from the file. We pass the address to the starting location of the array *(we may pass the array name directly or the address of the first element of the array. Please refer to the chapter on pointers)*. The only difference between the two functions is that the ANSI version accepts a *'char'* buffer whereas the wide character version accepts a 'wide character' buffer. The ANSI version of the function reads ANSI characters *(1 byte each)* from the file and fills the provided buffer with the read string. The wide character version reads wide characters *(1 to 4 bytes each depending on the architecture and file open mode)* from the file and fills the provided buffer with the wide character string.

We pass the size of the array as *'iNumChars'* to the functions. The functions read a maximum of *'iNumChars – 1'* characters from the file. So, the functions keep reading characters from the file until *'iNumChars - 1'* characters have been read or either a newline or the end-of-file is reached, whichever happens first. The functions then append a NULL character at the end to mark the end of the string. An important thing to remember is that if both the functions encounter a newline character while reading, they retain the newline character as the last character of the string *(followed by a NULL character)*.

If the functions encounter an error while reading, they return NULL and the provided buffer remains unchanged.

12.4.4 WRITING AND READING FORMATTED DATA

Till now we learned file handling functions which read and write only specific type of data viz. Character, integer or strings. It would make our life far easy if we have functions which help us write and read multiple items at a time and that too belonging to different data types. We have the functions **'fprintf'** and **'fscanf'** which help us to do just that. **'fprintf'** is very similar to the *'printf'* function and **'fscanf'** is very similar to the *'scanf'* function. The *'printf'* function generates the output to the default output device whereas you can specify the output stream to the *'fprintf'* function which generally is a file. So, whatever you write using *'fprintf'* goes to the specified stream which may be a file handle. Similarly, the *'scanf'* function reads the input from standard input device, whereas you can specify the input stream in case of the *'fscanf'* function. The function will read the input from the specified stream, format the input and fill the variables with the formatted input data. Let us start our discussion with *'fprintf'* function.

ANSI → int **fprintf**(FILE *fp, const char *pszFormat, ...);
Wide Character → int **fwprintf**(FILE *fp, const wchar_t *pszFormat, ...);

We can see that the function is very similar to the *'printf'* function except that it accepts an additional parameter in the form of the file stream identifier. The format specification too is similar to the *'printf'* function and the function accepts variable number of arguments. An example of its usage is:

fprintf(fp, "The student details are: %s, %d, %f", szName, iRoll, 81.5);

The function returns the total number of characters written to the file. The function returns a negative value when it encounters an error.

The *'fscanf'* function has the following prototype:

ANSI → int **fscanf**(FILE *fp, const char *pszFormat, *argument-list*);
Wide Character → int **fwscanf**(FILE *fp, const wchar_t *pszFormat, *argument-list*);

The functions read data from the stream *(given as 'fp')* and store them according to the parameter format into the locations pointed by the additional arguments *(following the parameter 'pszFormat')*. The additional arguments should point to variables of the type specified by their corresponding format specifier within the format string.

We can see that the function is very similar to the *'scanf'* function except that it accepts an additional parameter, which is the file stream identifier. The format specification too is similar to the *'scanf'* function. An example of its usage is:
                fscanf(fp, "%d %s", &iItemCode, szItemName);
where *'iItemCode'* is an existing integer variable and *'szItemName'* is a character array.

The function returns the total number of items successfully read and formatted to the specified arguments list. This may be equal to the expected number of items or be less *(even zero)* due to a matching *(format)* failure, a read error, or on reaching the end of file. The function returns EOF when it encounters an error.

To understand the above functions, we will write a program which accepts the student name, address, registration number and class from the user. The program then writes these data to a file.

```c
#include <stdio.h>

/* Defined Values. */
#define MAX_STUDENTS    10
#define ARRAYSIZE(x)    sizeof(x)/sizeof(x[0])

/* Structure Definitions. */
typedef struct _STUDENTDETAILS
{
    char           szName[50];
    char           szAddress[100];
    char           szRegNo[20];
    unsigned int uClass;

}STUDENTDETAILS;

/* Forward Declarations. */
int AcceptDetails(STUDENTDETAILS *pDetails);
int SaveDetails(FILE *fp, STUDENTDETAILS *pDetails);

int main(void)
{
    STUDENTDETAILS Details = { 0 };
    int             i       = 0;
    int             iReturn = 0;
    FILE            *fp      = NULL;

    fp = fopen("Student.dat", "w");
    if (!fp)
    {
        iReturn = -1;
```

```
            goto EXIT;
    }

    for (; i < MAX_STUDENTS; i++)
    {
        iReturn = AcceptDetails(&Details);
        if (0 > iReturn)
        {
            break;
        }

        iReturn = SaveDetails(fp, &Details);
        if (0 > iReturn)
        {
            break;
        }
    }

EXIT:
    if (fp)
    {
        fclose(fp);
        fp = NULL;
    }

    return iReturn;
}

int AcceptDetails(STUDENTDETAILS *pDetails)
{
    size_t cchLen = 0;

    if (!pDetails)
    {
        return -1;
    }

    memset(pDetails, 0, sizeof(STUDENTDETAILS));

    /* Accept the student's name from the user. The 'fgets' function accepts a string
       from the specified stream, which in our case is the standard input device 'stdin'.
       'fgets' function keeps reading characters from the input stream until a newline
       character ('\n'), end of file (EOF) or the end of the buffer is found. The
       function NULL terminates the string but also retains the newline character. As
       we do not require the newline character to be present in our string, we overwrite
       it with a '\0' character making it as the new end of the string. We have used
       'fgets' instead of 'scanf' function because the 'scanf' function stops reading
       from the input as soon as it encounters a whitespace character. This makes 'scanf'
       unviable for accepting strings like name and address which may contain spaces. */
    printf("\nEnter the student's name: ");
    fgets(pDetails->szName, ARRAYSIZE(pDetails->szName), stdin);
    cchLen = strlen(pDetails->szName);

    if (cchLen > 0 && '\n' == pDetails->szName[cchLen - 1])
        pDetails->szName[cchLen - 1] = '\0';

    printf("Enter the student's address: ");
    fgets(pDetails->szAddress, ARRAYSIZE(pDetails->szAddress), stdin);
    cchLen = strlen(pDetails->szAddress);

    if (cchLen > 0 && '\n' == pDetails->szAddress[cchLen - 1])
        pDetails->szAddress[cchLen - 1] = '\0';
```

```
    printf("Enter the registration number: ");
    scanf("%s", pDetails->szRegNo);

    printf("Enter the class: ");
    scanf("%u", &pDetails->uClass);

    return 0;
}

int SaveDetails(FILE *fp, STUDENTDETAILS *pDetails)
{
    if (!fp || !pDetails)
    {
        return -1;
    }

    fprintf(fp, "%s\n%s\n%s\n%u\n",
            pDetails->szName,
            pDetails->szAddress,
            pDetails->szRegNo,
            pDetails->uClass);

    return 0;
}
```

We have accepted and saved the details to a file. Let us now read the saved data and show it to the user.

```
int LoadDetails(FILE *fp, STUDENTDETAILS *pDetails)
{
    int     iReturn = -1;
    size_t  cchLen  = 0;

    if (!fp || !pDetails)
    {
        return -1;
    }

    memset(pDetails, 0, sizeof(STUDENTDETAILS));

    /* 'fgets' function keeps reading characters from the file until a newline
       character ('\n'), end of file (EOF) or the end of the buffer occurs. The
       function retains the newline character. As we do not require the newline
       character to be present in our string, we overwrite it with a '\0' character
       making it as the new end of the string. We have used 'fgets' instead of
       'fscanf' function because the 'fscanf' function stops reading from the input
       as soon as it encounters a whitespace character. This makes 'fscanf' nonviable
       for accepting strings like name and address which may contain spaces. */

    if (NULL == fgets(pDetails->szName, ARRAYSIZE(pDetails->szName), fp))
    {
        goto EXIT;
    }
    cchLen = strlen(pDetails->szName);

    if (cchLen > 0 && '\n' == pDetails->szName[cchLen − 1])
        pDetails->szName[cchLen - 1] = '\0';

    if (NULL == fgets(pDetails->szAddress, ARRAYSIZE(pDetails->szAddress), fp))
    {
        goto EXIT;
    }
    cchLen = strlen(pDetails->szAddress);
```

```
        if (cchLen > 0 && '\n' == pDetails->szAddress[cchLen - 1])
            pDetails->szAddress[cchLen - 1] = '\0';

        if (0 >= fscanf(fp, "%s", pDetails->szRegNo))
        {
            goto EXIT;
        }

        /* When reading an integer value, 'fscanf' does not read the newline character.
           As a result, the newline character will be read during the next read
           iteration upon which 'szName' will contain only the newline character.
           To prevent this from happening, we ask the 'fscanf' function to read a
           single character after reading the class (uClass). As we have used '*'
           in this format specifier '%*c', the character is read but ignored and
           dropped. This essentially forwards the read pointer past the newline. */
        if (0 >= fscanf(fp, "%u%*c", &pDetails->uClass))
        {
            goto EXIT;
        }

        iReturn = 0;

EXIT:
        return iReturn;
}

int PrintDetails(STUDENTDETAILS *pDetails)
{
    if (!pDetails)
    {
        return -1;
    }

    printf("Student Name: %s\n", pDetails->szName);
    printf("Student Address: %s\n", pDetails->szAddress);
    printf("Student Registration Number: %s\n", pDetails->szRegNo);
    printf("Student Class: %u\n\n", pDetails->uClass);

    return 0;
}

int main(void)
{
    STUDENTDETAILS Details = { 0 };
    FILE           *fp      = NULL;

    fp = fopen("Student.dat", "r");
    if (!fp)
    {
        return -1;
    }

    while (LoadDetails(fp, &Details) >= 0)
    {
        PrintDetails(&Details);
    }

    fclose(fp);
    fp = NULL;

    return 0;
}
```

12.5 WRITING-TO AND READING-FROM A BINARY FILE

Till now we focused on writing and reading in textual format. The biggest disadvantage of using textual format is that we have to write each individual items separately. Moreover, we have to take care of the encoding of the text we intend to write or read. If we are working with data types like integer or float, we need to use formatted output and input for writing and reading data. This involves additional processing overheads as the data is converted to string and back. To overcome these disadvantages, C provides us with two functions *'fwrite'* and *'fread'* which enable us to write and read data as is i.e. the way they are represented in memory.

When we use functions like *'fwrite'* and *'fread',* we need to open the files in binary format mode. We have to specify the additional flag **'b'** in the *'mode'* parameter of *'fopen'* function *(refer to the section on 'fopen')*. When using *'fwrite'* on integer or real values, the data is not converted to textual format but are written as they are represented in memory. Hence, when reading the data back using *'fread'*, the data does not require to be converted back.

The biggest advantage of the functions *'fwrite'* and *'fread'* is that they allow writing and reading data in bulk. For *'fwrite',* it is like dumping the entire memory representation of the data directly to disk, and for *'fread',* it is like retrieving the entire dumped data from the disk to the memory. For this reason, these two functions are much faster when operating on large amounts of data than their textual counterparts.

Writing and reading data in bulk reduces coding time for data types like structures and unions. Rather than writing each individual item *(member or field)* of the structure separately, we may write the entire structure data directly at one go using *'fwrite'*. Similarly, we may read the entire structure data directly using a single call to *'fread'*.

Now, let us have a look at the prototypes of the two functions starting with *'fwrite'*:

size_t **fwrite**(const void *pData, size_t ItemSize, size_t ItemCount, FILE *fp);

The function writes an array of *'ItemCount'* elements, each with a size of *'ItemSize'* bytes, from the memory location pointed by *'pData'* to the specified file *(identified using 'fp')*. The data is written at the current position within the file. For example, if we are writing an array of structure data, we need to specify the array name *(or the address of the first element of the array)* as *'pData'*. We will specify the size of each array element *(equivalent to the structure size)* as *'ItemSize'*. The number of array elements we intend to write should be specified for *'ItemCount'*.

In place of writing the entire array data at one go, we may utilize a loop within which we will write each array element using the *'fwrite'* function. Each iteration of the loop will write a single array element by specifying the element address as *'pData'*, the element size as *'ItemSize'* and 1 (one) as *'ItemCount'*. In the next iteration, we will increment to point to the next array element.

After writing the data, position indicator of the file is automatically advanced by the total number of bytes written. The function returns the total number of elements *(items)* written to the file. If the number of elements written is different from *'ItemCount'*, we can assume that there was an error which prevented the function from writing all the data.

Now, let us have a look at the *'fread'* function:

size_t **fread**(void *pData, size_t ItemSize, size_t ItemCount, FILE *fp);

The function reads an array of *'ItemCount'* elements, each with a size of *'ItemSize'* bytes, to the memory location pointed by *'pData'* from the specified file *(identified using 'fp')*. The data is read from the current position within the file. We must make sure that the memory location pointed by *'pData'* is large enough to hold the read data, which typically must be at-least of *(ItemSize * ItemCount)* bytes.

After reading the data, position indicator of the file is automatically advanced by the total number of bytes read. The function returns the total number of elements *(items)* read from the file. If the number of elements read is different from *'ItemCount'*, we can assume that there was an error which prevented the function from reading all the data.

We will understand the behavior of the two functions better using two programs. In both the programs we will accept details of items used in a consumer shop. Each item detail will be stored in a single structure variable.

In our first program, we will accept each item's detail from the user and immediately save that data to a file. This will be done in each iteration. After accepting and saving the details, we will start reading the data back from the file. We will read each item individually and print its details. This approach is convenient in situations where we are not sure regarding the count of items we are going to save to the file or read from the file.

In our second program, we will declare an array of the structure and will accept the details of all the items in the array. We will then save the entire array at one go to the file. When reading the data back from the file, we will read the entire data to our array at one go.

PROGRAM-1
```
#include <stdio.h>
#include <ctype.h>

/* Structure Definition. */
typedef struct _ITEMDETAILS
{
    int    iItemCode;
    char   szItemName[50];
    float  fltItemRate;

}ITEMDETAILS;

/* Function which accepts the details from the user. */
int AcceptDetails(ITEMDETAILS *pDetails)
{
    int iReturn = 0;
```

```c
    do
    {
        if (!pDetails)
        {
            break;
        }

        printf("\nEnter the item code: ");
        scanf("%d", &pDetails->iItemCode);

        printf("Enter the item name: ");
        scanf("%s", pDetails->szItemName);

        printf("Enter the item rate: ");
        scanf("%f", &pDetails->fltItemRate);

        iReturn = 1;

    } while (0);

    return iReturn;
}

/* Function for printing the item details to the console. */
int PrintDetails(ITEMDETAILS *pDetails)
{
    int iReturn = 0;

    do
    {
        if (!pDetails)
        {
            break;
        }

        printf("\n\nItem code: %d", pDetails->iItemCode);
        printf("\nItem name: %s", pDetails->szItemName);
        printf("\nItem rate: %f", pDetails->fltItemRate);

        iReturn = 1;

    } while (0);

    return iReturn;
}

int main()
{
    /* Variable Declaration and Initialization. */
    ITEMDETAILS ItemDetails = { 0 };
    char        chContinue  = 'y';
    size_t      iReturn     = 0;
    FILE        *fp         = NULL;

    /* Open the file for writing. */
    fp = fopen("Items.dat", "wb");
    if (!fp)
    {
        /* Failed to create the file. Bail out with a message.*/
        printf("Failed to create the file. Stopping...");
        goto EXIT;
    }
```

```
        do
        {
            /* Accept the details from the user in our structure variable.*/
            AcceptDetails(&ItemDetails);

            /* Write the entire structure contents directly to the file at
               the current file position which will be advanced after the write. */
            iReturn = fwrite(&ItemDetails, sizeof(ItemDetails), 1, fp);
            if (1 != iReturn)
            {
                printf("\nError writing to file. Continuing to read...");
                break;
            }

            printf("Press Y/y to continue: ");
            chContinue = getchar();

        } while ('y' == tolower(chContinue));

        /* Close the file and reopen it for reading. */
        fclose(fp);
        fp = NULL;

        fp = fopen("Items.dat", "rb");
        if (!fp)
        {
            /* Failed to open the file. Bail out with a message.*/
            printf("Failed to open the file for reading...");
            goto EXIT;
        }

        /* Keep reading until the end of file is reached. */
        while (1 == fread(&ItemDetails, sizeof(ItemDetails), 1, fp))
        {
            /* Print the details. */
            PrintDetails(&ItemDetails);
        }
EXIT:
    if (fp)
    {
        fclose(fp);
        fp = NULL;
    }

    printf("\n\n");
    return 0;
}
```

PROGRAM-2

For this program, we will have identical *'ITEMDETAILS'* structure definition as **Program-1**. We will also have identical *'AcceptDetails'* and *'PrintDetails'* function definition as **Program-1**. So, we are not re-specifying those over here and are just concentrating on the 'main()' function which differs between the two.

```
#define MAX_ITEMS    10

int main()
{
```

```
    /* Variable Declaration and Initialization. */
    ITEMDETAILS ItemDetails[MAX_ITEMS] = { 0 };
    int         iCount                 = 0;
    size_t      iReturn                = 0;
    FILE        *fp                    = NULL;

    /* Open the file for writing. */
    fp = fopen("Items.dat", "wb");
    if (!fp)
    {
        /* Failed to create the file. Bail out with a message.*/
        printf("Failed to create the file. Stopping...");
        goto EXIT;
    }

    /* Accept the details from the user in our structure array.*/
    for (iCount = 0; iCount < MAX_ITEMS; iCount++)
    {
        AcceptDetails(&ItemDetails[iCount]);
    }

    /* Write the details to the file at one go. */
    iReturn = fwrite(ItemDetails, sizeof(ItemDetails[0]), iCount, fp);
    if (iReturn != iCount)
    {
        /* Failed to write the data to the file. Bail out...*/
        printf("\nFailed to write the data to the file. Stopping...");
        goto EXIT;
    }

    /* Close the file and reopen it for reading. */
    fclose(fp);
    fp = NULL;

    fp = fopen("Items.dat", "rb");
    if (!fp)
    {
        /* Failed to open the file. Bail out with a message.*/
        printf("Failed to open the file for reading...");
        goto EXIT;
    }

    memset(ItemDetails, 0, sizeof(ItemDetails));

    /* Read the entire file at one go. */
    iReturn = fread(ItemDetails, sizeof(ItemDetails[0]), iCount, fp);
    if (iReturn != iCount)
    {
        /* Failed to read the data from the file. Bail out...*/
        printf("\nFailed to read the data from the file. Stopping...");
        goto EXIT;
    }

    /* Print all the read items. */
    for (iCount = 0; iCount < iReturn; iCount++)
    {
        /* Print the details. */
        PrintDetails(&ItemDetails[iCount]);
    }

EXIT:
    if (fp)
    {
```

```
        fclose(fp);
        fp = NULL;
    }

    printf("\n\n");
    return 0;
}
```

12.6 MISCELLANEOUS FILE MANAGEMENT FUNCTIONS

Apart from the input and output functions, C has some additional functions which help in working with files.

- int **fgetpos**(FILE *fp, fpos_t *pos);
  The function retrieves the current byte position within the file *(identified by 'fp')*. This is the position where the next read or write operation will occur, if not changed. The variable *'pos'* needs to be declared by the caller and is filled with the current position after the call completes. *'fpos_t'* is compiler defined and may be a type-defined name for *'long'* or *'long long'*. The function returns 0 *(zero)* in case of success and a non-zero value in case of an error.

- int **fsetpos**(FILE *fp, const fpos_t *pos);
  The function sets the current byte position to *'pos'*. This is the position where the next read or write operation will occur. The variable *'pos'* needs to be declared and set by the caller. It may also be filled using a previous call to *'fgetpos'*. The function returns 0 *(zero)* in case of success and a non-zero value in case of an error.

- long int **ftell**(FILE *fp);
  The function returns the current byte position within the file *(identified by 'fp')*. It is very similar to *'fgetpos'* except that it returns a *'long'* value instead of *'fpos_t'* for *'fgetpos'*. So, this function will fail if the file size is larger than 2 GB. There are compiler specific functions which overcome this limit *(ex: '_ftelli64' in Microsoft VC or 'ftello' in POSIX)*. In case of an error, this function returns -1.

- int **fseek**(FILE *fp, long int lOffset, int iOrigin);
  The function sets the current byte position of the file *(identified by 'fp')*. 'iOffset' is the number of bytes of offset from *'iOrigin'*. When 'iOffset' is positive, the file position moves forward. *'iOffset'* can be negative, implying that the file position be moved backwards as respect to *'iOrigin'*. *'iOrigin'* may have the following compiler-defined values:
  SEEK_SET: As respect to beginning of the file.
  SEEK_CUR: As respect to current byte position within the file.
  SEEK_END: As respect to the end of the file.
  As the function accepts a *'long'* value as *'iOffset'*, we are limited to operating with 2 GB limit. There are compiler specific functions which overcome this limit *(ex: '_fseeki64' in Microsoft VC or 'fseeko' in POSIX)*. The function returns 0 *(zero)* if successful, and a non-zero value in case of an error.

- void **rewind**(FILE *fp);
  Sets the byte position to the beginning of the file.

- FILE * **freopen**(const char *pszFilename, const char *pszMode, FILE *fp);
  The function reopens the file stream with different file or mode. If a new filename is specified as *'pszFilename'*, the function closes the existing file. The function then opens the file specified by *'pszFilename'* using the specified mode *'pszMode'*, and associates it with the file stream handle *'fp'*, just like *'fopen'* would do. If *'pszFilename'* is specified as NULL, the function attempts to change the file open mode to *'pszMode'*. If the function succeeds, it returns the same pointer *'fp'* specified as the third parameter to the function. If the function fails, it returns NULL.

- int **remove**(const char *pszFilename);
  Deletes the file whose name is specified as *'pszFilename'*. The operation is performed directly on the file identified by *'pszFilename'*. *'pszFilename'* may be an absolute path to a file. If only the name of the file is specified, it is assumed that the file resides in the current working directory. The file does **not** need to be opened for the file to be deleted. The function returns 0 *(zero)* if the file was deleted, and a non-zero value in case of an error.

- int **rename**(const char *pszOldname, const char *pszNewname);
  The function renames the file or directory specified by *'pszOldname'* to the name specified by *'pszNewname'*. The old name must be the path of an existing file or directory and the new name must not be an existing file or directory. We can also use this function to move a file from one directory to another by giving a different path in the *'pszNewname'* argument. However, the function cannot move a directory.

- FILE * **tmpfile**(void);
  The function creates a temporary file in **'wb+'** mode *(refer to 'fopen')* with a filename guaranteed to be different from any other existing file. The file is created in the current working directory. The file is automatically deleted when the file is closed using *'fclose'* or the program terminates. If the function fails, the return value is NULL.

- char * **tmpnam**(char *pszStr);
  The function returns a string containing a filename different from the name of any existing file. This enables us to safely create a temporary file without the risk of overwriting an existing file. If *'pszStr'* is NULL, *'tmpnam'* leaves the result in an internal static buffer. Thus any subsequent calls to *'tmpnam'* will destroy this value. It is recommended that the caller provides a buffer *(char array)* for *'pszStr'*. The function will then populate this buffer with the generated temporary filename. The buffer must be large enough to hold the temporary filename.

DYNAMIC MEMORY ALLOCATION

[CHAPTER-13]

13.1 INTRODUCTION

During programming, many a times we may face situations where we are unsure regarding the amount of data we are going to deal with. The amount of data is determined during execution of the program, and so we are completely in the dark when coding. Consider an example where we are accepting marks obtained by students of different classes and calculating the rank and total percentage obtained by each student. Not only the number of students change, but also the number of subjects change depending on the class. How do we provision the memory for such dynamic nature of data? For such situations, we have what we call *dynamic memory allocation*. As the name suggests, in this mechanism the memory allocation is entirely handled dynamically during execution of the program. Dynamic memory allocation or *dynamic memory management* allow us to allocate additional memory as per our requirement and also free those when they are not required. Dynamic memory allocation is extensively used in concepts like *linked lists* and *trees* which we will learn later in our book.

13.2 C PROGRAM – MEMORY LAYOUT

Before going deeper into dynamic memory allocation, let us understand the memory layout of a C program.

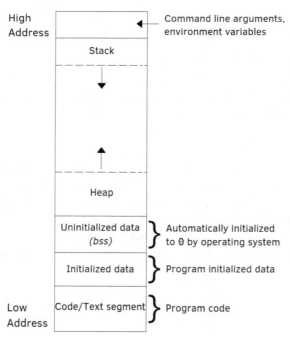

A C program contains many components such as the program code, function local variables, global variables, static variables, dynamically allocated memory space etc. All these need to be provided with some memory space to operate. The processor pulls these data from the memory rather than the disk. So, all these components need to be present in the memory for the CPU to work on them. A program may be saved to disk, but is loaded to memory before it is run, and the entire execution operates from the memory itself.

Code or Text segment:
This section contains the executable instructions. It is the machine code of the compiled program. This segment is mostly read-only as it is not allowed to be accessed by the program code. This segment is shareable so that only a single copy needs to be in memory for frequently executed programs, such as text editors etc. Only one shareable segment optimizes memory utilization of the operating system.

Initialized data segment:
Initialized data segment contains the global variables and static variables that are initialized by the programmer within the program. This segment may contain two types of data – initialized read-only data or initialized read-write data. Read-only data are the ones which are initialized during their declaration and cannot be changed thereafter, such as a constant global variable. Read-write data are the ones which can be altered any time during the program execution, such as normal global variables.

Uninitialized data segment:
Uninitialized data segment, also known as the *'bss'* segment, is named after an ancient assembler operator that stood for 'block started by symbol'. Data in this segment is automatically initialized to 0 *(zero)* by the operating system before the program starts. This segment contains all global and static variables that have not been explicitly initialized in the source code by the programmer. As for an example, a static variable declared as *'static int iValue;'* or a global variable declared as *'float g_fltRate;'* will be put in this segment.

Stack segment:
This is the segment where automatic variables are stored. Also, each time a function is called, the address *(next instruction location within the code segment)* of where to return to *(after the function completes)* is saved in this segment. Assume, function *'f1'* calls the function *'f2'*. The next instruction location is within the caller function *'f1'* and is the instruction which needs to be executed after the function *(f2)* call completes. The newly called function *(f2)* then allocates room on the stack for storing its automatic and temporary variables. This is how recursive functions also work. Each time a recursive function calls itself, a new stack space is used for the new call. So one set of variables belonging to one instance does not interfere with the variables from another recursive instance of the function.

Heap segment:
Heap is the segment which stores the data that are dynamically allocated. All dynamically allocated data goes into this segment. We use the C functions *'malloc'*, *'calloc'* and *'realloc'* to allocate memory dynamically from this segment. We use the C function *'free'* to free the dynamically allocated space which are no longer required. When using the allocation functions, we specify the amount of memory *(in*

bytes) we require, and consecutive memory location from this segment is allotted to us. After the memory is allotted, the starting address *(memory location)* of the allotted region is returned to us. So, essentially we declare a pointer which points to this starting address. Unlike stack segment, the data within heap segment may be shared between functions of the program, shared libraries or even dynamically loaded modules of the program. Just like stack segment, data in this segment is uninitialized and may contain garbage value after being allotted.

13.3 ALLOCATING MEMORY

We may allocate memory using the C function **'malloc'**. The function reserves a contiguous block of memory from the heap segment and returns the starting address of the block. The function needs to be specified the number of bytes *(memory-size)* to be be allocated and the function returns a *void pointer* pointing to the starting location of the allocated memory. Returning a void pointer allows us to typecast it to a pointer of any type. So, the function returns only the block of requested memory space. What we store in that memory space *(int, float, char, structure, string...)* depends on us, provided the allocated space is equal or larger than the data we are trying to store. The function has the following form:

void* malloc(size_t SizeInBytes);

The returned void pointer can be type-casted to a pointer of any desired type. If the function fails to allocate the requested space, it returns a **NULL pointer**. Few example usages of the function are:

```
/* Allocate space for a single double variable */
double *pdblRate = NULL;

pdblRate = (double *) malloc(sizeof(double));
*pdblRate = 62872.7372;
```

```
/* Allocate space for an array of integers */
int iCounter = 0;
int *prgiValues = NULL;

prgiValues = (int *) malloc(100 * sizeof(int));
for (iCounter = 0; iCounter < 100; iCounter++)
{
    prgiValues[iCounter] = iCounter;
}
```

```
/* Allocate space to store a character string */
char *pszName = NULL;

pszName = (char *) malloc(13 * sizeof(char));
strcpy(pszName, "David Miller");
```

```
/* Allocate space for an array of structures */
int iCounter = 0;
struct ITEMDETAILS *pDetails = NULL;
```

```
pDetails = (struct ITEMDETAILS *) malloc(sizeof(struct ITEMDETAILS) * 100);
for (iCounter = 0; iCounter < 100; iCounter++)
{
    pDetails[iCounter].iItemID = iCounter;
}
```

```
/* Allocate space for an array of structures */
int iCounter = 0;
struct ITEMDETAILS *pDetails = NULL;
struct ITEMDETAILS *pMove = NULL;

pDetails = (struct ITEMDETAILS *) malloc(sizeof(struct ITEMDETAILS) * 100);
for (iCounter = 0, pMove = pDetails; iCounter < 100; iCounter++, pMove++)
{
    pMove->iItemID = iCounter;
}
```

When we allocate a space and assign it to a pointer, the pointer points to the starting address of the allocated space.

Please note that the allocated memory space initially contains garbage data and we should avoid accessing the value of any location before initializing it. We should also be careful regarding overflowing our allocated memory space i.e. trying to access a memory location outside of what was allotted to us. Please note that we **cannot** determine the size of the reserved memory space by using the 'sizeof' operator on the returned memory pointer. Using the 'sizeof' operator on the pointer will return the memory space used by the pointer variable itself and not the memory space pointed by it. This will typically be 4 bytes on a 32-bit architecture and 8 bytes on a 64-bit architecture. In our above image, the returned (sizeof) value will be the space used by the 'ptr' variable itself and not the memory space pointed by the 'ptr' pointer variable.

C provides another memory allocation function called **'calloc'** which allows allocating memory space at run time. It is similar to 'malloc' except for the following two differences:

1. When allocating an array, we need to calculate the total space required by the array (number of array elements multiplied by the size of each element) and specify that to 'malloc'. In case of 'calloc', we do not require to do this calculation. We specify the number of elements of the array and the size of each element as two different parameters to the function 'calloc'. The function calculates the size required before doing the allocation.

2. In case of 'malloc', the newly allocated space is uninitialized and contains garbage data. 'calloc'

initializes the newly allocated space to 0 *(zero)*. So, every byte of the allocated memory space will contain the value 0 *(zero)* after allocation by *'calloc'*.

The general form of the *'calloc'* function is:

void* **calloc**(size_t *NumElements*, size_t *SizeOfEachElement*);

Allocates a block of memory for an array of *'NumElements'* elements, each of *'SizeOfEachElement'* bytes long, and initializes all its bytes to 0 *(zero)*. So, effectively it allocates a memory block of *(NumElements * SizeOfEachElement)* bytes.

The function returns a pointer to the starting address of the allocated memory space which can be type-casted to any desired type. If the function fails, it returns a NULL pointer.

C11 provided us with another memory allocation function called '**aligned_alloc**'. We have read in section 10.11 *'Aligning Addresses'*, the importance of aligning addresses of certain variables. The '**_Alignas**' keyword we discussed, helps us align compile time variables *(variable declared during design time)*. How do we achieve the same when allocating memory dynamically? The answer is *'aligned_alloc'*. The function has the following declaration:

void * **aligned_alloc**(size_t *Alignment*, size_t *SizeInBytes*);

The function allocates *'SizeInBytes'* bytes of uninitialized storage space where the starting address location is aligned to a multiple of *'Alignment' (power of 2)*.

13.4 ALTERING ALLOCATED MEMORY SIZE

It is very likely that later in our program we discover that the previously allocated memory is not sufficient to hold all our data *(or array elements)* and we need additional space for more data *(or array elements)*. It is also possible that we later realize that we had been over ambitious and allocated too much space, much more than what we require. In both these cases, we can change the already allocated memory size using the help of another function called '**realloc**'. The function name is the short form of *reallocation* of memory. The general form of the function is:

void* **realloc**(void *ptr*, size_t *NewSizeInBytes*);

The function changes the size of the memory block pointed to by *'ptr'* to the new size *'NewSizeInBytes'*. The function may move the memory block to a new location *(whose address is returned by the function)*. If the new requested memory space is larger than the previously allocated space, the contents of the old memory space is entirely copied to the new location. If the new requested memory space is smaller, the contents of the old memory space up to a maximum of the newly requested space is copied to the new location. Hence in simple words, the content of the memory block is preserved up to the lesser of the old and new sizes.

The function returns a pointer pointing to the address of the starting location of the newly allocated memory block. The new memory block may or may not begin at the same location as the old block. If the function does not find enough additional contiguous space in the same region, it will allocate a newly requested space in another location and return that address. The function also frees the old memory location after the transfer to the new location. If it is able to allocate the space in the old location itself, it will return the same address as *'ptr'*. An example usage of the *'realloc'* function is:

$$\text{void *ptr} = \text{malloc}(50 * \text{sizeof(int)});$$
$$\text{ptr} = \textbf{realloc}(\text{ptr}, 100 * \text{sizeof(int)});$$

13.5 RELEASING ALLOCATED SPACE

Dynamically allocated space need to be freed by the programmer when it is no longer required. We should not keep holding onto memory space when not needed, as memory space is limited. When we release a memory block, it becomes available again for allocating. We free an already allocated memory space using the function **'free'**. Memory allocated using *'malloc'*, *'calloc'*, *'aligned_alloc'* or reallocated using *'realloc'* can be freed using this function. The general form of the function is:

$$\text{void } \textbf{free}(\text{void *ptr});$$

'ptr' is the pointer pointing to the memory block allocated using the functions *'malloc'*, *'calloc'*, *'aligned_alloc'* or reallocated using the function *'realloc'*. Using an invalid address in *'ptr'* may result in undesirable effects.

13.6 SAMPLE PROGRAM

Let us write a program which accepts the details of the books in a library. For simplicity, we will accept only two details related to the books – their IDs and their names. We will use a structure to hold the information regarding each book. We will hold all the accepted information using an array of the structures in memory. Each element of the array will have details regarding one book. As we do not know beforehand regarding the number of book details the user wants to enter, we will allocate memory as required during run time. If our already allocated space is not large enough to store any more data, we will reallocate the memory for a larger space. After we have accepted all the details, we will print those.

```
#include <stdio.h>
#include <stdlib.h>
#include <ctype.h>

/* Defined Values */
#define SIZE_INC_COUNT  10

/* Defined Structures */
typedef struct _BOOKDETAILS
{
    int   iBookID;
    char  szBookName[100];

}BOOKDETAILS, *PBOOKDETAILS;

int main(void)
{
    /* Variable Declaration & Initialization. */
    PBOOKDETAILS pBooks        = NULL; /* Same as stating BOOKDETAILS *pBooks */
    PBOOKDETAILS pMove         = NULL;
    int          iCurArraySize = 0;
```

```
int           idxInput    = 0;
char          chContinue  = 'y';

/* Keep accepting book details till the user chooses to continue.
   We will continue till the user presses 'Y' or 'y'. */
for ( ; 'y' == tolower(chContinue); idxInput++)
{
    if (idxInput >= iCurArraySize)
    {
        /* The user wants to continue, but we have run out of array elements.
           If we have not yet allocated any memory for the array, we will use
           'calloc', and if we need to add to already allocated space, we will
           use 'realloc'. 'iCurArraySize' tracks our current allocated array
           size which is incremented everytime we request for more space. */
        iCurArraySize += SIZE_INC_COUNT;

        if (0 == idxInput)
        {
            /* We have not allocated any memory space yet. So, we use 'calloc'. */
            pBooks = (PBOOKDETAILS)calloc(iCurArraySize, sizeof(BOOKDETAILS));
        }
        else
        {
            /* We need more space. So, we request a larger memory space. */
            pBooks = (PBOOKDETAILS)realloc(pBooks, iCurArraySize * sizeof(BOOKDETAILS));
        }

        if (NULL == pBooks)
        {
            printf("\nFailed to allocate sufficient memory. Stopping...");
            break;
        }
    }

    printf("Enter the book ID: ");
    scanf("%d", &pBooks[idxInput].iBookID);

    printf("Enter the book name: ");
    fgets(pBooks[idxInput].szBookName, 100, stdin);

    printf("\nPress 'Y/y' to continue: ");
    chContinue = getchar();

    printf("\n");
}

/* We have accepted the data from the user. Let us now print the data.
   For accepting the data, we have demonstrated using the array index.
   For printing the data, we will use pointers and pointer arithmetic.
   We will not increment the 'pBooks' pointer but use a separate pointer
   'pMove'. When freeing the allocated memory block, we need to specify
   the starting address of the memory block to the function 'free'. As,
   'pBooks' points to the starting address, we can use that later in
   our program to free the allocated memory block/space. */
if (pBooks != NULL)
{
    for (pMove = pBooks; (pMove - pBooks) < idxInput; pMove++)
    {
        printf("Book ID: %d, Book name: %s", pMove->iBookID, pMove->szBookName);
    }

    /* We have completed using our allocated memory. Now, free it. */
    free(pBooks);
```

```
        pBooks = NULL;
    }

    printf("\n");
    return 0;
}
```

13.7 THINGS TO REMEMBER

1. The memory allocation functions *'malloc'*, *'calloc'* and *'realloc'* may fail, in which case they will return NULL. Before trying to use the returned pointer for any operation, we must verify that the pointer is not NULL. Trying to use a NULL pointer will generate a memory fault leading to a program crash.

2. Never provide an invalid or NULL pointer to the function *'free'*. If any of the memory allocation functions failed and returned NULL, we have nothing to free.

3. Always be careful regarding the amount of memory we have reserved. We should never try to access a location outside the allocated memory block. Though pointer arithmetic is possible for locations beyond the memory block *(example: incrementing a pointer to a location beyond the memory block)*, we should **never** try to access or manipulate those locations.

4. When freeing a memory block, always provide the address of the starting location of the memory block to the function *'free'*.

5. We should not rely too much on dynamic memory allocation. Too many number of allocations and deallocations lead to memory fragmentation. This may affect the performance of our program. Also, when memory becomes fragmented, contiguous memory locations may cease to exist, leading to memory allocation failures.

COMMAND LINE ARGUMENTS

[CHAPTER-14]

14.1 INTRODUCTION

On many occasions we may want our program to be non-interactive. The program may also need to work as a background or hidden process and be invoked from other processes for helping them accomplish certain tasks. If our program needs to work with certain input values, how do other programs pass those values to us? The answer is command line arguments. Command line arguments are parameters supplied to the program when it is invoked. They are used when we need to control our program or pass values to our program from outside. Also, rather than hard-coding our program with specific values, we may accept the values as command line arguments from the user. When executing the program, command-line arguments are specified after the program name with each argument separated from the other by a space. They are passed into the *'main()'* function of the program by the operating system. Examples of invoking a program using command line arguments are:

myprog1 *inputfile.dat outputfile.dat*

myprog2 *http://www.mydomain.com/*

14.2 'main' FUNCTION REVISITED

Till now we have been mainly dealing with *'main'* function accepting nothing *('void')* as its parameter. Instead of *'void'*, it may have two specific types of parameters which enable it to accept command line options for the program. Any command line arguments we specify when invoking the program are passed to the *'main'* function as parameters to it. The prototype or declaration of such a *'main'* function is as follows:

ANSI →	int **main**(int argc, char *argv[]); **or** int **main**(int argc, char **argv);
Wide Character →	int **wmain**(int argc, wchar_t *argv[]); **or** int **wmain**(int argc, wchar_t **argv);

Description of the parameters are:
- **argc** (*argument count*): It is an integer value specifying the count of arguments passed to the program from the command line. The program name is considered as the first argument and thus, the value of *'argc'* is at-least 1. Each command line argument following the program name when invoking *(executing)* the program increments the value of *'argc'*. So, *'argc'* will have a value of 4 for a command line as *'myprogram value1 value2 value3'*.
- **argv** (*argument vector*): An array of null-terminated strings. The first string *(argv[0])* is the program name, and each following string *(argv[1], argv[2], ...)* is an argument passed to the program from the command line. As the program name is considered as an argument, we will

always have the program name in *'argv[0]'*. All subsequent strings *(argv[1], argv[2], ...)* depend on whether our program was invoked using any additional command line arguments or not. So, the last valid string will be *'argv[argc – 1]'*. The last pointer *(argv[argc])* is always NULL. If the program was invoked as *'myprogram inputfile.dat outputfile.dat'*, *'argv[0]'* will have the string *'myprogram'*, *'argv[1]'* will have the string *'inputfile.dat'* and *'argv[2]'* will have the string *'outputfile.dat'*.

14.3 PASSING COMMAND LINE ARGUMENTS

While passing command line arguments to a program, we need to keep the following in mind:
- Each command line argument must be separated by a space.
- The program name is always the first argument *(argv[0])* in the list.
- If a command line argument contains spaces, it must be placed within quotes. In case quotes are not used, each individual token will be treated as a separate command line argument.
  Correct --> myprogram "This is a test string"
  Incorrect --> myprogram This is a test string
- The maximum number of command line arguments that can be passed to a program is operating system dependent.

14.4 SAMPLE PROGRAMS

1. In our first program, we will copy one file to another. We will accept two command line arguments corresponding to two filenames. The first filename is the input file i.e. the file to be copied. The second filename is the target file i.e. the one which needs to be created. The program opens the first file, creates the second and copies all the data *(byte at a time)* to the second file.

```c
#include <stdio.h>

int CopyFile(char *pszInputFile,
             char *pszOutputFile)
{
    /* Variable Declaration and Initialization. */
    FILE        *fp      = NULL;
    FILE        *tp      = NULL;
    int          iReturn = 0;
    unsigned char cValue  = 0;

    do
    {
        if (!pszInputFile || !pszOutputFile)
        {
            iReturn = -1;
            break;
        }

        /* Open the input file for reading. */
        fp = fopen(pszInputFile, "rb");
        if (!fp)
        {
            iReturn = -2;
```

```c
            break;
        }

        /* Open the output file for writing. */
        tp = fopen(pszOutputFile, "wb");
        if (!tp)
        {
            iReturn = -3;
            break;
        }

        /* Read each byte from the input file and write that to
           the output file. Continue, till all the bytes are read. */
        while (1 == fread(&cValue, sizeof(cValue), 1, fp))
        {
            if (1 != fwrite(&cValue, sizeof(cValue), 1, tp))
            {
                iReturn = -4;
                break;
            }
        }

    } while (0);

    if (fp)
    {
        fclose(fp);
        fp = NULL;
    }

    if (tp)
    {
        fclose(tp);
        tp = NULL;
    }

    return iReturn;
}

int main(int argc, char *argv[])
{
    int iReturn = 0;

    if (argc != 3)
    {
        printf("Usage: myprogram <InputFilename> <OutputFilename>\n\n");
        return -1;
    }

    /* Copy the file. */
    iReturn = CopyFile(argv[1], argv[2]);
    if (iReturn == -2)
    {
        printf("Error opening input file %s\n\n", argv[1]);
    }
    else if (iReturn == -3)
    {
        printf("Error creating output file %s\n\n", argv[2]);
    }
    else if (iReturn == -4)
    {
        printf("Error writing to output file %s\n\n", argv[2]);
    }
```

```
        else if (iReturn == 0)
        {
            printf("File successfully copied.\n\n");
        }
        else
        {
            printf("Error copying file.\n\n");
        }

        return iReturn;
}
```

2. In our next program we will calculate the compound interest on bank deposits. Compound interest is that interest which is added back to the principal sum, so that the interest is earned on that added interest too during the next compounding period. The shorter the compounding period the higher will be the maturity amount. Compounding frequency is the frequency at which the interest is calculated *(ex. every month, every quarter, every twelve months)*. A monthly compounding *(compound frequency of 12)* will earn a higher maturity amount than a half-yearly compounding *(compound frequency of 2)*, as the interest on interest is calculated much more frequently. The formula for annual compound interest is:

$$A = P * (1 + r / n)^{(n * t)}$$

Where:
A = The amount receivable including interest after the maturity period
P = The principal investment amount (the initial deposit)
r = The annual rate of interest
n = The number of times the interest is compounded per year
t = The period of interest

In the program we will accept the principal investment amount, annual rate of interest, compounding frequency and the period of investment through the command line. We will then calculate the total maturity amount for the investment.

```
/* Header Files */
#include <stdio.h>

/* Defined Structures */
typedef struct _CMPDINT
{
    double dblPrincipal;
    float  fltInterestRate;
    int    iCompoundFrequency;
    float  fltPeriod;
    double dblMaturityAmount;

}CMPDINT;

void CalculateMaturity(CMPDINT *pcmpdint)
{
    /* Variable Declaration & Initialization */
    double dblRate   = 0;
    double dblPeriod = 0;
```

```c
    if (pcmpdint)
    {
        /* fltInterestRate is in percentage. Convert to decimals. */
        dblRate   = (double)pcmpdint->fltInterestRate / 100;

        dblRate   = 1 + (dblRate / pcmpdint->iCompoundFrequency);
        dblPeriod = pcmpdint->iCompoundFrequency * (double)pcmpdint->fltPeriod;

        pcmpdint->dblMaturityAmount = pcmpdint->dblPrincipal * pow(dblRate, dblPeriod);
    }
}

int main(int argc, char *argv[])
{
    int       iReturn = -1;
    CMPDINT cmdint;

    if (argc != 5)
    {
        printf("Usage: myprogram <Principal> <Rate> <Frequency> <Period [Years]>\n\n");
        return iReturn;
    }

    cmdint.dblPrincipal      = atof(argv[1]);
    cmdint.fltInterestRate   = atof(argv[2]);
    cmdint.iCompoundFrequency = atoi(argv[3]);
    cmdint.fltPeriod         = atof(argv[4]);

    if (cmdint.dblPrincipal <= 0)
    {
        printf("Principal amount must be greater than 0.\n\n");
    }
    else if (cmdint.fltInterestRate <= 0)
    {
        printf("Interest rate must be greater than 0.\n\n");
    }
    else if (cmdint.iCompoundFrequency > 12 || cmdint.iCompoundFrequency < 1)
    {
        /* 12 --> monthly compounding.
            4 --> quarterly compounding.
            2 --> half yearly compounding.
            1 --> yearly compounding. */
        printf("Compound frequency must be between 1-12.\n\n");
    }
    else if (cmdint.fltPeriod <= 0)
    {
        printf("Period must be greater than 0.\n\n");
    }
    else
    {
        CalculateMaturity(&cmdint);
        printf("Total maturity amount will be %lf.\n\n", cmdint.dblMaturityAmount);
        iReturn = 0;
    }

    return iReturn;
}
```

PREPROCESSOR DIRECTIVES

[CHAPTER-15]

15.1 INTRODUCTION

C Preprocessor directives are special statements which are used to make a program portable, easy to read, easy to modify, efficient and being conditionally compiled. As the name suggests, preprocessor directives are processed before the source code is passed through the compiler. Before a source code is sent to the compiler, it is analyzed by the preprocessor for any such statements and if found, the source code is modified *(in memory)* depending on the statements and then sent to the compiler. All preprocessor directives begin with the character **'#'** which needs to be the first non-blank character in the line. Also preprocessor directives do not end with a semicolon. We are very accustomed to the preprocessor directives **'#define'** and **'#include'**. All preprocessor directives can be divided into three categories:

- File inclusion directives
- Macro directives
- Compiler control directives

15.2 FILE INCLUSION DIRECTIVES

From the start of our book we have been using statements like *'#include <stdio.h>'*. It is a file inclusion statement which includes the specified header file during compilation. So, what do statements like these actually do? Whenever we use the **'#include'** directive, we are essentially asking the preprocessor to copy the entire contents of the specified file at the exact location where the *'#include'* directive is specified. So, essentially the directive gets replaced by the contents of the file mentioned in the directive. This makes the source code file contain the contents of the included file. All this is done in memory before sending the modified source code to the compiler for compilation. The actual source code file present in the disk isn't affected in any way.

The included file may further include other files. Included files generally contain function declarations *(system header files contain system library function declarations)*, type-defined values, defined macros, structure or union declarations etc. When the included file is specified within *double-quotation marks* in the *'#include'* directive, the file is first searched in the current directory and then in the standard directories. If specified within the pair '<>' *(less than and greater than symbols)*, the file is searched only in the standard directories. If the included file is not found, an error is reported and the compilation stops.

We may create our own header files to be included within our source code files. When we have functions, structures, type-defined identifiers, macros *(defined values)* etc., which are needed across multiple source code files within our project, we send their declarations to header files. Header files act as common repository for all these declarations. The body of a declared function *(definition)* may be written in any one of the source code files of the project. Due to the function declaration being present in the header file, including the header file allows us to call the function from a different source code file *(other than the one where it is defined)*. The declaration provides the compiler with the information regarding the function name, the arguments accepted and its return type. The compiler does not check for the existence of the body *(definition)* of the function, which is the responsibility of the linker. The linker links all the object files *(an object file is the compiled representation of a source code file)* together, and checks for the existence of the function implementations in the combined *(linked)* output.

Assume we have a project with two source code files *(source1.c and source2.c)* and one header file *(header1.h)*. We have one function *(MyFunction1)* which has been defined in *'source1.c'*. Another function *'MyFunction2'* is defined in *'source2.c'* but needs to call the function *'myFunction1'* to perform certain tasks. As *'myFunction1'* is not present in the source file *'source2.c'*, the compiler will raise an error if we try to call the function from *'myFunction2'*. To overcome the error, we may specify the declaration of the function *'myFunction1'* within the header file *'header1.h'*, and include that header file within the source code file *(source2.c)* from where the call to the function is made. Similarly, structures, unions, type-defined values or macros *(defined values)* may be defined in a header file, which in turn is included in the source code files wherever they are used.

15.3 MACRO DIRECTIVES

We have already seen the use of *'#define'* statement which replaces a defined name by a token wherever the name appears within the source code file. The use of the *'#define'* statement to define the name corresponding to the token is called *Macro Definition (or simply a macro),* and the **process** of substituting the defined name with the token within the source code file is called *Macro Substitution.* The preprocessor is responsible for achieving the macro substitution by replacing all occurrences of the defined name with the corresponding token. Let us reiterate the general form of a *'#define'* statement as:

#define   *symbolic-name*   *value*

Wherever the *symbolic-name* appears in the source code file, it is replaced with the *value* specified corresponding to the name. The *value* can be a string, a character, an integer, a real value, a group of code statements or even another macro. There must be at-least one space each between *'#define'*, *symbolic name* and *value*. The *symbolic name* must be a valid C name.

The different forms of macro substitution are:
1. Simple macro substitution
2. Macro substitution using arguments
3. Nested macro substitution
4. Standard Predefined Macros

15.3.1 SIMPLE MACRO SUBSTITUTION

We have been using simple macro substitution throughout our book. We associate a simple token *(like a number, character or a string)* with a defined name. Wherever the preprocessor finds that name within the source code file, it replaces that name with the specified token. The modified code is then sent to the compiler for compilation. Have a look at the next example:

```
#include <stdio.h>
#define MAX_ELEMENTS 10
int main(void)
{
    int rgNumbers[MAX_ELEMENTS] = { 0 };
    int idx = 0;
    for (; idx < MAX_ELEMENTS; idx++)
    {
        rgNumbers[idx] = idx * idx;
    }
    return 0;
}
```

In the above program, the preprocessor replaces the defined name 'MAX_ELEMENTS' with 10 wherever it finds that name. So, essentially we have declared an array 'rgNumbers' of 10 elements. Also, the comparison 'idx < MAX_ELEMENTS' is expanded to 'idx < 10' by the preprocessor before the compiler takes over.

It is a convention to write the macro name in all capital letters. This helps us to identify them as symbolic constants and distinguish them from other variables. Though, within the source code, the macro name is substituted with the expression with which it is associated, a similar text *(as the macro name)* appearing within a string are not replaced. If we have a macro as below:

#define MAXNUM   5

All occurrences of 'MAXNUM' will be replaced by 5, starting after the line of definition of the macro to the end of the source code file. If we have code segment as below:

```
int iTotal = MAXNUM * iRate;
printf("MAXNUM = %d.", MAXNUM);
```

The above code segment will be changed to the following during preprocessing:

```
int iTotal = 5 * iRate;
printf("MAXNUM = %d.", 5);
```

Notice that the string 'MAXNUM = %d.' is left unchanged.

A macro definition may have something more than a simple constant value. It may include expressions which expand to meaningful expressions wherever they are used. They may include other macro names too. Some examples are:

```
#define PI    3.141592
#define DOUBLE_PI    (PI * 2)
#define MAXVAL    8 * 64
#define INT_SIZE    sizeof(int)
```

The second macro *(DOUBLE_PI)* above, uses the previously defined macro *'PI'* in its expression. So, wherever we use the macro name *'DOUBLE_PI'*, it is first replaced by the expression *'(PI * 2)'* and then to *'(3.141592 * 2)'*. Similarly, wherever we use the macro name *'INT_SIZE'*, it is replaced by the expression *'sizeof(int)'*.

We may pretty much use any expression within a macro, which replaces the macro name wherever the macro name is used. Some more interesting macros are:

```
#define PRINTHELLO    printf("Hello")
#define GREATER_THAN   >
#define EQUAL_TO    ==
#define LESS_THAN    <
#define INCREMENT    ++
```

The above macros can be used as below:

```
#include <stdio.h>
int main(void)
{
    int iCount = 0;
    PRINTHELLO;
    if (10 GREATER_THAN 5)
        INCREMENT iCount;
    if (5 EQUAL_TO 5)
        INCREMENT iCount;
}
```

15.3.2 MACRO SUBSTITUTION USING ARGUMENTS

We can define macros whose use look like a function call. We use the same *'#define'* directive, but put a pair of parentheses immediately following the macro name. These type of macros may or may not accept arguments. To define a macro that uses arguments, we specify parameters between the pair of parentheses in the macro definition. These parameters must be valid C identifiers, separated by commas. White space character may optionally be present between the parameters, but, no white space is allowed between the macro name and the left parenthesis. Consider the below example where the macro finds the greater number between two numbers.

```
#define MAX(x, y)   (x > y)?x:y
int main(void)
{
    printf("The greater number is %d.", MAX(5, 7));
}
```

To invoke a macro that accepts arguments, we write the name of the macro followed by a list of actual arguments within the parentheses, separated by commas. The number of actual arguments must equal the number of formal parameters specified in the macro definition. Invoking a macro is also known as a *macro call (similar to a function call).* When a macro is called, the preprocessor substitutes the expression, replacing the formal parameters with the actual parameters. So in our above example, when we make the macro call *'MAX(5, 7)'*, the macro expression *'(x > y)?x:y'* is replaced by *'(5 > 7)?5:7'*.

We should be very careful in making a macro call as macro argument replacements may result into a value which we did not expect. The macro arguments are **not** evaluated before expanding the macro. This can be explained using a very simple example:

```
#define CUBE(x)    (x * x * x)
int main(void)
{
    printf("The cube is: %d.\n\n", CUBE(3 + 2));
    return 0;
}
```

What do we expect when we run the above program? We expect to print the result as 125 *(5 * 5 * 5)*. But, what we will actually print is 17. This is because the preprocessor performs a blind text substitution of the formal parameter *'x'* with the actual parameter *'3 + 2'*. So, what we essentially get after the text substitution is *'3 + 2 * 3 + 2 * 3 + 2'*, which gives us the final result as 17. This is not the result we expected! To achieve the desired result, we need to enclose the actual parameters within parentheses. This changes our macro call to *'CUBE((3 + 2))'*. Notice the extra parenthesis surrounding the *'3 + 2'*. What we get after the macro substitution in this case is:

$$'(3 + 2) * (3 + 2) * (3 + 2)'$$

This gives us the expected result. But, macro calls may be present in a lot of places within the program. Missing the parentheses even in a single place will produce erroneous result for our program. An effective way to make the macro call error free is to change the macro itself as below:

$$\text{#define CUBE(x)   ((x) * (x) * (x))}$$

This makes our macro to be expanded properly, even if we miss the extra parentheses during the macro call.

The arguments passed to macros can be concatenated using **token pasting operator** *(##)*. When a macro is expanded, the two tokens on either side of the '##' operator are combined into a single token. It is also possible to concatenate two numbers to form a single number. Consider the below example:

```
#include <stdio.h>
#define MERGE(x, y) x##y
int main()
{
    printf("%d\n", MERGE(76, 81));
    printf("%s\n\n", MERGE("I Love ", "C Programming"));
}
```

Output:
```
7681
I Love C Programming
```

C provides another operator called **stringizing operator** *(#)* which converts macro parameters to string literals. The actual parameters to the macro are not changed or affected. Wherever the stringizing operator precedes the use of the argument within the macro, it transforms that to a string literal. All other locations pertaining to the use of the argument without a preceding stringizing operator remain unchanged and follow their original behavior.

```c
#include <stdio.h>

#define printline(x)  printf(#x "\n")
#define printvalue(x) printf(#x " is %d\n", x)

int main(void)
{
    int a = 5;
    int b = 10;

    printline(I love football);
    printvalue(a + b);

    return 0;
}
```

Output:
```
I love football
a + b is 15
```

If we have multiple lines of expression in our macro, each line must end with a backslash '\'. The last line of the expression does not need to have the backslash '\'. Have a look at the next example:

```c
#include <stdio.h>
#include <stdlib.h>

#define FREE_ARRAY(x) if (x != NULL) \
                      {               \
                          free(x);   \
                          x = NULL;  \
                      }

int main(void)
{
    int  i   = 0;
    int *ptr = (int *)malloc(10 * sizeof(int));
    if (ptr)
    {
        for (; i < 10; i++)
            ptr[i] = i;
    }

    FREE_ARRAY(ptr);
    return 0;
}
```

15.3.3 NESTED MACRO SUBSTITUTION

We may have a macro which is dependent on the outcome of another macro. We may use the other macro within the definition of this macro. In other words, we may have nested macros wherein the macro definition of one macro contains the use of other macros. Consider the following examples:

```
#define NUM_ROWS    10
#define NUM_COLS    4
#define TOTAL_ELEMENTS    (NUM_ROWS * NUM_COLS)
#define SQUARE(x)   (x * x)
#define CUBE(x)   (SQUARE(x) * x)
#define QUAD(x)   (CUBE(x) * x)
```

The macro which is used within another macro needs to be defined first. For the containing macro, the preprocessor expands each sub *(contained)* macro until there are no more macros to expand. If we are using the macro *'QUAD'* in our code, it will be expanded in the following order:

- The first expansion of '(CUBE(x) * x)' yields the following:
  ((SQUARE(x) * x) * x), where 'CUBE(x)' is expanded to '(SQUARE(x) * x)'.
- The second expansion of '((SQUARE(x) * x) * x)' yields the following:
  (((x * x) * x) * x), where 'SQUARE(x)' is expanded to '(x * x)'.

Macros can also be used as parameters of other macros. For example, we may do the following:

```
#define SQUARE(x)   (x * x)
#define HALF(x)   (x / 2)
#define HALF_SQUARE(x)   HALF(SQUARE(x))
```

The macro 'HALF_SQUARE' finds the half of the square of a number. So, if we provide 6 as the argument to the macro, it will generate the result as '((6 * 6) / 2)' = 18. This means the output of 'SQUARE' will act as the input of 'HALF' producing the result for 'HALF_SQUARE'.

Similarly, we may nest a macro within itself during the macro call. Few paragraphs ago, we had discussed a macro 'MAX' which finds the maximum of two numbers. We may modify its call to find the maximum of three numbers as below:

MAX(x, MAX(y, z))

15.3.4 STANDARD PREDEFINED MACROS

There are certain predefined macros which are defined by most C compilers. These macros help achieve certain tasks easily. Some are:

- __FILE__: This macro expands to the name of the current source file, in the form of a C string constant. It specifies the name of the file in which this macro is specified *(called)*.
- __FUNCTION__: This macro expands to a C string constant constituting the name of the function in which this macro is specified.
- __LINE__: This macro expands to the current line number within the source file, in the form of an integer constant. It specifies the line number of the location where this macro is specified.
- __DATE__: This macro expands to the date on which the preprocessor is being run, in the form of a C string constant. So, generally this expands to the date of compilation of the source file in which this macro is specified.
- __TIME__: This macro expands to the time at which the preprocessor is being run, in the form of a C string constant. So, generally this expands to the time of compilation of the source file in

which this macro is specified.

Usage example:
```
printf("File: %s, Function: %s, Line: %d, Date and time of compilation: %s %s.\n\n",
    __FILE__, __FUNCTION__, __LINE__, __DATE__, __TIME__);
```

15.3.5 UNDEFINING A MACRO

If a macro ceases to be useful, we may undefine it with the '**#undef**' directive. We may also require a macro to behave differently from a different point within the program. For such situations, we may undefine the macro and redefine it with the new meaning. '#undef' takes a single argument, which is the name of the macro to undefine. It takes the following form:

#undef MACRO_NAME

15.3.6 VARIADIC MACROS

Introduced in C99, variadic macros are macros that accept a variable number of arguments and are very similar to functions which do the same. On most occasions a variadic macro is used as a pass thru to a function accepting variable number of arguments. The arguments within the variable arguments list **cannot** be individually accessed within the macro.

In a variadic macro, a sequence of three dots *(ellipsis)* '...' is used to indicate that one or more arguments must be passed. The ellipsis may be specified as the final formal argument in the macro definition. The macro may forward the variable argument list to a variadic function using the keyword '**__VA_ARGS__**'. The general form of a variadic macro is:

#define MACRO_NAME(Fixed-Arguments, ...)   Macro-Body

Let us explain variadic macros using a simple example:

```c
#include <stdio.h>

#define PRINT_IF_ZERO(x, ...) if (!x) { printf(__VA_ARGS__); }
#define PRINT1(...)          printf(__VA_ARGS__)
#define PRINT2(format, ...)  printf(format, __VA_ARGS__)

int main(void)
{
    float fltPrice = 1.89;
    char  szItem[] = "Tomatoes";

    PRINT_IF_ZERO(0, "%s %s is $%f\n", "The price of", szItem, fltPrice);

    PRINT_IF_ZERO(1, "This line will not print");
    PRINT_IF_ZERO(5, "%s", "This line too will not print");

    PRINT1("%s %s is $%f\n", "The price of", szItem, fltPrice);
    PRINT2("%s %s is $%f\n", "The price of", szItem, fltPrice);

    return 0;
}
```

15.4 COMPILER CONTROL DIRECTIVES

Compiler control preprocessor directives are statements which change the behavior of the compiler when compiling the program. The compiler will work according to the instructions specified using the directives. The compiler control preprocessor directives are of the following types:

- Conditional preprocessor statements
- Pragma directives
- Diagnostic preprocessor statements

15.4.1 CONDITIONAL PREPROCESSOR STATEMENTS

A conditional preprocessor statement is a directive that instructs the preprocessor to include or exclude a piece of code in the final output code to be passed onto the compiler. A conditional preprocessor statement is very similar to an 'if' statement in C, except for the fact that an 'if' statement is evaluated during execution of the program whereas a conditional preprocessor statement is evaluated before a source code is sent for compilation. The purpose of conditional preprocessor statement is to allow different code segments to be included in the program depending on certain conditions *(like a defined value etc.)* at the time of compilation.

A program may need to use different set of code depending on the machine or operating system in which it is going to run. The code for one operating system may not work on another operating system *(operating system specific APIs etc.)*. We use conditional compilation to avoid the portion of the code which will not work on a specific operating system. The conditional compilation is achieved using a preprocessor condition where the invalid code can be avoided from the program.

A preprocessor condition whose result is always false is also used to exclude code *(code which is not required right now)* from the program but keep it as a sort of comment for future reference.

Now let us discuss the different types of conditional preprocessor directives:

1. **#ifdef:** This is the simplest form of conditional preprocessor directive. It is paired with a **'#endif'** directive, and consists of a block of code *(controlled code)* specified between the *(#ifdef-#endif)* pair. The general form of such a directive is given below:

    #ifdef *MACRONAME*
    Controlled code
    #endif

    The controlled code will be included in the output of the preprocessor *(and thus compiled)* if and only if *'MACRONAME'* is defined. *'MACRONAME'* must be defined in the source file before the *'#ifdef'* check, for the conditional check to be successful. The controlled code may include further preprocessor statements including other conditional preprocessor directives. This means that just like 'if' statements, we may have nested conditional preprocessor statements. The inner conditional statements are evaluated only if the outer conditions succeed. Like the curly braces ('{' and '}') in nested 'if' statements, *'#endif'* always matches the nearest *'#ifdef'*.

In the below example, the controlled code within *(#ifdef-#endif)* will get executed as *'MAX_BUFFER'* is defined. Commenting or removing the *'MAX_BUFFER'* definition will make the controlled code to be skipped from compilation.

```
#define MAX_BUFFER    128

#ifdef MAX_BUFFER

#define NUM_ELEMENTS    MAX_BUFFER/sizeof(int)
int g_rgiValues[NUM_ELEMENTS];

#endif
```

2. **#ifndef:** This is very similar in usage to *'#ifdef'*, except for the fact that it works just the opposite. In this case, the controlled code is included only if *'MACRONAME'* is not defined.

> **#ifndef** *MACRONAME*
> *Controlled code*
> **#endif**

3. **#if:** Unlike *'#ifdef'* which only checks for the existence of a macro, *'#if'* directive allows us to test the value of an arithmetic expression. If the value of the expression evaluates to 'true' *(non zero)*, the controlled code within the *'#if-#endif'* pair is included in compilation. The general form of the directive is:

> **#if** *expression*
> *Controlled code*
> **#endif**

'expression' is a valid C expression, which may contain:
a) Integer constants.
b) Character constants.
c) Arithmetic, bitwise, relational and logical operators.
d) Macros. All macros in the expression are expanded before actual computation of the expression's value is performed.
e) Use of defined operator, which lets us check whether macros are defined or not.

4. **#if-#else:** *'#else'* acts as an extension to the *'#if'* directive. *'#else'* also contains a controlled code, which is sent for compilation only if the *'#if'* conditional check fails. The general form of the directive is:

> **#if** *expression*
> *Controlled code 1*
> **#else**
> *Controlled code 2*
> **#endif**

If *'expression'* evaluates to true *(non zero)*, *'Controlled code 1'* is compiled, else, *'Controlled code 2'* is compiled.

5. **#if-#elif-#else:** *'#if-#elif-#else'* is a further extension of the *'#if'* directive. *'#elif'* behaves very similarly to 'else if' statement, except for the fact that it is a preprocessor directive and the rules corresponding to *'#if'* directive must apply to *'#elif'* too. This means the *'expression'* corresponding to the *'#elif'* directive must follow the same rules as the *'#if'* directive. A *'#elif'* directive is evaluated only if all previous *'#if'* and *'#elif'* directives evaluate to zero *(their corresponding expressions have evaluated to false)*. The general form of the *'#elif'* directive is:

```
#if expression1
Controlled code 1

#elif expression2
Controlled code 2

#elif expression3        /* Optional block */
Controlled code 3

#else
Controlled code 4
#endif
```

'expression3' is evaluated only if the result of both expressions *'expression1'* and *'expression2'* have evaluated to zero. Subsequently, if *'expression3'* evaluates to true *(non zero)*, the *'Controlled code 3'* gets compiled. *'Controlled code 4'* is included in compilation only if all previous *'#if'* and *'#elif'* directives evaluate to zero.

Usage example:

```
#define LOGLEVEL 7

#if LOGLEVEL == 0
#define LOG_BUFFER_SIZE    10

#elif LOGLEVEL < 5
#define LOG_BUFFER_SIZE    50

#elif LOGLEVEL >= 5 && LOGLEVEL <= 10
#define LOG_BUFFER_SIZE    100

#else
#define LOG_BUFFER_SIZE    200

#endif
```

6. **defined:** The *'defined'* operator is used in *'#if'* and *'#elif'* expressions to test whether a name is defined as a macro. It evaluates to non zero, if *'MACRONAME'* is defined as a macro and zero, if it is not defined. Thus, *'#if defined' MACRONAME* is precisely equivalent to *'#ifdef' MACRONAME*. Usage example:

#if defined *(MACRONAME1)* || **defined** *(MACRONAME2)*

evaluates to non zero, if either of *'MACRONAME1'* or *'MACRONAME2'* is defined as a macro.

15.4.2 Pragma DIRECTIVES

The **'#pragma'** directive is used to access compiler specific preprocessor extensions. It is used to specify how a compiler should process its input. The *'#pragma'* directives are compiler specific and may vary from one compiler to another. Some common *'#pragma'* statements are:

1. **#pragma once:** It indicates that the file, in which the *pragma* is stated, will be included only once by the compiler during a build. It is mainly stated at the start of a header file to instruct the compiler to include that header file just once during the compilation of a source file.

   This can be explained using an example. Say, we have two header file *'header1.h'* and *'header2.h'* and a source file *'source1.c'*. The header file *'header2.h'* in turn includes *'header1.h'* and the source file includes both the header files. So, the source file gets the reference to *'header1.h'* twice, once when it directly includes *'header1.h'* and the next via *'header2.h'* *(header2.h includes header1.h)*. This can result into compilation error as the compiler will get reference to all declarations declared in *'header1.h'* twice. One way to prevent the compiler error is to use this directive at the start of the header file *'header1.h'*, which makes the *'header1.h'* to be included only once during the build.

   Another way in which we can achieve this same objective *(without the use of #pragma once)* is to put all declarations in *'header1.h'* *(entire header1.h contents)* within a *'#ifndef'* directive. But, clearly using the statement *'#pragma once'* is much simpler than doing the following:

   ```
   #ifndef _HEADER1_H_INCLUDED_
   #define _HEADER1_H_INCLUDED_
   /* Specify all declarations here */
   #endif
   ```

2. **#pragma comment:** Places a comment into an object or executable file. It has the below form:

   #pragma comment(*Comment-Type, Comment-String*)

   The *'Comment-Type'* can be the following:
   a) **compiler** – Places the name and version number of the compiler in the object file. *'Comment-String'* is not used and ignored.
   b) **exestr** – Places *'Comment-String'* in the executable file. *'Comment-String'* is any programmer specified string. This is mostly used to put copyright information within an object or executable file.
   c) **lib** – Links the specified library with the executable. The *'Comment-String'* parameter

specifies the name *(and possibly the path)* of the library to link.

d) **linker** – Places a linker option within the object file. The *'Comment-String'* specifies the linker option.

e) **user** – Places a general comment in the object file. The *'Comment-String'* contains the text of the comment.

Usage examples:
#pragma comment*(compiler)*
#pragma comment*(lib, "mylib.lib")*

3. **#pragma warning:** Allows us to selectively modify the behavior of compiler warning messages during compilation. It has the following form:

#pragma warning*(Warning-Specifier : Warning-Number-list)*

The *'Warning-Specifier'* can be the following:

a) **once** – Makes the compiler display the warning message corresponding to the *'Warning-Number'* only once during the compilation. Example: *#pragma warning(once : 4381)* displays the warning 4381 only once.

b) **disable** – Stops the compiler from displaying the listed warnings. The warning numbers are specified in the *'Warning-Number-list'*. Example: *#pragma warning(disable : 4327 154)* prevents the compiler from showing the warnings 4327 and 154.

c) **error** – Forces the compiler to report the specified warnings as errors. Example: *#pragma warning(error : 4257)* makes the compiler report 4257 as an error *(instead of a warning)*. This forces the compilation to stop immediately.

C99 introduced the **_Pragma operator** to address a major problem with *'#pragma'*. *'#pragma'* being a directive, cannot be produced as the result of a macro expansion making them unsuitable to be used within macros. Being an operator, *_Pragma* can be embedded within macros. It has the following syntax:

_Pragma*(String-Literal)*

where *'String-Literal'* can be either a normal or wide-character string enclosed within double quotes. It is a compiler specific directive which may vary from one compiler to another.

15.4.3 DIAGNOSTIC PREPROCESSOR STATEMENTS

Diagnostic preprocessor statements are of two types:

1. **#error:** The directive *'#error'* causes the preprocessor to report a fatal error and stop compilation. The string following *'#error'* is used as the error message. Example:

```
#ifdef _32BIT_
#error "This program will not work on 32 bit architecture."
#endif
```

2. **#warning:** Similar to *'#error'*, but makes the preprocessor issue a warning and continue the processing.

3. **_Static_assert** *(static_assert)***:** Tests an expression at compile time. If the specified expression

is false, the compiler displays the specified message and stops the compilation, otherwise it has no effect. '_Static_assert' keyword or 'static_assert' macro were included from C11 and their general form are:

$$\_Static\_assert(expression,\ message);$$

Or

$$static\_assert(expression,\ message);$$

Some examples are:

```
_Static_assert(sizeof(int) >= 4, "sizeof(int) should be greater or equal to 4");
static_assert(sizeof(void *) == 4, "The program compiles only for 32-bit");
```

15.5 SAMPLE PROGRAM

1. N-Queens problem deals with the placing of N chess queens on a N × N Chessboard so that no two queens can attack each other, i.e. no two queens are in the same line - diagonally, horizontally or vertically. Our program will solve the problem for a defined 'N'. The chess board is visualized as a two-dimensional N x N array where an element value of '1' indicates a queen's position. For example, following is an array representation for a 4-Queen solution:

$$\{\ 0,\ 1,\ 0,\ 0\ \}$$
$$\{\ 0,\ 0,\ 0,\ 1\ \}$$
$$\{\ 1,\ 0,\ 0,\ 0\ \}$$
$$\{\ 0,\ 0,\ 1,\ 0\ \}$$

We use the backtracking algorithm for solving the N-Queens problem. We will place queens one by one in different columns, starting from the left-most column. Before placing a queen in a column, we will check for clashes (diagonally and horizontally) with already placed queens. We do not require to check vertically as we place only a single queen in each column eliminating the possibility of two queens appearing in the same column. In the current column 'n', we try each row to find a row for which there is no clash.

a) If we find such a row, we mark this array element '[row][column]' with '1' i.e. as part of the solution, and do a recursive call to find queen placements for the next remaining columns.

b) If we do not find such a row for the entire current column 'n', we return false. During our recursive call 'n - 1' (while processing the previous column 'n - 1'), we get the result from the nth recursion as false, and we backtrack. We then try to find a different row for the 'n - 1' column (than the one which was previously found) with no clash.

If we do not find any, we return false. In turn, the recursive call for the 'n - 2' column gets the result as false and that too backtracks and tries to find a different row (than the one which was previously found). The backtrack continues until a column finds a different row with no clash and we again start moving forward.

The program prints a 'Q' at the location where a queen is placed and a '#' in all other locations.

```c
#include <stdio.h>

#define NUM_QUEENS    7
```

```
/* If your compiler does not support C99 or above, comment the following. */
#define C99_SUPPORTED

#ifndef C99_SUPPORTED
#define _Bool int
#endif

#ifndef false
#define false   0
#endif

#ifndef true
#define true    1
#endif

_Bool CanPlace(unsigned int rgiBoard[NUM_QUEENS][NUM_QUEENS],
               int          iRow,
               int          iColumn)
{
    /* Variable declaration and initialization. */
    int i = 0;
    int j = 0;

    /* Check if a queen appears in this same row which means a clash. We need to
       check only till 'iColumn' as all later columns are yet to be processed. */
    for (j = 0; j < iColumn; j++)
    {
        if (0 != rgiBoard[iRow][j])
        {
            /* Its a clash. A queen appears in this row but in a different column. */
            return false;
        }
    }

    /* Check upper-left diagonal of this element for a clash. */
    for (i = iRow, j = iColumn; i >= 0 && j >= 0; i--, j--)
    {
        if (0 != rgiBoard[i][j])
        {
            /* There is a clash in the upper-left diagonal. */
            return false;
        }
    }

    /* Check lower-left diagonal of this element for a clash. */
    for (i = iRow, j = iColumn; i < NUM_QUEENS && j >= 0; i++, j--)
    {
        if (0 != rgiBoard[i][j])
        {
            /* There is a clash in the lower-left diagonal. */
            return false;
        }
    }

    /* There are no clash for this row. */
    return true;
}

_Bool PlaceQueen(unsigned int rgiBoard[NUM_QUEENS][NUM_QUEENS],
                 int          iColumn)
{
    /* Variable declaration and initialization. */
    int    iRow    = 0;
```

```c
    _Bool fPlaced = false;

    /* All queens are already placed. Return true. */
    if (iColumn >= NUM_QUEENS)
    {
        return true;
    }

    /* Try to find a row for this column where we will have no clash. */
    for (; iRow < NUM_QUEENS; iRow++)
    {
        /* Check if the queen can be placed in this row. */
        if (CanPlace(rgiBoard, iRow, iColumn))
        {
            /* We found a row with no clash. Mark this array element as a
               possible solution. Note: This is not the final solution as it
               may change if no possible location is found in a later column. */
            rgiBoard[iRow][iColumn] = 1;

            /* Use recursion to find the queen placements for the
               remaining columns to the right. */
            if (PlaceQueen(rgiBoard, iColumn + 1))
            {
                /* This column and all later columns are solved. So, this row is
                   the correct position for this column and we abondon the search. */
                fPlaced = true;
                break; /* break out of the for loop. */
            }

            /* Queen's placement could not be found in one of the later columns. So
               in this column, we need to find a different row for the queen which
               may resolve the clash in the later column. In a single word: BACKTRACK */
            rgiBoard[iRow][iColumn] = 0;
        }
    }

    return fPlaced;
}

void PrintBoard(unsigned int rgiBoard[NUM_QUEENS][NUM_QUEENS])
{
    /* Variable declaration and initialization. */
    int iRow    = 0;
    int iColumn = 0;

    printf("The solution for the %u-Queens problem is:", NUM_QUEENS);
    for (; iRow < NUM_QUEENS; iRow++)
    {
        printf("\n");
        for (iColumn = 0; iColumn < NUM_QUEENS; iColumn++)
        {
            printf("%c ", (0 != rgiBoard[iRow][iColumn]) ? 'Q' : '#');
        }
    }
}

int main(void)
{
    /* Variable declaration and initialization. */
    unsigned int rgiBoard[NUM_QUEENS][NUM_QUEENS] = { 0 };

    if (!PlaceQueen(rgiBoard, 0))
    {
```

```
        /* Returned 0 (false). ['!' of '!= 0' means '== 0'] */
        printf("Failed to find a solution to the %u-Queens problem.\n\n",
               NUM_QUEENS);
    }
    else
    {
        /* We found a solution. Print the result. */
        PrintBoard(rgiBoard);
        printf("\n\n");
    }

    return 0;
}
```

DEPRECATED FUNCTIONS

[CHAPTER-16]

Just like most other computer languages, advancements have been made in C too, with newer versions released over the years. Each new version has come with new features and most importantly security enhancements. Many old library functions had security flaws which made them prone to memory faults, hack attacks and overflow issues. Simple programming error could lead these functions to go kaput leading to the program crash. As these functions were already in use by many applications around the world, changing their behavior, their signature *(prototype)* or removing them entirely were not feasible. So, newer version of these functions were developed where the functions had a similar but different name and were recommended to be used in new applications. Though the signature was changed for many of the new version functions, the changes were very limited and bore resemblance to the older ones. The old functions were deprecated and not recommended to be used any more. Though we may still use these functions, but, the compiler will generate a warning if we try to do so. We must remember that future versions of C may remove these functions entirely. Some of the library functions which have been deprecated and their newer secure counterparts are given below:

Sr. No.	Deprecated (ANSI Version)	Recommended (ANSI Version)	Deprecated (Wide Char Version)	Recommended (Wide Char Version)
1	asctime	asctime_s	_wasctime	_wasctime_s
2	atof	strtod	_wtof	wcstod
3	atoi	strtol	_wtoi	wcstol
4	atol	strtol	_wtol	wcstol
5	atoll	strtoll	_wtoll	wcstoll
6	bsearch	bsearch_s		
7	ctime	ctime_s	_wctime	_wctime_s
8	fopen	fopen_s	_wfopen	_wfopen_s
9	fprintf	fprintf_s	fwprintf	fwprintf_s
10	freopen	freopen_s	_wfreopen	_wfreopen_s
11	fscanf	fscanf_s	fwscanf	fwscanf_s
12	getenv	getenv_s	_wgetenv	_wgetenv_s
13	gets	gets_s	_getws	_getws_s
14	gmtime	gmtime_s		
15	localtime	localtime_s		
16	mbsrtowcs	mbsrtowcs_s		
17	mbstowcs	mbstowcs_s		
18	memcpy	memcpy_s	wmemcpy	wmemcpy_s
19	memmove	memmove_s	wmemmove	wmemmove_s
20	printf	printf_s	wprintf	wprintf_s
21	qsort	qsort_s		

Sr. No.	Deprecated (ANSI Version)	Recommended (ANSI Version)	Deprecated (Wide Char Version)	Recommended (Wide Char Version)
22	scanf	scanf_s	wscanf	wscanf_s
23	setbuf	setvbuf		
24	snprintf	_snprintf_s	_snwprintf	_snwprintf_s
25	sprintf	sprintf_s	swprintf	swprintf_s
26	sscanf	sscanf_s	swscanf	swscanf_s
27	strcat	strcat_s	wcscat	wcscat_s
28	strcpy	strcpy_s	wcscpy	wcscpy_s
29	strerror	strerror_s	_wcserror	_wcserror_s
30	strncat	strncat_s	wcsncat	wcsncat_s
31	strncpy	strncpy_s	wcsncpy	wcsncpy_s
32	strtok	strtok_s	wcstok	wcstok_s
33	vfprintf	vfprintf_s	vfwprintf	vfwprintf_s
34	vfscanf	vfscanf_s	vfwscanf	vfwscanf_s
35	vprintf	vprintf_s	vwprintf	vwprintf_s
36	vscanf	vscanf_s	vwscanf	vwscanf_s
37	vsnprintf	vsnprintf_s	_vsnwprintf	_vsnwprintf_s
38	vsprintf	vsprintf_s	vswprintf	vswprintf_s
39	vsscanf	vsscanf_s	vswscanf	vswscanf_s

Note: Not all compilers support the newer version functions.

BEST PROGRAMMING PRACTICES

[CHAPTER-17]

17.1 INTRODUCTION

As programmers we should always try to write code in a way that makes it:
- Better readable
- Easily understandable
- Better manageable
- Easily maintainable
- Prevent errors from creeping in
- Make our programs more robust

In this chapter, we will understand the techniques which help achieve the above points. Lets start...

17.1.1 DOCUMENTATION

Provide adequate documentation within the entire code using the help of comments. At every critical code segment, we should explain the reason for doing something in a particular way. Comments should be provided explaining the logic and the control flow. Most programs require future maintenance where they need to be reworked *(for adding features and fixing bugs)*. The maintenance may not be done by the original programmers. The rework may also be performed after a considerable amount of time for which even the original programmers too lose track and forget the logic used. So, it becomes essential that we make the program understandable for future reference. But, we should not become over enthusiastic and fill our program with more comments than the actual code :-) itself. Documentation must be just enough to make the program better understandable. Too much documentation will reduce the readability of the program and too less documentation will make it difficult to be understood. Documentation helps make the program understandable, manageable and maintainable.

17.1.2 AVOID USING DEPRECATED FUNCTIONS

Use of deprecated functions make our program error prone and susceptible to hacker and virus attacks. So, always try to use the newer version of the functions. See the chapter on 'Deprecated Functions' for a list of deprecated functions and their recommended alternatives. This technique prevents errors from creeping in our program and makes it more robust.

17.1.3 TABS

The source code editor *(IDE)* should be configured to replace tabs with spaces. Tab stops should be set at four spaces. This ensures that we will see the code in the same way irrespective of the editor in which they are viewed.

17.1.4 INDENTATION

Every new scope should be indented by four spaces *(one tab stop)*. Every time a new scope is introduced, either through the use of a compound statement or the use of braces, indentation of all the statements contained within the new scope should be increased by one *(four spaces)*.

17.1.5 LINE LENGTH

No line should exceed the width of a typical source code editor which is approximately 80-100 characters. A longer line should be broken into multiple lines using line breaks.

17.1.6 BLANK LINES

We can use a single blank line to separate areas of functionality within a method. For example, we could use a blank line after a loop construct to separate it from the below statements. Two *(or three)* blank lines can be used to separate the end of one method from the beginning of another.

17.1.7 FILE HEADER

Every file *(whether header or source)* should start with a comment header. The header should explain the purpose of the file, its creation date, modification history and copyright information *(if any)*. The format of the header must be consistent across all the files. A file header may look as below:

```
/*------------------------------------------------------------------------
** File: MySource.c
**
** Desc: Description of the file. Long description should be broken into multiple
**       lines and also indented like this.
**
**       2017/06/19 - Sudripta Nandy - Initial implementation.
**       2017/11/17 — Sudripta Nandy — Fixed bug #68.
**
** Copyright (c) 2017-2018, MyCompany. All rights reserved.
**----------------------------------------------------------------------*/
```

17.1.8 FUNCTION HEADER

Every function should start with a comment header. The header should explain the purpose of the function, the description of the parameters it accepts, and the possible return values.

```
/*------------------------------------------------------------------------
** Name: MyFunction
** Desc: The description of the function. Long description should be broken into
**       multiple lines and also indented like this.
**
** Parameters:
**       Parameter1: Description of first parameter.
**       Parameter2: Description of second parameter. Long description should
**                   be broken into multiple lines and also indented like this.
**
** Returns:
**       0: Description of when it returns 0.
**       1: Description of when it returns 1.
//----------------------------------------------------------------------*/
```

17.1.9 BRACES

When a code block starts, we may opt to place the opening brace in the same line as the start of the block statement *(if, for, while etc.)* or as separately on the following line. The former option is called the **K&R style**, and the latter is called the **Allman style**. Either style is acceptable, but it should be used consistently across the entire program. The K&R style makes the code more compact but at the cost of readability as the opening brace may be easily overlooked. The Allman style makes the opening and closing braces clearly visible.

```
/* K&R Style */
if (x < 5) {
    printf("x is less than 5");
}

/* Allman Style */
while (x > 0)
{
    x--;
}
```

17.1.10 PREVENT MULTIPLE INCLUSIONS

All include *(header)* files should be protected from being included multiple times during compilation. It can be done in various ways. The preferred way is to use the '#pragma once' directive. Please refer to the topic on '#pragma once' under section 15.4.2.

17.1.11 FUNCTION POINTERS

It is recommended to type-define function pointers. It makes the code cleaner, better readable and easier to understand.

17.1.12 USE OF PARENTHESIS

Wherever we have doubt about operator precedence or associativity, we may use parenthesis to sequence the execution of the operations. Use of parenthesis within complex statements also improve readability allowing us to easily understand the sequence of execution of the operations. When we are working with bitwise operators, use of parenthesis is highly recommended.

$$a = ((iValue \; \& \; 7) << 4);$$

17.1.13 BOOLEAN COMPARISONS

We should never compare a boolean value for equality or inequality with *'true'* or 1. Comparisons should always be done for equality or inequality with *'false'* or 0 *(zero)*. We must remember that any non-zero value represents *'true'*. The exact value of *'true'* may differ between programming languages. A function which returns a boolean value may return any non-zero value to denote a *'true'* outcome *(value)*. So, comparing the returned value with *'true'* *(in the caller function)* may give us incorrect results. Comparisons for equality or inequality with 'false' are permissible because *'false'* is always 0.

We may also use the NOT (!) operator for checking equality or inequality with *'false'*.

17.1.14 COMPARING CONSTANTS

When a constant value *(or a defined value)* is used within a comparison, it should be placed on the left side of the comparison. This will force the compiler to issue an error when we accidentally use '=' instead of '=='.

if (0 == x) */* Recommended */*

if (x == 0) */* Not recommended as we may mistakenly write (x = 0) */*

17.1.15 ALWAYS CHECK RETURN VALUES

When a caller calls another function, it must always check the value returned by the called function before continuing with its execution. The called function might have failed which may result into errors if further processing continues. In worst cases, the program may hit a memory fault and crash. For this reason, every function that has a return code should have its return code checked. Though we may have situations where it is safe to continue even if a called function fails. For rest of the functions, we must check their return code before continuing.

17.1.16 BLOCK STATEMENTS

All block control statements like conditional or loop constructs *(if statements, while statements, for statements etc.)* should be enclosed within opening and closing brace pair. Even if the constructs contain a single statement, they must be enclosed within braces.

```
/* Recommended */
if (x < 5)
{
    x++;
}
```
```
/* Not Recommended */
if (x < 5)
    x++;
```

17.1.17 SWITCH STATEMENTS

A switch statement must be indented as below:

```
switch (variable)
{
    case value1:
        ....
        break;

    case value2:
        ....
        break;
```

```
            default:
               ....
            break;
    }
```

A common bug with *'switch'* statements is to forget placing a *'break'* after executing a *'case'* label. Each case code block should be ended with a break statement. If our logic desires an intentional fall thru to the next 'case' block, we must clearly mark the fall thru using a comment.

17.1.18 DISABLING OUT CODE

When a portion of code is not needed right now, but may make a possible comeback in the future, should **not** be removed and retained as a **non** working code. To make a piece of code non working, we may comment that portion of the code **or** put that code within a **'#if'** block *(preferable)* as below:

```
#if 0
    Obsolete code
#endif
```

We should, using a comment put an explanation behind the reason for disabling the code.

17.1.19 SHORT FUNCTIONS ARE BEAUTIFUL

Long functions are not only harder to maintain but also difficult to understand. Ideally, functions should be able to fully fit onto the screen at one time. Functions longer than approximately 50 lines should be examined to see if they can be broken up into smaller functions. This isn't a hard and fast rule, but will produce more maintainable code.

17.1.20 LIMIT EXIT POINTS FROM FUNCTIONS

Having more than one exit point in a function which allocates memory, risks memory leaks. A common bug is to forget freeing *(deallocate)* an allocated memory when we return early from a function. When our function allocates memory from heap using *'malloc'* or *'calloc'*, we will leak memory if we forget freeing them using *'free'*. If we return early from multiple places, we have to remember freeing the allocations before every point of return. Even if all of these cases are handled, maintenance of the code may be cumbersome and difficult. So, we should try to limit the number of exit points from a function.

There are multiple ways to limit the number of exit points from a function. We will discuss two of them:
- Using **goto**: We may put a label before a single exit point of the function. The label will be followed by all the clean up code *(deallocation etc.)* required for the function. Every location which desires a return from the function, will use a *goto* statement to catapult the control to the label. The construct will be something similar to the following:

```
void MyFunc(void)
{
    int *ptr = NULL;
```

```
ptr = (int *) malloc(10 * sizeof(int));
if (NULL == ptr)
{
   goto CLEANUP;
}
....
....
if ( ... )
{
   goto CLEANUP;
}
....
....
CLEANUP:
if (NULL != ptr)
{
   free(ptr);
   ptr = NULL;
}
}
```

- Using **do-while** construct: We have been using this construct in most of our programs. In this approach, we put most of our function code *(except the variable declarations)* within a *do-while* construct. This *do-while* construct is a bit unique in the sense that it does not loop, and its body is executed just once. We make this a single execution loop by making the loop condition such that it never fulfills. But being an exit-controlled loop, the loop body gets executed once even when the loop condition fails. The construct will be something similar to the following:

```
void MyFunc(void)
{
   int *ptr = NULL;
   do
   {
      ptr = (int *) malloc(10 * sizeof(int));
      if (NULL == ptr)
      {
         break;
      }
      ....
      ....
      if ( ... )
      {
         break;
      }
```

```
                    ....
                    ....
                 } while(0);

                 if (NULL != ptr)
                 {
                    free(ptr);
                    ptr = NULL;
                 }
              }
```

Though both the above approaches work, the second approach is desirable. This is because, the use of *goto* brings its own side effects **(refer section 6.8)**. Also, use of *goto* statements reduces program optimization leading to inefficient programs.

17.1.21 INITIALIZE VARIABLES

This is one of the most basic rules of C programming. Uninitialized C variables *(except static and global variables)* contain garbage values. If we do not initialize them, we may end up comparing them with incorrect values. Pointer variables must be initialized to NULL. Initializing variables also help us during clean up of the variables before we exit the function. If a variable is supposed to be allocated, we must compare its value with NULL before attempting to use it or deallocate it. This prevents us from trying to access an invalid memory location. After a successful deallocation, we must again make the pointer variable point to NULL to prevent its further use.

17.1.22 VARIABLE NAMING CONVENTIONS

We should always name variables according to their usage. By looking at a variable name we should be able to understand its purpose, its scope and its type. We should also be able to understand whether a variable is a constant, an array, a string or a pointer. This ensures easy understanding of the program. Some of the variable naming conventions are:
- Always precede global variable names with with a **'g_'** and static variable names with a **'s_'**.
- A single character variable should start with a **'c'**, an integer variable should start with an **'i'**, a float variable should start with a **'flt'**, a double should start with a **'dbl'** and a boolean variable should start with an **'f'**.
- An array should start with a **'rg'** and a pointer variable should start with a **'p'**.
- ANSI character string should start with **'sz'** and a wide character string should start with **'wsz'**.
- Constants should have all UPPERCASE names.
- Most importantly, the name of a variable should indicate its purpose or use.

Examples:
g_fltRate *(global float variable)*, g_rgiRates[10] *(global integer array)*, s_fToggle *(static boolean variable)*, szName[100] *(character string)*, pszName *(pointer to a string)*, piQuantity *(pointer to an integer)*, MAX_LENGTH *(defined constant value)*.

LINKED LISTS

[CHAPTER-18]

18.1 INTRODUCTION

A list is a group of items organized sequentially. Arrays are one type of lists. We can access array elements using their index or by incrementing a pointer to point to the desired element. As the array elements are sequentially arranged, accessing array elements are quick. But, arrays have some major disadvantages. We need to know the required size of an array beforehand. An array cannot be resized as per our growing need. We may resize an array only if we dynamically allocate the array space from heap using the functions *'malloc'* or *'calloc'*. But, to resize such an array we need to reallocate the array to a new location which is not only time consuming but also a processor intensive task. Moreover, there is no guarantee that we will get enough contiguous free memory space for the new allocation. To overcome this, if we over predict our requirement when creating the array, we will be wasting memory and may quickly run out of memory for other tasks.

In many practical applications, it is impossible to predict our requirement at the beginning. We need to keep allocating as per our requirement. So, arrays make a very inefficient solution to such problems. An efficient solution can be reached with a very different approach using a new kind of list. In this approach, we make each item of the list a part of a structure along with a pointer pointing to the next such structure. In the same sequence, the next structure too contains a **link** *(pointer)* to the structure coming after it. These links allow us to move forward within the list. Optionally, a structure may also contain another **link** pointing back to the previous structure *(the structure coming before it)*. This optional back link allows us to move back within the list.

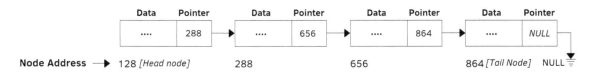

The above figure shows a typical representation of a *single linear linked list*. A single data structure within the list is called a *'node'*. The above figure contains four nodes. A linked list is stated as *'single'*, if we only have a forward link in the linked list. This means that a node only points to the next node within the list. A node lacks a pointer to the previous node within the list. A linked list is called as *'linear'*, if the last node within the list points to NULL, which marks the end of the list.

The first logical node within a list is called the *head node* and the last logical node within the list is called the *tail node*. In the above figure we can see that the head node has a starting memory address of 128 and the tail node has a starting memory address of 864. Similarly, the two middle nodes have addresses of 288 and 656 respectively. We can see that the nodes are **not** allocated consecutive memory locations. A node is assigned a memory address wherever enough consecutive free space is available to just accommodate that node itself. The previous node in the list is then made to point to this newly allocated node.

There are various advantages and disadvantages of using linked lists and they are:

Advantages:
- With arrays we need to have a clear idea regarding the number of elements that are going to be required. Except for dynamic allocation, arrays cannot be expanded or contracted as per requirement. Even for dynamically allocated arrays, expanding or contracting the array is a time consuming and processor intensive task. Linked lists can be easily expanded and contracted as per requirement. Adding a new node or deleting an existing node are low resource operations for linked lists.
- Insertion or deletion of a node is much simpler to do in linked lists.
- Array elements are assigned contiguous memory locations for which a large chunk of free contiguous memory space is required for the allocation to be successful. On the other hand, the nodes of a linked list are non contiguous in memory location. Each node is allocated a different location wherever enough free memory capable of containing that node is available. This makes multiple small memory locations to be allocated for a linked list, unlike a large chunk of contiguous memory for arrays. So, memory availability is better guaranteed for linked lists.

Disadvantages:
- Unlike arrays, random access of linked list nodes is not possible. We have to access nodes sequentially starting from the first or last node. For searching and access of elements, arrays are faster than linked lists.
- As random access is not possible, we cannot do binary search with linked lists.
- Extra memory space for pointers is required with each node of the list.
- Pointer arithmetic for element access can be used with arrays but not with linked list. This again makes element access and retrieval quicker for arrays.

For situations where the number of elements are fixed with no requirement of insertion or deletion of elements, arrays are preferred. For all other cases, linked list make a much better choice.

18.2 LINKED LIST TYPES
There are four possible types of linked list, and they are:
1. Single linear linked list
2. Double linear linked list
3. Single circular linked list
4. Double circular linked list

18.2.1 SINGLE LINEAR LINKED LIST
The example linked list discussed in **section 18.1** is a single linear linked list. The nodes in this list

contain a single pointer pointing to the next node in the list. These nodes do **not** have a back pointer which points to the previous node. This makes the list inoperable for backward traversal, and we can only move forward within the list. An example of the node structure of a single linear linked list is:

```
struct ITEMDETAILS
{
    int iItemID;
    char szItemName[50];
    float fltItemRate;
    struct ITEMDETAILS *pNext;
};
```

'iItemID', 'szItemName' and 'fltItemRate' mark the data portion of the node and 'pNext' is the pointer to the next node. Optionally, we may type-define the structure for easy usage across our program. Our example program *(provided a little later)*, does exactly the same.

Our program will have a pointer *(possibly global)* which will point to the starting node *(Head)* of the list. When the list does not have any nodes, this pointer will point to NULL. Otherwise, this pointer will always point to the head node of the list. Optionally, we may have a pointer which points to the last node *(Tail)* of the list. This pointer too points to NULL when there are no nodes in the list.

Adding nodes to the end of the list is a simple task. If our list is empty, we mark the new node as *'Head'* node of the list. In case of a non-empty list, we make the *'pNext'* pointer of the *'Tail'* node point to the newly created node. We make the *'pNext'* pointer of the new node point to NULL and mark the new node as the new *'Tail'* node of the list.

Inserting a new node between two existing nodes is a little more tricky task. If a new node needs to be inserted between two nodes *('A'* and *'B')*, we make the *'pNext'* pointer of the previous node *('A')* point to the new node and the *'pNext'* pointer of the new node point to the next node *('B')*.

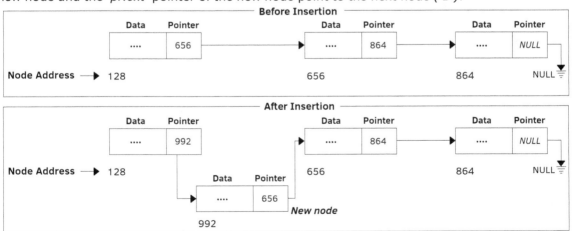

Deleting an existing node requires us to readjust the *'pNext'* pointer of the previous node. If the node to be deleted is the *'Head'* node of our list, we make the node following the current *'Head'* node *(the node to be deleted)* as the new *'Head'* node of the list. In all other cases, we make the *'pNext'* pointer of the previous node point to the node which comes after the node to be deleted.

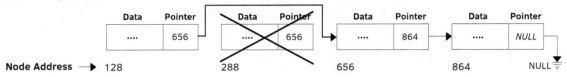

Now, let us understand single linear linked list using a program. In the program, we will hold the electricity consumption details corresponding to the customers of an electric company. The user will provide the total units consumed in a month by a consumer. The consumers will be identified by a unique consumer ID. We will allow the user to add/insert node to the list, delete node from the list and traverse the list.

```c
#include <stdio.h>
#include <stdlib.h>

typedef struct _CONSUMPTIONINFO
{
    long lConsumerID;
    int  iUnitsConsumed;

    struct _CONSUMPTIONINFO *pNext;

}CONSUMPTIONINFO, *PCONSUMPTIONINFO;

PCONSUMPTIONINFO pHead = NULL;

/* The function creates a new node and adds it to the list. The function adds the nodes in
   ascending order based on the consumer ID. */
void AddNodeSorted(void)
{
    CONSUMPTIONINFO *pNewNode = NULL;
    CONSUMPTIONINFO *pMove    = NULL;

    do
    {
        /* Allocate the new node. */
        pNewNode = (CONSUMPTIONINFO *) malloc(sizeof(CONSUMPTIONINFO));
        if (NULL == pNewNode)
        {
            printf("Failed to allocate memory for the new node.\n");
            break;
        }

        /* Accept the consumer details from the user. */
        printf("Enter the consumer ID: ");
        scanf("%ld", &pNewNode->lConsumerID);

        printf("Enter the total units consumed: ");
        scanf("%d", &pNewNode->iUnitsConsumed);

        if (NULL == pHead || pNewNode->lConsumerID < pHead->lConsumerID)
        {
            /* If our list is empty, or the consumer ID of the new node is less than the
               previous 'Head' node (i.e. the smallest in the list), our new node needs
```

to be the new 'Head' node of the list.

If our list was empty, the 'pNext' pointer of the new node must point to NULL. This is because the newly created node is not only the first node, but also the last node of the list. In case of an empty list 'pHead' is NULL, which makes the statement 'pNewNode->pNext = pHead' the same as 'pNewNode->pNext = NULL'. New (Empty list): |N| --> NULL

If the list was non empty and the new node needs to be the new 'Head' node, the statement 'pNewNode->pNext = pHead' makes the 'pNext' pointer of the new node point to the previous starting (Head) node. We then make our 'pHead' pointer point to the newly created node, i.e. the newly created node now becomes the new 'Head' node of the list.
Previously: |3| --> |5| --> |9| --> NULL
Updated (New value 2): |2| --> |3| --> |5| --> |9| --> NULL */

```
        pNewNode->pNext = pHead;
        pHead           = pNewNode;
    }
    else
    {
        /* Locate the position to insert the new node. */
        for (pMove = pHead; pMove->pNext != NULL; pMove = pMove->pNext)
        {
            if (pNewNode->lConsumerID < pMove->pNext->lConsumerID)
            {
                break;
            }
        }

        /* The new node will be placed after 'pMove'. Make the new node point to the
           node which 'pMove' was pointing to. We then make 'pMove' point to the new
           node. If 'pMove' is at |5|,
           Previously:                |3| --> |5| --> |9| --> NULL
           Updated (New value 7): |3| --> |5| --> |7| --> |9| --> NULL */
        pNewNode->pNext = pMove->pNext;
        pMove->pNext    = pNewNode;
    }

    printf("Node successfully added\n");

} while (0);
}

/* The function accepts the consumer ID and deletes the first occurring node with that
   consumer ID. */
void DeleteNode(void)
{
    CONSUMPTIONINFO *pMove  = NULL;
    CONSUMPTIONINFO *pPrev  = NULL;
    long             lConID = -1;

    do
    {
        if (NULL == pHead)
        {
            break;
        }

        /* Accept the consumer ID to delete. */
        printf("Enter the consumer ID to delete: ");
        scanf("%ld", &lConID);
```

```
    if (pHead->lConsumerID == lConID)
    {
        /* We need to delete the 'Head' node. Make the node following the 'Head'
           node as the new 'Head' node. If there are no nodes after the 'Head'
           node, then 'pHead' will now point to NULL. After update, 'pMove' points
           to |3| and 'pHead' points to |5|.
           Previously:                |3| --> |5| --> |9| --> NULL
           Updated (Delete value 3): |5| --> |9| --> NULL */

        pMove = pHead;
        pHead = pHead->pNext;
    }
    else
    {
        /* Locate the node with the consumer ID. 'pPrev' points to the node which
           precedes the node to delete. 'pMove' points to the node to delete. */
        for (pPrev = pHead, pMove = pHead->pNext; pMove != NULL;
             pPrev = pMove, pMove = pMove->pNext)
        {
            if (pMove->lConsumerID == lConID)
            {
                break;
            }
        }

        if (NULL != pMove)
        {
            /* We found the node to delete. Make the previous (preceding)
               node (pPrev) point to the node following the node to delete.
               'pPrev' points to |3| and 'pMove' points to |5|.
               Previously:                |3| --> |5| --> |9| --> NULL
               Updated (Delete value 5): |3| --> |9| --> NULL */
            pPrev->pNext = pMove->pNext;
        }
    }

    if (NULL != pMove)
    {
        /* We found the node to delete. Free the node memory. */
        free(pMove);
        pMove     = NULL;
        printf("Node successfully deleted.\n");
    }
    else
    {
        printf("No node with the given consumer ID found.\n");
    }

} while (0);
}

/* The function traverses the entire list and prints each node's values. */
void TraverseList(void)
{
    CONSUMPTIONINFO *pMove = pHead;

    for (; NULL != pMove; pMove = pMove->pNext)
    {
        printf("Consumer ID: %ld, Units Consumed: %d\n",
               pMove->lConsumerID, pMove->iUnitsConsumed);
    }
}
```

```
int main(void)
{
    int iOption = 0;

    while (4 != iOption)
    {
        printf("\n1. Add node\n2. Delete node\n3. Traverse list\n4. Exit");
        printf("\n\nEnter your option (1-4): ");
        scanf("%d", &iOption);
        printf("\n");

        switch (iOption)
        {
            case 1:
                AddNodeSorted();
                break;
            case 2:
                DeleteNode();
                break;
            case 3:
                TraverseList();
                break;
            default:
                break;
        }
    }

    /* Memory cleanup before exit. */
    for (PCONSUMPTIONINFO pMove = pHead; NULL != pMove; pMove = pHead)
    {
        pHead = pHead->pNext;
        free(pMove);
    }

    return 0;
}
```

18.2.2 DOUBLE LINEAR LINKED LIST

Every node in this list contain two pointers, one pointing to the previous node in the list and another pointing to the next node. The *'pPrev'* pointer of the *'First/Head'* node, and the *'pNext'* pointer of the *'Last/Tail'* node point to NULL. As we have a back pointer too in every node within the list, the list becomes suitable for backward traversal, and we not only can move forward but also backward within the list. An example of the node structure of a double linear linked list is:

```
struct ITEMDETAILS
{
    int iItemID;
    char szItemName[50];
    float fltItemRate;
    struct ITEMDETAILS *pPrev;
    struct ITEMDETAILS *pNext;
};
```

'pPrev' is the pointer to the previous node and *'pNext'* is the pointer to the next node.

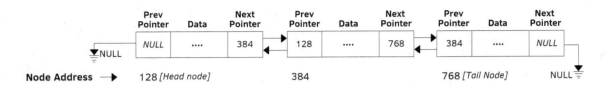

We will have an almost equivalent code as of a single linear linked list when adding a node at the end of the list. Additionally, we will also make the *'pPrev'* pointer of our new node point to the previous *'Tail'* node.

If a new node needs to be inserted between two nodes *('A' and 'B')*, we make the *'pNext'* pointer of the previous node *('A')* point to the new node, the *'pPrev'* pointer of the new node point to the previous node *('A'),* the *'pNext'* pointer of the new node point to the next node *('B')* and the *'pPrev'* pointer of the next node *('B')* point to the new node.

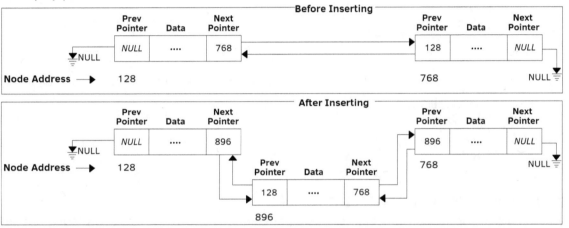

In case of delete, if the node to be deleted is the *'Head'* node of our list, we make the node following the current *'Head'* node as the new *'Head'* node. If we are deleting a node say *'B'* situated between nodes *'A'* and *'C',* we will make the *'pNext'* pointer of *'A'* point to *'C',* and the *'pPrev'* pointer of *'C'* point to *'A'.* This will make *'B'* get disconnected from the linked list.

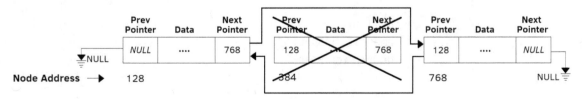

In our next program, we will use the same case situation as the single linear linked list program. The only difference is that we will now use a double linear linked list instead. The *'TraverseList'* function will be exactly similar to the previous program, and so we are not reproducing the same over here.

```c
#include <stdio.h>
#include <stdlib.h>

typedef struct _CONSUMPTIONINFO
{
    long lConsumerID;
    int  iUnitsConsumed;

    struct _CONSUMPTIONINFO *pPrev;
    struct _CONSUMPTIONINFO *pNext;

}CONSUMPTIONINFO, *PCONSUMPTIONINFO;

PCONSUMPTIONINFO pHead = NULL;

/* The function creates a new node and adds it to the list. The function adds the nodes
   in ascending order based on the consumer ID. */
void AddNodeSorted(void)
{
    CONSUMPTIONINFO *pNewNode  = NULL;
    CONSUMPTIONINFO *pPrevNode = NULL;
    CONSUMPTIONINFO *pMove     = NULL;

    do
    {
        /* Allocate the new node. */
        pNewNode = (CONSUMPTIONINFO *) malloc(sizeof(CONSUMPTIONINFO));
        if (NULL == pNewNode)
        {
            printf("Failed to allocate memory for the new node.\n");
            break;
        }

        /* Accept the consumer details from the user. */
        printf("Enter the consumer ID: ");
        scanf("%ld", &pNewNode->lConsumerID);

        printf("Enter the total units consumed: ");
        scanf("%d", &pNewNode->iUnitsConsumed);

        if (NULL == pHead || pNewNode->lConsumerID < pHead->lConsumerID)
        {
            /* If our list is empty, or the consumer ID of the new node is less
               than the previous 'Head' node (i.e. the smallest in the list),
               our new node needs to be the new 'Head' node of the list. */

            /* Make 'pNext' pointer of 'pNewNode' point to the old 'Head' node. */
            pNewNode->pNext = pHead;
            if (NULL != pHead)
            {
                /* Make 'pPrev' pointer of the old 'Head' node point to the new node.
                   This makes our new node get positioned at the start of the list. */
                pHead->pPrev = pNewNode;
            }

            /* As 'pNewNode' now becomes the new starting node,
               its 'pPrev' pointer needs to point to NULL. */
            pNewNode->pPrev = NULL;
            pHead           = pNewNode; /* 'pNewNode' is now the new 'Head'. */
        }
        else
```

```
        {
            /* Locate the position to insert the new node.
               The new node will come in between 'pPrevNode' and 'pMove'.
               |pPrevNode| --> |pNewNode| --> |pMove| ->
               For easier explanation, we are using two pointers 'pPrevNode'
               and 'pMove'. This can instead be done using a single pointer. */
            for (pPrevNode = pHead, pMove = pHead->pNext; pMove != NULL;
                 pPrevNode = pMove, pMove = pMove->pNext)
            {
                if (pNewNode->lConsumerID < pMove->lConsumerID)
                {
                    break;
                }
            }

            /* Make the 'pNext' pointer of the new node point to 'pMove' i.e.
               the node (or NULL) which will come after this new node. */
            pNewNode->pNext = pMove;
            /* Make the 'pPrev' pointer of the new node point to 'pPrevNode'
               i.e. the node which will come before this new node. */
            pNewNode->pPrev = pPrevNode;
            /* As the new node will come after 'pPrevNode', make the 'pNext'
               pointer of the previous node 'pPrevNode' point to the new node. */
            pPrevNode->pNext = pNewNode;
            if (NULL != pMove)
            {
                /* As the new node will come before 'pMove', make the 'pPrev'
                   pointer of the next node 'pMove' point to the new node. */
                pMove->pPrev = pNewNode;
            }
        }

        printf("Node successfully added\n");

    } while (0);
}

/* The function accepts the consumer ID and deletes the first
   occurring node with that consumer ID. */
void DeleteNode(void)
{
    CONSUMPTIONINFO *pMove       = NULL;
    CONSUMPTIONINFO *pPrevNode   = NULL;
    long             lConID      = -1;

    do
    {
        if (NULL == pHead)
        {
            break;
        }

        /* Accept the consumer ID to delete. */
        printf("Enter the consumer ID to delete: ");
        scanf("%ld", &lConID);

        if (pHead->lConsumerID == lConID)
        {
            /* We need to delete the 'Head' node. Make the node following the
               'Head' node as the new 'Head' node. If there are no nodes after
               the 'Head' node, then 'pHead' will now point to NULL. */

            /* We make 'pMove' point to the node to delete. */
```

```c
        pMove           = pHead;
        /* The second node becomes the new 'Head' node. */
        pHead           = pHead->pNext;

        if (NULL != pHead)
        {
            /* Being the new 'Head' node, it's 'pPrev' must now point to NULL. */
            pHead->pPrev = NULL;
        }
    }
    else
    {
        /* Locate the node with the consumer ID.
           'pPrevNode' points to the node which precedes the node to delete.
           'pMove' points to the node to delete. */
        for (pPrevNode = pHead, pMove = pHead->pNext; pMove != NULL;
             pPrevNode = pMove, pMove = pMove->pNext)
        {
            if (pMove->lConsumerID == lConID)
            {
                break;
            }
        }

        if (NULL != pMove)
        {
            /* We found the node to delete. Make the previous (preceding)
               node (pPrevNode) point to the node following the node to delete. */
            pPrevNode->pNext = pMove->pNext;
            if (NULL != pMove->pNext)
            {
                /* Make the 'pPrev' pointer of the later (succeeding) node point
                   to the previous (preceding) node of the node to delete. */
                (pMove->pNext)->pPrev = pPrevNode;
            }
        }
    }

    if (NULL != pMove)
    {
        /* We found the node to delete. Free the node memory. */
        free(pMove);
        pMove = NULL;
        printf("Node successfully deleted.\n");
    }
    else
    {
        printf("No node with the given consumer ID found.\n");
    }

} while (0);
}

int main(void)
{
    int iOption = 0;

    while (3 != iOption)
    {
        printf("\n1. Add node\n2. Delete node\n3. Exit");
        printf("\n\nEnter your option (1-3): ");
        scanf("%d", &iOption);
        printf("\n");
```

```
        switch (iOption)
        {
            case 1:
                AddNodeSorted();
                break;
            case 2:
                DeleteNode();
                break;
            default:
                break;
        }
    }

    /* Memory cleanup before exit. */
    for (PCONSUMPTIONINFO pMove = pHead; NULL != pMove; pMove = pHead)
    {
        pHead = pHead->pNext;
        free(pMove);
    }

    return 0;
}
```

18.2.3 SINGLE CIRCULAR LINKED LIST

The node structure and list construction of single circular linked list is similar to single linear linked list. The only difference is that, in the case of single circular linked list, the *'Last/Tail'* node of the list points back to the *'First/Head'* node, making the list arrangement circular.

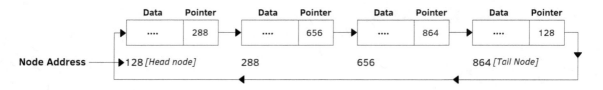

Our program will have two pointers *(possibly global)*, where one will point to the *'Head'* of the list and the other to the *'Tail'*. When the list does not have any nodes, both these pointers will point to NULL. Theoretically speaking, being a circular list, the list does not have any head or tail. But for easy implementation we consider one node *(generally the first added node)* as the *'Head'* of the list and the node preceding it *(generally the last added node)* as the *'Tail'*.

When adding a new node to the end of the list, if our list is empty, we mark the new node as both head and tail of the list. Being a circular linked list, its *'pNext'* pointer will be made to point to the node itself *(i.e. when we have only a single node in the list)*. In case of a non-empty list, we make the *'pNext'* pointer of the *'Tail'* node point to the newly created node, and the *'pNext'* pointer of the new node point to the *'Head'* node. We mark this new node as the new tail of the list.

Inserting a new node, or deleting an existing node is very similar to a single linear linked list. The only difference is that while doing these two operations, we should always remember to maintain the circularity of the list *(the Tail node should point to the Head node).* In case a node is getting inserted after the 'Tail' node, we should mark it as the new 'Tail' node and in case the 'Tail' node is getting deleted, we should make the node situated before the current 'Tail' node as the new 'Tail' node.

In our next program we will use a single circular linked list. In this program, we will not add the nodes in sorted order, but will add the new nodes at the *tail/end* of the list. Being a circular linked list, the list has no *'Tail'*. By *'Tail'*, we mean the position after the last added node.

```c
#include <stdio.h>
#include <stdlib.h>

typedef struct _CONSUMPTIONINFO
{
    long lConsumerID;
    int  iUnitsConsumed;

    struct _CONSUMPTIONINFO *pNext;

}CONSUMPTIONINFO, *PCONSUMPTIONINFO;

PCONSUMPTIONINFO pHead = NULL;
PCONSUMPTIONINFO pTail = NULL;

/* The function creates a new node and adds it to the end of the list i.e. after
   the previous 'Tail' node. The newly added node now becomes the new 'Tail' node. */
void AddNode(void)
{
    CONSUMPTIONINFO *pNewNode = NULL;

    do
    {
        /* Allocate the new node. */
        pNewNode = (CONSUMPTIONINFO *)malloc(sizeof(CONSUMPTIONINFO));
        if (NULL == pNewNode)
        {
            printf("Failed to allocate memory for the new node.\n");
            break;
        }

        /* Accept the consumer details from the user. */
        printf("Enter the consumer ID: ");
        scanf("%ld", &pNewNode->lConsumerID);

        printf("Enter the total units consumed: ");
        scanf("%d", &pNewNode->iUnitsConsumed);

        if (NULL == pHead)
        {
            /* Being the only node in the list, our next pointer will point to
               ourselves. The new node will be marked as both 'Head' and 'Tail'. */
            pNewNode->pNext = pNewNode;
            pHead = pTail   = pNewNode;
        }
        else
        {
            /* Insert the new node between the 'Tail' node and the 'Head' node. */
            pNewNode->pNext = pHead;
            pTail->pNext    = pNewNode;
            /* Mark this node as the new 'Tail' node. */
            pTail           = pNewNode;
        }
```

```
            printf("Node successfully added\n");

    } while (0);
}

/* The function accepts the consumer ID and deletes the first
   occurring node with that consumer ID. */
void DeleteNode(void)
{
    CONSUMPTIONINFO *pPrevNode = NULL;
    CONSUMPTIONINFO *pMove     = NULL;
    long            lConID     = -1;

    do
    {
        if (NULL == pHead)
        {
            break;
        }

        /* Accept the consumer ID to delete. */
        printf("Enter the consumer ID to delete: ");
        scanf("%ld", &lConID);

        /* Start searching from the 'Head' node for the given consumer ID. We will
           keep searching until we are back pointing to the 'Head' node again.
           'pPrevNode' is the node which precedes the node 'pMove'.
           --> |pPrevNode| --> |pMove| ->
           Being a circular list, the 'Tail' node points to the 'Head' node. */
        pPrevNode = pTail;
        pMove     = pHead;
        do
        {
            if (pMove->lConsumerID == lConID)
            {
                /* We found the node to delete. */
                if (pHead == pTail)
                {
                    /* Our 'Head' and 'Tail' nodes are the same. This means that we
                       have only one node in our list and we are about to delete
                       that one too. So, we will be left with no nodes in the list. */
                    pHead = pTail = NULL;
                }
                else if (pMove == pHead)
                {
                    /* We are about to delete our 'Head' node. So, now we need to
                       adjust our 'Head' pointer to the next node in the list. */
                    pHead = pHead->pNext;
                }
                else if (pMove == pTail)
                {
                    /* We are about to delete our 'Tail' node. So, the node before
                       the 'Tail' node now becomes the new 'Tail' node. */
                    pTail = pPrevNode;
                }

                /* We are about to delete the node 'pMove'. So, make the next pointer
                   of the previous node point to the node which comes after 'pMove'.
                   If the node to delete (pMove) is |7|, make the next pointer of
                   the node |4| point to the node |8|.
                   Previously:    --> |3| --> |4| --> |7| --> |8| --> |9| ->
                   Updated:       --> |3| --> |4| --> |8| --> |9| -->    */
```

```c
                pPrevNode->pNext = pMove->pNext;

                free(pMove);
                pMove = NULL;
                printf("Node successfully deleted.\n");

                break;
            }

            /* Go to the next node in the list. */
            pPrevNode = pMove;
            pMove     = pMove->pNext;

        } while (pMove != pHead);

        if (NULL != pMove)
        {
            printf("No node with the given consumer ID found.\n");
        }

    } while (0);
}

void TraverseList(void)
{
    CONSUMPTIONINFO *pMove = pHead;

    if (NULL == pHead)
    {
        printf("List is empty. No items to show.\n");
        return;
    }

    do
    {
        printf("Consumer ID: %ld, Units Consumed: %d\n",
                pMove->lConsumerID, pMove->iUnitsConsumed);

        /* Go to the next node in the list. */
        pMove = pMove->pNext;

    } while (pMove != pHead);
}

int main(void)
{
    int iOption = 0;

    while (4 != iOption)
    {
        printf("\n1. Add node\n2. Delete node\n3. Traverse list\n4. Exit");
        printf("\n\nEnter your option (1-4): ");
        scanf("%d", &iOption);
        printf("\n");

        switch (iOption)
        {
            case 1:
                AddNode();
                break;
            case 2:
                DeleteNode();
                break;
```

```
        case 3:
            TraverseList();
            break;
        default:
            break;
    }
}

/* Memory cleanup before exit. */
for (PCONSUMPTIONINFO pMove = pHead; NULL != pMove; pMove = pHead)
{
    pHead = pHead->pNext;
    free(pMove);
}

return 0;
}
```

18.2.4 DOUBLE CIRCULAR LINKED LIST

The node structure and list construction of a double circular linked list is similar to a double linear linked list. The only difference is that, in the case of double circular linked list, the *'Tail'* and *'Head'* nodes are connected to each other, making the list arrangement circular.

Just like single circular linked list, we will have two pointers *(possibly global)*, one pointing to the *'Head'* and the other pointing to the *'Tail'* of the list.

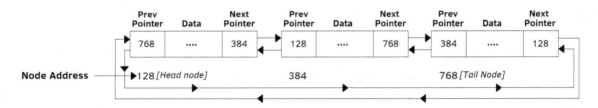

When adding a new node to the end of the list, if our list is empty, we mark the new node as both head and tail of the list. Being a double circular linked list, both *'pPrev'* and *'pNext'* pointers will be made to point to the node itself *(i.e. when we have only a single node in the list)*. In case of a non-empty list, we make the *'pNext'* pointer of the *'Tail'* node point to the newly created node, *'pPrev'* pointer of the new node point to the *'Tail'* node, the *'pNext'* pointer of the new node point to the *'Head'* node, and the *'pPrev'* pointer of the *'Head'* node point to the new node. We mark this new node as the new tail of the list.

Inserting a new node, or deleting an existing node is very similar to a double linear linked list. The only difference is that while doing these two operations, we should always remember to maintain the circularity of the list. In case a node is getting inserted after the *'Tail'* node, we should mark it as the new *'Tail'* node and in case the *'Tail'* node is getting deleted, we should make the node situated before the current *'Tail'* node as the new *'Tail'* node.

In our next program we will use a double circular linked list. The *'TraverseList'* function will be exactly similar to the previous program *(for single circular linked list)*, and so we are not reproducing the same over here.

```c
#include <stdio.h>
#include <stdlib.h>

typedef struct _CONSUMPTIONINFO
{
    long lConsumerID;
    int  iUnitsConsumed;

    struct _CONSUMPTIONINFO *pPrev;
    struct _CONSUMPTIONINFO *pNext;

}CONSUMPTIONINFO, *PCONSUMPTIONINFO;

PCONSUMPTIONINFO pHead = NULL;
PCONSUMPTIONINFO pTail = NULL;

/* The function creates a new node and adds it to the end of the list i.e. after the
   previous 'Tail' node. The newly added node now becomes the new 'Tail' node. */
void AddNode(void)
{
    CONSUMPTIONINFO *pNewNode = NULL;

    do
    {
        /* Allocate the new node. */
        pNewNode = (CONSUMPTIONINFO *)malloc(sizeof(CONSUMPTIONINFO));
        if (NULL == pNewNode)
        {
            printf("Failed to allocate memory for the new node.\n");
            break;
        }

        /* Accept the consumer details from the user. */
        printf("Enter the consumer ID: ");
        scanf("%ld", &pNewNode->lConsumerID);

        printf("Enter the total units consumed: ");
        scanf("%d", &pNewNode->iUnitsConsumed);

        if (NULL == pHead)
        {
            /* Being the only node in the list, our next and prev pointer will point
               to ourselves. The new node will be marked as both 'Head' and 'Tail'. */
            pNewNode->pNext = pNewNode;
            pNewNode->pPrev = pNewNode;
            pHead     = pTail = pNewNode;
        }
        else
        {
            /* Insert the new node between the 'Tail' node and the 'Head' node. */
            pNewNode->pNext = pHead;
            pNewNode->pPrev = pTail;
            pHead->pPrev    = pNewNode;
            pTail->pNext    = pNewNode;
            /* Mark this node as the new 'Tail' node. */
            pTail           = pNewNode;
        }

        printf("Node successfully added\n");
```

289

```
        } while (0);
}

/* The function accepts the consumer ID and deletes the first
   occurring node with that consumer ID. */
void DeleteNode(void)
{
    CONSUMPTIONINFO *pMove  = NULL;
    long            lConID = -1;

    do
    {
        if (NULL == pHead)
        {
            break;
        }

        /* Accept the consumer ID to delete. */
        printf("Enter the consumer ID to delete: ");
        scanf("%ld", &lConID);

        /* Start searching from the 'Head' node for the given consumer ID. We will
           keep searching until we are back pointing to the 'Head' node again. */
        pMove = pHead;
        do
        {
            if (pMove->lConsumerID == lConID)
            {
                /* We found the node to delete. */
                if (pHead == pTail)
                {
                    /* Our 'Head' and 'Tail' nodes are the same. This means that we
                       have only one node in our list and we are about to delete
                       that one too. So, we will be left with no nodes in the list. */
                    pHead = pTail = NULL;
                }
                else if (pMove == pHead)
                {
                    /* We are about to delete our 'Head' node. So, now we need to
                       adjust our 'Head' pointer to the next node in the list. */
                    pHead = pHead->pNext;
                }
                else if (pMove == pTail)
                {
                    /* We are about to delete our 'Tail' node. So, the node before
                       the 'Tail' node now becomes the new 'Tail' node. */
                    pTail = pTail->pPrev;
                }

                /* We are about to delete the node 'pMove'. So, make the next pointer
                   of the previous node point to the node which comes after 'pMove'.
                   If the node to delete (pMove) is |7|, make the next pointer of
                   the node |4| point to the node |8|.
                   Previously:     --> |3| --> |4| --> |7| --> |8| --> |9| -->
                   Updated:        --> |3| --> |4| --> |8| --> |9| -->       */
                (pMove->pPrev)->pNext = pMove->pNext;
                /* Similarly, make the prev pointer of the next node point to the node
                   which comes before 'pMove'. If the node to delete (pMove) is |7|,
                   make the prev pointer of the node |8| point to the node |4|.
                   Previously:     <-- |3| <-- |4| <-- |7| <-- |8| <-- |9| <--
                   Updated:        <-- |3| <-- |4| <-- |8| <-- |9| <--       */
                (pMove->pNext)->pPrev = pMove->pPrev;
```

```c
                free(pMove);
                pMove = NULL;
                printf("Node successfully deleted.\n");

                break;
            }

            /* Go to the next node in the list. */
            pMove = pMove->pNext;

        } while (pMove != pHead);

        if (NULL != pMove)
        {
            printf("No node with the given consumer ID found.\n");
        }

    } while (0);
}

int main(void)
{
    int iOption = 0;

    while (3 != iOption)
    {
        printf("\n1. Add node\n2. Delete node\n3. Exit");
        printf("\n\nEnter your option (1-3): ");
        scanf("%d", &iOption);
        printf("\n");

        switch (iOption)
        {
        case 1:
            AddNode();
            break;
        case 2:
            DeleteNode();
            break;
        default:
            break;
        }
    }

    /* Memory cleanup before exit. */
    for (PCONSUMPTIONINFO pMove = pHead; NULL != pMove; pMove = pHead)
    {
        pHead = pHead->pNext;
        free(pMove);
    }

    return 0;
}
```

STACKS AND QUEUES

[CHAPTER-19]

19.1 INTRODUCTION

Stacks and Queues are two different storage and retrieval mechanisms in data structures. The choice of usage of a mechanism depends on the problem in hand. Both the mechanisms can be implemented using arrays and linked lists in C.

19.2 STACKS

A **stack** is an ordered list in which all insertion and deletion of elements are made at one end only, called the top. As a real life example, we can visualize this as a stack of books where we need to take the top items off the stack in order to get things lying under them. A stack is implemented using **LIFO** *(Last In First Out)* arrangement, where the last added element is the first one to be taken out or retrieved.

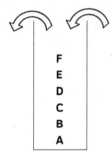

If the elements 'A', 'B', 'C', 'D', 'E', 'F' are added to the stack *(in the given order)*, then the first element to be retrieved must be 'F' and the last will be 'A'.

In case of computer programming, the sequence in which nested functions are called and completed may be visualized as similar to a stack where the last called function completes first. When we are using recursion, we get a similar stack behavior where the last called instance of the function completes first. As a matter of fact, the operating system maintains the function call information *(function address, function variables etc.)* in a stack arrangement.

The addition of an item to a stack is called **push** and the retrieval or deletion of an item from the stack is called **pop**. Apart from *push* and *pop*, we can also perform the following two operations on a stack:
- **peek:** It returns the item at the top of the stack without removing it from the stack.
- **IsEmpty:** Checks whether a stack contains any items or not.

We will now write two programs where the first one implements a stack using an integer array and the second one implements the stack using a single linear linked list.

19.2.1 STACK USING ARRAY

In our next program we will try to implement a stack using an integer array. We will accept numbers from the user and store them in the array. The entire arrangement of store, display and remove will be done in LIFO.

```c
#include <stdio.h>

/* Defined values */
#define MAX_STACK_ELEMENTS 10

/* Global variables */
/* The stack array. */
int g_rgiValues[MAX_STACK_ELEMENTS];
/* The variable which keeps track of the number of elements in the stack.
   It also helps keep track of the top index of the stack. */
int g_iCurStackCount;

/* Function which adds/pushes a new element on to the stack. */
void PushElement(void)
{
    if (MAX_STACK_ELEMENTS == g_iCurStackCount)
    {
        printf("The stack is full. No more items can be added to the stack.\n");
    }
    else
    {
        printf("Enter the value to add: ");
        scanf("%d", &g_rgiValues[g_iCurStackCount]);
        g_iCurStackCount++;
    }
}

/* Function which removes/pops an element out of the stack. */
void PopElement(void)
{
    if (0 == g_iCurStackCount)
    {
        printf("The stack is empty. No items to pop.\n");
    }
    else
    {
        g_iCurStackCount--;
        printf("Value popped: %d.\n", g_rgiValues[g_iCurStackCount]);
    }
}

int main(void)
{
    int iOption = 0;

    while (3 != iOption)
    {
        printf("\n1. Add element\n2. Remove element\n3. Exit");
        printf("\n\nEnter your option (1-3): ");
        scanf("%d", &iOption);
        printf("\n");

        switch (iOption)
        {
```

```
            case 1:
                PushElement();
                break;
            case 2:
                PopElement();
                break;
            default:
                break;
        }
    }

    return 0;
}
```

We are adding the values to the end of the array by pushing the values with increasing array index. During pop, we are displaying and removing the values starting from the end of the array and continuing towards the front. This makes the last pushed values get popped out first *(LIFO)*.

19.2.2 STACK USING LINKED LIST

In our next program, we will implement a stack using a single linear linked list. Similar behaviour can also be achieved using the other types of linked lists.

```c
/* Header Files */
#include <stdio.h>
#include <stdlib.h>

/* Structure Definition */
typedef struct _CONSUMPTIONINFO
{
    long lConsumerID;
    int  iUnitsConsumed;

    struct _CONSUMPTIONINFO *pNext;

}CONSUMPTIONINFO, *PCONSUMPTIONINFO;

PCONSUMPTIONINFO pHead = NULL;

/* The function creates a new node and adds it to the start of the list
   creating a stack arrangement. It makes the new node the 'Head' of the list
   i.e. the last added node becomes the first (Head) node of the list. */
void Push(void)
{
    CONSUMPTIONINFO *pNewNode = NULL;

    do
    {
        /* Allocate the new node. */
        pNewNode = (CONSUMPTIONINFO *) malloc(sizeof(CONSUMPTIONINFO));
        if (NULL == pNewNode)
        {
            printf("Failed to allocate memory for the new node.\n");
            break;
        }

        /* Accept the consumer details from the user. */
        printf("Enter the consumer ID: ");
        scanf("%ld", &pNewNode->lConsumerID);
```

```
        printf("Enter the total units consumed: ");
        scanf("%d", &pNewNode->iUnitsConsumed);

        pNewNode->pNext = pHead;
        pHead           = pNewNode;

        printf("Node successfully added\n");

    } while (0);
}

/* The function pops the first (Head) node from the list i.e. the last
   added node is popped first (LIFO). The node following the 'Head' node
   becomes the new 'Head' node. */
void Pop(void)
{
    CONSUMPTIONINFO *pMove = NULL;

    do
    {
        if (NULL == pHead)
        {
            printf("The list is empty. Nothing to pop.\n");
            break;
        }

        printf("Consumer ID: %ld, Units Consumed: %d\n",
               pHead->lConsumerID, pHead->iUnitsConsumed);

        pMove = pHead;
        pHead = pHead->pNext;
        free(pMove);
        pMove = NULL;

        printf("Node successfully popped\n");

    } while (0);
}

int main(void)
{
    int iOption = 0;

    while (3 != iOption)
    {
        printf("\n1. Add node\n2. Delete node\n3. Exit");
        printf("\n\nEnter your option (1-3): ");
        scanf("%d", &iOption);
        printf("\n");

        switch (iOption)
        {
        case 1:
            Push();
            break;
        case 2:
            Pop();
            break;
        default:
            break;
        }
    }
```

```
/* Memory cleanup before exit. */
for (PCONSUMPTIONINFO pMove = pHead; NULL != pMove; pMove = pHead)
{
    pHead = pHead->pNext;
    free(pMove);
}

return 0;
}
```

In the above program, we are adding the new nodes to the front of the list. The newest node is also made the *'Head'* node of the list. We are popping the values from the front of the list producing a stack arrangement i.e. the last added node is popped first.

19.3 QUEUES

A **queue** is another ordered list in which insertion and deletion of elements happen at opposite ends. We can visualize queue as a pipe in which we push items from one end of the pipe and the items come out from the other end. Another example of a real life approach of queuing systems is whilst waiting in line at a food store – the first in line will be the first to leave, with new people being added at the end of the queue. A queue is implemented using **FIFO** *(First In First Out)* arrangement, where the first added element is the first one to be taken out or retrieved. The elements are inserted from one end of the queue called the **rear** *(also called the tail)* and are removed from the other end called the **front** *(also called the head)*.

If the elements 'A', 'B', ..., 'J', 'K' are added to the queue *(in the given order)*, then the first element to be retrieved must be 'A' and the last will be 'K'.

In case of computer programming, the operating system maintains the program information of the multiple programs running at a time using a queue.

The process of adding an element to a queue is called **enqueue** and the process of removal of an element is called **dequeue**. Apart from *enqueue* and *dequeue,* we can also perform the following two operations on a queue:
  • **peep:** It returns the item at the front of the queue without removing it from the queue.
  • **IsEmpty:** Checks whether a queue contains any items or not.

19.3.1 QUEUE USING ARRAY

Our first example on queue will be to implement the queue using an array. If we add *(enqueue)* values to the end of the array and keep removing *(dequeue)* the values from the front *(start)* of the array, we will soon reach the top of the array *(the maximum array index)*, even if we have free space *(array elements whose values have been dequeued/removed)* at the front of the array.

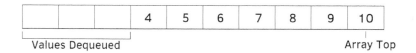

			4	5	6	7	8	9	10

Values Dequeued   Array Top

To solve this problem, we can resort to enqueue and dequeue of the values using a circular arrangement where new values are enqueued again from the front *(after we reach the array top)*, if we have available space at the front of the array.

```c
#include <stdio.h>

/* Defined values */
#define MAX_QUEUE_ELEMENTS 10

/* Global variables */
/* The queue array. */
int g_rgiValues[MAX_QUEUE_ELEMENTS];
/* Variable which keeps track of the start index of the queue i.e. it
   keeps track of the first queue element. In simpler words it points to
   the index of the element which can next be dequeued. */
int g_iStart = 0;
/* Variable which keeps track of the end index of the queue i.e. it points
   to the last enqueued element in the array. */
int g_iEnd = -1;
/* Variable which tracks the total numbers of elements currently in the queue. */
int g_iTotalElements = 0;

/* Function which adds/enqueues a new element to the queue. */
void EnqueueElement(void)
{
    if (MAX_QUEUE_ELEMENTS == g_iTotalElements)
    {
        printf("The queue is full. No more items can be added.\n");
    }
    else
    {
        if (MAX_QUEUE_ELEMENTS == (g_iEnd + 1))
        {
            /* We have reached the array's highest index. Now, wrap around. */
            g_iEnd = -1;
        }

        g_iEnd++;
        g_iTotalElements++;
        printf("Enter the value to add: ");
        scanf("%d", &g_rgiValues[g_iEnd]);
    }
}

/* Function which removes/dequeues an element from the queue. */
void DequeueElement(void)
{
    if (0 == g_iTotalElements)
    {
        printf("The queue is empty. No items to dequeue.\n");
    }
    else
    {
        printf("Value dequeued: %d.\n", g_rgiValues[g_iStart]);
```

```
        if (MAX_QUEUE_ELEMENTS == (g_iStart + 1))
        {
            /* We have reached the array's highest index. Now, wrap around. */
            g_iStart = -1;
        }

        g_iStart++;
        g_iTotalElements--;
    }
}

int main(void)
{
    int iOption = 0;

    while (3 != iOption)
    {
        printf("\n1. Add element\n2. Remove element\n3. Exit");
        printf("\n\nEnter your option (1-3): ");
        scanf("%d", &iOption);
        printf("\n");

        switch (iOption)
        {
        case 1:
            EnqueueElement();
            break;
        case 2:
            DequeueElement();
            break;
        default:
            break;
        }
    }

    return 0;
}
```

'g_iStart' moves forward when items are dequeued. As more items are dequeued 'g_iStart' moves further forward, creating a vacuum at the front of the array. After 'g_iEnd' reaches 'MAX_QUEUE_ELEMENTS', it starts occupying the vacuum left behind at the front of the array when values were dequeued. This way both 'g_iStart' and 'g_iEnd' move in a circular fashion. Assume, we have added the values 1, 2, 3, 4, 5, 6, 7, 8, 9, 10 in the given sequence. No more items can be enqueued as the queue has reached its maximum capacity. We then dequeue the values 1, 2, and 3. This means our 'g_iStart' has moved to the value 4 *(array index 3)*, creating a free space for 3 new elements at the front of the array. We can then again resume adding new elements to the queue from the front of the array. So, 'g_iEnd' loops back to the front of the array. If we add new values 11, 12 and 13, they will then be placed at the array indices 0, 1 and 2 respectively. 'g_iStart' will then point to 3 *(array index)* and 'g_iEnd' will point to 2 *(array index)*.

19.3.2 QUEUE USING LINKED LIST

We will now implement a queue using a single linear linked list in our next program. We will have two pointers in our program, one pointing to the start of the list *'Head'* and another pointing to the end *'Tail'*. We will enqueue values to the end of the list and dequeue from the front resulting in a FIFO behavior.

```c
#include <stdio.h>
#include <stdlib.h>

typedef struct _CONSUMPTIONINFO
{
    long lConsumerID;
    int  iUnitsConsumed;

    struct _CONSUMPTIONINFO *pNext;

}CONSUMPTIONINFO, *PCONSUMPTIONINFO;

PCONSUMPTIONINFO pHead = NULL;
PCONSUMPTIONINFO pTail = NULL;

/* The function creates a new node and adds it to the end of the list
   creating a queue arrangement. It makes the new node the 'Tail' of the list. */
void Enqueue(void)
{
    CONSUMPTIONINFO *pNewNode = NULL;

    do
    {
        /* Allocate the new node. */
        pNewNode = (CONSUMPTIONINFO *) malloc(sizeof(CONSUMPTIONINFO));
        if (NULL == pNewNode)
        {
            printf("Failed to allocate memory for the new node.\n");
            break;
        }

        /* Accept the consumer details from the user. */
        printf("Enter the consumer ID: ");
        scanf("%ld", &pNewNode->lConsumerID);

        printf("Enter the total units consumed: ");
        scanf("%d", &pNewNode->iUnitsConsumed);

        pNewNode->pNext = NULL;

        if (NULL == pHead)
        {
            /* This is the only node in the list. */
            pHead = pTail = pNewNode;
        }
        else
        {
            /* Make the previous 'Tail' node point to this new node. */
            pTail->pNext = pNewNode;
            /* Make this node as the new 'Tail' node of the list. */
            pTail        = pNewNode;
        }

        printf("Node successfully added.\n");

    } while (0);
}

/* The function dequeues the first (Head) node from the list i.e. the first added node is
   popped first (FIFO). The node following the 'Head' node becomes the new 'Head' node. */
```

```c
void Dequeue(void)
{
    CONSUMPTIONINFO *pMove = NULL;

    do
    {
        if (NULL == pHead)
        {
            printf("The list is empty. Nothing to dequeue.\n");
            break;
        }

        printf("Consumer ID: %ld, Units Consumed: %d\n",
                pHead->lConsumerID, pHead->iUnitsConsumed);

        pMove = pHead;
        pHead = pHead->pNext;
        free(pMove);
        pMove = NULL;

        printf("Node successfully dequeued.\n");

    } while (0);
}

int main(void)
{
    int iOption = 0;

    while (3 != iOption)
    {
        printf("\n1. Add node\n2. Delete node\n3. Exit");
        printf("\n\nEnter your option (1-3): ");
        scanf("%d", &iOption);
        printf("\n");

        switch (iOption)
        {
        case 1:
            Enqueue();
            break;
        case 2:
            Dequeue();
            break;
        default:
            break;
        }
    }

    /* Memory cleanup before exit. */
    for (PCONSUMPTIONINFO pMove = pHead; NULL != pMove; pMove = pHead)
    {
        pHead = pHead->pNext;
        free(pMove);
    }

    return 0;
}
```

TREES

[CHAPTER-20]

20.1 INTRODUCTION

One of the disadvantages of using an unsorted array or linked list to store data is the time needed to search an item. Since both are linear arrangements, the time required to search an item is proportional to the size of the array or list. To overcome such problems, we have another kind of data structure called 'Tree'. A tree is a non-linear data structure where the stored data is organized hierarchically with each node *(called the parent node)* capable of pointing to two or more nodes *(called the child nodes)*, and the child nodes may optionally point back to the parent node. The structure of a *tree* is similar to that of an inverted real life tree which is grounded via the root.

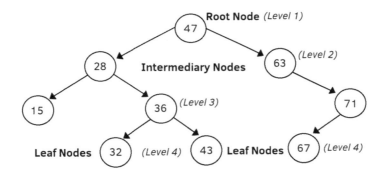

A tree may have *zero* or more nodes. If it has no nodes, the tree is called a **null** or **empty** tree.

The topmost node in the tree is called the **Root** node. There is only one *root* node in a tree. The nodes which do not have any child nodes are called **Leaf** or **External** nodes and are at the bottom of the tree. All the nodes which come in between the *root* node and the *leaf* nodes are called the **Intermediary** or **Internal** nodes.

A node is called the **parent** of another node if it directly points to the other node. Conversely, a node is called the **child** of another node *(parent)* if it is directly pointed to by the other node. In the above diagram, the node with the value *36* is the *parent* of the nodes with values *32* and *43 (child nodes)*. Nodes which have the same parent are called the **siblings**.

A node is called a **descendant** of another node if it can be reached by repeated iteration from the other node. In the above diagram the node with the value *43* is a descendant of the node *28* but not of the node *63*. A **subtree** of a tree is a tree consisting of a node 'A' and all the descendants of the node 'A'. So every node in a tree contains a *subtree* of itself and all its descendants with the node as the *root* of that *subtree*. The *subtree* corresponding to the *root* node is the entire tree itself. In our example tree, the node with key value 36 is the *root of the subtree* with nodes 32, 36 and 43. The root of the entire tree is the node with key value 47. The number of *subtrees* of a node is called its **degree**.

The number of connections in-between a node and the *root* node of a tree is called the **level** of a node, which is equal to '1+' the number of connections. So, the *root* node itself is at level 1.

The connection between one node and another is called the **edge.** The number of *edges* on the longest path between a node and a leaf is called its **height**. In the above diagram, the *height* of the node with value *47* is 3 and that of *36* is 1. The *height* of a tree is equal to the height of its *root* node.

The **depth** of a node is the number of *edges* between the node and the *root* of the tree. The node with value *63* has a *depth* of 1.

In this chapter we will discuss about two types of trees – Binary Search Trees and AVL Trees.

20.2 BINARY SEARCH TREES

A **binary tree** is a tree data structure where each node has at most two children, which are referred to as the left child and the right child of the node. The tree shown in **section 20.1** is an example of a binary tree. **Binary search trees** are special type of *binary trees* where the nodes are arranged according to their values. They are also called **ordered** or **sorted** binary trees as their nodes appear in a sorted order.

A binary search tree (***BST** in short)* allows quick search, addition and removal of items. BST arranges its nodes in sorted order, so that searches can use the principle of binary search.

Binary search is a search algorithm that finds a target value within a sorted sequence of values. Binary search compares the target value to the middle element of the sequence. If unequal, half of the sequence in which the target cannot lie is eliminated and the search continues on the other half. This process continues until the target value is found or its possibility of existence in the sequence is eliminated.

In case of BST, the entire binary tree is arranged in such a way which makes the nodes with key values smaller than the root node lie to the left of the root node, and nodes with key values larger than the root node lie to the right of it. This principle is followed for every node in the tree, making the entire tree sorted. To summarize, we may define a BST as a binary tree which has the following properties:
- The left subtree of a node contains only nodes with key values less than the node's key value.
- The right subtree of a node contains only nodes with key values greater than the node's key value.
- The left and right subtrees too must be binary search trees themselves.
- There must be no two nodes with the same key value.

Consider the next BST:

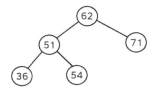

We start searching for a given value from the root node in BST and continue downwards in either the left subtree or the right subtree depending on the value to search. We compare the search value with the key value of a node. If same, we return the node. If the search value is smaller than the node's key value, we recur down the left subtree of the node. Otherwise we recur down its right subtree.

Assume, we are searching for the value 54 in the above BST. We will start from the root node of the tree and compare its key value with the search value. As the search value is less than the root node's key value, we will move down the left subtree of the root node. Now, we will be at the node with value '51'. As the search value is greater than the node's value, we will move down its right subtree, getting us to the node with value '54' *(our desired node)*.

In a BST, we can traverse the nodes in four different ways:
- **Inorder traversal:** For every node, all nodes present in its left subtree is traversed first, followed by that node itself and then by the nodes in its right subtree. This traversal technique produces the output in sorted order on the node key values.
- **Preorder traversal:** For every node, its own value is printed first, followed by all nodes present in its left subtree, and then by the nodes in its right subtree.
- **Postorder traversal:** For every node, all nodes present in its left branch is traversed first, followed by the nodes in its right branch, and then that node itself.
- **Level order traversal:** The nodes are traversed level by level starting from the root node to the leaf nodes. For each level, the nodes are traversed from left to right. This is an inefficient traversal technique in terms of space and time requirements, and hence rarely used.

Now, let us write our first binary search tree. The program allows the user to add nodes, delete nodes, search values, and perform inorder, preorder and postorder traversal.

```
/* Header Files */
#include <stdio.h>
#include <stdlib.h>

/* Structure Definition */
typedef struct _NODE
{
    /* This node's value. */
    int         iNodeValue;
    /* The pointer which points to the left child of this node. */
    struct _NODE *pLeftChild;
    /* The pointer which points to the right child of this node. */
    struct _NODE *pRightChild;

} NODE;
```

```c
/* Function which creates and returns a new node. */
NODE *CreateNode(int iValue)
{
    /* Allocate the node. */
    NODE * pNode = (NODE *) malloc(sizeof(NODE));
    if (pNode)
    {
        pNode->iNodeValue = iValue;
        pNode->pLeftChild = pNode->pRightChild = NULL;
    }

    return pNode;
}

/* Searches the BST for the node with the given value. */
NODE *SearchValue(NODE *pNode, int iValue)
{
    do
    {
        if (NULL == pNode)
        {
            /* The value was not found. */
            printf("The value %d could not be found.\n", iValue);
            break;
        }

        if (pNode->iNodeValue == iValue)
        {
            /* Found the node with the given value. */
            printf("Found the node with value %d.\n", pNode->iNodeValue);
            break;
        }
        else if (iValue < pNode->iNodeValue)
        {
            /* The value is smaller than this node's value. So, the value
               should come in the left branch of this node. */
            pNode = SearchValue(pNode->pLeftChild, iValue);
        }
        else
        {
            /* The value is larger than this node's value. So, the value
               should come in the right branch of this node. */
            pNode = SearchValue(pNode->pRightChild, iValue);
        }

    } while(0);

    return pNode;
}

/* Function which performs in-order traversal. For every node, all nodes present in its
   left branch is traversed first, followed by that node itself and then by the nodes in
   its right branch. This traversal technique always prints the nodes in sorted order.
   LEFT CHILD, NODE, RIGHT CHILD. */
void InOrderTraversal(NODE *pNode)
{
    if (NULL != pNode)
    {
        /* Traverse the left branch of this node. All nodes present in the left branch
           of this node has been traversed when the (first) below recursive call
           completes for this node. This means all values smaller than this node's
           value has been printed when this recursive call ends. */
        InOrderTraversal(pNode->pLeftChild);
```

```c
        /* The left branch of this node has been printed. Now, print this node's value. */
        printf("%d, ", pNode->iNodeValue);

        /* Traverse the right branch of this node. All nodes present in the right branch
           of this node has been traversed when the below recursive call completes. */
        InOrderTraversal(pNode->pRightChild);
    }
}

/* Function which performs pre-order traversal. For every node, its own value is
   printed first, followed by all nodes present in its left branch, and then by
   the nodes in its right branch. NODE, LEFT CHILD, RIGHT CHILD. */
void PreOrderTraversal(NODE *pNode)
{
    if (NULL != pNode)
    {
        /* First, print this node's value. */
        printf("%d, ", pNode->iNodeValue);

        /* Now, traverse the left branch of this node. */
        PreOrderTraversal(pNode->pLeftChild);

        /* Now the right branch. */
        PreOrderTraversal(pNode->pRightChild);
    }
}

/* Function which performs post-order traversal. For every node, all nodes
   present in its left branch is traversed first, followed by the nodes in its
   right branch, and then that node itself. LEFT CHILD, RIGHT CHILD, NODE. */
void PostOrderTraversal(NODE *pNode)
{
    if (NULL != pNode)
    {
        /* First, traverse the left branch of this node. */
        PostOrderTraversal(pNode->pLeftChild);

        /* Now the right branch. */
        PostOrderTraversal(pNode->pRightChild);

        /* Left and right branches of this node has been traversed.
           Now, print this node's value. */
        printf("%d, ", pNode->iNodeValue);
    }
}

/* Function which adds a new node with given value in the BST.
   A new value is always added at a leaf position and is never inserted
   in-between nodes. The new node always becomes a new leaf node. We start
   comparing values from root till we hit a leaf position. Once a leaf position
   is found, the new node is added at that position, connecting it to its parent. */
NODE *AddNode(NODE *pNode, int iValue)
{
    if (NULL == pNode)
    {
        /* We have found the position where this node needs to be added. This node
           will now become a new leaf node. We will create the new node and its
           address will be returned and then assigned to the left/right pointer
           (depending on the below 'if' condition check) of the parent node. */

        return CreateNode(iValue);
    }
```

```
    /* Check if the value is smaller than this node's value. If smaller, the value
       should come in the left branch of this node. We will start moving down the
       left branch until we find the position where the value needs to be added.
       Similarly, if the value is larger, we will find the value's position in the
       right branch of this node. If this is the node under which the new node
       should come, the next recursive call will create the new node and return its
       address. We will then assign the returned address to the left/right pointer
       (depending on the successful 'if' check below) of this node. */
    if (iValue < pNode->iNodeValue)
    {
        pNode->pLeftChild = AddNode(pNode->pLeftChild, iValue);
    }
    else if (iValue > pNode->iNodeValue)
    {
        pNode->pRightChild = AddNode(pNode->pRightChild, iValue);
    }
    else
    {
        printf("Duplicate value not allowed.\n");
    }

    /* This is an existing node. Return its (unchanged) node address. */
    return pNode;
}

/* Finds the node with the minimum value under the given 'pNode' subtree. */
NODE *FindMinValueNode(NODE *pNode)
{
    /* Start from the given node and continue down its left branch. */
    NODE *pCurrent = pNode;

    if (pCurrent)
    {
        /* Loop down to find the leftmost leaf which will have the minimum value. */
        while (NULL != pCurrent->pLeftChild)
        {
            pCurrent = pCurrent->pLeftChild;
        }
    }

    return pCurrent;
}

/* Deletes the node with the given value. If the value is less than the node's
   value, we move down the left branch in search of the value. If larger, we move
   down the right branch. If the value is not found, the function returns NULL.
   If a node's value matches the given value, we de-link the node from the tree.
   While de-linking, we may face the following scenarios:
   1. The node is a leaf node: Delete the node and return NULL. The parent of the
      deleted leaf node starts pointing to NULL in place of the leaf node.
   2. The node has only one child node: Delete the node and return the address of
      the child node of this node. This makes the child node take the position of
      the deleted node.
   3. The node has two child nodes: If the node to delete is 'A', find the node with
      the lowest value in the right subtree of 'A' (the node to delete). The lowest
      value will be the left-most leaf. Assuming 'B' is the leaf node with the lowest
      value in the right sub-tree of 'A', replace the value of 'A' with that of 'B'.
      Now, delete the node 'B' as done in #1. So, in effect 'B' replaces 'A'. */
NODE *DeleteNode(NODE *pNode, int iValue)
{
    NODE *pTemp = NULL;
```

```
    do
    {
        if (NULL == pNode)
        {
            /* The given value does not exist in the tree. */
            printf("The value %d does not exist.\n", iValue);
            break;
        }

        /* Check if the given value is smaller than this node's value. If smaller,
            the value should be in the left branch/subtree of this node. If larger,
            the value should be in the right branch. If same, we delete the node. */
        if (iValue < pNode->iNodeValue)
        {
            /* Look in the left branch/subtree of this node. */
            pNode->pLeftChild = DeleteNode(pNode->pLeftChild, iValue);
        }
        else if (iValue > pNode->iNodeValue)
        {
            /* Look in the right branch/subtree of this node. */
            pNode->pRightChild = DeleteNode(pNode->pRightChild, iValue);
        }
        else
        {
            /* We found the node with the given value. */
            if (NULL == pNode->pLeftChild)
            {
                /* The node either has no child nodes or only right child node.
                    Delete this node and make its child node take its position. */
                pTemp = pNode->pRightChild;
                free(pNode);
                pNode = pTemp;
                break;
            }
            else if (pNode->pRightChild == NULL)
            {
                /* The node has only one child node and it is the left child.
                    Delete this node and make its child node take its position. */
                pTemp = pNode->pLeftChild;
                free(pNode);
                pNode = pTemp;
                break;
            }

            /* The node has two child nodes. Find the node with the lowest value in
                the right subtree of this node. Assuming this node to be 'A', we try to
                find a node 'B' with the lowest value in the right subtree of 'A'. */
            pTemp = FindMinValueNode(pNode->pRightChild);

            /* Replace this node's value with that of the node with the
                lowest value in its right sub-tree. */
            pNode->iNodeValue = pTemp->iNodeValue;

            /* We have shifted the value/data of 'B' to the node 'A' essentially,
                replacing the value of 'A'. Now, delete the node 'B' as it has now
                become a duplicate and no longer required. */
            pNode->pRightChild = DeleteNode(pNode->pRightChild, pTemp->iNodeValue);
        }

    } while (0);

    return pNode;
}
```

```c
/* Deletes the entire tree. */
void DeleteTree(NODE *pNode)
{
    if (NULL == pNode)
    {
        return;
    }

    /* Delete the left subtree of this node. */
    DeleteTree(pNode->pLeftChild);
    /* Delete the right subtree of this node. */
    DeleteTree(pNode->pRightChild);

    /* Now delete this node itself. */
    free(pNode);
    pNode = NULL;
}

int main(void)
{
    int    iOption = 0;
    int    iValue  = 0;
    NODE *pRoot    = NULL;

    while (7 != iOption)
    {
        printf("\n1. Add node");
        printf("\n2. Remove node");
        printf("\n3. Inorder traversal");
        printf("\n4. Preorder traversal");
        printf("\n5. Postorder traversal");
        printf("\n6. Search value");
        printf("\n7. Exit");
        printf("\n\nEnter your option (1-7): ");
        scanf("%d", &iOption);
        printf("\n");

        switch (iOption)
        {
        case 1:
            printf("Enter the value to add: ");
            scanf("%d", &iValue);
            if (NULL == pRoot)
            {
                pRoot = AddNode(pRoot, iValue);
            }
            else
            {
                AddNode(pRoot, iValue);
            }
            break;

        case 2:
            printf("Enter the value to delete: ");
            scanf("%d", &iValue);
            pRoot = DeleteNode(pRoot, iValue);
            break;

        case 3:
            InOrderTraversal(pRoot);
            break;
```

```
        case 4:
            PreOrderTraversal(pRoot);
            break;

        case 5:
            PostOrderTraversal(pRoot);
            break;

        case 6:
            printf("Enter the value to search: ");
            scanf("%d", &iValue);
            SearchValue(pRoot, iValue);
            break;

        default:
            break;
        }

        printf("\n");
    }

    /* Clean up by deleting the entire tree. */
    DeleteTree(pRoot);
    pRoot = NULL;

    return 0;
}
```

20.3 AVL TREES

An **AVL tree** *(named after inventors Adelson, Velski and Landis)* is a self-balancing binary search tree. By self-balancing we mean that the heights of the two child subtrees of any node differ by at most one. If at any moment *(during node addition or deletion)* the height difference becomes more than 1, re-balancing is done to restore this property. Re-balancing is done by rearrangement or rotation of the nodes of the tree starting from the location of the change *(addition or deletion)* till the *root* node. The difference between the heights of the left subtree and the right subtree is called the **Balance Factor**. The *balance factor* of every node within an AVL tree must be one of the three values -1, 0 or 1.

Lets check out the below binary search trees. The first one is an unbalanced BST and contains a balance factor outside the values -1, 0 or 1. The second tree is a balanced BST and contains a favorable balance factor of 0 for each node. Both the trees contain the exact same nodes but arranged a little differently. The arrangement of the nodes make the first one *unbalanced* and second one *balanced*.

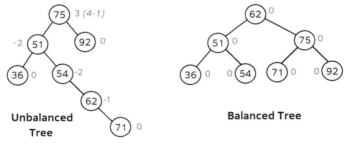

Assume, we require to search for the value 71 in both the above trees. In the first tree, we will need to traverse through the nodes 75, 51, 54 and 62 to reach our desired node containing the value. In the second tree, we will require to traverse through the nodes 62 and 75 only to reach our desired node. For applications that require to do a lot of searching, using a balanced BST may improve the application efficiency significantly.

Search efficiency may increase many-fold for a balanced BST, because the concept of binary search can be effectively used. In an unbalanced BST a branch may become so elongated that searching a node may become almost equivalent to a sequential search. This kind of a situation kills the very purpose of using a BST. This is where an AVL tree comes to the rescue which guarantees that the tree always remains balanced.

20.3.1 AVL ROTATIONS
To balance itself, an AVL tree may perform the following four kinds of rotations:
- **Right rotation:** An AVL tree may become unbalanced, if a new node is inserted in the left subtree of an existing node. In such a case the tree needs a *right rotation*. Right rotation is also desired when an existing node is deleted from the right subtree. The re-balancing of the tree needs to be done starting from the position of unbalance to the tree root. In the below image, the node *'C'* has been added in the left subtree of a node *'B'*. This makes the parent node *'A'* of node *'B'* get unbalanced with a balance factor of 2 *(fig-1)*. This is because *'A'* was already having only one child node *'B' (no right subtree)*, when the node *'C'* was added to the left of node 'B'. When this situation arises, we need to do a *right rotation* as depicted in the below image *(fig-2, fig-3)*.

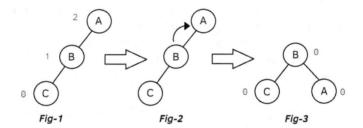

Fig-1   Fig-2   Fig-3

- **Left rotation:** An AVL tree may become unbalanced, if a new node is inserted in the right subtree of an existing node. In such a case the tree needs a *left rotation*. Left rotation is also desired when an existing node is deleted from left subtree. The re-balancing of the tree needs to be done starting from the position of unbalance to the tree root. In the below image, the node *'C'* has been added in the right subtree of node *'B'* which makes the parent node *'A'* of node *'B'* get unbalanced with a balance factor of -2 *(fig-1)*. This is because *'A'* was already having only one child node *'B' (no left subtree)*, when the node *'C'* was added to the right of node 'B'. When this situation arises, we do a *left rotation* as depicted in the next image *(fig-2, fig-3)*.

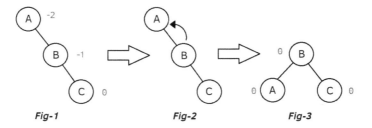

Fig-1   Fig-2   Fig-3

- **Right-Left rotation:** We need a double rotation when a situation as in *fig-1* of the below image arises due to a node addition or deletion. *Right-Left rotation* is a combination of right rotation followed by a left rotation as shown in the figures *2 to 5*.

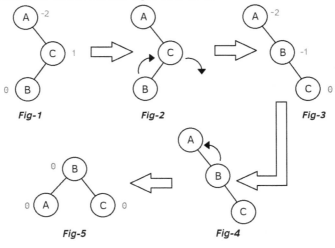

- **Left-Right rotation:** When the situation as shown in *fig-1* of the below image arises due to a node addition or deletion, we need a *Left-Right rotation*. Left-Right rotation is a combination of left rotation followed by a right rotation as shown in the figures *2 to 5*.

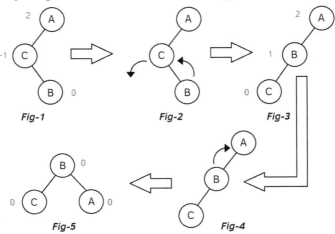

In our next program, we will create an AVL tree and perform node additions and deletions on it. Being a BST, the search and traversal methods *(inorder, preorder and postorder)* are exactly the same as our previous BST example program. Hence, we have skipped these functions over here.

```c
#include <stdio.h>
#include <stdlib.h>

#ifndef max
#define max(a,b)     (((a) > (b)) ? (a) : (b))
#endif

typedef struct _NODE
{
    /* This node's value. */
    int             iNodeValue;
    /* The pointer which points to the left child of this node. */
    struct _NODE *pLeftChild;
    /* The pointer which points to the right child of this node. */
    struct _NODE *pRightChild;
    /* The height of this node in the AVL tree. */
    int             iHeight;

} NODE;

/* Function which creates and returns a new node. */
NODE *CreateNode(int iValue)
{
    NODE * pNode = (NODE *) malloc(sizeof(NODE));
    if (pNode)
    {
        pNode->iNodeValue = iValue;
        pNode->iHeight    = 0;
        pNode->pLeftChild = pNode->pRightChild = NULL;
    }

    return pNode;
}

/* Function which returns the height of the given node. */
int GetNodeHeight(NODE *pNode)
{
    if (NULL == pNode)
    {
        return -1;
    }

    return pNode->iHeight;
}

/* Gets the difference in height of the left branch with that
   of the right branch of a given node. */
int GetHeightDiff(NODE *pNode)
{
    if (NULL == pNode)
    {
        return 0;
    }

    return (GetNodeHeight(pNode->pLeftChild) - GetNodeHeight(pNode->pRightChild));
}
```

```
/* Function which right rotates a subtree under the given node 'pNodeA'
   ('pNodeA' is the root node of that subtree).
     A                    B
    /                    / \
   B         =>         D   A
  / \                      /
 D   C                    C
*/
NODE *RotateRight(NODE *pNodeA)
{
    if (NULL == pNodeA || NULL == pNodeA->pLeftChild)
    {
        return pNodeA;
    }

    NODE *pNodeB = pNodeA->pLeftChild;
    NODE *pNodeC = pNodeB->pRightChild;

    /* 'pNodeB' was smaller than 'pNodeA'. So, 'pNodeA' goes to right of 'pNodeB'.
       'pNodeC' was smaller than 'pNodeA' (was in its left branch) but, larger than
       'pNodeB'. So, it goes to the right branch of 'pNodeB' but left of 'pNodeA'.
       Right of 'pNodeB' was previously 'pNodeC', but now its 'pNodeA'.
       Left of 'pNodeA' was previously 'pNodeB', but now its 'pNodeC'. */
    pNodeB->pRightChild = pNodeA;
    pNodeA->pLeftChild  = pNodeC;

    /* Update the heights of the readjusted nodes. */
    pNodeA->iHeight = max(GetNodeHeight(pNodeA->pLeftChild),
                      GetNodeHeight(pNodeA->pRightChild)) + 1;

    pNodeB->iHeight = max(GetNodeHeight(pNodeB->pLeftChild),
                      GetNodeHeight(pNodeB->pRightChild)) + 1;

    /* 'pNodeB' is the new root of this subtree. */
    return pNodeB;
}

/* Function which left rotates a subtree under the given node 'pNodeA'
   ('pNodeA' is the root node of that subtree).
 A                    B
  \                  / \
   B       =>       A   D
  / \                \
 C   D                C
*/
NODE *RotateLeft(NODE *pNodeA)
{
    if (NULL == pNodeA || NULL == pNodeA->pRightChild)
    {
        return pNodeA;
    }

    NODE *pNodeB = pNodeA->pRightChild;
    NODE *pNodeC = pNodeB->pLeftChild;

    /* 'pNodeB' was larger than 'pNodeA'. So, 'pNodeA' goes to left of 'pNodeB'.
       'pNodeC' was larger than 'pNodeA' (was in its right branch) but, smaller than
       'pNodeB'. So, it goes to the left branch of 'pNodeB' but right of 'pNodeA'.
       Left of 'pNodeB' was previously 'pNodeC', but now its 'pNodeA'.
       Right of 'pNodeA' was previously 'pNodeB', but now its 'pNodeC'. */
    pNodeB->pLeftChild  = pNodeA;
```

```
        pNodeA->pRightChild = pNodeC;

        /* Update the heights of the readjusted nodes. */
        pNodeA->iHeight = max(GetNodeHeight(pNodeA->pLeftChild),
                            GetNodeHeight(pNodeA->pRightChild)) + 1;

        pNodeB->iHeight = max(GetNodeHeight(pNodeB->pLeftChild),
                            GetNodeHeight(pNodeB->pRightChild)) + 1;

        /* 'pNodeB' is the new root of this subtree. */
        return pNodeB;
}

/* Checks if a subtree under the node 'pNode' has become unbalanced. If so,
   this function rebalances the subtree and returns the new root node for
   that subtree (Previous root node for the subtree was 'pNode'). */
NODE *RebalanceSubTree(NODE *pNode)
{
    int iBalance = 0;

    do
    {
        if (NULL == pNode)
        {
            break;
        }

        /* Update the height of the given node. */
        pNode->iHeight = 1 + max(GetNodeHeight(pNode->pLeftChild),
                                GetNodeHeight(pNode->pRightChild));

        /* Check if the subtree under this node has become unbalanced or not. */
        iBalance = GetHeightDiff(pNode);

        /* If unbalanced, we will have 4 cases: */

        /* Right Rotation Case */
        if (iBalance > 1 && 0 <= GetHeightDiff(pNode->pLeftChild))
        {
            /* The left branch of the subtree is longer. So, we need to rotate
               towards right. Rotate and set the new root node of the subtree. */
            pNode = RotateRight(pNode);
        }
        /* Left Rotation Case */
        else if (iBalance < -1 && 0 >= GetHeightDiff(pNode->pRightChild))
        {
            /* The right branch of the subtree is longer. So, we need to rotate
               towards left. Rotate and set the new root node of the subtree. */
            pNode = RotateLeft(pNode);
        }
        /* Left-Right Rotation Case */
        else if (iBalance > 1 && 0 > GetHeightDiff(pNode->pLeftChild))
        {
            /* The first left rotation. */
            pNode->pLeftChild = RotateLeft(pNode->pLeftChild);
            /* Now the right rotation of the main subtree. */
            pNode = RotateRight(pNode);
        }
        /* Right-Left Rotation Case */
        else if (iBalance < -1 && 0 < GetHeightDiff(pNode->pRightChild))
        {
            /* The first right rotation. */
            pNode->pRightChild = RotateRight(pNode->pRightChild);
```

```
            /* Now the left rotation of the main subtree. */
            pNode = RotateLeft(pNode);
        }

    } while (0);

    /* Return the new root of the rebalanced subtree. */
    return pNode;
}

/* Function which adds a new node with the given value in the AVL tree. The node
   addition logic is exactly same as that of BST. Additionally, after the node is
   added to the tree, we start rebalancing the tree starting from the parent node
   of the newly added node and continuing upwards. */
NODE *AddNode(NODE *pNode, int iValue)
{
    if (NULL == pNode)
    {
        return CreateNode(iValue);
    }

    if (iValue < pNode->iNodeValue)
    {
        pNode->pLeftChild = AddNode(pNode->pLeftChild, iValue);
    }
    else if (iValue > pNode->iNodeValue)
    {
        pNode->pRightChild = AddNode(pNode->pRightChild, iValue);
    }
    else
    {
        printf("Duplicate value not allowed.\n");
        return pNode;
    }

    /* The node has been added. Now rebalance the subtree, if required.
       After rebalancing, we return the new root node of this subtree
       to the previous recursive call. */
    return RebalanceSubTree(pNode);
}

/* Finds the node with the minimum value under the given 'pNode' subtree. */
NODE *FindMinValueNode(NODE *pNode)
{
    NODE *pCurrent = pNode;

    if (pCurrent)
    {
        /* Loop down to find the leftmost leaf which will have the minimum value. */
        while (NULL != pCurrent->pLeftChild)
        {
            pCurrent = pCurrent->pLeftChild;
        }
    }

    return pCurrent;
}

/* Deletes the node with the given value. The node deletion logic is very similar
   to that of BST. Additionally, after the node is deleted, we start rebalancing
   the tree starting from the same level as the deleted node and continuing upwards. */
NODE *DeleteNode(NODE *pNode, int iValue)
{
```

```c
    NODE *pTemp = NULL;

    do
    {
        if (NULL == pNode)
        {
            /* The given value does not exist in the tree. */
            printf("The value %d does not exist.\n", iValue);
            break;
        }

        if (iValue < pNode->iNodeValue)
        {
            /* Look in the left branch/subtree of this node. */
            pNode->pLeftChild = DeleteNode(pNode->pLeftChild, iValue);
        }
        else if (iValue > pNode->iNodeValue)
        {
            /* Look in the right branch/subtree of this node. */
            pNode->pRightChild = DeleteNode(pNode->pRightChild, iValue);
        }
        else
        {
            /* We found the node with the given value. */
            if (NULL == pNode->pLeftChild)
            {
                /* The node either has no child nodes or only right child node. */
                pTemp = pNode->pRightChild;
                free(pNode);
                pNode = pTemp;
                break;
            }
            else if (pNode->pRightChild == NULL)
            {
                /* The node has only one child node and it is the left child. */
                pTemp = pNode->pLeftChild;
                free(pNode);
                pNode = pTemp;
                break;
            }
            else
            {
                /* The node has two child nodes. */
                pTemp = FindMinValueNode(pNode->pRightChild);
                pNode->iNodeValue  = pTemp->iNodeValue;
                pNode->pRightChild = DeleteNode(pNode->pRightChild, pTemp->iNodeValue);
            }
        }

        if (NULL == pNode)
        {
            break;
        }

        /* If our subtree has become unbalanced, rebalance it. We will continue
           rebalancing upwards as we keep coming out of the recursive calls. */
        pNode = RebalanceSubTree(pNode);

    } while (0);

    return pNode;
}
```

```c
/* Deletes the entire tree. */
void DeleteTree(NODE *pNode)
{
    if (NULL == pNode)
    {
        return;
    }

    /* Delete the left subtree of this node. */
    DeleteTree(pNode->pLeftChild);
    /* Delete the right subtree of this node. */
    DeleteTree(pNode->pRightChild);

    /* Now delete this node itself. */
    free(pNode);
    pNode = NULL;
}

int main(void)
{
    int   iOption = 0;
    int   iValue  = 0;
    NODE *pRoot   = NULL;

    while (3 != iOption)
    {
        printf("\n1. Add node");
        printf("\n2. Remove node");
        printf("\n3. Exit");
        printf("\n\nEnter your option (1-3): ");
        scanf("%d", &iOption);
        printf("\n");

        switch (iOption)
        {
        case 1:
            printf("Enter the value to add: ");
            scanf("%d", &iValue);
            pRoot = AddNode(pRoot, iValue);
            break;

        case 2:
            printf("Enter the value to delete: ");
            scanf("%d", &iValue);
            pRoot = DeleteNode(pRoot, iValue);
            break;

        default:
            break;
        }

        printf("\n");
    }

    /* Clean up by deleting the entire tree. */
    DeleteTree(pRoot);
    pRoot = NULL;

    return 0;
}
```

20.4 SPACE AND TIME COMPLEXITIES

Sometimes, there may be multiple ways to solve a problem. We need to know the performance of the different algorithms and choose the best one to solve a particular problem. Space and Time complexities help us analyze the performance of an algorithm.

Space Complexity of an algorithm is the total memory used by the algorithm with respect to its input size. In simpler words, it is a measure of the amount of memory an algorithm needs. It is stated in terms of the Big O notation. Big O notation is a mathematical notation that indicates the behavior of a function when the input tends towards a particular value or infinity. Description of the Big O notation is beyond the scope of this book.

Time complexity is the computational complexity that estimates the time taken for running an algorithm. In other words it signifies the total time required by the algorithm to run till its completion. It is estimated by counting the number of elementary operations performed by the algorithm. Just like space complexity, time complexity too is stated in terms of the Big O notation.

The space and time complexities of binary search trees are:

Complexities	Average	Worst
Space	O(n)	O(n)
Time *(Search Node)*	O(log(n))	O(n)
Time *(Add Node)*	O(log(n))	O(n)
Time *(Delete Node)*	O(log(n))	O(n)

The space and time complexities of AVL trees are:

Complexities	Average	Worst
Space	O(n)	O(n)
Time *(Search Node)*	O(log(n))	O(log(n))
Time *(Add Node)*	O(log(n))	O(log(n))
Time *(Delete Node)*	O(log(n))	O(log(n))

20.5 FULL BINARY TREES

A **full binary tree** is a tree in which every node has either 0 or 2 children. So, every node other than the leaves have two children. In other words, we will have **no nodes** containing only one child. A full binary tree is sometimes called a **proper binary tree**.

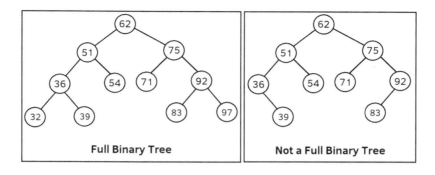

Full Binary Tree   Not a Full Binary Tree

20.6 PERFECT BINARY TREES

A **perfect binary tree** is a binary tree in which all interior nodes have two children and all leaf nodes are at the same depth or level. It may be considered as a full binary tree whose leaf nodes are all at the same depth or level. Hence, all perfect binary trees are full binary trees but, not the other way round.

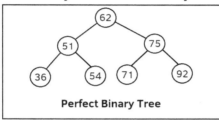

Perfect Binary Tree

20.7 COMPLETE BINARY TREES

A **complete binary tree** is a binary tree in which at every level *(except the last)*, is completely filled, and all nodes are as far left as possible.

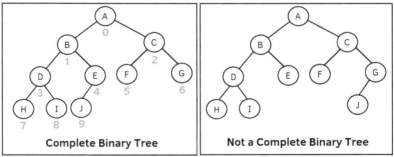

Complete Binary Tree   Not a Complete Binary Tree

A complete binary tree can also be represented using an array where each element of the array constitute a node of the tree. If a node is assumed to be at the array element index 'n', its child nodes will be at the array element indices '2n + 1' *(left child)* and '2n + 2' *(right child)* respectively. In the previous image of the complete binary tree, the numbers beneath each node is the node's index when the tree is represented using an array. Hence, the array representation of the tree will look as below:

A	B	C	D	E	F	G	H	I	J

SORTING AND SEARCHING

[CHAPTER-21]

21.1 INTRODUCTION

In our previous chapter we learned Binary Search Trees and AVL Trees which help us arrange values in sorted order. But, these algorithms are limited to be used in tree structures only. If we are dealing with arrays or linked lists, we need to use algorithms better suited for these data structures. Every sorting algorithm has affinity towards a specific type of data structure and performs best for that data structure. For other data structures, the algorithm's performance may degrade substantially. We need to do careful selection of our sorting algorithm depending on the kind of data structure we are dealing with. In this chapter we will discuss sorting mechanisms which work on arrays or linked lists.

21.2 QUICKSORT

QuickSort was developed by Tony Hoare in the year 1959. It is a very efficient sorting algorithm and works with the principle of divide and conquer. It divides/partitions a set of values into two halves and sorts each half recursively. At each recursive call, it picks a value to act as a **pivot** (central value) and arranges all values in such a way so that the values less than the pivot lie to the left of the pivot and larger values lie to its right. So, all values to the left of the pivot are smaller than all values positioned to the right of the pivot. We then repeat this process with each of the individual halves recursively and continue till there are not enough items to partition and sort. This makes each of the individual halves too getting sorted. The steps can be summarized as below:
* Pick an element, called the pivot, from the set.
* *Partition:* Rearrange the array so that all elements with values less than the pivot come before the pivot, while all elements with values greater than the pivot come after it (equal values can go either way). This makes all values to the left of the pivot to be less than all values positioned to the right of the pivot.
* Recursively apply the above steps to the two separate sub-sets (one lying to the left of the pivot and another to the right).

Its best to explain the logic using a simple example. Assume we have an array with five elements 7, 5, 2, 9 and 8. We do the following steps:
1. Take 7 as the pivot.
2. Partition the values. After partitioning we get 5, 2, 7, 9, 8.
3. Sort the first set 5, 2.
   a) Take 5 as the pivot.
   b) Partition the values. After partitioning we get 2, 5.
4. The array has now become 2, 5, 7, 9, 8.
5. Sort the second set 9, 8.
   a) Take 9 as the pivot.

  b) Partition the values. After partitioning we get 8, 9.
6. The array has now become 2, 5, 7, 8, 9.

Quicksort is best suited to work with arrays, though we may use it to sort linked lists too. But, its best performance is achieved when working with arrays.

Let us now implement the algorithm using two programs. The first program will sort an array using the Quicksort algorithm and the second will do the same on a linked list.

PROGRAM 1: QUICKSORT AN ARRAY

During each recursive call we work within two logical boundaries *'iLow'* and *'iHigh'* corresponding to two array indices. The array section between *'iLow'* and *'iHigh'* consists of the elements which need to be partitioned and sorted. At every recursive call, we first partition the array into two halves - *'iLow'* to *'iPivot'* and *'iPivot + 1'* to *'iHigh'*.

While **partitioning**, we *start* with the value of the *'iLow'* index element as the pivot value. We take two counters where the first one moves from left to right *(increments starting from 'iLow')* and the second one moves from right to left *(decrements starting from 'iHigh')* until they cross. All left positioned values *(traversed using the first counter)* which are greater than or equal to the pivot value are swapped with all right positioned values which are smaller than the pivot value *(traversed using the second counter)*. This makes lesser values to take the lower indices and the higher values take higher indices. We then return a middle value within the array section as the *final* pivot value.

Following the partitioning, we get two partitioned halves - *'iLow'* to *'iPivot'* and *'iPivot + 1'* to *'iHigh'*. We recursively sort these two individual halves again. In every recursive call we repeat the same process of dividing the array section into two halves and sorting.

```c
#include <stdio.h>

/* The partition needs to be done from 'iLow' to 'iHigh'. We take 'prgiValues[iLow]'
   as the starting pivot value. We take two counters, one starting from 'iLow' and
   incrementing, and another starting from 'iHigh' and decrementing. We continue until
   both these counters cross, the moment when all the values have been partitioned. */
int Partition(int *prgiValues, int iLow, int iHigh)
{
    int iPivot = prgiValues[iLow];
    int i      = iLow - 1;
    int j      = iHigh + 1;
    int iTemp  = 0;

    while (1)
    {
        do
        {
            i++;

        } while (i <= j && prgiValues[i] < iPivot);

        do
        {
```

```
            j--;

        } while (j >= i && prgiValues[j] > iPivot);

        if (i >= j)
        {
            break;
        }

        /* Here, we have 'prgiValues[i] >= iPivot' and 'prgiValues[j] <= iPivot'.
           But, we should actually have 'prgiValues[i]' less than 'iPivot' and
           'prgiValues[j]' greater than 'iPivot'.
           Hence, swap the values of these two locations. */
        iTemp          = prgiValues[i];
        prgiValues[i] = prgiValues[j];
        prgiValues[j] = iTemp;
    }

    return j;
}

void Quicksort(int *prgiValues, int iLow, int iHigh)
{
    int iPivot = 0;

    if (iLow < iHigh)
    {
        /* Partition the array into two halves. */
        iPivot = Partition(prgiValues, iLow, iHigh);
        /* Sort the first partitioned half. */
        Quicksort(prgiValues, iLow, iPivot);
        /* Sort the second partitioned half. */
        Quicksort(prgiValues, iPivot + 1, iHigh);
    }
}

int main(void)
{
    int rgiValues[]       = { 23, 28, 78, 62, 11, 5, 68, 92, 34, 51, 15, 85, 47 };
    int iArrayNumElements = sizeof(rgiValues) / sizeof(rgiValues[0]);
    int idx               = 0;

    Quicksort(rgiValues, 0, iArrayNumElements - 1);

    printf("The array after sorting: \n");
    for (; idx < iArrayNumElements; idx++)
    {
        printf("%d, ", rgiValues[idx]);
    }
    printf("\n\n");

    return 0;
}
```

PROGRAM 2: QUICKSORT A LINKED LIST

The next program has a little variation from the previous program. As we are working with linked list, rather than values *(as in the case of arrays)*, the nodes themselves are rearranged due to sorting. This may lead to a change in the head and tail nodes. The previous head and tail nodes may not be in their same positions within the list. So, we need to update the original 'Head' and 'Tail' pointers of the caller function to the new 'Head' and 'Tail' nodes respectively upon completion of the sort.

Within each recursive call, we are working with a section of the list at a time. We are partitioning the list into two, and individually sorting the two partitions. But during the entire operation, both the partitions continue to remain as part of the main list. When a list section is partitioned, the nodes get rearranged and the start and end nodes of that section may change to some other nodes. So, the link between the starting node *(of the section)* and the node preceding it *(within the main list)* will need to be re-established. Similarly, the link between the last node of a list section and the node succeeding it will need to be re-established.

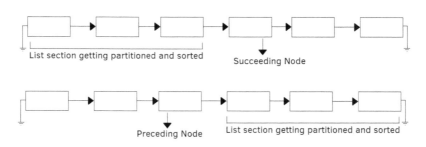

List section getting partitioned and sorted   Succeeding Node

Preceding Node   List section getting partitioned and sorted

```c
#include <stdio.h>
#include <stdlib.h>

/* Defined Values */
#define MAX_ITEMS    10

typedef struct _NODE
{
    int             iNodeValue; /* This node's value. */
    struct _NODE *pNext;        /* The pointer which points to the next node. */
    struct _NODE *pPrev;        /* The pointer which points to the previous node. */

} NODE;

/* In this function we will take the start node as the pivot. All nodes with values
   less than the pivot node will be placed before the pivot node, and all nodes with
   values greater or equal will be placed after the pivot node. We start traversing
   the nodes starting from the node following the pivot node to the end node. We stop
   when we have gone past the end node. During traversing, we compare each node's
   value with the pivot value. All nodes with values greater than the pivot are left
   unchanged (as they are already positioned after the pivot node). All nodes with
   values less than the pivot are re-positioned before the pivot node. When a node
   with lesser value is found, it is put at the start of this list section and made
   the new start node of this section. After the function completes we may have a new
   start node and an end node as the nodes may get re-arranged (the position of the
   previous end node may change or nodes may come before the previous start node). So
   on completion, we update the 'ppStart' and 'ppEnd' pointers with the new addresses. */
NODE *Partition(NODE **ppStart, NODE **ppEnd)
{
    NODE *pPivot    = *ppStart;         /* We take the start node as the pivot */
    NODE *pPrevNode = *ppStart;
    NODE *pMove     = pPrevNode->pNext; /* We start from the node after the start */
    NODE *pEndMarker = (*ppEnd)->pNext; /* We partition till we reach this location. */

    while (pMove != pEndMarker)
    {
```

```c
        if (pMove->iNodeValue < pPivot->iNodeValue)
        {
            /* This node's value is less than the pivot. Position it before the pivot. */
            /* Disconnect 'pMove' from current location. */
            pPrevNode->pNext = pMove->pNext;
            if (NULL != pMove->pNext)
            {
                pMove->pNext->pPrev = pPrevNode;
            }

            /* Connect 'pMove' to the start of the list section and
               mark it as the new 'start' of the list. */
            pMove->pPrev       = (*ppStart)->pPrev;
            (*ppStart)->pPrev = pMove;
            pMove->pNext       = *ppStart;
            *ppStart = pMove;

            /* Make 'pMove' again point to the location from
               where we will resume traversing. */
            pMove              = pPrevNode->pNext;
        }
        else
        {
            /* 'pPrevNode' always points to the node preceding 'pMove'. */
            pPrevNode = pMove;
            pMove     = pMove->pNext;
        }
    }

    /* Update the new end of the list. */
    *ppEnd = pPrevNode;

    return pPivot;
}

/* The function accepts the start (ppStart) and end (ppEnd) nodes of the list
   which needs to be sorted. It also accepts the node address (in pPreStart)
   which precedes the start node. After partitioning, our start and end nodes
   may change for which we need to re-link 'pPreStart' with the new start node.
   After completion, the pointers 'ppStart' and 'ppEnd' are updated with the
   addresses of the new start and end nodes respectively. */
void Quicksort(NODE *pPreStart, NODE **ppStart, NODE **ppEnd)
{
    NODE *pPivot     = NULL;
    NODE *pPivotNext = NULL;

    if (NULL != *ppStart && NULL != *ppEnd && *ppStart != *ppEnd)
    {
        /* Partition the list into two. */
        pPivot = Partition(ppStart, ppEnd);
        if (NULL != pPreStart)
        {
            /* The start node might have changed. */
            pPreStart->pNext = *ppStart;
        }

        /* Sort the first partitioned half. */
        Quicksort(pPreStart, ppStart, &pPivot);
        pPivotNext = pPivot->pNext;
        /* Sort the next partitioned half. */
        Quicksort(pPivot, &pPivotNext, ppEnd);
    }
}
```

```c
int main(void)
{
    NODE *pHead  = NULL;
    NODE *pTail  = NULL;
    NODE *pNew   = NULL;
    NODE *pMove  = NULL;

    int    iCount = 0;

    /* Create the linked list. */
    for (; iCount < MAX_ITEMS; iCount++)
    {
        pNew = (NODE *)malloc(sizeof(NODE));
        if (NULL == pNew)
        {
            break;
        }

        printf("Enter the node's value: ");
        scanf("%d", &pNew->iNodeValue);

        if (NULL == pHead)
        {
            pHead        = pNew;
            pNew->pPrev = NULL;
        }
        else
        {
            pTail->pNext = pNew;
            pNew->pPrev  = pTail;
        }

        pTail         = pNew;
        pTail->pNext = NULL;
    }

    if (NULL != pHead)
    {
        Quicksort(NULL, &pHead, &pTail);

        printf("\nThe list after sorting:\n");
        for (pMove = pHead; NULL != pMove; pMove = pMove->pNext)
        {
            printf("%d, ", pMove->iNodeValue);
        }

        /* Cleanup the list before exit. */
        for (pMove = pHead; NULL != pMove; pMove = pHead)
        {
            pHead = pHead->pNext;
            free(pMove);
            pMove = NULL;
        }

        printf("\n\n");
    }

    return 0;
}
```

21.3 MERGE SORT

Like Quicksort, Merge Sort is also a divide and conquer algorithm. It was invented by John von Neumann in the year 1945. It divides a list of items in two halves, recurs itself to sort the two halves individually and then merges the two sorted halves. It breaks down a list of items into several sublists until each sublist consists of a single element. It then combines/merges the smaller sorted lists in a way which produces a sorted merged-list. A merge sort works as follows:

- Divide the unsorted list into n sublists, with each containing just one element.
- Merge these sublists *(two sublists at a time)* to produce a new sorted sublist. Continue doing so until there is only one sublist remaining. This will be the sorted list.

The process is better explained in the below image. Assume, we are sorting an array 7, 4, 3, 9, 8, 6, 5.

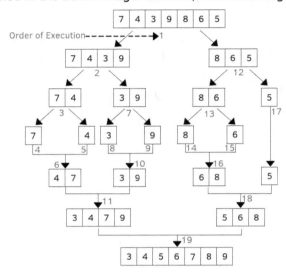

The entire array is divided into two sub-sections '7, 4, 3, 9' and '8, 6, 5' respectively. The sub-section '7, 4, 3, 9' is further divided into two sub-sections '7, 4' and '3, 9'. The sub-section '7, 4' is again divided into two sub-sections '7' and '4', after which no further divisions are possible. We now merge the two sub-sections '7', '4' to produce the sorted sequence '4, 7'. Similarly, the sub-section '3, 9' is divided into two sub-sections '3' and '9', and then merged back together to produce '3, 9'. The sorted sections '4, 7' and '3, 9' are now merged together to produce the sorted sequence '3, 4, 7, 9'. We now move towards the right sub-section *('8, 6, 5')* of the main array and similarly divide and sort it to produce the sequence '5, 6, 8'. We then merge the two sub-sections '3, 4, 7, 9' and '5, 6, 8' to produce our final sorted result as '3, 4, 5, 6, 7, 8, 9'.

Merge sort can not only be used on arrays but also is very effective for linked lists. Unlike Quicksort, which is naturally inclined towards arrays, merge sort is somewhat inclined more towards linked lists. For arrays merge sort requires a similar sized array *(as the array to be sorted)* to work as a temporary cache while performing the sort. For linked lists, there is no such requirement and hence, its space complexity is better than merge sort on arrays.

Now let us use two programs to understand the merge sort algorithm. The first program performs merge sort on an array and the second program performs merge sort on a linked list.

PROGRAM 1: MERGE SORT AN ARRAY

```
#include <stdio.h>

void Merge(int *prgiSource, int *prgiTarget, int idxBegin, int idxMiddle, int idxEnd)
{
    int i = idxBegin;
    int j = idxMiddle + 1;
    int k = idxBegin;

    /* Both the sections (idxBegin to idxMiddle and idxMiddle to idxEnd) are already
       in sorted order from previous recursive calls. Now, we scan these two sections
       concurrently and copy the next lower value out of these two sections to the
       target array. Assume that the two sections have the values as:
       Section 1: 17, 23, 26, 42.
       Section 2: 25, 29, 37, 45.
       We compare the values 17 from section 1 and 25 from section 2. As 17 is lower,
       we copy the value to target. Next, we compare the values 23 from section 1
       and 25 from section 2. We copy 23 to target array as it is lower. Then we
       compare 26 from section 1 with 25 from section 2. We copy 25 to target. We
       next compare 26 from section 1 with 29 from section 2. We copy 26. Next, we
       compare 42 from section 1 with 29 from section 2. We copy 29. Similarly,
       we now compare 42 from section 1 with 37 from section 2. The process continues.
       When there are no items left in one section, we copy rest of the items in the
       other section to the target array.
       We get the final output as:
       17, 23, 25, 26, 29, 37, 42, 45. */

    while (i <= idxMiddle && j <= idxEnd)
    {
        if (prgiSource[i] <= prgiSource[j])
        {
            prgiTarget[k] = prgiSource[i];
            i++;
        }
        else
        {
            prgiTarget[k] = prgiSource[j];
            j++;
        }

        k++;
    }

    /* Now copy the remaining items in section 1 to the target (if any left). */
    for (; i <= idxMiddle; i++, k++)
    {
        prgiTarget[k] = prgiSource[i];
    }

    /* Now copy the remaining items in section 2 to the target (if any left). */
    for (; j <= idxEnd; j++, k++)
    {
        prgiTarget[k] = prgiSource[j];
    }
}
```

```c
void MergeSort(int *prgiSource, int *prgiTarget, int iBegin, int iEnd)
{
    int iMiddle = 0;

    if (iEnd - iBegin < 1)
    {
        /* There is just 1 or less item left to be split and sort. This is
           the exit criteria of our recursion and we start coming out. */
        return;
    }

    /* Split the set of items from the middle. */
    iMiddle = (iBegin + iEnd) / 2;

    /* Recursively split and sort the items in the first section. We are
       deliberately reversing the positions of the source and target in both
       the below recursive calls to 'MergeSort'. We are making the subsequent
       recursive calls and getting the sorted output in 'prgiSource' (the
       two calls to 'MergeSort'). We are then using the 'prgiSource' as the
       source array for the call to the function 'Merge' for joining the two
       sorted sections in 'prgiSource'. 'Merge' function then generates the
       final sorted output in 'prgiTarget'. */
    MergeSort(prgiTarget, prgiSource, iBegin, iMiddle);
    /* Recursively split and sort the items in the second section. */
    MergeSort(prgiTarget, prgiSource, iMiddle + 1, iEnd);

    /* Merge the two sections. */
    Merge(prgiSource, prgiTarget, iBegin, iMiddle, iEnd);
}

int main(void)
{
    /* The array to sort. */
    int rgiValues[]        = { 23, 98, 78, 62, 11 };
    /* The array which works as a temporary cache during sorting. */
    int rgiTemp[sizeof(rgiValues) / sizeof(rgiValues[0])] = { 0 };
    int iArrayNumElements = sizeof(rgiValues) / sizeof(rgiValues[0]);
    int idx               = 0;

    /* In Merge sort we need an equal sized buffer (as the array to sort)
       to work as temporary cache during sorting. */
    for (idx = 0; idx < iArrayNumElements; idx++)
    {
        /* Copy the entire contents of the array to our buffer. */
        rgiTemp[idx] = rgiValues[idx];
    }

    /* Now, sort the buffer contents back to our original array. */
    MergeSort(rgiTemp, rgiValues, 0, iArrayNumElements - 1);

    /* Print the array after sorting. */
    printf("The array after sorting: \n");
    for (idx = 0; idx < iArrayNumElements; idx++)
    {
        printf("%d, ", rgiValues[idx]);
    }

    printf("\n\n");

    return 0;
}
```

PROGRAM 2: MERGE SORT A LINKED LIST

```c
#include <stdio.h>
#include <stdlib.h>

typedef struct _NODE
{
    /* This node's value. */
    int         iNodeValue;
    /* The pointer which points to the next node. */
    struct _NODE *pNext;

} NODE;

/* Defined Values */
#define MAX_ITEMS  10

/* The function merges the two given lists together and returns the 'Head' of
   the merged list. 'pStart1' is the 'Head' of the first list to merge and
   'pStart2' is the 'Head' of the second list. */
NODE *Merge(NODE *pStart1, NODE *pStart2)
{
    NODE *pStartMerged = NULL;
    NODE *pMoveMerged  = NULL;
    NODE *pNodeToAdd   = NULL;

    do
    {
        if (NULL == pStart1)
        {
            /* The first list is empty. So, our merged list will be the same
               as the second list, which already is sorted. */
            pStartMerged = pStart2;
            break;
        }
        else if (NULL == pStart2)
        {
            /* The second list is empty. So, our merged list will be the same
               as the first list, which already is sorted. */
            pStartMerged = pStart1;
            break;
        }

        /* Traverse both the lists and attach the node with the next lower value to
           the merged list. The next starting node in both the lists will have the
           smallest value in their respective lists (as both the lists are sorted).
           We continue merging until any one of the sub-lists becomes empty. */
        while (NULL != pStart1 && NULL != pStart2)
        {
            if (pStart1->iNodeValue <= pStart2->iNodeValue)
            {
                pNodeToAdd = pStart1;
                pStart1    = pStart1->pNext;
            }
            else
            {
                pNodeToAdd = pStart2;
                pStart2    = pStart2->pNext;
            }
```

```
                    if (NULL == pMoveMerged)
                    {
                        pStartMerged = pMoveMerged = pNodeToAdd;
                    }
                    else
                    {
                        pMoveMerged->pNext = pNodeToAdd;
                        pMoveMerged        = pMoveMerged->pNext;
                    }

                    pMoveMerged->pNext = NULL;
            }

            /* Now move the remaining items in list-1 to the merged list (if any). */
            while (NULL != pStart1)
            {
                pMoveMerged->pNext = pStart1;
                pStart1            = pStart1->pNext;
                pMoveMerged        = pMoveMerged->pNext;
                pMoveMerged->pNext = NULL;
            }

            /* Now move the remaining items in list-2 to the merged list (if any). */
            while (NULL != pStart2)
            {
                pMoveMerged->pNext = pStart2;
                pStart2            = pStart2->pNext;
                pMoveMerged        = pMoveMerged->pNext;
                pMoveMerged->pNext = NULL;
            }

    } while (0);

    return pStartMerged;
}

/* Splits the list starting with 'pHead' into two separate lists. The first
   separated list constitute front half of the source list, and the second
   separated list constitute the second half. We then return the address of
   the starting node of the two split lists using the pointers 'ppStart1' and
   'ppStart2'. The function uses slow/fast pointer strategy while traversing
   the source list for splitting. The slow pointer moves one node at a time
   and the fast pointer moves two pointers at a time. */
void SplitList(NODE *pHead, NODE **ppStart1, NODE **ppStart2)
{
    NODE *pFast = NULL;
    NODE *pSlow = pHead;

    do
    {
        if (NULL == pSlow || NULL == pSlow->pNext)
        {
            /* We have less than two nodes in the source list. */
            *ppStart1 = pHead;
            *ppStart2 = NULL;
            break;
        }

        /* 'pFast' pointer starts from one ahead of the 'pSlow' pointer. */
        pFast = pSlow->pNext;

        /* Advance the slow pointer by one node and the fast pointer by two nodes. */
        while (NULL != pFast)
```

```
            {
                pFast = pFast->pNext;
                if (NULL != pFast)
                {
                    pSlow = pSlow->pNext;
                    pFast = pFast->pNext;
                }
            }

        /* The first separated list starts from 'pHead' till 'pSlow'. */
        *ppStart1    = pHead;
        /* The second separated list starts from 'pSlow->pNext' till end. */
        *ppStart2    = pSlow->pNext;
        /* The last node of the first separated list must point to NULL marking
           its end. The following statement splits the source list into two. */
        pSlow->pNext = NULL;

    } while (0);
}

/* The 'Head' node of the original list may change after the sort completes. This
   is because the previous 'Head' node might not have the smallest value in the list.
   The node with the smallest value in the list becomes the new 'Head' node. So, we
   need to update the original 'pHead' pointer of the caller function to the new
   'Head' node of the list. Hence, we accept the pointer to the 'pHead' pointer as the
   function argument which enables us to update the 'Head' pointer of the caller. */
void MergeSort(NODE **ppHead)
{
    NODE *pStart1 = NULL;
    NODE *pStart2 = NULL;

    if (NULL == *ppHead || NULL == (*ppHead)->pNext)
    {
        /* We have 0 or 1 node in this list. No sorting required. */
        return;
    }

    SplitList(*ppHead, &pStart1, &pStart2);

    /* Recursively split and sort the first separated list. */
    MergeSort(&pStart1);
    /* Recursively split and sort the second separated list. */
    MergeSort(&pStart2);

    /* Merge the two sections. */
    *ppHead = Merge(pStart1, pStart2);
}

int main(void)
{
    NODE *pHead  = NULL;
    NODE *pTail  = NULL;
    NODE *pNew   = NULL;
    NODE *pMove  = NULL;

    int   iCount = 0;

    /* Create the linked list. */
    for (; iCount < MAX_ITEMS; iCount++)
    {
        pNew = (NODE *)malloc(sizeof(NODE));
        if (NULL == pNew)
        {
```

```
                break;
        }

        printf("Enter the node's value: ");
        scanf("%d", &pNew->iNodeValue);

        if (NULL == pHead)
        {
            pHead = pNew;
        }
        else
        {
            pTail->pNext = pNew;
        }

        pTail         = pNew;
        pTail->pNext = NULL;
    }

    if (NULL != pHead)
    {
        MergeSort(&pHead);

        printf("\nThe list after sorting:\n");
        for (pMove = pHead; NULL != pMove; pMove = pMove->pNext)
        {
            printf("%d, ", pMove->iNodeValue);
        }

        /* Cleanup the list before exit. */
        for (pMove = pHead; NULL != pMove; pMove = pHead)
        {
            pHead = pHead->pNext;
            free(pMove);
            pMove = NULL;
        }

        printf("\n\n");
    }

    return 0;
}
```

21.4 BINARY HEAP

Before moving to our next sorting algorithm *'heap sort'*, let us understand the concept of **'Binary Heap'** which drives the *'heap sort'* algorithm. A binary heap is a binary tree with two additional constraints:

1. **Shape property**: A binary heap is a *complete binary tree* (refer **section 20.7**).
2. **Heap property:** A node's value is either *greater than or equal to (>=)* or *less than or equal to (<=)* the value of its child nodes. This property holds true for every node *(except leaf nodes)* in the tree.

Binary heap where the parent node's value is *greater than or equal to (>=)* the value of its child nodes is called **Max Heap**. Similarly, binary heap where the parent node's value is *less than or equal to (<=)* the value of its child nodes is called **Min Heap**.

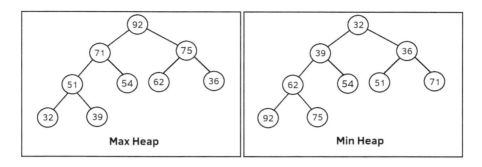

21.5 HEAP SORT

Heap sort was invented by J. W. J. Williams in the year 1964. Heap sort divides the values into two sections – unsorted *(heap section)* and sorted. It iteratively shrinks the unsorted section by extracting the largest element and moving that to the sorted section. Heap sort can be performed in place without requiring additional memory.

Heap sort algorithm works in the following manner for sorting an array in **ascending order**:
1. Visualize the entire array as a *complete binary tree* (refer **section 20.7**).
2. Build a *Max Heap* from the array values.
3. This makes the largest item to be stored at the root of the heap. Swap it with the last item of the heap. Post the swap, the last item of the heap will have the largest value within the heap.
4. Mark the last item of the heap as the starting location of the *sorted section*.
5. Reduce the size of the heap by 1.
6. Build a *Max Heap* from the remaining values of the heap.
7. Repeat steps 3 to 6 till the size of the heap is greater than 1.

And for **descending order**, we do the following:
1. Visualize the entire array as a *complete binary tree* .
2. Build a **Min Heap** from the array values.
3. This makes the **smallest** item to be stored at the root of the heap. Swap it with the last item of the heap. Post the swap, the last item of the heap will have the **smallest** value within the heap.
4. Mark the last item of the heap as the starting location of the *sorted section*.
5. Reduce the size of the heap by 1.
6. Build a **Min Heap** from the remaining values of the heap.
7. Repeat steps 3 to 6 till the size of the heap is greater than 1.

The function which constructs the in-place heap during heap sort is generally named *'Heapify'*. Now, let us understand the algorithm using a simple example. Assume, we are sorting an array with element values *'7, 4, 6, 2, 1, 3, 5'*.

Steps	Array Elements
After heapifying the entire array	7, 4, 6, 2, 1, 3, 5
After swap [1]	5, 4, 6, 2, 1, 3, 7

After re-heapifying the heap section [1]	6, 4, 5, 2, 1, 3, **7**
After swap [2]	3, 4, 5, 2, 1, 6, 7
After re-heapifying the heap section [2]	5, 4, 3, 2, 1, **6, 7**
After swap [3]	1, 4, 3, 2, 5, 6, 7
After re-heapifying the heap section [3]	4, 2, 3, 1, **5, 6, 7**
After swap [4]	1, 2, 3, 4, 5, 6, 7
After re-heapifying the heap section [4]	3, 2, 1, **4, 5, 6, 7**
After swap [5]	1, 2, 3, 4, 5, 6, 7
After re-heapifying the heap section [5]	2, 1, **3, 4, 5, 6, 7**
After swap [6]	1, 2, 3, 4, 5, 6, 7
After re-heapifying the heap section [6] *(Final Sorted Result)*	**1, 2, 3, 4, 5, 6, 7**

NOTE: *The numbers within third brackets '[]' in column 1 indicate the iteration count. The numbers stated in **bold** in column 2 constitute the sorted section within the array.*

Heap sort performs best on arrays. Although it is somewhat slower than a well-implemented Quicksort, it has the advantage of a better worst-case execution time of O(n log n) against O(n^2) of Quicksort.

Given below is a program which will help us understand the algorithm better.

```c
#include <stdio.h>

/* Swaps the values of two variables. */
void SwapValues(int *pValue1, int *pValue2)
{
    int iTemp = 0;

    if (NULL != pValue1 && NULL != pValue2)
    {
        iTemp    = *pValue1;
        *pValue1 = *pValue2;
        *pValue2 = iTemp;
    }
}

/* If we visualize the array as a binary tree, this function heapifys'
   a subtree rooted at array element location 'iRoot'. 'iNumElements'
   refers to the number of elements in the subtree under 'iRoot'. */
void Heapify(int *prgiValues, int iNumElements, int iRoot)
{
    /* Start with the assumption that we have the largest value at the root. */
    int idxLargest    = iRoot;

    /* Being a complete binary tree, if 'iRoot' is the index of the root element,
       it's left child will be at the array location (2 * iRoot + 1) and the right
       child will be at the array location (2 * iRoot + 2). */
    int idxLeftChild  = 2 * iRoot + 1;
    int idxRightChild = 2 * iRoot + 2;

    /* Check if we have any left child of this node. We do not have any left child
```

334

```
        if its supposed index is greater or equal to the number of elements. */
    if (idxLeftChild < iNumElements)
    {
        if (prgiValues[idxLeftChild] > prgiValues[idxLargest])
        {
            /* The left child's value is greater than the largest value
               (Currently, the root element's value). */
            idxLargest = idxLeftChild;
        }
    }

    /* Now, do the same for the right child too (as was done for the left). */
    if (idxRightChild < iNumElements)
    {
        if (prgiValues[idxRightChild] > prgiValues[idxLargest])
        {
            /* The left child's value is greater than the largest value (the larger
               of the root element's value and the left child's value). */
            idxLargest = idxRightChild;
        }
    }

    if (idxLargest != iRoot)
    {
        /* The root element does not have the largest value. One of its
           child has the largest value. So, we need to swap the two values
           to get the largest value at the root. */
        SwapValues(&prgiValues[iRoot], &prgiValues[idxLargest]);

        /* Our subtree rooted at 'idxLargest' has changed due to the swap.
           We need to re-heapify it. */
        Heapify(prgiValues, iNumElements, idxLargest);
    }
}

/* The main driver function for the sort procedure. 'prgiValues' is the array
   to sort and 'iNumElements' is the total number of elements in the array. */
void HeapSort(int *prgiValues, int iNumElements)
{
    int idx = 0;

    /* Heapify the entire array. If we visualize the array as a complete binary
       tree, where each array element acts as a tree's node, the child nodes
       of a node/element 'A' will be at the array indices '(2 * Index of A) + 1'
       and '(2 * Index of A) + 2'. On doing heapify, the value of every node/element
       will be more than the values of its children. The last non-leaf (Internal)
       node of the tree will be at the array index (iNumElements / 2 - 1). We start
       heapify-ing from the subtree rooted at this node and continue upwards until
       we have heapify-ed the entire array. */
    for (idx = iNumElements / 2 - 1; idx >= 0; idx--)
    {
        Heapify(prgiValues, iNumElements, idx);
    }

    /* The element at the root will have the highest value within the heap. One by one
       extract an element (from the root position) of the heap and swap it with the end
       of the heap. We then mark this end as the new start position of the sorted
       sequence. We continue doing so until there are no elements left in the heap
       and all elements have moved to the sorted portion. If the array currently has
       the values '7, 6, 4, 5, 2, 1, 3, 8, 9', where '7, 6, 4, 5, 2, 1, 3' is the
       heap portion and '8, 9' is the sorted portion, we swap 7 with 3. This makes
       our array become '3, 6, 4, 5, 2, 1, 7, 8, 9' where '7, 8, 9' is the new sorted
       portion. After the swap, we will need to re-heapify our heap portion which has
```

```
        become '3, 6, 4, 5, 2, 1' due to the swap. */
    for (idx = iNumElements - 1; idx >= 1; idx--)
    {
        SwapValues(&prgiValues[0], &prgiValues[idx]);
        Heapify(prgiValues, idx, 0);
    }
}

int main(void)
{
    int rgiValues[]       = { 7, 4, 8, 6, 2, 1, 9, 3, 5 };
    int iArrayNumElements = sizeof(rgiValues) / sizeof(rgiValues[0]);
    int idx               = 0;

    HeapSort(rgiValues, iArrayNumElements);

    printf("The array after sorting: \n");
    for (; idx < iArrayNumElements; idx++)
    {
        printf("%d, ", rgiValues[idx]);
    }
    printf("\n\n");

    return 0;
}
```

21.6 INSERTION SORT

Insertion sort works by inserting items to a list. When inserting an item to the list, the list is examined and the correct position of the new item is found *(as per the sorted order)*, and the item is inserted to that position in the list. Insertion sort works with the assumption that the items currently in the list are already in sorted order from previous rounds of sorted insertions. Insertion sort removes one element from the input data, scans the sorted list to find the location it belongs to, and inserts it there. It repeats until no input elements remain.

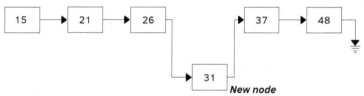

New node

Insertion sort is a very simple sorting algorithm but is much less efficient on large lists than more advanced algorithms such as *Quicksort*, *Merge sort* and *Heap sort*. Insertion sort is efficient when working with small lists and is effective when we are building the list in sorted order from the ground up itself. It performs very well when the input data is mostly sorted, and the algorithm has been optimized for that purpose. Insertion sort does not require any additional memory space while performing the sort.

Insertion sort performs poorly for arrays because of the fact that element insertions within arrays is a time-consuming and processor-intensive task. Insertion sort works good with linked lists as node insertions can be easily performed on linked lists.

The function *'AddNodeSorted'* within the program listed under **section 18.2.1** of *chapter 18* performs insertion sort while inserting new items to the list.

21.7 BUBBLE SORT

Bubble sort is a very simple sorting algorithm. It repeatedly traverses the list to be sorted, compares each pair of adjacent items and swaps them if they are in the wrong order. The repeated traversal takes place until no further swaps are needed, which indicates that the list is sorted.

There are few variations of the sorting algorithm achieving varying levels of optimization. In our approach, we will consider two sections within our array – unsorted and sorted. The sorted section contains the values which have already been sorted and have been placed at their desired positions, hence, requiring no further comparisons and sort. We will only work on the unsorted section, which at the start of the procedure spans the entire array to be sorted. As we keep sorting, the size of the unsorted section shrinks and the sorted section expands.

At each pass, we will compare adjacent elements until we reach the end of the unsorted section, which is: *'Number of array elements – Number of elements already sorted'*. The number of iterations *(Pass)* we do on the unsorted section is equal to the number of elements in the array minus 1. This is because when all elements except the last have already been placed in their correct positions, the last element is the only one left *(in the unsorted section)* and is already in its desired position within the array.

We further optimize the algorithm to detect an already sorted input array, and thus save ourselves from useless processing. At each pass *(traversal of the unsorted section)*, we check whether we required to swap any values. If none of the values were swapped during a pass, it means that all values in the unsorted section are already in sorted order and require no further processing.

Assume, we are sorting the array '5, 2, 4, 1, 3'. The algorithm will work as follows:

Pass 1
5, 2, 4, 1, 3 -> **2, 5**, 4, 1, 3   *[Swapped as 5 > 2].*
2, **5, 4**, 1, 3 -> 2, **4, 5**, 1, 3   *[Swapped as 5 > 4].*
2, 4, **5, 1**, 3 -> 2, 4, **1, 5**, 3   *[Swapped as 5 > 1].*
2, 4, 1, **5, 3** -> 2, 4, 1, **3, 5**   *[Swapped as 5 > 3].*

Pass 2
2, 4, 1, 3, 5 -> **2, 4**, 1, 3, 5
2, **4, 1**, 3, 5 -> 2, **1, 4**, 3, 5   *[Swapped as 4 > 1].*
2, 1, **4, 3**, 5 -> 2, 1, **3, 4**, 5   *[Swapped as 4 > 3].*

Pass 3
2, 1, 3, 4, 5 -> **1, 2**, 3, 4, 5   *[Swapped as 2 > 1].*
1, **2, 3**, 4, 5 -> 1, **2, 3**, 4, 5

Pass 4
1, **2**, 3, 4, 5 -> 1, **2**, 3, 4, 5

Bubble sort works best with arrays and should be avoided with linked lists. Although the algorithm is simple, it is slow for most input data. It gives a much better performance when the input data set is small and is mostly in sorted order. The advantage bubble sort has over most other sorting algorithms *(except insertion sort)* is the ability to detect that the list is sorted and thus, skip much of the unnecessary processing.

Let us now write a program which implements the bubble sort algorithm.

```c
#include <stdio.h>

void BubbleSort(int *prgiValues, int iNumElements)
{
    if (NULL == prgiValues)
    {
        return;
    }

    int i        = 0;
    int j        = 0;
    int iTemp    = 0;
    int iSwapped = 0;

    /* 'i' accounts for the passes we do on the unsorted section. We do not need a
       pass for the last unsorted item as it is the only one left in the unsorted
       section and thus occupying the only available position within the array. */
    for (; i < iNumElements - 1; i++)
    {
        iSwapped = 0;

        for (j = 0; j < iNumElements - i - 1; j++)
        {
            /* At each pass on the unsorted section, we go till the end of the
               unsorted section within the array. 'i' is the number of passes
               we have already performed and thus equals the number of elements
               occupying the sorted section (already sorted). */

            /* Compare the adjacent elements and swap if required. */
            if (prgiValues[j] > prgiValues[j + 1])
            {
                iTemp              = prgiValues[j];
                prgiValues[j]      = prgiValues[j + 1];
                prgiValues[j + 1]  = iTemp;
                iSwapped           = 1;
            }
        }

        if (0 == iSwapped)
        {
            /* We did not require to do any swaps. This means all the values in
               the unsorted section are already in sorted order and require no
               further processing. */
            break;
        }
    }
}
```

```
int main(void)
{
    int rgiValues[]       = { 7, 4, 6, 2, 1, 3, 5 };
    int iArrayNumElements = sizeof(rgiValues) / sizeof(rgiValues[0]);
    int idx               = 0;

    BubbleSort(rgiValues, iArrayNumElements);

    printf("The array after sorting: \n");
    for (; idx < iArrayNumElements; idx++)
    {
        printf("%d, ", rgiValues[idx]);
    }
    printf("\n\n");

    return 0;
}
```

21.8 SELECTION SORT

Just like *heap sort*, **selection sort** too divides an array into two sections – *sorted* and *unsorted*. Initially, the sorted section is empty and the unsorted section spans the entire array. As the sort progresses, more values are transferred from the unsorted section to the sorted section making the sorted section expand and the unsorted section shrink. This continues until there are no values left in the unsorted section. The sorted section occupies the start of the array *(left)* and the unsorted section occupies the end *(right)*.

At each iteration, the algorithm scans the unsorted section of the array to find the element with the least *(or highest in case of descending sort)* value. When its found, its value is swapped with the value of the left-most element of the unsorted section. Post the swap, the sorted section is expanded by one element *(to include the left-most element from the unsorted section)* and the unsorted section is shrinked by one element *(to exclude the left-most element)*.

The steps for sorting an array with 'n' elements in ascending order can be summarized as below:
1. Scan the unsorted section for the element with the least value.
2. Swap its value with the left-most element in the unsorted section.
3. Increment the starting index of the unsorted section.
4. Repeat steps 1 to 3 for 'n-1' times.

Note: *For sorting in descending order, we will search for the element with the largest value (instead of the least value) in step 1.*

Assume we are sorting an array 7, 2, 9, 3, 4. The sort operation will be performed in the following steps:
- 7, 2, 9, 3, 4 -> **2**, **7**, 9, 3, 4   *[Unsorted section start index: 0]*
- 2, 7, 9, 3, 4 -> 2, **3**, 9, **7**, 4   *[Unsorted section start index: 1]*
- 2, 3, 9, 7, 4 -> 2, 3, **4**, 7, **9**   *[Unsorted section start index: 2]*
- 2, 3, 4, 7, 9 -> 2, 3, 4, **7**, **9**   *[Unsorted section start index: 3, Final sorted result]*

Though selection sort is a very simple algorithm, it performs poorly in comparison to some other algorithms like Quicksort, Merge sort and Heap sort. Insertion sort too, in most cases perform better than selection sort. The Heap sort algorithm, though very similar to the selection sort algorithm, performs much better due to the use of binary heaps.

Selection sort works best with arrays, though, we may use it on linked lists too. The *program-1* in **section 5.5** of *chapter 5*, performs selection sort on an array. Here, we will write a program which will perform selection sort on a linked list.

```c
#include <stdio.h>

/* Defined Values */
#define MAX_ITEMS    10

typedef struct _NODE
{
    /* This node's value. */
    int          iNodeValue;
    /* The pointer which points to the next node. */
    struct _NODE *pNext;

} NODE;

void SelectionSort(NODE *pHead)
{
    NODE *pMove1 = NULL;
    NODE *pMove2 = NULL;
    NODE *pMin   = NULL;
    int   iTemp  = 0;

    /* 'pMove1' marks the start of the unsorted section.
       Initially, it is the entire list. */
    for (pMove1 = pHead; NULL != pMove1->pNext; pMove1 = pMove1->pNext)
    {
        /* Start with the assumption that the start node of the
           unsorted section has the least value. If we find a node
           with a lesser value, we will mark it as the new 'min'. */
        pMin = pMove1;

        /* Scan the entire unsorted section and try to find the
           node with the least value. */
        for (pMove2 = pMove1->pNext; NULL != pMove2; pMove2 = pMove2->pNext)
        {
            if (pMove2->iNodeValue < pMin->iNodeValue)
            {
                /* A new 'min' node is found. */
                pMin = pMove2;
            }
        }

        if (pMove1 != pMin)
        {
            /* The 'min' node is not the same as 'pMove1'. Swap their values. */
            iTemp               = pMin->iNodeValue;
            pMin->iNodeValue    = pMove1->iNodeValue;
            pMove1->iNodeValue  = iTemp;
        }
    }
}
```

```c
int main(void)
{
    NODE *pHead  = NULL;
    NODE *pTail  = NULL;
    NODE *pNew   = NULL;
    NODE *pMove  = NULL;

    int   iCount = 0;

    /* Create the linked list. */
    for (; iCount < MAX_ITEMS; iCount++)
    {
        /* Allocate the new node. */
        pNew = (NODE *) malloc(sizeof(NODE));
        if (NULL == pNew)
        {
            break;
        }

        printf("Enter the node's value: ");
        scanf("%d", &pNew->iNodeValue);

        if (NULL == pHead)
        {
            /* The list is empty. This is the first node of the list. */
            pHead = pNew;
        }
        else
        {
            pTail->pNext = pNew;
        }

        pTail        = pNew;
        pTail->pNext = NULL;
    }

    if (NULL != pHead)
    {
        SelectionSort(pHead);

        printf("\nThe list after sorting:\n");
        for (pMove = pHead; NULL != pMove; pMove = pMove->pNext)
        {
            printf("%d, ", pMove->iNodeValue);
        }

        /* Cleanup the list before exit. */
        for (pMove = pHead; NULL != pMove; pMove = pHead)
        {
            pHead = pHead->pNext;
            free(pMove);
            pMove = NULL;
        }

        printf("\n\n");
    }

    return 0;
}
```

21.9 BINARY SEARCH TREE

Just like *insertion sort*, we could build a **BST** from the ground up yielding us a sorted list at every stage of our list. When we are creating the list by adding items to it, we build it as a **binary search tree** or an **AVL tree**. The *inorder* traversal of the tree will generate the output in sorted order. This strategy helps us attain a very favourable space and time complexities.

21.10 SPACE AND TIME COMPLEXITIES

The space and time complexities of the various sorting algorithms are:

Algorithm	Space	Time (Best)	Time (Average)	Time (Worst)
Merge sort	O(n) with arrays and O(log(n)) with linked lists	$O(n \log(n))$	$O(n \log(n))$	$O(n \log(n))$
Quick sort	O(n)	$O(n \log(n))$	$O(n \log(n))$	$O(n^2)$
Heap sort	O(1)	$O(n \log(n))$	$O(n \log(n))$	$O(n \log(n))$
Insertion sort	O(1)	O(n)	$O(n^2)$	$O(n^2)$
Bubble sort	O(1)	O(n)	$O(n^2)$	$O(n^2)$
Selection sort	O(1)	$O(n^2)$	$O(n^2)$	$O(n^2)$

21.11 SEARCHING

When searching for an item within a list, we can opt for any of the following methods:
- Linear search
- Binary search
- Binary search tree
- Jump search

21.11.1 LINEAR SEARCH

Linear search is the simplest form of searching which involves searching every element within the list until the desired element is found. This searching method is also called **sequential search**. We start the search from the initial element of the list and continue searching until we have found the desired element or we have reached the end of the list. Though linear search is an extremely slow search technique, the advantage it has over most other search techniques is the fact that the input list need not be in sorted order. Linear search can be performed on almost all types of lists *(arrays, linked lists etc.)*. The time complexity of a linear search is O(n).

21.11.2 BINARY SEARCH

Binary search works only on a sorted list. It searches a sorted array by repeatedly dividing the search range in half and testing the middle element. The middle element is returned, if its value equals the search value. In an ascending ordered list, if the search value is less than the value of the element in the middle, the search continues in the lower half of the range. If the search value is more, the search continues in the upper half. We continue doing so until we find the search value or there are no elements in a range.

Assume, we are searching for a value *'iSrch'* within a sorted array *'arr'*. The array is sorted in ascending order and contains *'N'* number of elements. Two variables *'iStart'* and *'iEnd'* are declared, and initialized with the values 0 *(zero)* and *'N-1'* respectively. We look at the flowchart for binary searching such an array:

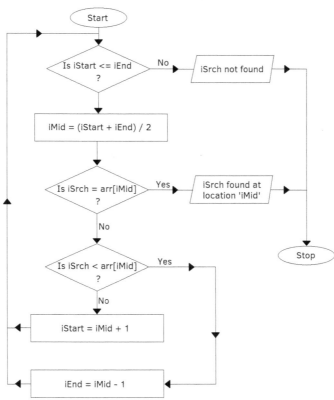

The time complexity of binary search is O(log(n)). Not only *binary search* has a simple implementation but also, it is very efficient. Let us understand it using a small program.

```c
#include <stdio.h>

int BinarySearch(int *prgiValues,
                 int  iNumElements,
                 int  iSrchValue)
{
    int iStart     = 0;
    int iEnd       = iNumElements - 1;
    int iMid       = 0;
    int iItemIndex = -1;

    while (iStart <= iEnd)
    {
        /* Find the middle index between the start and end indices. */
        iMid = (iStart + iEnd) / 2;
        if (iSrchValue == prgiValues[iMid])
        {
            /* Found the value. */
```

```
                iItemIndex = iMid;
                break;
            }
            else if (iSrchValue < prgiValues[iMid])
            {
                /* The search value should lie in the lower half. */
                iEnd = iMid - 1;
            }
            else
            {
                /* The search value should lie in the upper half. */
                iStart = iMid + 1;
            }
        }

        return iItemIndex;
    }

    int main(void)
    {
        /* 'rgiValues' must be sorted in ascending order. */
        int rgiValues[]        = { 10, 14, 19, 23, 27, 36, 39, 48, 53, 57, 59, 61 };
        int iArrayNumElements = sizeof(rgiValues) / sizeof(rgiValues[0]);
        int idx               = 0;
        int iSrchValue        = 23;

        /* Now, Search the value. */
        idx = BinarySearch(rgiValues, iArrayNumElements, iSrchValue);

        if (idx < 0)
        {
            printf("The value %d could not be found.", iSrchValue);
        }
        else
        {
            printf("The value %d is at array index %d.", iSrchValue, idx);
        }

        printf("\n\n");
        return 0;
    }
```

21.11.3 BINARY SEARCH TREE

We may arrange the data as a *binary search tree*, which will enable us to easily search for an item within the tree using the very principles of a binary search tree *(refer **section 20.2**)*. Search is very efficient for a BST as it uses binary search for the purpose. We can achieve best search performance only if the BST is balanced like an AVL tree. For a balanced BST, we will achieve a time complexity of O(log(n)).

21.11.4 JUMP SEARCH

Jump search also called **block search** checks fewer elements *(than a linear search)* by skipping ahead some elements. Like *binary search*, jump search too needs the array to be in sorted order. The algorithm uses a jump interval to jump a specific number of elements while keeping a track of the position it held before the jump. The elements spanning the last position to the jump location constitute the *current block*. The jump location is also called the *jump step* or simply *step*. The algorithm keeps jumping elements till the value of the jump step is less than the search value *(greater in case the array is sorted* *in descending order)*. If the search value is found to be less or equal, it will most likely be present in the current block. We then perform a linear search in the current block for the value.

Assume we are searching the value '17' within the array 2, 5, 9, 11, 15, 17, 21, 27, 31. We set our jump interval as 3. We hold the last position *(before the jump)* in the variable *'iStart'* and the position after the jump *(jump step)* in *'iStep'*. The elements between *'iStart'* and *'iStep'* constitute the *current block*.

- iStart is initialized to 0 *(zero)* and iStep is initialized to 3 *(jump interval)*.
- iStep *(value 11)* is less than search value 17. This makes us to continue the jump search.
- iStart becomes 4 and iStep becomes 6.
- iStep *(value 21)* is more than search value 17. The search value should lie in the current block *(array index 4 to array index 6)*.
- Perform linear search in the current block *(array index 4 to array index 6)*.

Jump search is an improvement over *linear search* but, is less efficient than *binary search.* It is prudent to use binary search instead of jump search wherever possible. The only advantage of jump search over binary search is that we generally require lesser number of backward jumps than in binary search. For jump search, we mostly move forward, and resort to backward traversal only when we are doing linear search within the identified block. Jump search has a time complexity of O(sqrt(n)).

```c
#include <stdio.h>

int JumpSearch(int *prgiValues,
               int  iNumElements,
               int  iSrchValue)
{
    int iStart     = 0;
    int iIncrement = sqrt(iNumElements);
    int iStep      = iIncrement;
    int iItemIndex = -1;

    /* Find the block where our search value may be present. Jump search
       by skipping 'iIncrement' elements each time till the search value is
       more than the step element's value. */
    for (; iStep < iNumElements; iStep += iIncrement)
    {
        if (iSrchValue <= prgiValues[iStep])
        {
            /* The search value (if present) should lie in this block. */
            break;
        }

        iStart = iStep + 1;
    }

    if (iStep >= iNumElements)
    {
        /* We have crossed the end of the array. Re-adjust to the array end. */
        iStep = iNumElements − 1;
    }

    /* We found the block. Perform linear search within this block (moving backwards). */
    for (; iStep >= iStart; iStep--)
    {
        if (iSrchValue > prgiValues[iStep])
```

```
        {
            /* We crossed the location where the value could have existed. This means
                the search value does not exist in the array. Assume we are searching the
                value 8 within the block of values 6, 7, 9. We start from the value 9
                and move backwards. We will stop at the value 7 when our search value
                of 8 becomes greater than the element's value (meaning the search value
                does not exist). We perform backward search as it achieves better
                performance when a step value is equal to the search value. */
            break;
        }
        else if (iSrchValue == prgiValues[iStep])
        {
            iItemIndex = iStep;
            break;
        }
    }

    return iItemIndex;
}

int main(void)
{
    /* 'rgiValues' must be sorted in ascending order. */
    int rgiValues[]        = { 10, 14, 19, 23, 27, 36, 39, 48, 53, 57, 59, 61 };
    int iArrayNumElements = sizeof(rgiValues) / sizeof(rgiValues[0]);
    int idx               = 0;
    int iSrchValue        = 57;

    /* Now, Search the value. */
    idx = JumpSearch(rgiValues, iArrayNumElements, iSrchValue);

    if (idx < 0)
    {
        printf("The value %d could not be found.", iSrchValue);
    }
    else
    {
        printf("The value %d is at array index %d.", iSrchValue, idx);
    }

    printf("\n\n");
    return 0;
}
```

THREADING AND SYNCHRONIZATION

[CHAPTER-22]

Note: *Native support for threads and synchronization was introduced from C11 onwards. Not all compilers support these features.*

22.1 THREADS

Thread is the smallest executable unit of a process consisting of a program counter, a stack and a thread ID. A process may break up its tasks into multiple units with each unit getting executed in parallel. This not only achieves operational efficiency but also scalability. A word processor application may divide its work into multiple threads with each thread performing its tasks in parallel. One thread may be given the responsibility of interacting with the user *(the UI layer)*, another thread may be performing spell and grammar check and another thread may be caching/saving the document to the disk.

In today's world, most processors come with multiple cores, with each core capable of performing tasks independently. This makes it prudent to allocate the tasks between multiple threads. Each thread may be allotted a separate processing core for which the entire task gets completed faster.

Each thread has its own set of tasks and its own path of execution within the process. All threads of the same process share memory of that process. The threads may communicate between each other using shared resources like variables.

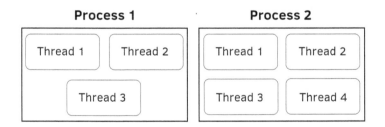

Threads can be utilized when:
- A process has multiple tasks which need to performed independently of the others.
- One of the tasks may block and it is desired to allow the other tasks to proceed without getting blocked by the time consuming task.

Every program has at-least one thread, even if it does not create any more threads. A program which does not create any further threads is called a *single-threaded* application. Prior to this chapter, all our examples were single-threaded where all the work was performed from the 'main' function itself *(optionally helped by many system/helper functions)*. This thread is called the *main/primary* thread. A program which creates additional threads *(called secondary threads)* is called a *multi-threaded* application.

22.1.1 WHY MULTI-THREADED – FOR AND AGAINST

Multithreaded applications have the following advantages:

- **Responsiveness:** One thread may remain responsive while the other threads are blocked or slowed down doing intensive operations. For example in a single threaded application, the application may seem to have become unresponsive when it is busy performing a time-consuming operation. In a multi-threaded application the blocking task may be shifted to a separate thread for which the user-interaction thread remains responsive.
- **Parallel execution:** In a multi-core or multi-CPU environment, resource intensive tasks may be broken into multiple units with each unit getting executed in parallel.
- **Economy:** An application can serve multiple clients concurrently using multiple threads. Rather than using multiple processes of the program *(with one process serving one client)*, it is more economical to use threads within a single application, with one thread serving one client. Process creation is more expensive than creating threads.
- **Resource sharing:** All threads within a process can share the same resources available to the process. Rather than creating separate processes with their own set of resource requirements, it is much cheaper to create threads within a process.

Some of the disadvantages of multithreaded applications are:

- **Deadlocks:** In a multithreaded application, we can easily get into deadlocks, if care is not taken while writing the code. We will read about deadlocks a little later in this chapter.
- **Thread crashes:** An illegal operation performed by one thread may crash the entire process. Thus, one misbehaving thread can disrupt the processing of all the other threads within the application.

22.1.2 WRITING MULTI-THREADED PROGRAMS IN C

In C, a thread can be created using the **'thrd_create'** function which has the following form:

$$\text{int } \textbf{thrd\_create}(\text{thrd\_t } *pThread, \text{thrd\_start\_t } pFunc, \text{void } *pArg);$$

where:

'pThread' receives an identifier to the newly created thread. The caller provides a pointer to a **'thrd_t'** identifier and the function *'thrd_create'* fills the identifier with information related to the newly created thread. *'thrd_t'* is generally a structure containing all information related to the thread. The format of *'thrd_t'* may vary between compilers.

'pFunc' is a pointer to the thread procedure/function. Just like a program begins with the 'main' function, a thread procedure acts as the base function for a secondary thread. A thread procedure must have the following form:

*int FunctionName(void *pArg);*

The *'pArg'* argument provided to the *'thrd_create'* function is forwarded as an argument to the thread procedure *'pFunc'* when creating the thread. The function *'thrd_create'* returns the enumeration value *'thrd_success'* if successful, *'thrd_nomem'* if there was insufficient memory, and *'thrd_error'* in case of an error.

There are additional thread handling functions in C, which are:

int thrd_equal(thrd_t ThrID1, thrd_t ThrID2): Checks whether *'ThrID1'* and *'ThrID2'* refer to the same thread. Non-zero if same, and zero otherwise.

thrd_t thrd_current(void): Returns the thread identifier of the calling thread.

int thrd_sleep(const struct timespec *pDuration, struct timespec *pRemain): Blocks the execution of the calling thread until *'pDuration'* time elapsed. *'pRemain' (if not NULL)* will receive the remaining time.

void thrd_yield(void): Suspend the current thread allowing other threads to run.

_Noreturn void thrd_exit(int iReturn): Terminates the calling thread. *'iReturn'* is the thread return value.

int thrd_join(thrd_t Thr, int *pReturn): Blocks the current thread until the thread identified by *'Thr'* ends. *'pReturn'* receives the thread return value from *'Thr'*.

int thrd_detach(thrd_t Thr): Detaches the thread identified by *'Thr'*. The resources held by the thread will be freed automatically once the thread exits.

22.1.3 OUR FIRST MULTI-THREADED PROGRAM

In our first multi-threaded application we will keep it simple. From the 'main()' function we will create 5 threads, one after the other. We will pass a thread index as the parameter to the thread procedure when creating the thread. After a thread is created, it will print a simple message involving the thread index it received from the 'main' function during its creation. The primary/main thread will wait *(within function 'main')* for the created thread to end. When the thread completes, the primary thread will create the next thread using the same thread procedure.

```c
#include <stdio.h>
#include <string.h>
#include <time.h>
#include <threads.h>

// Thread procedure.
int ThreadFunc(void *pData)
{
    struct timespec ts = { 0 };

    if (NULL == pData)
    {
        // We got no arguments. Print a general message.
```

```
        printf("\nThis is the thread speaking.");
    }
    else
    {
        // 'pData' argument points to an integer which contains
        // this thread's index. We will print that index.
        int iThreadIndex = *(int *)pData;
        printf("\nThis is thread %d speaking.", iThreadIndex);
    }

    // Wait 2 seconds before stopping this thread.
    ts.tv_sec = 2;
    thrd_sleep(&ts, NULL);

    return 0;
}

int main(void)
{
    thrd_t ThreadID = { 0 };
    int    iSuccess = 0;
    int    iThreadIdx = 1;
    int    iThreadRes = 0;

    // We will create 5 threads one after the other. After creating a thread
    // we will wait for the thread to end before creating the next thread.
    for (; iThreadIdx <= 5; iThreadIdx++)
    {
        memset(&ThreadID, 0, sizeof(ThreadID));

        // Create the thread.
        iSuccess = thrd_create(&ThreadID, &ThreadFunc, &iThreadIdx);
        if (thrd_success != iSuccess)
        {
            // The thread creation failed. Stop.
            break;
        }

        // Wait for the thread to complete execution.
        iSuccess = thrd_join(ThreadID, &iThreadRes);
        if (thrd_success != iSuccess)
        {
            break;
        }
    }

    printf("\n\n");
    return 0;
}
```

22.2 SYNCHRONIZATION

We create multiple threads with each thread working in parallel to the other. What happens:

- When one thread depends on the output of another. An intermediate or final result produced by one thread is required for continuation by another thread.
- When more than one thread access and make changes to a shared resource *(a global variable, a thread parameter sent to multiple threads etc.)*. For example, we have two threads 'A' and 'B', both having access to two shared integer variables 'x' and 'y'. Thread 'A' needs to calculate the result of the formula *'(x * y)/(x + y)'*. 'A' calculates (x * y), but before it gets a chance to

calculate (x + y), thread 'B' changes the values of 'x' and 'y'. Now, thread 'A' will produce an erroneous result as it used different values of 'x' and 'y' when calculating (x * y) and (x + y) respectively.

The only solution to the above problems is to synchronize the execution between the threads. Threads can be synchronized to:

1. Execute critical section of a code *(such as accessing the value of a shared variable)* in such a manner that no two threads do the same concurrently. The threads synchronize their execution so that when one thread is executing the critical section, other threads wait for their turn.
2. Wait on a code section which is dependent on the result of execution of another thread. This can be explained using a simple real life example. Suppose two people go to a movie theatre. One waits at the theatre gate and the other goes to purchase the tickets. The first person cannot get into the theatre without the ticket and thus, needs to wait for the other person to complete the purchase.

In C, the synchronization as in *#1* above can be achieved using a mutex whereas *#2* can be achieved with a combination of mutex and a conditional variable.

22.2.1 MUTEX

Mutex, a short form of mutual exclusion enables two or more threads to access common resource in such a way that no two threads do the same at the same time. Every thread which needs to access a shared resource needs to first place a lock on the mutex. The thread which locks the mutex, gets the chance to access the resource, and all other threads wait to place a lock on the mutex before continuing. Only one thread can lock a mutex at a time.

A mutex can be of three types:

1. **Plain:** Any attempt to lock a plain mutex would either fail or block when the mutex is already locked, even if the same thread had placed the lock. If a thread having a lock on a mutex tries to lock it again, it will get blocked.
2. **Recursive:** A thread trying to lock an already locked mutex will succeed if and only if the locking thread is the one that already holds the lock.
3. **Timed:** A mutex that supports timeout.

Mutex handling in C

Before a mutex is used, it must be initialized. A mutex is initialized using the '**mtx_init**' function. It has the following form:

int **mtx_init**(mtx_t *pMutex, int *iType*);

'**mtx_t**' is the mutex identifier and is generally a structure containing all information related to the mutex. The format of *'mtx_t'* may vary between compilers. *'iType'* refers to the type of mutex which can be:

*   **mtx_plain:** A plain mutex.
*   **mtx_recursive:** A recursive mutex.

- **mtx_timed:** A plain mutex supporting timeout.
- **mtx_recursive | mtx_timed:** A recursive mutex supporting timeout.

The following C functions can be utilized to lock a mutex:
int mtx_lock(mtx_t *pMutex);
The function blocks the current thread until the mutex pointed to by *'pMutex'* gets locked. The function does not return until it successfully locks the mutex, making the calling thread wait on the function. The function returns the enumeration value *'thrd_success'* if successful, and *'thrd_error'* otherwise.

int mtx_timedlock(mtx_t *pMutex, const struct timespec *pTS);
Blocks the current thread until the timed mutex pointed to by *'pMutex'* is locked or until the specified time pointed to by *'pTS'* has been reached, whichever occurs first. The function returns *'thrd_success'* if successful, *'thrd_timedout'* if the timeout time has been reached before the mutex is locked, and *'thrd_error'* in case of an error.

int mtx_trylock(mtx_t *pMutex);
The function tries to lock the mutex pointed to by *'pMutex'* without blocking. It returns immediately if the mutex is already locked. The function returns *'thrd_success'* if successful, *'thrd_busy'* if the mutex is already locked, and *'thrd_error'* in case of an error.

Once a thread which had locked a mutex, has completed working with the shared resource, it needs to unlock the mutex to enable other threads *(waiting to acquire a lock on the mutex)* gain access to the shared resource. A mutex is unlocked using the function:
int mtx_unlock(mtx_t *pMutex);

When a mutex is no longer required, it needs to be destroyed using the function:
void mtx_destroy(mtx_t *pMutex);

<u>**Synchronization example using a mutex**</u>
In our next program we will create two threads. Each thread will have a different thread procedure – thread 1 will be operated using *'ThreadProc1'* and thread 2 will be operated using *'ThreadProc2'*. There will be a shared variable *'iSharedValue'* which will be accessed and modified by both the threads.

'iSharedValue' is part of a structure *'_THREADPARAMS'*. The structure variable is part of the primary thread in function 'main' and will be provided as thread parameters when creating the secondary threads. The secondary threads will receive the structure variable as an argument in their respective thread procedures.

Both the threads will increment and print the member value *'iSharedValue'*. The thread 1 is required to print only the odd values of *'iSharedValue'* and thread 2 is required to print only the even values.

As both the threads are making changes to a common variable, we will require a mutex to control access to the variable by both the threads. Concurrent changes to the value of the variable may yield unexpected results where thread 1 may print an even value whereas thread 2 may print an odd value. This can be explained using a simple example: Thread 1 increments the value to 5 but, before it gets a chance to print the value, thread 2 increments the value to 6. Thread 1 now prints the current value 6.

To save ourselves from these erroneous output, we are using the '_THREADPARAMS' member variable 'mutex' which is accessible to both the threads. Before accessing or modifying the shared variable 'iSharedValue', both the threads place a lock on the mutex. When a lock is successfully placed by one thread, the other thread waits for the mutex to be unlocked before using the variable. The mutex is unlocked by the same thread which placed the lock once its work with the variable has been completed. The mutex is locked using the function 'mtx_lock'. If the mutex is **not** already locked, the function locks the mutex and returns immediately. If the mutex is already locked, the function waits for the mutex to be unlocked before placing a lock and returning. When the function has returned, we can be sure that the mutex has been locked by the calling thread and we can safely access the shared resource.

Once a thread places a lock on the mutex, it needs to unlock the same using the function 'mtx_unlock', once it has completed working with the shared resource. If a thread places a lock on the mutex but forgets to unlock it, we will get into a state of partial deadlock where another thread waits indefinitely for the mutex to be unlocked. If say, thread 1 places a lock on the mutex but forgets to unlock the same, thread 2 will indefinitely wait on the function call 'mtx_lock' to place a lock on the mutex, which never happens, as thread 1 never releases the lock.

The program waits *(in the primary thread, 'main' function)* for the user to hit the 'enter' key to stop the execution. Once the key is hit, the program sets the variable 'fStopThread' to true, which makes the secondary threads to stop. As only one thread *(primary thread)* is making changes to the shared variable 'fStopThread' and the other two threads are only reading its value, we can afford to keep this variable outside the scope of synchronization.

```c
#include <stdio.h>
#include <string.h>
#include <time.h>
#include <stdbool.h>
#include <threads.h>

typedef struct _THREADPARAMS
{
    int    iSharedValue;
    mtx_t mutex;
    bool  fStopThread;

}THREADPARAMS, *PTHREADPARAMS;

bool IsEven(int iValue)
{
    if (0 == (iValue % 2))
    {
        return true;
    }

    return false;
}
```

```c
int ThreadProc1(void *pData)
{
    int             iThreadExitCode = 0;
    struct timespec ts              = { 0 };
    bool            fChanged        = false;
    PTHREADPARAMS   pParam;

    do
    {
        if (NULL == pData)
        {
            iThreadExitCode = -1;
            break;
        }

        ts.tv_sec = 1;

        pParam = (PTHREADPARAMS)pData;

        while (!pParam->fStopThread)
        {
            // Before getting access to the shared value, we need
            // to get a lock status on the mutex. A lock status
            // will mean no other thread has a lock on the mutex
            // and thus, no other thread is accessing the value.
            mtx_lock(&pParam->mutex);

            // We are signalled to go. We can now make changes to
            // shared values as the other thread is waiting on us.
            if (IsEven(pParam->iSharedValue))
            {
                pParam->iSharedValue++;
                printf("\nThread 1: Shared value is now odd. "
                        "It's value is %d.", pParam->iSharedValue);
                fChanged = true;
            }

            // Our work on the shared value is complete. We may
            // now release the mutex so that other threads can now
            // access the shared value.
            mtx_unlock(&pParam->mutex);

            if (fChanged)
            {
                // We have just changed the value. Sleep for a second
                // and let the other thread make the change.
                thrd_sleep(&ts, NULL);
                fChanged = false;
            }
        }

    } while (0);

    return iThreadExitCode;
}

int ThreadProc2(void *pData)
{
    int             iThreadExitCode = 0;
    struct timespec ts              = { 0 };
    bool            fChanged        = false;
    PTHREADPARAMS   pParam;
```

```c
    do
    {
        if (NULL == pData)
        {
            iThreadExitCode = -1;
            break;
        }

        ts.tv_sec = 1;

        pParam = (PTHREADPARAMS)pData;

        while (!pParam->fStopThread)
        {
            // Before getting access to the shared value, we need
            // to get a lock status on the mutex. A lock status
            // will mean no other thread has a lock on the mutex
            // and thus, no other thread is accessing the value.
            mtx_lock(&pParam->mutex);

            // We are signalled to go. We can now make changes to
            // shared values as the other thread is waiting on us.
            if (!IsEven(pParam->iSharedValue))
            {
                pParam->iSharedValue++;
                printf("\nThread 2: Shared value is now even. "
                       "It's value is %d.", pParam->iSharedValue);
                fChanged = true;
            }

            // Our work on the shared value is complete. We may
            // now release the mutex so that other threads can now
            // access the shared value.
            mtx_unlock(&pParam->mutex);

            if (fChanged)
            {
                // We have just changed the value. Sleep for a second
                // and let the other thread make the change.
                thrd_sleep(&ts, NULL);
                fChanged = false;
            }
        }

    } while (0);

    return iThreadExitCode;
}

int main(void)
{
    thrd_t       ThreadID1   = { 0 };
    thrd_t       ThreadID2   = { 0 };
    int          iSuccess    = 0;
    int          iThreadRes  = 0;
    THREADPARAMS Param       = { 0 };

    do
    {
        printf("Press enter to stop the program...");

        Param.fStopThread  = false;
        Param.iSharedValue = 0;
```

```
        // Create the mutex.
        iSuccess = mtx_init(&Param.mutex, mtx_plain);
        if (thrd_success != iSuccess)
        {
            // The mutex creation failed. Stop.
            break;
        }

        // Create the first thread.
        iSuccess = thrd_create(&ThreadID1, &ThreadProc1, &Param);
        if (thrd_success != iSuccess)
        {
            // The thread creation failed. Stop.
            break;
        }

        // Create the second thread.
        iSuccess = thrd_create(&ThreadID2, &ThreadProc2, &Param);
        if (thrd_success != iSuccess)
        {
            // The thread creation failed. Stop.
            break;
        }

        // Wait for the user to press enter to stop the execution.
        getchar();

    } while (0);

    // Ask the threads to stop.
    Param.fStopThread = true;
    // Wait for the threads to stop.
    thrd_join(ThreadID1, &iThreadRes);
    thrd_join(ThreadID2, &iThreadRes);

    // Destroy the mutex.
    mtx_destroy(&Param.mutex);

    printf("\n\n");
    return 0;
}
```

22.2.2 CONDITION VARIABLE

A condition variable is a form of synchronization which combines a lock *(mutex)* with a signalling mechanism. It is used when threads need to wait for a resource to become available. Condition variables enable threads to atomically release a lock and enter a sleeping state. The thread remains in sleeping state until another thread signals a change in the condition variable. After a thread is woken, it re-acquires the lock *(mutex)* it released when it entered the sleeping state.

A condition variable is best utilized in a producer-consumer scenario, where one thread acts as the producer and another as consumer. The producer thread generates some data in a queue buffer which are consumed by the consumer thread. The consumer has to wait *(for the producer to produce)* if the queue is empty and the producer has to wait *(for the consumer to consume)* if the queue is full. As both producer and consumer act on the same buffer, the buffer must be protected using a mutex.

When the queue goes empty, the consumer releases its lock on the mutex and goes into sleep.

Releasing the lock enables the producer to acquire the lock and start generating the data. The consumer remains in sleep mode until the producer signals the consumer that the queue is no more empty. Upon being signalled so, the consumer immediately acquires back the lock on the mutex. Getting signalled and acquiring back the lock is all done atomically. This same mechanism is also followed by the producer. In a producer-consumer scenario, we can have multiple producers and consumers.

Using Condition Variables in C
Before a condition variable is used, it must be initialized. A condition variable is initialized using the '**cnd_init**' function. It has the following form:

int cnd_init(cnd_t *pCond);

'**cnd_t**' is the condition variable identifier and is generally a structure containing all information related to the condition variable. The format of '*cnd_t*' may vary between compilers.

A thread may go into sleep based on the condition variable using any of the following functions:
int cnd_wait(cnd_t *pCond, mtx_t *pMutex);
'*pMutex*' is the identifier of the mutex which needs to be released before the thread goes into sleep. As soon as the condition '*pCond*' gets signalled, a lock on '*pMutex*' is atomically acquired and the thread gets woken up.

int cnd_timedwait(cnd_t *pCond, mtx_t *pMutex, const struct timespec *pTS);
The function is similar to '*cnd_wait*' except that this function waits for a maximum of '*pTS*' duration. The mutex is locked again before the function returns.

When a thread is sleeping on a condition, it can be awakened using any of the following functions:
int cnd_signal(cnd_t *pCond);
Signals a waiting thread to wake up.

int cnd_broadcast(cnd_t *pCond);
Signals all threads which are waiting on the condition.

When a condition variable is no longer required, it must be destroyed using the function:
void cnd_destroy(cnd_t *pCond);

Synchronization example using condition variables
In our program we will create a producer-consumer relationship. We will have a fixed size buffer which will act as repository for the values being exchanged between the producers and consumers. We will have one or more threads acting as producers and consumers. Producer threads will write values to the shared buffer and the consumer threads will read the values.

A consumer cannot read a value until the producer produces it. Once a value is read, that value gets discarded from the buffer i.e. its buffer position becomes available to be re-utilized. The values are written to the buffer in a circular fashion i.e. once the top of the buffer fills up, writing starts from the start of the buffer *(if free space is available)*.

When the buffer gets full, the producers need to wait for the consumers to consume some items and free up space. The producers go into a sleeping wait state when this condition occurs. Similarly when the buffer gets empty, the consumers need to wait for the producers to produce some items.

```c
#include <stdio.h>
#include <time.h>
#include <string.h>
#include <stdbool.h>
#include <threads.h>

// Defined values
#define BUFFER_SIZE              10
#define NUM_PRODUCERS            2
#define NUM_CONSUMERS            2
#define PRODUCER_SLEEP_TIME      1
#define CONSUMER_SLEEP_TIME      3

// The shared buffer
unsigned long g_rguBuffer[BUFFER_SIZE];

// The value of the last item produced (written) by the producers
unsigned long g_ulLastItemValue;
// The total number of items produced (written) by the producers
unsigned long g_ulTotalItemsProduced;
// The total number of items consumed (read) by the consumers
unsigned long g_ulTotalItemsConsumed;

// The total number of items currently in the buffer
int    g_iItemsInBuffer;
// The next index position to be read. The items are located in circular
// fashion starting from this index to the last produced item
int    g_iItemStartIndex;

mtx_t g_mutex;

// The condition variable used to notify the producers that the buffer is not full
cnd_t g_BufferNotFull;
// The condition variable used to notify the consumers that the buffer is not empty
cnd_t g_BufferNotEmpty;

bool   g_fStopApp;

int ProducerProc(void *pData)
{
    int              iProducerID  = 0;
    int              iNextItemIdx = 0;
    struct timespec ts           = { 0 };

    if (NULL != pData)
    {
        iProducerID = *((int *)pData);
    }

    ts.tv_sec = PRODUCER_SLEEP_TIME;

    while (!g_fStopApp)
    {
        thrd_sleep(&ts, NULL);

        mtx_lock(&g_mutex);
```

```
        while (BUFFER_SIZE <= g_iItemsInBuffer && !g_fStopApp)
        {
            // Buffer is full. Wait for the consumers to consume items
            // and signal us that the buffer is no more full.
            // We are releasing our mutex on this condition 'g_BufferNotFull'
            // so that the consumers get the chance to consume items.
            // As soon as this condition is met (signalled by the consumers)
            // we will again automatically attain the lock on the mutex.
            // This is done atomically within the function call 'cnd_wait'.
            cnd_wait(&g_BufferNotFull, &g_mutex);
        }

        if (g_fStopApp)
        {
            // The primary thread is asking us to stop.
            // Release the mutex, signal the waiting consumers and stop.
            goto UNLOCKMUTEX;
        }

        // We are operating in a circular fashion within the array. If
        // there are no free space at the top (end) of the array, we wrap
        // around and start from the beginning of the array, only on the
        // condition that the beginning of the array is free i.e. the items
        // at the beginning have been consumed by the consumers. As
        // 'g_iItemsInBuffer' is less than 'BUFFER_SIZE', we definitely
        // have free space available in the array. This can be explained as:
        // Assuming our shared array contains 10 elements,
        // If the next item to be consumed is at index 2 and there are 8 items
        // in the array, then we will place the new item at the index 0.
        // If the next item to be consumed is at index 7 and there are 9 items
        // in the array, then we will place the new item at the index 6.
        // If the next item to be consumed is at index 1 and there are 8 items
        // in the array, then we will place the new item at the index 9.
        iNextItemIdx = (g_iItemStartIndex + g_iItemsInBuffer) % BUFFER_SIZE;

        // Fill the next item in the buffer.
        g_rguBuffer[iNextItemIdx] = ++g_ulLastItemValue;
        g_ulTotalItemsProduced++;
        g_iItemsInBuffer++;

        printf("\nProducer %d produced item %u at location %d.",
               iProducerID, g_ulLastItemValue, iNextItemIdx);

UNLOCKMUTEX:
        mtx_unlock(&g_mutex);

        // We have produced 1 item in the buffer. So, there is at-least one
        // item in the buffer and our buffer is not empty. Signal the consumer
        // that our buffer is not empty.
        cnd_signal(&g_BufferNotEmpty);
    }

    cnd_broadcast(&g_BufferNotEmpty);
    return 0;
}

int ConsumerProc(void *pData)
{
    int             iConsumerID = 0;
    unsigned long   ulItemValue = 0;
    int             iItemLoc    = 0;
    struct timespec ts          = { 0 };
```

```
        if (NULL != pData)
        {
            iConsumerID = *((int *)pData);
        }

        ts.tv_sec = CONSUMER_SLEEP_TIME;

        while (!g_fStopApp)
        {
            thrd_sleep(&ts, NULL);

            mtx_lock(&g_mutex);

            while (0 >= g_iItemsInBuffer && !g_fStopApp)
            {
                // Buffer is empty. Wait for the producers to produce items
                // and signal us that the buffer is no more empty.
                // We are releasing our mutex on this condition 'g_BufferNotEmpty'
                // so that the producers get the chance to produce items.
                // As soon as this condition is met (signalled by the producers)
                // we will again automatically attain the lock on the mutex.
                // This is done atomically within the function call 'cnd_wait'.
                cnd_wait(&g_BufferNotEmpty, &g_mutex);
            }

            if (g_fStopApp)
            {
                // The primary thread is asking us to stop.
                // Release the mutex, signal the waiting producers and stop.
                goto UNLOCKMUTEX;
            }

            ulItemValue = g_rguBuffer[g_iItemStartIndex];
            iItemLoc    = g_iItemStartIndex;
            g_iItemStartIndex++;
            g_ulTotalItemsConsumed++;
            g_iItemsInBuffer--;

            if (BUFFER_SIZE == g_iItemStartIndex)
            {
                g_iItemStartIndex = 0;
            }

            printf("\nConsumer %d consumed item %u from location %d.",
                    iConsumerID, ulItemValue, iItemLoc);

UNLOCKMUTEX:
            mtx_unlock(&g_mutex);

            // We have consumed 1 item in the buffer. So, the buffer is in no
            // way full. Signal the producer that our buffer is not full.
            cnd_signal(&g_BufferNotFull);
        }

        cnd_broadcast(&g_BufferNotFull);
        return 0;
}

int main(void)
{
        int     iSuccess   = 0;
        int     iThreadRes = 0;
```

```
thrd_t ProducerThread[NUM_PRODUCERS];
thrd_t ConsumerThread[NUM_CONSUMERS];
int    iProdThreadIDs[NUM_PRODUCERS];
int    iConThreadIDs[NUM_CONSUMERS];

do
{
    printf("Press enter to stop the program...");

    for (int idx = 0; idx < NUM_PRODUCERS; idx++)
    {
        memset(&ProducerThread[idx], 0, sizeof(thrd_t));
        iProdThreadIDs[idx] = idx + 1;
    }

    for (int idx = 0; idx < NUM_CONSUMERS; idx++)
    {
        memset(&ConsumerThread[idx], 0, sizeof(thrd_t));
        iConThreadIDs[idx] = idx + 1;
    }

    // Create the mutex.
    iSuccess = mtx_init(&g_mutex, mtx_plain);
    if (thrd_success != iSuccess)
    {
        // The mutex creation failed. Stop.
        break;
    }

    iSuccess = cnd_init(&g_BufferNotFull);
    if (thrd_success != iSuccess)
    {
        // Could not create the condition variable. Stop.
        break;
    }

    iSuccess = cnd_init(&g_BufferNotEmpty);
    if (thrd_success != iSuccess)
    {
        // Could not create the condition variable. Stop.
        break;
    }

    // Create the producer threads.
    for (int idx = 0; idx < NUM_PRODUCERS; idx++)
    {
        iSuccess = thrd_create(&ProducerThread[idx],
                               &ProducerProc,
                               &iProdThreadIDs[idx]);
        if (thrd_success != iSuccess)
        {
            // The thread creation failed. Stop.
            break;
        }
    }

    if (thrd_success != iSuccess)
    {
        // Thread creation failed. Stop.
        break;
    }

    // Create the consumer threads.
```

```
        for (int idx = 0; idx < NUM_CONSUMERS; idx++)
        {
            iSuccess = thrd_create(&ConsumerThread[idx],
                                    &ConsumerProc,
                                    &iConThreadIDs[idx]);
            if (thrd_success != iSuccess)
            {
                // The thread creation failed. Stop.
                break;
            }
        }

        if (thrd_success != iSuccess)
        {
            // Thread creation failed. Stop.
            break;
        }

        getchar();

    } while (0);

    g_fStopApp = true;

    for (int idx = 0; idx < NUM_PRODUCERS; idx++)
    {
        thrd_join(ProducerThread[idx], &iThreadRes);
    }

    for (int idx = 0; idx < NUM_CONSUMERS; idx++)
    {
        thrd_join(ConsumerThread[idx], &iThreadRes);
    }

    // Destroy the mutex.
    mtx_destroy(&g_mutex);

    // Destroy the condition variables.
    cnd_destroy(&g_BufferNotFull);
    cnd_destroy(&g_BufferNotEmpty);

    printf("\n\nTotal items produced %u and total items consumed %u.\n",
            g_ulTotalItemsProduced, g_ulTotalItemsConsumed);
    return 0;
}
```

22.3 DEADLOCK

When working with threads we should be very careful regarding deadlocks. When threads use synchronization *(very likely)* there is every chance to get into a deadlock, if care is not taken. A deadlock is a state in which each thread is waiting for another thread to take some action. It may occur when a thread enters a waiting state because a shared resource is held by another thread, which in turn is waiting for another resource held by another waiting thread. The wait occurs in a circular/partial-circular arrangement. This can be explained using a simple example. Suppose thread T1 is waiting on a mutex to be released by thread T2, which in turn is waiting on another mutex to be released by thread T3, which again is waiting for thread T4 to release another mutex. Thread T4 too is waiting for another mutex to be released by any of the earlier threads *(T1/T2/T3)*.

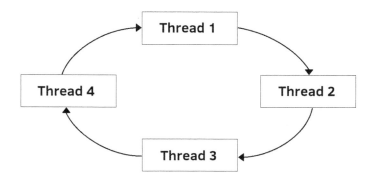

A deadlock may also occur in a much simpler scenario than the one discussed above. Assume, thread T1 is waiting for thread T2 for releasing mutex m1 and T2 is waiting for T1 to release another mutex m2. Result... we are in deadlock.

We can avoid deadlocks by:
- Eliminating or limiting the number of shared resources/dependencies between threads.
- No thread should try to lock one mutex while holding onto another.
- Eliminate all possibilities of a circular wait in threads. *Example: T1 waiting for --> T2 waiting for --> T3 waiting for --> T1.* The more mutexes we use, the greater is the chance of a circular wait.
- If a thread locks a mutex, its every code path should lead to unlocking the mutex. No thread should keep holding on to a mutex when not required.
- A thread should not hold a shared resource for an indeterministic amount of time.

We will deliberately get into a deadlock in our next program. We will have three threads where the primary thread *(thread 0)* waits for thread 1 to complete. Thread 1 in turn waits for thread 2 to unlock the mutex it is waiting on. Thread 2 waits on another mutex to be released by the primary thread *(thread 0)*. So, thread 0 is waiting for thread 1 to end, thread 1 is waiting on mutex 1 to be released by thread 2, and thread 2 is waiting on mutex 2 to be release by thread 0... a deadlock situation.

WARNING: The program will not end of its own. You will need to kill *(terminate)* the program. Before running this program, make sure that you know how to kill a program.

```c
#include <stdio.h>
#include <threads.h>

mtx_t g_mutex1 = { 0 };
mtx_t g_mutex2 = { 0 };

int ThreadProc1(void *pData)
{
    printf("\nThis is thread 1 and am moving into deadlock state.");
    mtx_lock(&g_mutex1);
    printf("\nThread 1: This message will never get printed.");
    return 0;
}
```

```c
int ThreadProc2(void *pData)
{
    printf("\nThis is thread 2 and am moving into deadlock state.");
    mtx_lock(&g_mutex2);

    // Unlock thread 1. But this statement will never be reached,
    // as we wait (above) indefinitely for mutex 2 to be unlocked
    // by the primary thread (thread 0).
    mtx_unlock(&g_mutex1);
    printf("\nThread 2: This message will never get printed.");
    return 0;
}

int main(void)
{
    thrd_t ThreadID1  = { 0 };
    thrd_t ThreadID2  = { 0 };
    int    iSuccess   = 0;
    int    iThreadRes = 0;

    do
    {
        // Create the first mutex.
        iSuccess = mtx_init(&g_mutex1, mtx_plain);
        if (thrd_success != iSuccess)
        {
            // The mutex creation failed. Stop.
            break;
        }

        // Create the second mutex.
        iSuccess = mtx_init(&g_mutex2, mtx_plain);
        if (thrd_success != iSuccess)
        {
            // The mutex creation failed. Stop.
            break;
        }

        // Attain a lock on both the mutexes.
        mtx_lock(&g_mutex1);
        mtx_lock(&g_mutex2);

        // Create the first thread.
        iSuccess = thrd_create(&ThreadID1, &ThreadProc1, NULL);
        if (thrd_success != iSuccess)
        {
            // The thread creation failed. Stop.
            break;
        }

        // Create the second thread.
        iSuccess = thrd_create(&ThreadID2, &ThreadProc2, NULL);
        if (thrd_success != iSuccess)
        {
            // The thread creation failed. Stop.
            break;
        }

        printf("\nThis is thread 0 and am moving into deadlock state.");
        // Wait for the thread 1 to complete. But, thread 1 will
        // never complete as it is waiting for thread 2 to unlock
        // the mutex (g_mutex1) which will never happen.
        thrd_join(ThreadID1, &iThreadRes);
```

```
        // Unlock thread 2. But this statement will never be reached,
        // as we wait (above) indefinitely for thread 1 to complete.
        mtx_unlock(&g_mutex2);

        printf("\nThread 0: This message will never get printed.");

    } while (0);

    // Destroy the mutexes.
    mtx_destroy(&g_mutex1);
    mtx_destroy(&g_mutex2);

    printf("\n\n");
    return 0;
}
```

Another example of getting into a deadlock...

```
#include <stdio.h>
#include <threads.h>

mtx_t g_mutex1 = { 0 };
mtx_t g_mutex2 = { 0 };

int ThreadProc1(void *pData)
{
    printf("\nThis is thread 1 and am moving into deadlock state.");
    mtx_lock(&g_mutex1);

    // Unlock thread 2. But this statement will never be reached, as we
    // wait (above) indefinitely for mutex 1 to be unlocked by thread 2.
    mtx_unlock(&g_mutex2);

    printf("\nThread 1: This message will never get printed.");
    return 0;
}

int ThreadProc2(void *pData)
{
    printf("\nThis is thread 2 and am moving into deadlock state.");
    mtx_lock(&g_mutex2);

    // Unlock thread 1. But this statement will never be reached, as we
    // wait (above) indefinitely for mutex 2 to be unlocked by thread 1.
    mtx_unlock(&g_mutex1);

    printf("\nThread 2: This message will never get printed.");
    return 0;
}

int main(void)
{
    thrd_t ThreadID1  = { 0 };
    thrd_t ThreadID2  = { 0 };
    int    iSuccess   = 0;
    int    iThreadRes = 0;

    do
    {
        // Create the first mutex.
        iSuccess = mtx_init(&g_mutex1, mtx_plain);
```

```c
        if (thrd_success != iSuccess)
        {
            // The mutex creation failed. Stop.
            break;
        }

        // Create the second mutex.
        iSuccess = mtx_init(&g_mutex2, mtx_plain);
        if (thrd_success != iSuccess)
        {
            // The mutex creation failed. Stop.
            break;
        }

        // Initially both mutexes will be locked. Mutex 1 is supposed to
        // be unlocked by thread 2 and mutex 2 is supposed to be unlocked
        // by thread 1. But, this will never happen due to the deadlock.
        mtx_lock(&g_mutex1);
        mtx_lock(&g_mutex2);

        // Create the first thread.
        iSuccess = thrd_create(&ThreadID1, &ThreadProc1, NULL);
        if (thrd_success != iSuccess)
        {
            // The thread creation failed. Stop.
            break;
        }

        // Create the second thread.
        iSuccess = thrd_create(&ThreadID2, &ThreadProc2, NULL);
        if (thrd_success != iSuccess)
        {
            // The thread creation failed. Stop.
            break;
        }

        // Wait for the thread 1 to complete. But, thread 1 will
        // never complete as it is waiting for thread 2 to unlock
        // the mutex (g_mutex1) which will never happen.
        thrd_join(ThreadID1, &iThreadRes);

    } while (0);

    // Destroy the mutexes.
    mtx_destroy(&g_mutex1);
    mtx_destroy(&g_mutex2);

    printf("\n\n");
    return 0;
}
```

C LIBRARY FUNCTIONS

[APPENDIX-1]

C language has a collection of very powerful library functions declared in multiple header files. From time to time, new functions are added to existing header files depending on the compiler and the C version we are working with. Also, new header files are created as per the changing requirements. Here we will discuss some of the major library functions.

Header File	Description
assert.h	Contains the assert macro which assists in detecting specific errors in debug versions of a program.
complex.h *(since C99)*	Complex number arithmetic functions.
ctype.h	Single character test and conversion functions.
errno.h	Macros for testing error codes reported by library functions.
float.h	Defines the limits of various float types (in macros).
limits.h	Defines the limits of various fundamental integral types depending on the architecture and compiler used (in macros).
locale.h	Defines localization specific settings, such as culture-specific date formats or country-specific currency symbols.
math.h	Mathematical functions.
stdarg.h	Provides types and macros which enable functions to accept variable number of arguments.
stdbool.h *(since C99)*	Contains macros for the Boolean data type.
stddef.h	Common macro definitions.
stdint.h *(since C99)*	Fixed-width integer types.
stdio.h	Standard input and output functions
stdlib.h	Some utility functions for string conversion, memory allocation, random number generation etc.
stdnoreturn.h *(since C11)*	Defines the *noreturn* macro to identify functions which will not return the control back to the caller function post their execution.
string.h	String handling functions.
time.h	Time information and manipulation functions.
wchar.h *(since C95)*	String manipulation functions *(wide character versions)*.
wctype.h *(since C95)*	Single character test and conversion functions *(wide character versions)*.
threads.h *(since C11)*	Threading and synchronization functions.

Note: *Many of the functions discussed in this appendix are deprecated and are replaced with their newer versions. Please refer to chapter-16 for a list of the deprecated functions and their replacements.*

assert.h

assert	If the argument expression of this macro equal to zero, a message is written to the standard error device and the program execution is terminated. The message will include the expression whose assertion failed, the name of the source file and the line number where it happened.

complex.h

cabs, cabsf, cabsl	Computes the complex absolute value.
carg, cargf, cargl	Computes argument of a complex number.
cimag, cimagf, cimagl	Computes the imaginary part of a complex number.
creal, crealf, creall	Computes the real part of a complex number.
conj, conjf, conjl	Computes the complex conjugate.
cproj, cprojf, cprojl	Computes the complex projection into Riemann sphere.
cexp, cexpf, cexpl	Computes the complex exponential.
clog, clogf, clogl	Computes the complex logarithm.
csqrt, csqrtf, csqrtl	Computes the complex square root.
cpow, cpowf, cpowl	Computes the complex power.
csin, csinf, csinl	Computes complex sine.
ccos, ccosf, ccosl	Computes complex cosine.
ctan, ctanf, ctanl	Computes complex tangent.
casin, casinf, casinl	Computes complex arc sine.
cacos, cacosf, cacosl	Computes complex arc cosine.
catan, catanf, catanl	Computes complex arc tangent.
csinh, csinhf, csinhl	Computes complex hyperbolic sine.
ccosh, ccoshf, ccoshl	Computes complex hyperbolic cosine.
ctanh, ctanhf, ctanhl	Computes complex hyperbolic tangent.
casinh, casinhf, casinhl	Computes complex hyperbolic arc sine.
cacosh, cacoshf, cacoshl	Computes complex hyperbolic arc cosine.
catanh, catanhf, catanhl	Computes complex hyperbolic arc tangent.

ctype.h (ANSI)/wctype.h (Wide Character)

ctype.h	wctype.h	
isalnum	iswalnum	Checks if the specified character is alphanumeric.
isalpha	iswalpha	Checks if the specified character is alphabetic
isblank	iswblank	Checks if the specified character is a blank character.
iscntrl	iswcntrl	Checks if the specified character is a control character.
isdigit	iswdigit	Checks if the specified character is a decimal digit.
isgraph	iswgraph	Checks if the specified character has graphical representation.

ctype.h	wctype.h	
islower	iswlower	Checks if the specified character is a lowercase letter.
isprint	iswprint	Checks if the specified character can be printed.
ispunct	iswpunct	Checks if the specified character is a punctuation character.
isspace	iswspace	Checks if the specified character is a white-space character.
isupper	iswupper	Checks if the specified character is an uppercase letter.
isxdigit	iswxdigit	Checks if the specified character is a hexadecimal digit.
tolower	towlower	Returns the lowercase equivalent of the given character.
toupper	towupper	Returns the uppercase equivalent of the given character.

errno.h

errno	An integer variable whose value indicates the last error faced by a standard library function. Its value can be changed within the program code.

float.h

FLT_RADIX	Base used for the floating-point types.
FLT_MANT_DIG DBL_MANT_DIG LDBL_MANT_DIG	Precision of the mantissa. 'FLT' is for float data type, 'DBL' is for double and 'LDBL' is for long double.
FLT_DIG DBL_DIG LDBL_DIG	Number of decimal digits that can be rounded to a floating point and back without any change to the value. 'FLT' is for float data type, 'DBL' is for double and 'LDBL' is for long double.
FLT_MIN_EXP DBL_MIN_EXP LDBL_MIN_EXP	Minimum value for the exponent that generates a normalized floating point number. 'FLT' is for float data type, 'DBL' is for double and 'LDBL' is for long double.
FLT_MIN_10_EXP DBL_MIN_10_EXP LDBL_MIN_10_EXP	Minimum value for the exponent of a Base-10 expression that generates a normalized floating point number. 'FLT' is for float data type, 'DBL' is for double and 'LDBL' is for long double.
FLT_MAX_EXP DBL_MAX_EXP LDBL_MAX_EXP	Maximum value for the exponent that generates a normalized floating point number. 'FLT' is for float data type, 'DBL' is for double and 'LDBL' is for long double.
FLT_MAX_10_EXP DBL_MAX_10_EXP LDBL_MAX_10_EXP	Maximum value for the exponent of a Base-10 expression that generates a normalized floating point number. 'FLT' is for float data type, 'DBL' is for double and 'LDBL' is for long double.
FLT_MAX DBL_MAX LDBL_MAX	Maximum value which can be finitely represented as a floating point number. 'FLT' is for float data type, 'DBL' is for double and 'LDBL' is for long double.
FLT_MIN DBL_MIN	Minimum value which can be finitely represented as a floating point number. 'FLT' is for float data type, 'DBL' is for double and 'LDBL' is for

LDBL_MIN	long double.
FLT_EPSILON DBL_EPSILON LDBL_EPSILON	Difference between 1 and the next smallest floating point number. 'FLT' is for float data type, 'DBL' is for double and 'LDBL' is for long double.
FLT_ROUNDS	Rounding mode of floating points operations. -1: Indeterminable 0: Towards zero 1: To the nearest number 2: Towards positive infinity 3: Towards negative infinity

limits.h

CHAR_BIT	Number of bits in a char.
SCHAR_MIN	Minimum possible value of a signed char.
SCHAR_MAX	Maximum possible value of a signed char.
UCHAR_MAX	Maximum possible value of an unsigned char.
CHAR_MIN	Minimum possible value of a char.
CHAR_MAX	Maximum possible value of a char.
MB_LEN_MAX	Maximum number of bytes in a multi-byte character, for any locale.
SHRT_MIN	Minimum possible value of a short int.
SHRT_MAX	Maximum possible value of a short int.
USHRT_MAX	Maximum possible value of an unsigned short int.
INT_MIN	Minimum possible value of an int.
INT_MAX	Maximum possible value of an int.
UINT_MAX	Maximum possible value of an unsigned int.
LONG_MIN	Minimum possible value of a long int.
LONG_MAX	Maximum possible value of a long int.
ULONG_MAX	Maximum possible value of an unsigned long int.
LLONG_MIN	Minimum possible value of a long long int.
LLONG_MAX	Maximum possible value of a long long int.
ULLONG_MAX	Maximum possible value of an unsigned long long int.

locale.h

struct lconv	Contains formatting info for numeric and monetary values.
setlocale	Sets or retrieves the locale information.
localeconv	Gets locale formatting information.

math.h

acos	Calculates inverse cosine.
asin	Calculates inverse sine.
atan	Calculates inverse tangent.
atan2	Calculates inverse tangent *(two parameters)*.
ceil	Returns the smallest whole number greater than the parameter.
cos	Calculates cosine.
cosh	Calculates hyperbolic cosine.
exp	Calculates the exponential value.
fabs	Calculates the absolute value of the floating point number.
floor	Returns the largest whole number **not** greater than the parameter.
fmod	Returns the floating point remainder for the division of the parameter1 by parameter2.
frexp	Returns mantissa and exponent of the floating point number.
ldexp	Multiplies a floating point number by an integral power of two.
log	Calculates natural logarithm.
log10	Calculates Base-10 logarithm.
modf	Breaks into fractional and integral parts.
pow	Returns parameter1 to the power of parameter2.
sin	Calculates sine.
sinh	Calculates hyperbolic sine.
sqrt	Calculates the square root.
tan	Calculates tangent.
tanh	Calculates hyperbolic tangent.

Below functions are available in C99 and above

acosh	Calculates inverse hyperbolic cosine.
asinh	Calculates inverse hyperbolic sine.
atanh	Calculates inverse hyperbolic tangent.
cbrt, cbrtf, cbrtl	Calculates the cube root.
copysign, copysignf, copysignl	Returns the value of parameter1 with the sign of parameter2.
erf, erff, erfl	Calculates error function.
erfc, erfcf, erfcl	Calculates complementary error function.
exp2, exp2f, exp2l	Calculates 2 to the power of the parameter.
expm1, expm1f, expm1l	Calculates exponential minus 1.
fdim, fdimf, fdiml	Returns positive difference.
fma, fmaf, fmal	Multiply and add.

fmax, fmaxf, fmaxl	Returns the largest of the parameter1 and parameter2.
fmin, fminf, fminl	Returns the smallest of the parameter1 and parameter2.
hypot, hypotf, hypotl	Calculates the hypotenuse.
ilogb, ilogbf, ilogbl	Calculates unbiased Base-2 exponent.
lgamma, lgammaf, lgammal	Calculates natural logarithm of absolute value of the gamma function.
llrint, llrintf, llrintl	Rounds to integer using current rounding mode *(returns long long)*.
lrint, lrintf, lrintl	Rounds to integer using current rounding mode *(returns long)*.
llround, llroundf, llroundl	Rounds to the nearest whole number *(returns long long)*.
lround, lroundf, lroundl	Rounds to the nearest whole number *(returns long)*.
log1p, log1pf, log1pl	Returns the natural logarithm of the parameter plus 1.
log2, log2f, log2l	Calculates the Base-2 logarithm.
logb, logbf, logbl	Extracts exponent from the floating point number.
nan	Returns a NaN from the provided string argument.
nearbyint, nearbyintf, nearbyintl	Rounds the floating point number to nearest whole number.
nextafter, nextafterf, nextafterl	Returns next re-presentable value after parameter1 and in the direction of parameter2.
nexttoward, nexttowardf, nexttowardl	Returns next re-presentable value after parameter1 and in the direction of parameter2 *(higher precision)*.
remainder, remainderf, remainderl	Computes the remainder of the quotient, rounded to the nearest integral value.
remquo, remquof, remquol	Computes the remainder of two values, and stores an integer value with the sign and approximate magnitude of the quotient in a location specified as a parameter.
rint, rintf, rintl	Rounds to integer using the current rounding mode.
round, roundf, roundl	Rounds to integer, rounding halfway cases away from zero.
scalbln, scalblnf, scalblnl	Scales parameter1 by FLT_RADIX raised to the power of the parameter2 *(where parameter2 is long int)*.
scalbn, scalbnf, scalbnl	Scales parameter1 by FLT_RADIX raised to the power of the parameter2 *(where parameter2 is int)*.
tgamma, tgammaf, tgammal	Returns the gamma function.
trunc, truncf, truncl	Rounds towards zero, returning the nearest integral value that is not larger in magnitude.
Macros	
fpclassify	Returns the floating-point classification of the parameter.
isfinite	Determines whether the argument has a finite value.
isinf	Determines whether the argument is infinite.
isnan	Checks if the argument is not a number.

signbit	Returns whether the argument is negative.
isgreater	Checks if parameter1 is greater than parameter2.
isgreaterequal	Checks if parameter1 is greater than or equal to parameter2.
isless	Checks if parameter1 is less than parameter2.
islessequal	Checks if parameter1 is less than or equal to parameter2.
islessgreater	Checks if parameter1 is less or greater than parameter2.

stdarg.h

va_list	Type for iterating the variable arguments list. Holds the information required for the macros 'va_start', 'va_arg' and 'va_end' to work.
va_start	Initializes a variable argument list.
va_arg	Retrieves the next argument in the list.
va_end	Marks the end of the use of the variable arguments list.
va_copy *(since C99)*	Copies a variable arguments list to another.

stdbool.h

bool	Expands to _Bool, the boolean data type.
true	Expands to the value 1.
false	Expands to the value 0 *(zero)*.

stddef.h

ptrdiff_t	Represents the result of any valid pointer subtraction operation.
size_t	Unsigned integral type.
NULL	Null pointer.
offsetof	Returns the offset value in bytes of the specified member field within the data structure or union.

stdint.h

Types

int8_t	Signed 8-bit integer.
uint8_t	Unsigned 8-bit integer.
int16_t	Signed 16-bit integer.
uint16_t	Unsigned 16-bit integer.
int32_t	Signed 32-bit integer.
uint32_t	Unsigned 32-bit integer.
int64_t	Signed 64-bit integer.
uint64_t	Unsigned 64-bit integer.

intmax_t	Signed integer type with maximum capacity.
uintmax_t	Unsigned integer type with maximum capacity.
Type ranges	
INT8_MIN	Minimum possible value of int8_t.
INT8_MAX	Maximum possible value of int8_t.
UINT8_MAX	Maximum possible value of uint8_t.
INT16_MIN	Minimum possible value of int16_t.
INT16_MAX	Maximum possible value of int16_t.
UINT16_MAX	Maximum possible value of uint16_t.
INT32_MIN	Minimum possible value of int32_t.
INT32_MAX	Maximum possible value of int32_t.
UINT32_MAX	Maximum possible value of uint32_t.
INT64_MIN	Minimum possible value of int64_t.
INT64_MAX	Maximum possible value of int64_t.
UINT64_MAX	Maximum possible value of uint64_t.
INTMAX_MIN	Minimum possible value of intmax_t.
INTMAX_MAX	Maximum possible value of intmax_t.
UINTMAX_MAX	Maximum possible value of uintmax_t.
SIZE_MAX	Maximum possible value of size_t.
PTRDIFF_MIN	Minimum possible value of ptrdiff_t.
PTRDIFF_MAX	Maximum possible value of ptrdiff_t.
SIG_ATOMIC_MIN	Minimum possible value of sig_atomic_t.
SIG_ATOMIC_MAX	Maximum possible value of sig_atomic_t.
WCHAR_MIN	Minimum possible value of wchar_t.
WCHAR_MAX	Maximum possible value of wchar_t.
WINT_MIN	Minimum possible value of wint_t.
WINT_MAX	Maximum possible value of wint_t.

stdio.h/wchar.h (Wide character)

stdio.h	**wchar.h**	
File open or close functions		
fopen	_wfopen	Creates or opens a file.
freopen	_wfreopen	Reopens a file stream with a different file or mode.
fflush		Flushes the data in the stream to the output device/disk.
setbuf		Sets the buffer for a stream.
setvbuf		Changes the stream buffering.

stdio.h	wchar.h	
fclose		Closes an already opened file.
Stream positioning functions		
fgetpos		Gets current position in the stream.
fsetpos		Sets the position indicator of the stream to the new position.
ftell		Gets the current position in the stream.
rewind		Sets position of the stream to the beginning.
fseek		Repositions stream position indicator to the new position.
Single character input or output functions		
fgetc	fgetwc	Reads a character from the stream.
fputc	fputwc	Writes a character to the stream.
getc	getwc	Reads a character from the stream.
putc	putwc	Writes a character to the stream.
ungetc	ungetwc	Ungets a character from stream. The file position indicator is repositioned to the location as was before the last *'get'* operation.
getchar	getwchar	Gets a character from the standard input device *(stdin)*.
putchar	putwchar	Writes a character to the standard output device *(stdout)*.
String input or output functions		
fgets	fgetws	Reads a string from the stream.
fputs	fputws	Writes a string to the stream.
gets	_getws	Gets a string from the standard input device *(stdin)*.
puts	_putws	Writes a string to the standard output device *(stdout)*.
Binary mode input or output functions		
fread		Reads a block of data from the stream.
fwrite		Writes a block of data to the stream.
Formatted input or output functions		
fprintf	fwprintf	Writes formatted data to the stream.
fscanf	fwscanf	Reads formatted data from the stream.
printf	wprintf	Writes formatted data to the standard output device *(stdout)*.
scanf	wscanf	Reads formatted data from the standard input device *(stdin)*.
snprintf *(since C99)*	_snwprintf	Writes formatted output to the provided buffer *(buffer size specified by caller)*.
sprintf	swprintf	Writes formatted data to the string.
sscanf	swscanf	Reads formatted data from the specified string.

stdio.h	wchar.h	
vfprintf	vfwprintf	Writes formatted data from variable argument list to the stream.
vfscanf *(since C99)*	vfwscanf	Reads formatted data from the stream into variable argument list.
vprintf	vwprintf	Writes formatted data from variable argument list to the standard output device *(stdout)*.
vscanf *(since C99)*	vwscanf	Reads formatted data from standard input device *(stdin)* into variable argument list.
vsnprintf *(since C99)*	_vsnwprintf	Writes formatted data from variable argument list to the provided buffer *(buffer size specified by caller)*.
vsprintf	vswprintf	Writes formatted data from variable argument list to string.
vsscanf *(since C99)*	vswscanf	Reads formatted data from string into variable argument list.
File system operation functions		
remove	_wremove	Removes the specified file.
rename	_wrename	Renames the specified file.
tmpfile		Creates a temporary binary file for read/write with a filename guaranteed to be unique.
tmpnam	_wtmpnam	Returns a string containing a filename different from any existing file.
Error handling functions		
clearerr		Clears all error indicators for the stream.
feof		Checks if the end of file indicator for the stream is set.
ferror		Checks if the error indicator for the stream is set.
perror		Interprets the value in 'errno' and prints it to the standard output error stream.
Macros		
BUFSIZ		Default buffer size.
EOF		End of file marker.
FILENAME_MAX		Maximum length of filenames.
FOPEN_MAX		Maximum simultaneous open streams.
NULL		Null pointer marker.
TMP_MAX		Maximum number of temporary files.

Note: *The functions with name starting with an underscore '_' are compiler specific and may not be available on all C compilers.*

stdlib.h (ANSI)/wchar.h (Wide character)

stdlib.h	wchar.h	
Type conversion functions		
atof	_wtof	Converts the given string to double.
atoi	_wtoi	Converts the given string to integer.
atol	_wtol	Converts the given string to long integer.
atoll *(since C99)*	_wtoll	Converts the given string to long long integer.
strtod	wcstod	Converts the given string to double. The function also sets parameter2 to point to the character following the number within the string.
strtof *(since C99)*	wcstof	Converts the given string to float. The function also sets parameter2 to point to the character following the number within the string.
strtol	wcstol	Converts the given string to long integer using the specified base. The function also sets parameter2 to point to the character following the number within the string.
strtold *(since C99)*	wcstold	Converts the given string to long double. The function also sets parameter2 to point to the character following the number within the string.
strtoll *(since C99)*	wcstoll	Converts the given string to long long integer using the specified base. The function also sets parameter2 to point to the character following the number within the string.
strtoul	wcstoul	Converts the given string to unsigned long integer using the specified base. The function also sets parameter2 to point to the character following the number within the string.
strtoull *(since C99)*	wcstoull	Converts the given string to unsigned long long integer using the specified base. The function also sets parameter2 to point to the character following the number within the string.
Dynamic memory management functions		
malloc		Allocates block of memory from heap.
calloc		Allocates a zero-initialized memory block from heap.
realloc		Re-allocates an existing block of memory.
free		Deallocates a memory block.
Mathematical		
abs		Returns the absolute value.
div		Returns the integral quotient and remainder after dividing parameter1 by parameter2 *(integer)*.
labs		Returns the absolute value as long integer.

stdlib.h	wchar.h	
ldiv		Returns the integral quotient and remainder after dividing parameter1 by parameter2 *(long integer)*.
llabs *(since C99)*		Returns the absolute value as long long integer.
lldiv *(since C99)*		Returns the integral quotient and remainder after dividing parameter1 by parameter2 *(long long integer)*.
Pseudo random number generation function		
rand		Generates random number.
srand		Initializes the random number generator using a seed value.
Environment management functions		
abort		Aborts current process, producing an abnormal program termination.
atexit		Sets the function to be executed when the program terminates.
exit		Terminates current process normally, performing all regular cleanup before terminating.
getenv	_wgetenv	Gets the environment string corresponding to the environment name specified as a parameter to the function.
system	_wsystem	Executes a system (OS) command.
Searching and sorting functions		
bsearch		Performs binary search in an array.
qsort		Sorts the specified array.
Multibyte/Wide character operation functions		
mblen		Gets the length of the multibyte character.
mbtowc		Converts multibyte sequence to wide character.
wctomb		Converts wide character to multibyte sequence.
mbstowcs		Converts multibyte string to wide character string.
wcstombs		Converts wide character string to multibyte string.
Macros and types		
EXIT_FAILURE		Program failure termination code.
EXIT_SUCCESS		Program success termination code.
MB_CUR_MAX		Maximum size of multibyte characters.
NULL		Null pointer.
RAND_MAX		Maximum value returned by the rand function.
size_t		Unsigned integral type.

Note: *The functions with name starting with an underscore '_' are compiler specific and may not be available on all C compilers.*

stdnoreturn.h

noreturn *(Since C11)*	Expands to _Noreturn which specifies that the function does not return to its point of invocation.

string.h (ANSI)/wchar.h (Wide Character)
[For detailed explanations, please refer to section 9.7.1]

string.h	wchar.h	
Copy functions		
memcpy	wmemcpy	Copies a block of memory from source to destination.
memmove	wmemmove	Moves a block of memory from source to destination.
strcat	wcscat	Appends a copy of the source string to the destination string.
strcpy	wcscpy	Copies the source string to the destination.
strncat	wcsncat	Appends a copy of the source string to the destination string, subject to a maximum of 'n' characters.
strncpy	wcsncpy	Copies the source string to the destination, subject to a maximum of 'n' characters.
Compare functions		
memcmp	wmemcmp	Compares one block of memory to another.
strcmp	wcscmp	Compares one string to another.
strcoll	wcscoll	Compares one string to another using the locale.
strncmp	wcsncmp	Compares one string to another, subject to a maximum of 'n' characters.
strxfrm	wcsxfrm	Copies a string from a source to destination after transforming it using the current locale.
Search functions		
memchr	wmemchr	Searches a maximum of 'n' characters for the first occurance of the given character within the given block of memory.
strchr	wcschr	Searches a string for the first occurance of the given character.
strcspn	wcscspn	Scans parameter1 *(string)* for the first occurrence of any of the characters in parameter2 *(string)*. It returns the index of the first occurrence.
strpbrk	wcspbrk	Scans parameter1 *(string)* for the first occurrence of any of the characters in parameter2 *(string)*. It returns a pointer to the first occurrence.
strrchr	wcsrchr	Searches a string for the last occurance of the given character.
strspn	wcsspn	Returns the index of the first character in parameter1 *(string)*, that does not belong to any of the characters in parameter2 *(string)*.

string.h	wchar.h	
strstr	wcsstr	Returns a pointer to the first occurance of parameter2 *(string)* in parameter1 *(string)*.
strtok	wcstok	A sequence of calls to this function splits parameter1 *(string)* into tokens, where every token is a sequence of contiguous characters separated from the next token by any of the delimiters *(characters)* specified in parameter2 *(string)*.
Miscelleneous functions		
memset	wmemset	Sets the first 'n' bytes of the block of memory pointed by parameter1 to the value specified in parameter2.
strerror	_wcserror	Gets a system error message string corresponding to the given error code.
strlen	wcslen	Returns the length of a string.

Note: *The functions with name starting with an underscore '_' are compiler specific and may not be available on all C compilers.*

time.h/wchar.h (Wide character)

time.h	wchar.h	
asctime	_wasctime	Converts the provided 'tm' structure to a string
clock		Returns the processor time *(clock ticks)* elapsed since the program started
ctime	_wctime	Converts the provided 'time_t' value to a string
difftime		Returns the difference *(in seconds)* between two times
gmtime		Converts the provided 'time_t' to 'tm' structure as UTC time
localtime		Converts the provided 'time_t' to 'tm' structure as local time
mktime		Returns the 'time_t' corresponding to the provided tm structure
strftime	wcsftime	Formats the time specified as 'tm' structure to a string
time		Returns the current system time
Types		
clock_t		Clock tick count
struct tm		Structure containing a date and time broken down into its components
time_t		The number of seconds elapsed since Jan 1, 1970, 00:00 hours UTC
Macros		
CLOCKS_PER_SEC		The number of clock ticks *(clock_t)* per second

Note: *The functions with name starting with an underscore '_' are compiler specific and may not be available on all C compilers.*

wchar.h

[Apart from the functions and macros already stated alongside other header files (in this appendix), 'wchar.h' has the following additional functions and macros]

btowc	Returns the wide character equivalent of the specified single byte character.
wctob	Converts the wide character to single byte character.
mbrlen	Returns the length of the specified multibyte character.
mbsinit	Checks if the provided 'mbstate_t' is at initial conversion state.
mbrtowc	Converts the provided multibyte sequence to a wide character.
mbsrtowcs	Converts the provided multibyte string to a wide character string.
wcrtomb	Converts the provided wide character to multibyte sequence.
wcsrtombs	Converts the provided wide character string to multibyte string.

Types

mbstate_t	Type that holds the state information when converting between multibyte characters and wide characters *(both ways)*.
wchar_t	Wide character type.
wint_t	Wide integer type to hold error codes too.

Macros

WCHAR_MAX	Maximum possible value of wchar_t.
WCHAR_MIN	Minimum possible value of wchar_t.
WEOF	Wide end of file marker.

threads.h

[For detailed explanations, please refer chapter 22]

Thread manipulation functions

thrd_create	Creates a new thread.
thrd_equal	Checks whether the two specified thread identifiers refer to the same thread.
thrd_current	Returns the thread identifier of the calling thread.
thrd_sleep	Blocks the execution of the calling thread for the specified amount of time.
thrd_yield	Suspends the current thread allowing other threads to run.
thrd_exit	Terminates the calling thread.
thrd_join	Blocks the current thread until the specified thread ends.
thrd_detach	Detaches the specified thread.

Synchronization functions [Mutex]

mtx_init	Initializes a mutex.
mtx_lock	Blocks the current thread until the given mutex gets locked.
mtx_timedlock	Blocks the current thread until the given timed mutex gets locked or the specified

	time elapses, whichever comes first.
mtx_trylock	Tries to lock the given mutex without blocking.
mtx_unlock	Unlocks the given mutex.
mtx_destroy	Destroys the given mutex.
Synchronization functions [Condition variables]	
cnd_init	Initializes a condition variable.
cnd_wait	Makes the current thread go into sleep state and remain so until the given condition variable gets signalled.
cnd_timedwait	Similar to 'cnd_wait' except that this function waits for a maximum of the given duration.
cnd_signal	Signals a waiting thread to wake up.
cnd_broadcast	Signals all threads which are waiting on the condition.
cnd_destroy	Destroys the given condition variable.
Types	
thrd_t	Thread identifier.
thrd_start_t	Pointer to a thread procedure.
mtx_t	Mutex identifier.
mtx_plain	Plain (non-recursive) mutex.
mtx_recursive	Recursive mutex.
mtx_timed	Timed mutex.
cnd_t	Condition variable identifier.

Note: Many of the functions discussed in this appendix are deprecated and are replaced with their newer versions. Please refer to chapter-16 for a list of the deprecated functions and their replacements.